A Ghetto Takes Shape

BLACKS IN THE NEW WORLD

August Meier, Series Editor

A Ghetto Takes Shape

Black Cleveland, 1870-1930

Kenneth L. Kusmer

UNIVERSITY OF ILLINOIS PRESS

Urbana   Chicago   London

LIBRARY OF CONGRESS CATALOGING IN PUBLICATION DATA

Kusmer, Kenneth L   1945–
  A ghetto takes shape.

  (Blacks in the new world)
  Bibliography: p.
  Includes index.
  1. Negroes–Cleveland–History.   2.   Cleveland–
History.   I.   Title.   II.   Series.
F499.C69N34   977.1′32′00496073   75–40113
ISBN 0–252–00289–X

FOR MY MOTHER
AND IN MEMORY OF MY FATHER

Contents

Many are the misapprehensions and misstatements as to the social environment of Negroes in a great Northern city. Sometimes it is said, here they are free; they have the same chance as the Irishman, the Italian, or the Swede; at other times it is said, the environment is such that it is really more oppressive than the situation in Southern cities. The student must ignore both of these extreme statements and seek to extract from a complicated mass of facts the tangible evidence of a social atmosphere surrounding Negroes, which differs from that surrounding most whites; of a different mental attitude, moral standard, and economic judgment shown toward Negroes than toward most other folk. That such a difference exists and can now and then plainly be seen, few deny; but just how far it goes and how large a a factor it is in the Negro problems, nothing but careful study and measurement can reveal.

W. E. B. Du Bois,
The Philadelphia Negro (1899)

Preface

Historically, the institution of slavery and the development of the black ghetto have been the two great factors that have shaped the experience of Afro-Americans in the United States. The ramifications of slavery have been the subject of almost constant scholarly debate since the beginning of this century; and during the past fifteen years the nature of the "peculiar institution" has received careful and detailed scrutiny by a number of competing schools of historical thought. In marked contrast, the development of the ghetto—a phenomenon of equal importance—has received comparatively little attention. I hope this volume will, in some small way, help to rectify this historiographical deficiency.

A Ghetto Takes Shape constitutes an attempt at what might be called comprehensive comparative history. Its chief aim is to trace a number of aspects of black life—economic, political, social, and cultural—in a single city over a period of sixty to one hundred years, and to show how changes in each of these aspects were integrally related to the developing ghetto. This study also proposes, however, to make the process of ghetto development more comprehensible by systematically surveying changing white attitudes toward blacks; by comparing, at as many points as possible, the position of blacks in the social order with the positions of immigrants and native whites; and by placing the growth of the ghetto in its urban as well as its purely racial context.

The need for comparative analysis in black urban history cannot be emphasized too strongly. In his influential article, "The Enduring Ghetto" (*Journal of American History*, 55, September 1968), the late Gilbert Osofsky concluded that "the essential structure and nature of the Negro ghetto have remained remarkably durable since the demise of slavery in the North. There has been an unending and tragic sameness about Negro life in the metropolis over the two centuries." While in many ways this statement may be true for New York (the city which Osofsky drew most of his examples) and perhaps for some other cities also, I do not think that it applies equally well to all urban areas. If we are to understand the black urban experience in its totality, we need to revise and move beyond ahistorical concepts like the "enduring ghetto" by exploring the variations that have existed in the history of black communities—in much the same manner that historians have already begun to study the diversity of slave societies in the New World. Did the ghetto as a geographical entity develop differently and at different times in various cities? Did the black communities of different cities have varying patterns of property ownership and occupational mobility? of family structure? of political participation? Thus far historians have seldom asked these questions because they have not considered the answers to be worth noting. Yet these questions are crucial to understanding why a race riot occurred in Chicago but not in Cleveland; why there was a "ghetto revolt" in the 1960s but not in the 1920s; why black leadership has been militant in one community and conservative in another; why in some cities the black ghetto has indeed been "enduring," while in others the quality of black life has fluctuated over time.

Besides studying the differences among ghettos, there is also a need to analyze more carefully differences within individual black communities. Contrary to popular assumption, the black ghetto is not an undifferentiated mass of slum dwellers. To use St. Clair Drake's expression, there are —and have been—many "folkways and classways" in the black community. The emphasis, in some quarters, on the "pathological" effects of racism (however important these effects may intrinsically be) has led to a neglect of the study of the historical development of class structure in the black community and the positive ways in which blacks have responded to the growth of the ghetto. The functions of black organizations, institutions, and leadership at the local level require much more study than they have thus far received. We cannot assume that local branches of nationwide black organizations always functioned in the same manner as their parent organizations; nor can we assume that the ideologies, divisions, and strategies of black leadership groups in specific cities necessarily duplicates, during any given time period, divisions among those black leaders who claimed to speak for larger constituencies.

Exploring differences among and within black communities, however, is not sufficient. For a more comprehensive understanding of the development of black ghettos, comparative studies of Afro-Americans and other groups in the population, especially immigrants, are needed. It is hardly possible to assess adequately the position of blacks in the social order without measuring their progress (or lack of progress) against general trends. In analyzing occupations and patterns of residential change, in particular, I have sought to draw parallels between the experience of blacks and that of native whites and the various immigrant groups.

It should be evident from the nature of the questions raised in this preface that no one study can possibly explain all of the ramifications of the development of black ghettos. That will take many studies of many cities. Therefore, although one of the purposes of this study is to show that there were important differences among black communities before 1930 (and especially before 1915), I make no claims for the typicality of the Cleveland model. In many ways the history of Cleveland's black population parallels that of other cities; in other ways that history is exceptional, perhaps, or even unique. Wherever possible, I have tried to follow the astute advice which Gunnar Myrdal gave scholars in an appendix entitled "Research in a Negro Community," in *An American Dilemma* (1944): "When only a single community can be studied it should not be assumed to be typical nor should the question of its uniqueness or typicality be ignored. Rather, the investigator must attempt to place it in the Southern scene, or in the American scene, or even in the whole Western Civilization scene, by comparing it with the average and range in many significant respects." Throughout the present study I have compared Cleveland's developing ghetto and its black population with their counterparts in many other communities in both the North and the South. I have noted similarities where they have existed, but I have also noted differences and attempted to account for them. I have tried, perhaps unsuccessfully at times, to avoid reducing a complex and variegated historical problem to a series of pat, easily digested formulas.

Of the many librarians who helped me during the long process of researching this study, a few stand out as particularly praiseworthy. A special word of thanks is due the staffs of the Ohio State Historical Society, the Sociology Division of the Cleveland Public Library, the Joseph Regenstein Library of the University of Chicago, and the Western Reserve Historical Society Library. At Western Reserve, Virginia Hawley (who has assisted countless researchers during her tenure at the Library) and Olivia Martin were especially helpful.

I would like to express my deep appreciation to James Louis, Henry Leonard, Allan Spear, Christopher Wye, Paul Finkelman, Stanley Katz, August Meier, and John Hope Franklin for taking the time and trouble to read the manuscript of this study at various stages in its development, to point out errors, and to offer valuable criticisms. Professor Franklin, in particular, rendered a great service in drawing my attention to a number of critical issues in black urban history. Paul Lammermeier, of Kent State University, generously lent me data from his forthcoming dissertation on nineteenth-century black communities of the Ohio River Valley. Thanks also must go to Richard L. Wentworth and Carole S. Appel, of the University of Illinois Press, for their patience and editorial guidance. My greatest debt is to August Meier. This study began as a master's thesis under his direction, and I can say unequivocally that without his encouragement and inspiration I would never have enlarged upon my original ideas and brought them to their present fruition. I would also like to thank Leon C. Soulé, whose lectures first introduced me to American history; his intellectual guidance and moral support over the years have been invaluable. None of the individuals mentioned in this paragraph, of course, is responsible for any errors of fact or judgment that remain in this volume.

During the period of time that book has been in the making I received financial assistance from Kent State University, the history department of the University of Chicago (the James L. Cate Fellowship), and the Ford Foundation. I am very grateful for this aid.

An earlier version of this study was typed by Martha Siegwarth and Vitalija Mekesa Butkus. I am glad to have this opportunity to thank them for the valuable help which they rendered at the time.

Finally, I want to thank Holly—for everything.

PART I

The Nineteenth-Century Heritage

CHAPTER 1

Almost Equal:
Black Cleveland before 1870

I

December 2, 1859, was a day that the citizens of Cleveland would not soon forget. That morning, John Brown had been executed at Charlestown, Virginia. As news of his death reached Cleveland, there was an immediate reaction among the populace. A number of shop-keepers closed their doors for the day. For one half hour, from 10:30 to 11 that morning, the bell of the Second Baptist Church tolled in com-memoration of the departed hero. One group of citizens stretched a banner, bordered in black, across Superior Avenue, with Brown's words, "I do not think I can better honor the cause I love than to die for it," inscribed on it. Flags hung at half staff in several places, and a general gloom settled over the usually bustling town on the shores of Lake Erie.

The weather that Tuesday seemed to match the mood of the people. It was a stormy day, and the sun failed to break through a thick layer of clouds; a fine drizzle that began in the morning turned first to sleet and then to snow. That evening Melodeon Hall, one of the city's largest auditoriums, was draped in mourning for a public meeting in memory of the man who had tried unsuccessfully to liberate the slaves at Harpers Ferry. The meeting proved to be one of the largest the young metropolis had witnessed up to that time. Fourteen hundred people—about one of every fifteen adults in the community—turned out for the occasion. Dur-ing the 1850s, southern slaveholders were fond of depicting the northern abolitionists as a rabble-rousing minority of troublemakers and ne'er-do-wells, bent on dividing communities and sundering the Union. The meeting at Melodeon Hall, however, belied at least the first half of this description: it contained a broad cross section of the community and included many people of wealth and standing. Among the speakers that night were two judges, three well-known ministers, and several aspiring local politicians, as well as John M. Langston, the prominent black abolitionist from Oberlin. One after another of these individuals rose to eulogize Brown, to condemn the state of Virginia for his execution, and to denounce the institution of slavery. "John Brown has gone to his grave," said one speaker, "and we can't call him back, but I propose that we baptise ourselves in his spirit, and stand upon a foundation of adamant in unalterable hostility to slavery." Several resolutions, adopted unanimously, highlighted the emotion-filled evening. "However much we may lament the death of the devoted Brown," read one of these that summed up the feelings of the crowd, "we are satisfied that his execution will bring confusion upon his enemies, and do more to overthrow the bulwarks of Slavery than a long life of philanthropic deeds with a peaceful exit. We honor his memory! Posterity will give him a monument as indestructable as their aspirations for FREEDOM."[1]

The outpouring of sentiment for John Brown was indicative of the growing sympathy of white Clevelanders, on the eve of the Civil War, for the plight of black Americans. Yet it had not always been this way. The delegates from the northeastern section of Ohio who attended the state Constitutional Convention in 1802 had evinced no marked concern for the rights of Negroes, and the constitution that emerged from the convention's deliberations was distinctly a white man's document. Slavery was excluded (by a single vote!), but blacks were denied suffrage and the right to give testimony in court against white persons, and they were declared ineligible to hold public office or to serve in the state militia. In addition to these constitutional provisions, a series of Black Laws were soon passed that further degraded the state's Afro-American population. Blacks were prohibited from settling in the state without filing a five-hundred-dollar bond. They were required to register their certificate of freedom in a county clerk's office before they could obtain employ-

---

[1] A Tribute of Respect, Commemorative of the Worth and Sacrifice of John Brown, of Ossawatomie: It Being a Full Report of the Speeches made and the Resolutions adopted by the citizens of Cleveland, at a meeting held in the Melodeon, on the evening of the day on which John Brown was sacrificed by the Commonwealth of Virginia; together with a Sermon, commemorative of the same sad event (Cleveland, 1859). Earlier in 1859 Brown had been able to live openly in Cleveland without fear of arrest, even though President James Buchanan had offered a large reward for his arrest. See Stephen B. Oates, To Purge This Land with Blood: A Biography of John Brown (New York, 1970), 267.

ment. They were excluded from jury service. Prior to 1848, the state made no provision for the public education of black youths; and when the legislature finally did pass laws pertaining to their education, it specifically allowed local communities to establish separate, segregated schools—an option that most localities readily accepted. Some of the Black Laws (such as the filing of bonds and certificates of freedom) were only sporadically enforced; most of the statutes limiting the freedom of blacks, however, were carried out to the letter.[2]

Prior to the mid-1830s, most of the citizens of Cleveland, Cuyahoga County, and the surrounding counties—an area known collectively as the Western Reserve—found the provisions of the Black Laws acceptable. There may well have been some individuals in Cleveland at that time who opposed the restrictive codes, but they were too few in number to be noticed by the local press. A more ambivalent attitude prevailed on the subject of slavery. As early as 1819, two men were convicted by a Cleveland jury on a charge of kidnapping when they attempted to return two fugitive slaves who had settled in the city to their master in western Virginia. This action, however, was unique for its time and constituted only the first faint stirrings of the militant abolitionism that would later take hold in the Reserve. When some Ohioans suggested, in the same year, that the state constitution be changed to allow slavery, the Cleveland *Register* vigorously protested that the "practice of trafficking in the human species is too contemptible an occupation for a citizen of Ohio." On the other hand, while opposing the introduction of slavery in Ohio, the paper did not object to the existence of the peculiar institution in those parts of the Union where it had already gained a foothold; and in the same edition the editors took note that a slave insurrection in Georgia had "been happily defeated." During the first two or three decades of the nineteenth century, most of the antislavery sentiment in Ohio was confined to those southern parts of the state that had been founded by Quakers. Western Reserve newspapers carried adver-

[2] Charles T. Hickok, *The Negro in Ohio, 1802–1870* (Cleveland, 1896), 33–39, 40–46; Helen M. Thurston, "The 1802 Constitutional Convention and [the] Status of the Negro," *Ohio History*, 81 (Winter 1972), 15–37; Robert E. Chaddock, *Ohio before 1850: A Study of the Early Influence of Pennsylvania and Southern Populations in Ohio*, Columbia University Studies in History, Economics, and Public Law, vol. 31, no. 2 (New York, 1908), 82–86; Franklin Johnson, *The Development of State Legislation Concerning the Free Negro* (New York, 1918), 161–63. For a survey of the legal disabilities facing Negroes throughout the North at this time, see Leon Litwack, *North of Slavery: The Negro in the Free States, 1790–1860* (Chicago, 1961), 64–112. See also Frank U. Quillin, *The Color Line in Ohio: A History of Race Prejudice in a Typical Northern State* (Ann Arbor, 1913), 13–34, 44–59.

tisements for fugitive slaves, and—notwithstanding the 1819 kidnapping case—runaways captured in northern Ohio were often routinely returned to their masters.[3]

In confronting the questions of slavery and race during the 1820s and much of the 1830s, the chief hallmark of white opinion in Cleveland was the desire to avoid sectional conflict. The Cuyahoga County Colonization Society was founded in 1826, and its proposed "solution" to the race question—gradual abolition and the colonization of blacks in Africa or South America—rapidly gained adherents and was soon being advocated by the Cleveland *Herald*, the city's leading newspaper at that time. The *Herald* defended the Colonization Society as "a highly useful institution" and opposed any scheme of emancipation that did not include a plan to reimburse the slave owners for the loss of their "property." Commenting in 1833 on the more militant advocates of abolition that were beginning to organize in New England, the *Herald* stated with satisfaction that "The visionary schemes of enthusiasts who would, to effect their purposes, jeopardize even our happy form of government, find but few advocates in this place [the Western Reserve]." Two years later a large proslavery meeting in the city resolved to "distinctly disclaim any right to interfere with the subject of slavery in the southern states" and condemned the abolitionists for menacing "the peace and permanence of the union. . . ."[4]

During the next two decades, however, while white sentiment throughout much of the North turned against the Negro in an effort to placate southern opinion, the attitude of people in the Western Reserve shifted dramatically in the opposite direction. Inundated by settlers from New England, many of whom were steeped in evangelical religion and were hospitable to reform causes of all types, the Reserve exhibited a growing hostility to slavery during the years preceding the Civil War. Much of northern Ohio became, in fact, a hotbed of abolitionism, and Cleveland and surrounding towns became regular stopping points on the underground railroad. "It is well known," William Wells Brown, the

[3] Cleveland *Herald*, November 14, 1820, January 2, 1821; Cleveland *Register*, April 27, June 8, 15, 1819, in Works Projects Administration, *The Annals of Cleveland* (Cleveland, 1937–38), III, 77, IV, 148, I, 499, 579, 587, 589 (hereafter cited as *Annals*); Chaddock, *Ohio before 1850*, 88–93; A. G. Riddle, "Rise of the Anti-Slavery Sentiment on the Western Reserve," *Magazine of Western History*, 6 (1887), 154; Wilbur Henry Siebert, *The Mysteries of Ohio's Underground Railroads* (Columbus, 1951), 26–132.

[4] Cleveland *Herald*, November 3, 1826, January 11, 25, 1828, April 9, 23, August 17, October 26, 1833; Cleveland *Whig*, September 16, 1835, in *Annals*, IX, 40, XI, 252, 253, XV, 138, 139, 141, XVIII, 107.

black abolitionist, noted in 1848, "that a great number of fugitives make their escape to Canada, by way of Cleaveland; and while on the lakes, I always made arrangements to carry them on the boat to Buffalo or Detroit, and thus effect their escape to the 'promised land.' The friends of the slave, knowing that I would transport them without charge, never failed to have a delegation when the boat arrived at Cleaveland." As one historian has noted, the Fugitive Slave Act of 1850 became virtually a dead letter throughout the Reserve; and local abolitionists, as illustrated most dramatically by incidents like the Oberlin-Wellington rescue of 1858, made it very difficult for southern slaveholders to capture runaways once they reached the northeastern part of the state.[5]

As a number of scholars have recently shown, supporters of the anti-slavery cause did not necessarily also favor racial equality. In Cleveland, however, the two ideas were frequently conjoined, and militant abolitionists were almost always in the forefront of the struggle for equal rights. Beginning in 1838, the Cuyahoga County Anti-Slavery Society began pressuring office-seekers to take a strong stand against the Black Laws, and during the 1840s the repeal of the codes became a leading issue on the Reserve. Even the moderate Cleveland *Herald* came out against the codes in 1844, stating that in the future such laws would "be cited as evidence of the barbarous character of the state of Ohio in the early part of the 19th century." In 1848 the abolitionist congressman Joshua Giddings and other "conscience Whigs" led a mass defection to the Free Soil party. The Reserve sent an entire slate of Free Soil legislators to the state capitol, where they held the balance of power and were partially responsible for the repeal of most of the state's notorious Black Laws. The region remained a stronghold of radicalism during the crisis of the next two decades. In the Ohio Constitutional Convention of 1851, the delegates from Cuyahoga County voted unanimously against the anti-Negro provisions that were eventually included in the revised document, and in 1867 the county voted heavily in favor of granting

[5] Riddle, "Rise of the Anti-Slavery Sentiment on the Western Reserve," 145–46; Chaddock, *Ohio before 1850*, 104; Samuel P. Orth, *A History of Cleveland, Ohio* (Chicago, 1910), I, 290–99; Karl Geiser, "The Western Reserve in the Anti-Slavery Movement, 1840–1860," Mississippi Valley Historical Society *Proceedings*, 5 (1911–12), 73–98; William C. Cochran, *The Western Reserve and the Fugitive Slave Law: A Prelude to the Civil War*, Western Reserve Historical Society Collections, no. 101 (Cleveland, 1920), 78–211; *The Narrative of William W. Brown, A Fugitive Slave* (Reading, Mass., 1969; first published 1848), 46, 48; Russell H. Davis, *Memorable Negroes in Cleveland's Past* (Cleveland, 1969), 23. The description of the Fugitive Slave Act as a "dead letter" in the Reserve was made by Wilbur Siebert; see his *Mysteries of Ohio's Underground Railroads*, 264–79.

suffrage to Ohio Negroes (unfortunately, a majority of the state's voters rejected the proposal). During the 1850s and 1860s Cleveland sent two Radical Republicans, Edward Wade and Rufus Spaulding, to Congress. The entire region remained staunchly Republican during the next half-century.[6]

[6] Cleveland *Herald and Gazette*, September 23, 1838; Cleveland *Herald*, October 5, 1839, December 20, 1844, November 1, 21, 1845; Cleveland *Whig*, February 10, 1847, in *Annals*, XXI, 394–95, XXII, 132, XXVII, 560–61, XXVIII, 189; Cochran *The Western Reserve and the Fugitive Slave Law*, 81, 84–85; Quillin, *The Color Line in Ohio*, 38–40, 43, 100 (map showing 1867 vote on Negro suffrage by counties); Theodore C. Smith, *The Liberty and Free Soil Parties in the Northwest* (New York, 1897), 23, 35, 90–91; Cleveland *Daily True Democrat*, December 9, 1848, October 1, 1852; Cleveland *Leader*, April 9, 1867; A. G. Riddle, "Recollections of the Forty-Seventh General Assembly of Ohio, 1847–48," *Magazine of Western History*, 6 (1887), 341–51 (the assembly actually met 1848–49); N. S. Townshend, "The Forty-Seventh General Assembly of Ohio—Comments upon Mr. Riddle's Paper," *ibid.*, 6 (1887), 623–28; Thomas A. Flinn, "Continuity and Change in Ohio Politics," *Journal of Politics*, 24 (1962), 521–44. Giddings's career is surveyed in George W. Julian, *The Life of Joshua R. Giddings* (Chicago, 1892), and in Jane H. Pease and William H. Pease, *Bound with Them in Chains: A Biographical History of the Antislavery Movement* (Greenwood, Conn., 1972).

Several scholars have contended that it was the small size of the black population in the counties of the Western Reserve that was responsible for the lenient racial attitudes of many whites. "The blacks were not numerous enough in the Western Reserve to excite hostility," said William Cochran (*The Western Reserve and the Fugitive Slave Law*, 80). Frank Quillin carried this thesis further; after surveying racial attitudes in different parts of Ohio in the nineteenth century, he concluded that "the greater the negro population, the greater the white man's prejudice" (*The Color Line in Ohio*, 73). While this contention has some validity, it would be a mistake to push the point too far. There was only a very rough correlation between proportional vote against Negro suffrage in 1867 (one of the most readily available indicators of prejudice) and the size of a county's black population. The four counties with the largest number of blacks did vote heavily against suffrage, but counties with moderate-sized or small black populations followed no set pattern. There were some parts of the state that contained very few Negroes but still strongly opposed equal rights, both in the Constitutional Convention of 1851 and in the suffrage vote. (See maps in *ibid.*, 74–75, 100–101.) In explaining the egalitarianism of some whites, one is inclined to give considerable weight to the statement of one delegate from the Reserve who attended the 1851 convention: "Our sympathy for them [blacks] does not spring from our ignorance of them, but from the conviction that they are human beings and therefore entitled to all the rights and privileges and sympathies due to humanity, and from the conviction that they, equally with other men, are susceptible of intellectual and moral elevation" (*ibid.*, 70). The ideology of Radical Republicanism in the Western Reserve (as in other abolitionist centers of the North) was based fundamentally upon a moral opposition to slavery, but it also frequently entailed a rejection of nativism and an acceptance of the idea of equality between the races. For a general discussion, see the brilliant study by Eric Foner, *Free Soil, Free Labor, Free Men: The Ideology of the Republican Party before the Civil War* (New York, 1970), especially chs. 4, 7, 8, and 9. Also useful is James McPherson, *The Struggle for Equality* (Princeton, N.J., 1964), ch. 6.

Whites in southern and central Ohio, where hostility to blacks was widespread and growing during the 1850s, often expressed incredulity over the egalitarian or antislavery sentiments of many Clevelanders. When the Cleveland *Leader*, the city's leading Republican paper, quoted Frederick Douglass at length on the Kansas-Nebraska controversy in 1855, it drew fire from a Columbus newspaper. "What is the matter with the *Leader*?" asked the Columbus editor. "Does it go for Fred[erick] Douglass[?] Will no white man do?" The response of the *Leader* was unequivocal. "We infinitely prefer Fred[erick] Douglas[s] to the Chicago [i. e., Stephen A.] Douglas, or any of the Nebraska conspirators. We judge men by their principle."[7]

Such statements did not represent the opinion of all segments of the white population of Cleveland. If the *Leader* reflected what was undoubtedly the dominant view in the community, the Cleveland *Plain Dealer*, its Democratic competitor, accurately mirrored the views of those whites who believed in Negro inferiority and distrusted the abolitionist fervor of the majority. Although it changed course a number of times on specific issues, the *Plain Dealer* generally supported the "popular sovereignty" position on the extension of slavery into the territories. The paper also backed the Fugitive Slave Act. "The right to reclaim fugitives from labor," it editorialized vehemently in January, 1859, "*is in the Constitution.*" For many years, the paper was not above making racist jibes at the black citizens of Cleveland, Oberlin, and elsewhere, and it looked to the voluntary colonization of Negroes in Africa, rather than the attainment of equal rights in the United States, as the key to the nation's racial problems. "We have ever contended that Africa was the spot, the quarter of the Globe," the paper's editor stated in 1859, "originally designed for them and to which our free colored population should be *encouraged*, not *driven*, to go. . . . This is a government of white men; let them establish a government of colored men."[8]

The persistence of such views in nineteenth-century Cleveland insured a residue of prejudice and discrimination and made the achievement of absolute equality on the part of the city's black residents an impossibility. But until the end of the nineteenth century, if not later, the views expressed by the *Plain Dealer* were very far from being dominant among whites in the community. The racial egalitarianism of most whites, combined with the fluid social and economic conditions preva-

---

[7] Cleveland *Leader*, November 10, 1855.
[8] Archer H. Shaw, *The Plain Dealer: One Hundred Years in Cleveland* (New York, 1942), 82; Cleveland *Plain Dealer*, January 13, 1859.

lent in a rapidly growing frontier city, made nineteenth-century Cleveland much less oppressive for blacks than most other municipalities in the United States.

II

The growth of Cleveland during the nineteenth century was remarkable. Prior to 1832 the village remained a small, struggling frontier settlement. But in that year the Ohio and Erie Canal, connecting the Ohio River and Lake Erie, was completed, and Cleveland became the northern terminus of that important waterway. This gave the town the economic boost that it needed, and the completion of the first railroad linkages to New York and Cincinnati in the 1850s insured Cleveland's commercial dominance of northern Ohio over all rivals. The total population of Cleveland increased from a few thousand in 1830 to over ninety thousand, four decades later. Yet even this was insignificant compared with the expansion that lay ahead.[9] (See Table 1.)

TABLE 1. *Negro population of Cleveland, 1850–1930*

Year	Total population	Negro population[a]	Percentage Negro	Percentage of increase Total population	Percentage of increase Negro population
1850	17,034	224	1.3		
1860	43,417	799	1.9	142.0	180.0
1870	92,829	1,293	1.4	107.0	62.1
1880	160,416	2,062	1.3	72.5	59.3
1890	261,353	3,035	1.2	63.0	46.9
1900	381,768	5,988	1.6	46.0	98.7
1910	560,663	8,448	1.5	46.9	40.9
1920	796,841	34,451	4.3	42.1	307.8
1930	900,429	71,899	8.0	13.0	108.3

SOURCE: U.S. Census Bureau Reports, 1850–1930.
[a] Figures for years before 1900 include Chinese, Japanese, and "civilized Indians." These groups, however, were very small compared with the Negro population.

Cleveland's black community was almost as old as the city itself, but it grew at a slower rate. The first permanent black resident was a free Negro who migrated from Maryland in 1809, only a dozen years after Moses Cleaveland had staked out his original claim on the shores of Lake Erie. By 1850 the black population had increased to more than three hundred and comprised 1.8 percent of the inhabitants of the

[9] Orth, *A History of Cleveland*, I, 98–116; Department of the Interior, Census Office, *Report on the Social Statistics of Cities*, pt. II (Washington, 1887), 377–78.

Forest City. During the following decade, this community of "free persons of color" (as they called themselves) almost tripled in size, and between 1860 and 1880 their numbers continued to grow at a steady, if somewhat slower, rate. At the close of the Reconstruction era there were slightly more than two thousand Afro-Americans residing in the city.[10] The demographic characteristics of this small but growing black community ran counter to almost all of the stereotypes—then and now— about black urban life. There was not, as in most eastern and southern cities, a higher proportion of females to males; in 1850 males constituted 51.8 percent of the Cleveland Negro population. Nor was there an unusually large number of children or young people in the city's black community. In 1850, 52.4 percent of the blacks residing in Cuyahoga County were under the age of twenty-one; but by 1880, as a result of the migration of childless adults from other states, this percentage declined to 39.9. Almost all of the black families (93.1 percent in 1850; 85.2 percent twenty years later) were headed by males, and large families were clearly the exception rather than the rule: in 1880 68.4 percent of all black households in the county contained four persons or less.[11]

[10] Harry E. Davis, "Early Colored Residents of Cleveland," *Phylon,* 4 (July 1943), 235–36.

[11] This information is taken from Thomas J. Goliber's study of manuscript census data, "Cuyahoga Blacks: A Social and Demographic Study" (M.A. thesis, Kent State University, 1972), 22–34. It is now becoming clear that the sociological description of urban black lower-class families as "disorganized" and "matriarchal" as a result of "the impact of urban life on the simple family organization and folk culture which the Negro has evolved in the rural South" (E. Franklin Frazier, *The Negro Family in the United States,* New York, 1939, 41) is far from accurate when applied to families of the nineteenth century. In 1880, 82 percent of black households in Boston had two parents, and southern black migrants who came to that city at that time did not seem to experience any trend toward family "disorganization." In Philadelphia, where conditions were worse than in Boston, there was a somewhat higher proportion of female-headed households, especially among the poorer black families. But there is reason to believe that Philadelphia was not typical in this regard. An extensive study of black families in Pittsburgh, Cincinnati, Louisville, and several smaller Ohio River Valley cities between 1850 and 1880 shows that nuclear, male-headed households were predominant at that time; the percentage of black families in 1880 headed by males in Ohio Valley communities averaged over 80 percent. See Elizabeth Pleck, "The Two-Parent Household: Black Family Structure in Late Nineteenth-Century Boston," *Journal of Social History,* 6 (Fall 1972), 3–31; Theodore Hershberg, "Free Blacks in Antebellum Philadelphia: A Study of Ex-Slaves, Freeborn and Socioeconomic Decline," *ibid.,* 5 (Winter, 1971), 186; John W. Blassingame, *Black New Orleans, 1860–1880* (Chicago, 1972), 79–104; Paul Lammermeier, "The Urban Black Family in the Nineteenth Century: A Study of Black Family Structure in the Ohio Valley, 1850–1880," *Journal of Marriage and the Family,* 35 (August 1973), 454. Herbert Gutman's forthcoming history of the black family in the United States will analyze this problem in great detail.

As early as 1860, most of Cleveland's black population resided on the East Side, and the center of the Negro community was the old haymarket district on Central Avenue. Prior to the 1880s, however, there was no noticeable trend toward the ghettoization of the black population. Before then, in fact, no ward in the city was more than five percent black; and although blacks were concentrated essentially in three wards (the First, Fourth, and Sixth), they were thoroughly integrated in each. No segregated neighborhoods as such existed. Nor were blacks housed primarily in multiple-unit dwellings; in 1880 almost 70 percent of the city's Negroes lived in single-household units.[12]

The residential distribution of blacks in Cleveland before 1880—a clustering in certain areas of the city coupled with a high degree of integration *within* those areas—was probably quite similar to that of most other cities. On the basis of recently completed research, it now appears that the pattern of life in nineteenth-century urban America was usually not amenable to the formation of ghettos, either black or immigrant. Although in a few isolated instances (the best example is the Irish in Boston) a significant level of residential segregation was in evidence, this was the result of unique local conditions. Generally speaking, the high geographic mobility of urban workers, the rapid growth of many cities, unpredictable patterns of land use, and the need for people of all classes to live fairly close to their place of employment made the strict residential separation of any one group or class difficult. To be sure, blacks—more so than immigrants or native whites—tended to be restricted quite often to the poorer sections of many cities, but this was primarily the result of economic factors (the lower income of many Negroes) and only indirectly the result of racial prejudice. And in spite of this, it seems doubtful that anything even remotely resembling a real black ghetto existed in American cities, north or south, prior to the 1890s.[13]

[12] William Ganson Rose, *Cleveland: The Making of a City* (Cleveland, 1950), 218, 235; Works Projects Administration, "The Peoples of Cleveland" (typewritten manuscript [1942], Cleveland Public Library), 185, 195; Goliber, "Cuyahoga Blacks," 53, 60.

[13] For perceptive comments on this point, see Zane L. Miller, *Boss Cox's Cincinnati* (New York, 1968), 11; Sam Bass Warner, Jr., *The Private City: Philadelphia in Three Periods of Its Growth* (Philadelphia, 1968), 56–57, and Sam Bass Warner, Jr. and Colin Burke, "Cultural Change and the Ghetto," *Journal of Contemporary History*, 4 (October 1969), 173–87. On geographic mobility, see Stephan Thernstrom and Peter R. Knights, "Men in Motion: Some Data and Speculations about Urban Population Mobility in Nineteenth-Century America," *Journal of Interdisciplinary History*, 1 (Fall 1970), 1–19. On the segregation of the Irish in Boston, see Oscar Handlin, *Boston's Immigrants: A Study in Acculturation*, rev. ed. (New

Chicago and New York may be partial exceptions to this observation. In the late nineteenth century, *some* blacks in these cities undoubtedly lived in all-black sections of perhaps a few square blocks in size. Although Chicago had no clear-cut ghetto at the time, most of its black population was residentially restricted at an early date. A good deal of this may have been one of the indirect results of the fire of 1871 that almost destroyed the city; it allowed various groups to resettle in new areas and provided an opportunity to exclude blacks from neighborhoods where they had previously resided. Even before the fire, however, Afro-Americans were more segregated in Chicago than elsewhere, and the exact reason for this is unclear. The key may lie in the peculiar distribution of the city's ethnic elements, especially in the perhaps accidental tendency of blacks to settle in an area so close to hostile immigrant groups.[14]

Conditions in New York and Chicago were not typical, however. Even in such relatively "racist" cities as Detroit and Cincinnati there is no evidence of the existence of well-defined ghettos before 1890. A historian of Detroit's nineteenth-century black community found that in 1880 "even in the area of highest Negro concentration, blacks and whites lived next to one another." Summarizing conditions in Cincinnati in 1880, another scholar notes that "while the black population was concentrated in the poorer areas of the city, two-thirds of them lived in mixed blocks, inhabited chiefly by low-income Irish immigrants." In a number of smaller, more recently founded cities, blacks were also fairly well integrated residentially, and may in addition have been dispersed over a much wider area of the city than in older urban centers.[15]

York, 1959), 88–100. Even in Boston the Irish were not confined to a single unified ghetto; clusters of Irish immigrants were located in many parts of the city.

[14] Gilbert Osofsky, *Harlem: The Making of a Ghetto, Negro New York, 1890–1930* (New York, 1966), 12; St. Clair Drake and Horace R. Cayton, *Black Metropolis: A Study of Negro Life in a Northern City* (New York, 1945), 46–47, 62. Osofsky's description, "Handfuls of small and densely populated ghettos, usually a block or two in length, were found throughout Manhattan," stretches the definition of ghetto too far, however. Such small units of population are more accurately portrayed as "clusters" or "enclaves" than as ghettos.

[15] David M. Katzman, *Before the Ghetto: Black Detroit in the Nineteenth Century* (Urbana, Ill., 1973), 69; Paul J. Lammermeier, "Cincinnati's Black Community: The Origins of a Ghetto, 1870–1880," in John H. Bracey, August Meier, and Elliott Rudwick, eds., *The Rise of the Ghetto* (Belmont, Calif., 1971), 26; W. E. B. Du Bois, *The Philadelphia Negro: A Social Study* (Philadelphia, 1899), 58–62 and the map preceding the title page. Prior to about 1880, the amount of residential segregation in southern cities was quite minimal. Although as early as 1850 some very small predominantly Negro sections existed on the outskirts of Richmond, New Orleans, and Charleston, South Carolina, as well as elsewhere in

Although fairly typical in their patterns of residency, in other respects the social and economic status of blacks in Cleveland throughout most of the nineteenth century was much superior to that of blacks in most other parts of the state or country. Prior to the passage of the Fifteenth Amendment, of course, all Negroes in Ohio were excluded from holding public office, and most were denied the right to vote.[16] But with these significant exceptions, most of the disabilities that free blacks suffered in other localities usually did not occur in Cleveland. Segregation in public accommodations, for example, was infrequent and usually short-lived. As late as 1883, the editor of Cleveland's weekly black newspaper, the *Gazette*, claimed that no hotel in the city excluded Negroes—a statement that could be made of few municipalities outside of New England at that time. Integrated facilities were also the rule rather than the

the South, these districts housed only a small minority of the aggregate black populations of these metropolises. At that time most southern black urban dwellers were servants who lived in or near the residences of the whites for whom they worked; but even self-employed black artisans and entrepreneurs tended to be residentially integrated. See Richard C. Wade, *Slavery in the Cities: The South, 1820–1860* (New York, 1964), 273–80; Karl E. Taeuber and Alma F. Taeuber, *Negroes in Cities: Residential Segregation and Neighborhood Change* (Chicago, 1965), 45–46; John W. Blassingame, "Before the Ghetto: The Making of the Black Community in Savannah, Georgia, 1865–1880," *Journal of Social History*, 6 (Summer 1973), 481.

[16] Many scholars incorrectly list Ohio among those states which categorically prohibited Negro voting before the Civil War. Although the constitution of Ohio stated that only white males were entitled to vote, the state Supreme Court in 1842 upheld the right of suffrage of mulattoes with less than one-half Negro blood, on the grounds that such persons were more white than Negro. (*Parker Jeffries* v. *John Ankeny et al.*, 11 Ohio 372; *Edwin Thacker* v. *John Hawk et al.*, 11 Ohio 377.) These decisions, as well as other liberal interpretations of the Black Laws, led to much bitterness among whites in central and southern Ohio, and in 1859 the state legislature passed a bill excluding from the franchise anyone with "a distinct and visible admixture of African blood." (*Ohio Laws, 1859,* 120.) Yet this legislation did not prevent mulattoes from voting in the Western Reserve. Shortly after the passage of the 1859 law Freeman Morris, a Cleveland tailor of one-quarter Negro ancestry, brought suit in common pleas court when an election judge denied him the right to vote. Judge John A. Foote, a Radical Republican, ruled in favor of Morris and declared the law unconstitutional. The decision was not appealed, and apparently mulattoes continued to vote without interference in Cleveland and perhaps in other parts of the state as well. (*Weekly Anglo-African*, July 30, 1859; Cleveland *Leader*, April 18, 1867, January 20, April 6, 1868; Russell H. Davis, "The Negro in Cleveland Politics: Negro Political Life Begins," Cleveland *Call and Post*, September 10, 1966.) In 1868 the state legislature passed a much more elaborate "visible admixture" law, this time allowing any bona fide white voter to challenge the vote of any person whom he suspected to be Negro. (*Ohio Laws, 1868–69,* 97.) The Ohio Supreme Court immediately declared this law unconstitutional also (*James Monroe et al.* v. *George Collins*, 17 Ohio State Reports 666), reasserting the doctrine it had laid down in 1842. With the passage of the Fifteenth Amendment in 1870, of course, all blacks in Ohio gained the right of suffrage.

exception in most of the city's restaurants, lecture halls, and other public facilities. "An indication of the civilized spirit of the city of Cleveland," boasted the *Leader* in 1865, "is found in the fact that colored children attend our schools, colored people are permitted to attend all public lectures and public affairs where the fashion and culture of the city congregate, and nobody is offended."[17]

The *Leader's* statement was not, unfortunately, accurate in every respect. Racial prejudice was not completely absent from mid-nineteenth-century Cleveland. When, for example, Frederick Douglass visited the city in 1852, he was allowed to lodge at the Forest City House but was denied the right to take his meals at the common table with the rest of the hotel's guests. In 1851 the first attempt was made to establish a "colored gallery" in a Cleveland theater (whether the move was successful, or how long the policy of segregation lasted, is unclear), and throughout the Reconstruction era the Cleveland Academy of Music successfully barred black patrons from its dress circle. The fact that the *Leader* castigated the proprietor of the Academy as a "negro hater" did not make it easier for blacks to accept the policy of segregation.[18]

While such examples of discrimination existed, however, they were not (at least prior to 1890), typical of conditions in the city. Most theaters and other public facilities did not segregate blacks, a fact that surprised and sometimes infuriated visitors from other parts of the country where rigid segregation was the rule. When two Texans traveling through the North in 1865 stopped at Cleveland for supper, they related that "[we] had not more than taken our seats at the principal hotel when two buck negroes deliberately seated themselves opposite." This proved too much for their "Southern raising" and they promptly "left the table in great disgust." In large measure (though not invariably) the policy of integrated facilities received the backing of the judges and juries who interpreted the laws. An attempt to segregate Negroes by one of the city's streetcar companies in 1864 lead to a court decision making integration mandatory. In another case brought before a local court in 1868, a young Afro-American who had been excluded from a city skating rink sued the owner of the establishment and won a settlement of three hundred dollars—a considerable sum at that time. Undoubtedly the possibility of such action on the part of the legal authorities made owners

[17] David A. Gerber, "Ohio and the Color Line: Racial Discrimination and Negro Responses in a Northern State, 1860–1915" (Ph.D. dissertation, Princeton University, 1971; to be published as *Black Ohio and the Color Line, 1860–1915*, Urbana, Ill., 1976), 102; Cleveland *Leader*, March 7, 1865.

[18] Cleveland *Daily True Democrat*, September 4, 1851, May 20, 1852; Cleveland *Leader*, March 7, 1865. See also *ibid.*, May 3, 1856.

and managers think twice before they tried to draw the color line.[19]

Nowhere, perhaps, was the spirit of racial fairness more pervasive than in the city's school system. Despite the fact that prior to 1887 Ohio law either made no provision at all for black education or made it easy for communities to establish separate schools, Cleveland's public schools were integrated at an early date. From 1832 to 1837, before the city's school system had been formally established, the black community (with some help from white philanthropists) irregularly supported its own school, and during the early 1840s the City Council helped subsidize a private school for black children. By the end of that decade, however, the public educational system had been completely integrated, and it would remain that way until well into the twentieth century. The early policy of exclusion was probably due to the fact that state law, prior to 1848, limited access to the public schools to white children. This prohibited municipalities from establishing even segregated public schools for blacks. In addition, the legislature had inserted a statement in the original Cleveland city charter of 1835 that the schools were to be "accessible to all *white* children," and this may have had an intimidating effect.[20]

Once Cleveland's schools were integrated, few whites in the city disputed the new policy, and those that did were not numerous enough to turn back the clock. In 1859, when a group of whites living in the Sixth Ward "offered to pay for the erection of a separate school house for the exclusive use of colored children, in order to eliminate the necessity of colored children mingling with white children," the city Board of Education firmly rejected the proposal. This is not surprising, since the president of the Board at the time was the Rev. James A. Thome, a leading abolitionist and insistent advocate of racial equality who also served as pastor of the West Side Congregational Church. Other board members were equally adamant in opposing a separate school for blacks. "In the Hudson Street [Sixth Ward] school," said William Fogg, "there are 16 colored children scattered in five different rooms. I am opposed to any action like seating three or four in rooms by themselves,

[19] Cleveland *Leader*, July 1, 1864, May 6, 1865; Gerber, "Ohio and the Color Line," 76.

[20] Cleveland *Herald and Gazette*, July 11, 1837, March 29, 1839; Cleveland *Herald*, November 30, December 28, 1839, July 16, 1842, May 17, November 30, 1843, in *Annals*, XX, 379, XXII, 228, 233, 234, XXV, 223, XXVI, 296, 298; Hickok, *The Negro in Ohio, 1802–1870*, 88; James H. Kennedy, *History of the City of Cleveland* (Cleveland, 1896), 276; William J. Akers, *Cleveland Schools in the Nineteenth Century* (Cleveland, 1901), 29; Quillin, *The Color Line in Ohio*, 33, 45, 67.

thereby creating distinction and degrading these unfortunate children in their schoolmates' eyes. . . . I don't think my child is disgraced or contaminated by sitting next to these colored children. . . . Rather than consent to what I consider an act of injustice and oppression to any class or race of children I would resign my seat as a member of the board." After the Civil War, all resistance to integrated education in Cleveland faded away. In 1871, in an editorial criticizing segregation, the *Leader* stated that there "is no sound or reasonable objection" to integration of the schools, and that "the opposition to it springs wholly from that small and narrow prejudice which is no longer tolerable in this country." Most Clevelanders shared this opinion and accepted integrated schools as a fact of life, even if whites in Detroit and elsewhere did not.[21]

III

If blacks in nineteenth-century Cleveland achieved near-equality in access to public facilities, they also found the door of economic opportunity open wider in the Forest City than most other communities. At the Ohio Constitutional Convention of 1851, one white delegate from Cleveland used the general social and economic status of the city's blacks as proof enough that all Negroes deserved the right to vote. "The truth is," argued the Cleveland representative, "that if we apply to them the same measure of qualification that we do to the whites, they are as well qualified to exercise the right of suffrage as thousands of white voters in this or any other State." In 1858 the *Leader* chimed in its agreement. The city's black community, it claimed, contained many "old, intelligent, industrious and respectable citizens, who own property, pay taxes, vote at elections, educate their children in public schools, and contribute to build up the institutions and to the advancement of the prosperity of the city." Visitors to the city often agreed with these assessments. When William Wells Brown returned to Cleveland while on a lecture tour in 1857, he remarked upon "the intelligence, industry, and respectability of the colored citizens. . . . Indeed they will compare favorably with an equal number of whites in any portion of Ohio. Some of them are in good circumstances and are engaged in businesses employing their own capital." Wrote abolitionist James Freeman Clarke in 1859, "The feeling toward them [blacks] in Cleveland and throughout the Western Reserve is very kind, and there

---

[21] Cleveland *Leader*, May 11, December 20, 1859, January 13, 1871; Eugene H. Roseboom, *The Civil War Era, 1850–1873* (Columbus, Ohio, 1944), 194; Cochran, *The Western Reserve and the Fugitive Slave Law,* 159n.

they do better than in most places. There you find them master carpenters, master painters, shopkeepers, and growing rich every year."[22]

To be sure, not all of the city's Afro-Americans were "growing rich every year." But Cleveland's black community could boast a sizable number of success stories. George Peake, the city's first permanent black resident, owned a one-hundred-acre tract of land and invented and patented a new type of hand mill that made the production of meal from grain much easier. Alfred Greenbrier, another early resident, bred horses and cattle and became widely known for the excellence of the stock he raised. Madison Tilly, one of Cleveland's most prominent black citizens and an early political leader until his death in 1887, employed an integrated labor force of one hundred men in his lucrative business as an excavating contractor. He enjoyed social contacts with many prominent whites and left his sons an estate estimated at between $25,000 and $30,000. Dr. Robert Boyd Leach, Cleveland's first Negro physician, earned a degree from the city's Western Homeopathic College, one of the few medical colleges in the country that admitted Negroes. Leach's successful practice brought middle-class respectability; his home, the *Leader* noted in 1858, contained "all the pleasant surroundings which well-directed industry and economy usually bring with competence when directed by good taste." Freeman H. Morris owned a tailoring establishment in the Dunham House; he was described by the *Daily True Democrat* in 1850 as "a first rate workman and those who patronize him will be more than satisfied."[23]

Clearly the most prosperous black man in Cleveland before 1870, however, was the barber John Brown. Born in Virginia of free parents, Brown came to Cleveland in 1828. He soon established himself as one of the city's leading barbers, and by the early 1840s his income was large enough for him to almost single-handedly support a free school for blacks for several years. Through a judicious investment in real estate, Brown was able to accumulate about $40,000 in property by the time of his death in 1869.[24]

These successful individuals were not, of course, representative of the

[22] Quillin, *The Color Line in Ohio*, 67; Davis, *Memorable Negroes in Cleveland's Past*, foreword, n.p.; Cleveland *Leader*, February 8, 1858, quoted in introduction to Allan Peskin, ed., *North into Freedom: The Autobiography of John Malvin, Free Negro, 1795–1880* (Cleveland, 1966; first published 1879), 14; James Freeman Clarke, "Condition of the Free Colored People of the United States," *Christian Examiner*, 5th ser., 4 (1859), 255.

[23] Davis, "Early Colored Residents of Cleveland," 235–37; Davis, *Memorable Negroes in Cleveland's Past*, 7, 13, 17; Cleveland *Leader*, March 11, 1858; Cleveland *Daily True Democrat*, September 24, 1850.

[24] Cleveland *Leader*, March 31, 1869; Peskin, ed., *North into Freedom*, 72n.

entire black community, and there were, in fact, far more blacks near the lower than the upper end of the economic spectrum. Many blacks were dockworkers or unskilled laborers of various sorts. It is important, however, to place the economic and occupational structure of nineteenth-century black Cleveland in the proper context before evaluating it. Before 1870 (if not later), unskilled labor made up a relatively larger share of *all* groups in the economy, so the mere fact that many blacks were in this category does not, in itself, prove that their economic status was grossly depressed. For a more thorough understanding of the socio-economic standing of blacks it is necessary to look at both the male *and* female occupational structure of Negroes and to measure these against their native-white and ethnic counterparts.

Table 2 gives a breakdown of occupations by racial and ethnic group for Cleveland (in the case of blacks, for Cuyahoga County) in 1870. It reveals that a larger proportion of blacks were in the two lowest categories, unskilled labor and domestic service, than any other group in the economy of the city at that time. But there were also sizable numbers of the foreign-born in these two categories, and there was not a great deal of difference between the proportion of Negroes and Irish in the service jobs. Much more important was the ability of Afro-American males to gain access to the skilled trades; this job category, in fact, comprised about one-third of the black male work force. The proportion of blacks doing skilled work was little different from the rest of the city's work force, and blacks were much more likely to be artisans than were Irish immigrants. In the higher job categories blacks did not fare as well (although the number of black males in the professions was not noticeably lower than average), but in the professional and clerical occupations the foreign-born did little better.[25]

An analysis of female occupations shows that black women did not suffer any noticeable occupational discrimination because of their *race*. Sixty-two percent of all employed black women in the city were personal or domestic servants of one kind or another in 1870. In this respect, however, blacks differed little from the rest of the labor force, since 65.7 percent of *all* employed women in Cleveland worked as domestics. Gender, rather than race, was clearly the determining factor: it was females per se, not black females, whose occupational status was depressed at the time. Furthermore—perhaps because of the "stability"

[25] For a discussion of the limitations of these data, see the footnotes to Table 2. The occupational classification system used in this study is based upon that developed by Alba M. Edwards in *An Alphabetical Index of Occupations by Industries and Social-Economic Groups* (Washington, 1937) and is discussed in Appendix I.

TABLE 2. *Occupational structure of Cleveland, by ethnic and racial group, 1870*

	Occupational category						
	Professional	Proprietary	Clerical	Skilled	Semiskilled	Unskilled	Domestic service
Males							
Negroes[a]	1.4%	3.2%	0.8%	31.7%	14.8%	29.6%	14.8%
All workers[b]	1.9	7.4	7.4	30.2	12.0	14.7	0.9
Females							
Negroes[a]	1.0	2.9	—	—	26.5	7.8	61.7
All workers	4.2	0.5	1.7	—	22.8	0.1	65.7
Total work force							
Negroes	1.3	3.2	0.7	26.2	16.8	25.9	22.9
Foreign-born (total)	1.1	5.3	2.2	29.7	12.8	15.9	10.0
Native whites	3.9	8.5	10.7	21.0	15.6	4.5	8.5
German immigrants	1.2	6.8	1.9	33.6	11.0	16.3	7.1
Irish immigrants	0.7	3.1	1.7	16.9	11.6	19.8	15.8
English and Welsh immigrants	1.0	5.1	3.0	34.8	17.8	7.4	6.4
All workers	2.2	6.5	5.6	26.4	13.5	12.7	9.5

SOURCE: Thomas Goliber, "Cuyahoga Blacks: A Social and Demographic Study, 1850–1880" (M.A. thesis, Kent State University, 1972), 64–96; Department of the Interior, Census Office, *Ninth Census, 1870* (Washington, 1873), I, 784.
[a] Data for Cuyahoga County. The raw data on Negro occupations were taken from Goliber's study; the data were reorganized, however, according to the classification system explained in Appendix I of this volume. All other data were computed from the 1870 published census.
[b] Because more occupations in the 1870 printed census than in the 1870 manuscript census were unclassifiable (see Appendix I), it is likely that the percentages of white workers in skilled, semiskilled, and unskilled work, as listed above, are somewhat underestimated.

of the Negro family and the superior economic opportunities afforded black males in nineteenth-century Cleveland—there was only a slight tendency for black women to be employed more frequently than whites. In 1870, women made up 13.3 percent of the total work force, while females comprised 17.5 percent of the Negro work force.[26]

By means of a proportionate weighting of the different occupational categories, it is possible to calculate an occupational index which measures the average occupational standing of any group in the economy. (Throughout this study, this index will be one of the main tools used to compare the position of blacks relative to other groups.)[27] Table 3 shows that there was much less differentiation between the occupa-

TABLE 3. *Occupational indexes, by racial and ethnic group, Cleveland, 1870*

	Occupational index
Males	
Negroes	510
All workers	422
Females	
Negroes	618
All workers	617
Total work force	
Negroes	531
Foreign-born (total)	477
Native whites	414
Germans	459
Irish	528
English and Welsh	447
All workers	455

SOURCE: Table 2.

tional standing of Afro-Americans and other racial and ethnic groups in 1870 than would later become evident. The mythical "average" black male worker stood almost one full occupational unit below his white counterpart. But the typical employed male, regardless of the color of his skin or place of birth, was more likely to be a manual laborer than

[26] Although the 1870 printed census does not provide enough information to analyze female occupations by specific ethnic group, it is almost certain that Irish women tended to be employed more often, and at lower paying jobs, than German or English women. In 1890 German and English immigrant women made up, respectively, 12.6 percent of the total work forces of their ethnic groups; however, 20.6 percent of all employed Irish immigrants were female. U.S. *Thirteenth Census, Occupations* (Washington, 1893), II, 654–55.

[27] The occupational index is explained in Appendix I.

anything else; only among native whites did white-collar workers make up even 10 percent of the total work force. Negroes and Irish immigrants were clearly at the bottom of the occupational ladder. Cleveland in 1870, however, was still to a large extent a commercial rather than an industrial city, and there was much less diversity in its job structure than there would be later. As a result, there were not very many "rungs" between the top and bottom of the occupational ladder, and the status discrepancy between the highest and lowest groups on the scale was considerably foreshortened.

At the close of the Civil War, a large minority of Cleveland's black population had an aura of middle-class respectability. As a result of their unusual educational and economic opportunities, a significant number of blacks in the Forest City were able to accumulate property. Mention has already been made of several early black residents who acquired modest fortunes by buying land that later grew tremendously in value. The acquisition of property, however, was not limited to these lucky few. In 1850 eighteen blacks (23.6 percent of all heads of households) owned $15,660 in real estate. According to Thomas J. Goliber's meticulous compilation of manuscript census data, the total value of real property owned by Cuyahoga County Negroes increased dramatically to $237,400 in 1870, while the total number of property owners rose to 101, or 27.8 percent of the heads of households. Furthermore, those owning property in 1870 included many unskilled laborers and domestic servants who, despite their low occupational standing, had over the years been able to acquire modest holdings. The average value of the real estate owned by black property holders in Cuyahoga County in 1870 was $2,350; the average wealth per person (real estate and personal property) for the entire black population was $198. At a time when the average annual income of many workers was less than $500, these sums were not insignificant.[28]

Although a thorough history of black economic status remains to be written, it is clear from the scattered studies that exist that the overall economic standing of Cleveland's black population was higher than

[28] Goliber, "Cuyahoga Blacks," 98–101. Comparison of the economic status of black Clevelanders with the rural free Negroes of North Carolina is instructive. In 1860 the average wealth per person of the latter was only $34. John Hope Franklin, *The Free Negro in North Carolina, 1790–1860* (Chapel Hill, N.C., 1943), 159. Even more striking are the data on blacks in rural Adams County, Mississippi, recently compiled by Herbert Gutman. In 1880 only 6 percent of the adult black males in Adams County were farmers who owned property, and only 1 percent were skilled artisans. See Gutman, "The World Two Cliometricians Made," *Journal of Negro History*, 60 (January 1975), 123 (revised and reprinted, Urbana, Ill., 1975, as *Slavery and the Numbers Game: A Critique of Time on the Cross*).

that of most black communities in the nineteenth century. Perhaps the only city where black economic status surpassed that of Cleveland was New Orleans. During the 1860–80 period the free Negroes of that polyglot metropolis were employed in an amazing variety of skilled, semi-skilled, and proprietary occupations, and were able to accumulate substantial property, despite the racial antipathy of many whites. Whether this pattern prevailed elsewhere in the South is open to question, however. The situation in Atlanta was much different. There, in 1870, seven out of ten blacks were listed as laborers or servants. At the same time the number of blacks in Baltimore "with jobs requiring no skill at all far outweighed those with skilled or business or professional positions," and few Negroes in that city were able to acquire property.[29]

In most northern cities (at least those that have been studied so far), blacks were largely restricted to low-paying unskilled jobs.[30] As early as 1860, many black communities contained a property-holding middle class and even, in some cases, an elite group of well-to-do entrepreneurs; but these groups usually remained quite small. In New York City in 1855, for example, 76.9 percent of employed Negro males were either unskilled laborers or (as was more often the case) domestic servants, and only 5.6 percent held skilled jobs; less than one Negro in ten owned taxable property. In 1847 only 6 percent of the blacks living in Philadelphia owned real estate. The pattern of occupations there was similar to that of New York, although a considerably higher proportion of blacks (16 percent) were able to gain access to the skilled trades. The free Negroes of Washington, D.C., did somewhat better; by 1860 approximately 14 percent owned real estate. Conditions in antebellum Boston were much more favorable. There, in 1850, the occupational status of

[29] Blassingame, *Black New Orleans*, 60–61, 68–69, 223–28; Richard J. Hopkins, "Occupational and Geographical Mobility in Atlanta, 1870–1896," *Journal of Southern History*, 34 (May 1968), 204; Richard P. Fuke, "Black Marylanders, 1864–68" (Ph.D. dissertation, University of Chicago, 1973), 102, 105.

[30] It is important to note that this may also have been true of many immigrant groups and even some native whites, especially in the eastern seaboard cities during the antebellum period. Quantitative studies have shown that the social order of the large urban centers was becoming increasingly stratified on the eve of the Civil War. Stuart Blumin, "Mobility and Change in Ante-Bellum Philadelphia," in Stephan Thernstrom and Richard Sennett, eds., *Nineteenth-Century Cities* (New Haven, Conn., 1969), 204–6; Edward Pessen, 'The Egalitarian Myth and the American Social Reality: Wealth, Mobility, and Equality in the 'Era of the Common Man,'" *American Historical Review*, 76 (October 1971), 989–1034. A thorough analysis of the place of blacks in the socioeconomic order of nineteenth-century America would examine regional variations in black occupations and wealth-holding, would survey differences among blacks, imigrants, and native whites in each region or city, and would trace changes in these variations over time. This type of analysis is beyond the scope of the present study.

blacks easily surpassed that of the newly arrived Irish immigrants, most of whom were unskilled laborers or servants. A surprisingly large number of Boston Negroes (8.5 percent) operated small businesses, and an equally high 47.8 percent were employed as skilled or semiskilled workers. Among eastern cities, Boston was clearly exceptional in the opportunities it afforded blacks. In the fast-growing metropolises of the West and Midwest, the economic status of blacks was probably a good deal higher than that of most eastern cities. But even in Pittsburgh and Cincinnati, the average wealth per person for blacks in 1870 was only about two-thirds that of Cleveland.[31]

[31] Robert Ernst, "The Economic Status of New York City Negroes, 1850–1863," *Negro History Bulletin*, 12 (March 1949), 139–43 (footnote 38 and the "Special Statistical Note" at the end of the article); Gilbert Osofsky, "The Enduring Ghetto," *Journal of American History*, 55 (September 1968), 248; *A Statistical Inquiry into the Condition of the People of Color, of the City and Districts of Philadelphia* (Philadelphia, 1849), 14, 17; Du Bois, *The Philadelphia Negro*, 179–81; Hershberg, "Free Blacks in Antebellum Philadelphia," 187, 198–99; Dorothy Provine, "The Economic Position of the Free Blacks in the District of Columbia, 1800–1860," *Journal of Negro History*, 58 (January 1973), 68–69; John Daniels, *In Freedom's Birthplace: A Study of the Boston Negroes* (Boston, 1914), 18–19; Handlin, *Boston's Immigrants*, 69–70, 250–51 (Table 13). The percentages for black occupations in New York and Boston were computed from the manuscript census data provided by Handlin and Ernst; the occupational classification system used is explained in Appendix I. The data on wealth-holding in Pittsburgh and Cincinnati were supplied by Paul Lammermeier of Kent State University, whose forthcoming dissertation on the black communities of cities along the Ohio River Valley will deal extensively with the question of black occupations and property ownership, as well as with family structure and other aspects of black life.
The most thorough study of an antebellum black community, Theodore Hershberg's "Free Blacks in Antebellum Philadelphia," concludes that there was "a remarkable deterioration in the socioeconomic condition of blacks from 1830 to the Civil War." While this was undoubtedly true of Philadelphia and a number of other cities, it is important to note that these circumstances did not prevail uniformly throughout the country. Although blacks everywhere suffered from prejudice and discrimination, they were often able, in spite of handicaps, to make considerable economic progress at the time. (On this point, see E. Franklin Frazier, *The Free Negro Family*, Nashville, 1932, 12–23; Provine, "Economic Position of Free Blacks," 61–72; Letitia Woods Brown, *Free Negroes in the District of Columbia, 1790–1846*, New York, 1972, 140; and Blassingame, *Black New Orleans*, 10–11. See also the 1850 occupational data assembled by Katzman, *Before the Ghetto*, 29, although Katzman draws oddly negative conclusions from his findings.) Furthermore, our understanding of the economic status of black Americans in the nineteenth century is still incomplete because of the almost total scholarly neglect of northern blacks who lived outside the larger cities. It is seldom realized that throughout most of the nineteenth century most blacks—like most whites—resided in rural areas or small towns. While in some of these communities blacks lived in wretched poverty, in others quite the opposite conditions were in evidence. In rural New England, southwestern Michigan, and the Quaker settlements of Ohio, Indiana, and Illinois, blacks encountered little animosity from their white neighbors and little competition from immigrants and may as a result have had a much

IV

The low level of prejudice and unusual economic opportunities that prevailed in Cleveland before 1870 did not lead to a sense of complacency among the city's Afro-Americans. Rather it engendered a feeling of pride and a strong belief that the barriers of inequality that existed throughout most of the United States (as well as the remnants still evident in Cleveland) could only be surmounted through concerted, militant action. Blacks expressed this attitude most vigorously in their denunciation of the Fugitive Slave Law. "We will exert our influence to induce slaves to escape from their masters," a meeting of Cleveland Negroes declared in 1850, "and will protect them from recapture against all attempts, whether lawful or not, to return them to slavery."[32]

Afro-Americans in Cleveland and throughout the Western Reserve participated actively in the abolitionist movement and aided fugitive slaves in gaining safe passage to Canada. Alfred Greenbrier's farm, for many years equipped with a number of secret hideouts, served as an important link in the underground railroad; and Greenbrier's fine horses, according to legend, helped provide the necessary transportation to the next station along the line. Several other black leaders, especially John Brown and John Malvin, regularly assisted escaped slaves. By the 1850s, the city's black community had organized a vigilance committee of five men and four women whose purpose was to find temporary residence, material aid, and sometimes jobs for fugitives until they could be safely transported to Canada. During one nine-month period in 1854–55, the committee assisted a total of 275 runaways.[33]

When civil war erupted in 1861, Cleveland's black citizens were among the first to express their desire to serve in the Union army. "Resolved," they stated in an April 19 meeting, "that today, as in the times of '76, and in the days of 1812, we are ready to go forth and do battle in

---

better chance to acquire property than did their counterparts in Philadelphia and New York. In 1870—to give one readily available example—fully 57 percent of the black families living in the southern Ohio community of Portsmouth owned real estate. (Lammermeier, "The Urban Black Family in the Nineteenth Century," 445.)

[32] Cleveland *Daily True Democrat*, September 30, 1850.

[33] Davis, *Memorable Negroes in Cleveland's Past*, 11; Peskin ed., *North Into Freedom*, 44–46, 73–74; Benjamin Quarles, *Black Abolitionists* (New York, 1969), 153. Whether Greenbrier's farm was really as important a station in the underground railroad as legend would have us believe is difficult to determine. As Larry Gara has pointed out in *The Liberty Line: The Legend of the Underground Railroad* (Lexington, Ky., 1961), the exploits of many abolitionists tended to grow larger in the minds of some as the Civil War era receded into the haze of memory.

the common cause of our country." Negroes in Cleveland, as elsewhere, however, were not immediately allowed the opportunity to join in the struggle against the Confederacy. No sooner had the city's blacks offered their services than H. B. Carrington, the state's adjutant general, informed them that the Ohio constitution (which excluded blacks from the militia) did not allow their enlistment. During the first two years of the war, Ohio governor David Tod continued to resist all offers of blacks to volunteer; as a result, a number of blacks from Cleveland (including the barber John Brown's two sons) and other Ohio cities traveled to Massachusetts to join the black regiment that had been established there. It was not until the summer of 1863 that the recruitment of Negro troops in Ohio was finally authorized; black Clevelanders who joined after that date served in the Fifth United States Colored Troops, a regiment recruited almost exclusively from Ohio. The black community aided the war effort on the home front as well by contributing liberally to the Soldiers' Aid Society and holding several fairs to benefit the Cleveland branch of the Freedmen's Aid Society.[34]

Three leaders who exemplified the activism and militancy of the Cleveland black community during its early years were John L. Watson, William Howard Day, and John Malvin. In the 1840s, Watson was active in the Young Men's Union Society, a black organization founded "for mutual assistance and improvement" of the black community. Watson, a barber, was a frequent speaker at the Lyceum organized by the YMUS for the purpose of debating the important issues of the day; in 1842 he served as secretary of the School Committee organized at that time to support black education in the city. Watson was a delegate to a number of the state conventions held by Ohio Negroes prior to the Civil War. His prestige among Ohio Negroes was such that in 1850 he was appointed president of the 1850 State Convention of Colored Citizens and was one of two individuals named by the convention to lecture throughout the state on behalf of Negro suffrage. Apparently Watson left the city after 1858, but for two decades he had served the black community well as one of its most dynamic leaders.[35]

[34] Peskin, ed., *North into Freedom*, 84–85; Benjamin Quarles, *The Negro in the Civil War* (Boston, 1953), 29, 191–93; Charles H. Wesley and Patricia Romero, *Negro Americans in the Civil War* (New York, 1967), 61–62; Cleveland *Leader*, February 2, 13, 1865.

[35] Cleveland *Herald and Gazette*, February 5, March 29, 1839; Cleveland *Herald*, March 6, 1841, January 8, July 16, 1842, April 13, 1843, in *Annals* XXII, 129, 131, XXIV, 141, XXV, 179, 223, XXVI, 187; Cleveland *Daily True Democrat*, January 21, 30, February 2, 1850; *Report of Proceedings of the Colored National Convention held at Cleveland, Ohio, on Wednesday, September 6, 1848* (Rochester, N.Y.,

Though a resident of Cleveland for only a few years, William Howard Day gained more national recognition than Watson as a result of his many activities on behalf of the race. After graduating from Oberlin College in 1847, Day served briefly as a local editor for the white *Daily True Democrat*; for several years he also worked as a librarian for the Cleveland Library Association, the antecedent of the present library system. He edited the first black newspaper in Cleveland, *The Aliened American*, a militant journal which lasted from 1853 to 1855, and also published briefly in 1855 a monthly, *The People's Exposition*. A leading participant in the antebellum Negro Convention Movement, Day worked tirelessly on behalf of racial justice in the United States and also lectured abroad to raise funds for the assistance of fugitive slaves who had fled to Canada.[36]

It was not Day, however, but John Malvin, known as "Father John" by the time of his death in 1880 at eighty-five, who best exemplified both the militancy of the city's early black leaders and the high degree to which successful blacks were integrated into the general life of the community. Malvin worked at a variety of occupations, most of which entailed close contact with whites. At various times he served as cook, a sawmill operator, a carpenter and joiner, and a canalboat captain—in the latter instance, presiding over a thoroughly integrated crew. Eventually Malvin bought a lake vessel and built up a considerable business transporting limestone across Lake Erie to supply the city's first iron foundries.[37]

In the early 1830s, when Cleveland was still a village and had no public educational system, Malvin helped organize a school for blacks. Throughout most of his life, however, he fought for racial equality and the admission of blacks to white institutions, rather than for separate

---

1848); Howard H. Bell, "A Survey of the Negro Convention Movement, 1830–1861" (Ph.D. dissertation, Northwestern University, 1953), 139.

[36] Cleveland *Daily True Democrat*, September 10, 1852, June 15, 1853; Cleveland *Leader*, January 10, June 5, 1855; Davis, "Early Colored Residents of Cleveland," 24–43; J. Reuben Sheeler, "The Struggle of the Negro in Ohio for Freedom," *Journal of Negro History*, 31 (April 1946), 224; Bell, "A Survey of the Negro Convention Movement," 17, 107, 118, 141, 156, 172–73; Cleveland *Aliened American*, April 9, 1853. Day was one of the most militant black leaders of his era, and he urged Afro-Americans to use violent means if necessary to help slaves escape from bondage. (See *Proceedings of the Convention of Colored Men of Ohio, held in the city of Cincinnati, on the 23rd, 24th, 25th and 26th Days of November, 1858*, Cincinnati, 1858, 17–18.) The black editor left Cleveland in 1858 and eventually settled in Harrisburg, Pennsylvania, where he served for many years on the Board of Education. Day died in 1900.

[37] Peskin, ed., *North into Freedom*, 49–87; Davis, "Early Colored Residents of Cleveland," 237–40.

black institutions. Malvin and his wife, Harriet, were charter members of the First Baptist Church; and when the church's first permanent home was constructed in 1835, they were successful in preventing the segregation of black members in a separate "colored gallery." Malvin was a prominent member of the Cleveland Anti-Slavery Society, served as a lecturer for that organization, and personally assisted runaway slaves who were seeking safe passage to the border to the north. Though to a lesser extent than Day, Malvin was active in the Negro Convention Movement, and in 1843 he and one R. Robinson were the first blacks from Cleveland to attend a national convention. The ship captain fought vigorously against the Black Laws and was a frequent speaker at mass meetings protesting the unequal treatment that Afro-Americans received at the hands of the state legislature.[38]

Almost all of Cleveland's early black leaders were integrationists, and their success in breaking down many of the racial barriers that afflicted the race elsewhere caused them to look more hopefully to the future than did their brethren in other parts of the union. As a result, the sentiment for black emigration to Africa or Latin America that arose among an increasing number of northern black leaders during the pessimistic 1840s and '50s did not find much response among Afro-Americans in the Forest City. In a series of meetings held in the winter of 1845–46, Cleveland blacks joined with delegates from other cities to denounce the American Colonization Society as a racist organization that could only hinder the quest for equal rights in the United States. And seven years later a Cleveland delegate to the Ohio State Convention of Colored Freemen attacked the ACS as a "nefarious and diabolical" organization and supported a resolution naming the Society as "one of our worst enemies."[39]

[38] Peskin, ed., *North into Freedom*, 63–67, 56–57; *Minutes of the National Convention of the Colored Citizens Held at Buffalo, On the 15th, 16th, 17th, 18th and 19th of August, 1843* (New York, 1843), 11, 17–19; *Report of Proceedings of the Colored National Convention . . . 1848, passim*; Cleveland *Daily True Democrat*, June 15, 1853; *Proceedings of the National Convention of Colored Men, held in the City of Syracuse, N.Y., October 4, 5, 6, 7, 1864* (Boston, 1864), 6, 11. It is interesting to note that Malvin, unlike Day, was not willing to urge blacks to take up arms against the slaveholders. In the Negro Convention of 1843, he was one of the principal speakers against Henry Highland Garnet's resolution advocating violent rebellion by slaves.

[39] *African Repository and Colonial Journal*, 22 (1846), 265; *Cleveland Aliened American*, April 9, 1853. For the general black response to the Colonization Society and emigrationism, see Louis Mehlinger, "The Attitude of the Free Negro toward African Colonization," *Journal of Negro History*, 1 (July 1916), 271–301, and Hollis R. Lynch, "Pan-Negro Nationalism in the New World, Before 1862," in Jeffrey Butler, ed., *Boston University Papers on Africa*, II, *African History* (Boston, 1966), 149–79.

The ACS was a white organization; black Clevelanders also, however, opposed the plans of black emigrationists. In a meeting of the black citizens of the city in 1846 the question of emigrating was brought up, but "resolutions were adopted opposing the plan." And when a black emigrationist convention met in Cleveland in 1854 to promote colonization outside of North America, the *Leader* remarked "that the objects of the convention met with but little favor from our colored citizens." On the very eve of the Civil War there apparently was some upsurge of interest in emigration. "It has been announced," the press reported in March of that year, "that a party of intelligent colored citizens, mostly of Cleveland, propose to visit Africa, some to establish immediate homes, others to learn what advantages are to be found for those who wish to go." Whether the proposed trip was actually carried out is unknown, but with the coming of the Civil War no further mention of migrating to Africa was made by black Clevelanders.[40]

Equal access to most public accommodations and the integrationist ideology of Cleveland's black leadership retarded the development of separate black institutions in the city. Blacks did organize a number of informal literary and cultural groups and formed several debating societies, and in 1841 a black temperance society was formed. But unlike most cities in Ohio and throughout the North, Cleveland during these decades had few *formal* black institutions. The city had no separate schools for Negroes. The *Aliened American* was one of the earliest black newspapers in the country, but its existence was short-lived; it was less a community newspaper, in fact, than an organ for Negro leaders throughout the Midwest who were engaged in various protest activities. The small size of Cleveland's black population and the generally favorable editorial stance and news coverage of the *Leader* delayed the establishment of a regularly published black weekly until 1883.[41]

[40] Cleveland *Herald*, April 9, 1846, in *Annals*, IXXX, 177; Cleveland *Leader*, August 25, 1854, March 19, 1859. One black leader who did play an active role in the emigrationist movement was William Howard Day. Throughout the early 1850s, Day attempted to remain neutral on the emigration issue, but in 1856 he came out strongly for the plan and during the next six years actively promoted black migration to Africa (Cleveland *Leader*, September 18, 1858; Bell, "A Survey of the Negro Convention Movement," 141, 156, 173, 202–03, 208). By 1856, however, Day was more a national than a local leader, and he did not speak for the majority of black Clevelanders in supporting emigration.

[41] Cleveland *Herald*, April 21, 1841, 1841, in *Annals*, XXIV, 287; Davis, "Early Colored Residents of Cleveland," 240; Cleveland *Daily True Democrat*, January 1, 1850. On black support of the Cleveland *Leader*, see a letter to the editor of the *Leader*, October 12, 1874. On the *Leader's* radicalism compared with most other Midwestern white newspapers, see V. Jacque Voegeli, *Free But Not Equal: The*

Thanks to men like John Malvin, a number of Cleveland churches remained integrated until late in the nineteenth century. Cleveland's first
black church, St. John's AME (African Methodist Episcopal), was
founded in 1830, but it grew very slowly during its first two or three
decades and was serviced primarily by a lower-class element who felt
out of place attending the staid services of the integrated congregations.
In 1855 it was reported that the church was having difficulty meeting
the salary of its pastor, R. M. Thompson, and had to hold a "donation
party" to cover these expenses temporarily. During the next ten years
St. John's apparently grew in size, and the congregation was able to
move from their old home on Bolivar Street to a newly constructed
edifice on Ohio Street and to furnish their new pastor, John A. Warren,
with a parsonage. By 1863 the church had seventy-six members and "85
scholars in its Sunday school." Though a notable improvement over
earlier years, this figure still represented only about 15 percent of the
black population of the city at that time.[42]

The existence of integrated schools, churches, and other institutions
meant that the group life of Cleveland's black citizens would, for some
time, be different in several respects from that of most other black communities. The use of black churches as all-purpose institutions proved
largely unnecessary. "In addition to being a center of religious devotion
and ceremony," Leon Litwack has said in describing the typical antebellum black church, "it was a school, a political meeting hall, a community recreation and social center, and not too infrequently, a haven
for fugitive slaves." Black Clevelanders, however, had less pressing need
for these functions that the church provided elsewhere, because they
shared the schools, the meeting halls, and to some extent the recreation
and social centers of the city with white citizens.[43]

In time all this would change. The growth of the commercial town of
Cleveland into a major industrial metropolis, bringing with it new patterns of residency and employment; the changing racial attitudes of
whites in the city as well as in the country as a whole; the influx of immigrants from southern and eastern Europe; the declining influence and
changing values of the white elite of New England stock that ruled the
city during the nineteenth century; the increasing migration of impoverished blacks from the South—all these changes (and more) would

Midwest and the Negro during the Civil War (Chicago, 1967), 5, 62, 79, 86–87,
164.
    [42] Rose, Cleveland, 124, 325; introduction to Peskin, ed., North into Freedom,
18; Cleveland Leader, November 21, 1855, September 22, 1863.
    [43] Litwack, North of Slavery, 188.

gradually alter the status of the black population of Cleveland and call forth diverse responses from the city's black leaders.

For the time being, however, black Clevelanders enjoyed a significant degree of racial equality. Their condition was not, it is true, unsullied by prejudice and discrimination, and even during the Civil War and Reconstruction years, when sympathy for black rights was at its peak, there were hints of trouble to come. When fraternal lodges began to become popular after the war, Cleveland Negroes found (with a few exceptions) that they had to set up separate fraternal orders if they wished to participate in this activity. The formation in 1864 of a black middle-class church, Mt. Zion Congregational, was further evidence that there were limitations to the white acceptance of blacks as equals. In 1874, in a striking reversal of some previous judicial decisions, a Cleveland judge upheld the right of the proprietor of the Academy of Music to exclude black patrons from the theater's dress circle. These were clouds on the horizon, but they were not, as yet, significant enough to be viewed as part of a dangerous trend.[44] The development of the ghetto, and all that it entailed, still lay in the future.

[44] Cleveland *Leader*, November 30, 1874. Separate black Masonic and Odd Fellows lodges in Cleveland dated to 1856, but during the early years of these institutions a few blacks were accepted in white lodges. The development of black lodges and churches is surveyed in Chapter 5.

PART II

The Black Community in Transition, 1870-1915

CHAPTER 2

Urban Change and the Roots of the Ghetto

The period between 1870 and 1915 may be called the formative years of the black ghetto in the United States. Clear-cut black ghettos emerged in only a few cities during this period, but in most metropolises there was a noticeable increase in the residential segregation of blacks in a few fairly well defined sections. The intensification of racism during the post-Reconstruction decades (as discussed in Chapter 3) was one cause of the development of ghettos; it was not, however, the sole factor involved. Racial prejudice has always existed in the United States, but black ghettos have not. In order to understand the phenomenon of ghettoization, it is necessary to study the urban context as well as the racial context in which it occurred.

The ghettos began to take shape when they did because a period of growing racial hostility coincided with an era of dramatic change in the patterns of urban life. Between the Civil War and World War I, urban society in America underwent an enormous transformation. The increase in population alone—the total number of urban dwellers expanded from 6,200,000 in 1860 to almost 42,000,000 a half-century later—astounded European visitors as much as it delighted American boosters. During these years, New York's population approached five million; Chicago's exceeded two million; and several other cities reached or neared the one-million mark. Size was but one part of the story, however. Equally important was the reorganization that accompanied this growth in numbers. In the large urban areas, the "walking city" of the middle decades of the nineteenth century, with its haphazard arrangement of stores, businesses, and residential areas, was rapidly being replaced by a much more tightly organized urban structure. New modes of transportation—the omnibus, the electric streetcar, and by the end of the 1890s, the elevated train and subway—made possible the beginning of the exodus to the suburbs or to outlying areas of the city and allowed urban populations to sort themselves out by racial, ethnic, or socioeconomic group. At the same time, the expansion and diversification of large industries led to a more rigid system of zoning regulations than previously had existed. The result was the emergence of huge urban centers tied together by a nexus of economic relationships, but divided geographically into numerous commercial, industrial, and residential districts.[1]

Although the growth of Chicago during this period represented the archetypical model for urban change, Cleveland was no less dramatically affected. A huge influx of immigrant labor and the annexation of a number of adjacent towns helped Cleveland mushroom from a medium-sized urban center of 93,000 in 1870 to the "sixth city" in the nation, and an important industrial center, by the eve of World War I (see Table 1). The city never developed a subway or elevated system (a decision which probably retarded the development of suburbs until the 1920s, when the automobile came into widespread use), but the introduction of the electric streetcar in the 1890s made the common pattern of residential dispersion within the city possible. Geographically, Cleveland became more tightly organized during these years. For several miles along its length, the Cuyahoga River Valley became a solid industrial belt. (After World War I, the expansion of this industrial belt to the east would have an impact on the city's black population.) Lower Euclid and Superior avenues and East 9th Street became the main commercial and financial district for the city. As increasing numbers of newly arrived immigrants settled on the near East Side of the city, the exodus of Cleveland's elite, native-white constituency from that section began. Although

---

[1] Charles N. Glaab, ed., *The American City: A Documentary History* (Homewood, Ill., 1963), 174; Blake McKelvey, *The Urbanization of America, 1865–1915* (New Brunswick, N.J., 1963), 35–46, 76–85; Sam Bass Warner, Jr., *Streetcar Suburbs: The Process of Growth in Boston, 1870–1900* (Cambridge, Mass., 1962); Sam Bass Warner, Jr., *The Private City: Philadelphia in Three Periods of Its Growth* (Philadelphia, 1968), 161–76; Joel Arthur Tarr, "From City to Suburb: The 'Moral' Influence of Transportation Technology," in Alexander B. Callow, Jr., ed., *American Urban History: An Interpretive Reader with Commentaries,* 2d ed. (New York, 1973), 204–5. The best overall view of these changes (using Chicago as a case study) is Sam Bass Warner, Jr., *The Urban Wilderness: A History of the American City* (New York, 1972), ch. 4.

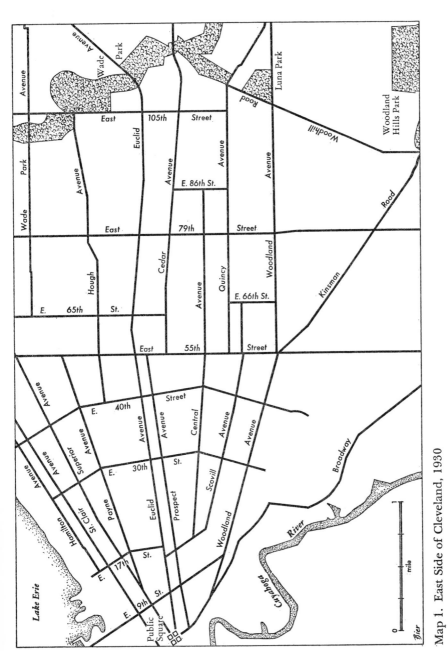

Map 1. East Side of Cleveland, 1930

much of Euclid Avenue (if not always the streets intersecting it) remained almost completely white as late as the 1950s, the noise of the
streetcars, coupled with the encroachment of business firms and the
foreign-born, persuaded most of the wealthy white families on that
thoroughfare to leave before World War I. Many of them resettled on
the quiet, tree-lined streets of the posh development beyond East 55th
Street between Hough and Euclid avenues. (This area would later become the center of the city's post–World War II black ghetto.) Simultaneously, many middle-class Clevelanders also moved east and north
of their previous, more centrally located residential areas, settling on the
equally respectable—if less exclusive—streets between Hough and Superior avenues.[2]

It was within this context of dramatic urban change that Cleveland's
black population expanded in size while simultaneously becoming more
restricted to certain parts of the city. In 1870, only thirteen hundred Negroes resided in the Forest City; by 1890, this number had increased to
three thousand. During the 1890s, the black population almost doubled
in size, but its growth rate fell off sharply during the next ten years. In
1910, the city contained eighty-five hundred black residents.

Migration from other states accounted for most of the growth of the
city's black community during these years. The black migration to Cleveland was part of a general drift of rural inhabitants to cities before World
War I. Declining or unstable economic conditions in many farming re-
gions, especially the South, caused many to move. Faced with a choice
between the stagnating economy of the rural South and the booming
factories of the North, the potential migrant had little trouble making a
decision. But as the black sociologist George Edmund Haynes astutely
noted, the beginnings of the black migration to the cities—a movement
which has not yet ended—was more the product of "unconscious social
forces" than reasoned alternatives. Blacks who migrated sought "better
opportunities," but they did not necessarily define opportunity solely in
economic terms. The desire for better schools, recreational facilities, and
the need (especially evident among the younger black generation that
had grown up since the Civil War) to escape the "hard, humdrum con-

[2] There is no thorough history of Cleveland for this period (or for that matter,
any other). I have relied chiefly on James B. Whipple, "Cleveland in Conflict: A
Study in Urban Adolescence, 1876–1900" (Ph.D. dissertation, Western Reserve
University, 1951); Archer H. Shaw, *The Plain Dealer: One Hundred Years in
Cleveland* (New York, 1942), 246–55; and the compilation of William Ganson
Rose, *Cleveland: The Making of a City* (Cleveland, 1950). On the slower growth
of Cleveland's suburbs, see W. Reynolds Farley, "Suburban Persistence" (M.A.
thesis, University of Chicago, 1963), 43–45.

ditions and poor accommodations on plantation and farm" undoubtedly played an important part in motivating these early migrants.[3]

It is likely that most of the black migrants who came to Cleveland before World War I were young—in their teens or twenties—and that males predominated. Unlike in most eastern and southern cities, the black populations of Cleveland and many other midwestern cities did not have a majority of females either before or, for that matter, after the World War I migration. In Cleveland in 1900 only 46.9 percent of the black population was female, and this percentage was even lower in many other cities beyond the Alleghenies. It is also likely that few of these migrants brought children with them. The impact of relatively youthful, childless migrants on Cleveland's black population is illustrated by the distribution by ages for different groups in 1910. The black community was not overburdened by an excessively large percentage of small children; it closely resembled the city's immigrant element, in fact, in that two-thirds of its population was between the ages of fifteen and forty-four. Only 2.4 percent of Cleveland's blacks were over sixty-five, and children under five years of age comprised only 6.1 percent of the total. (See Table 4.) This contrasted sharply with the native whites and second-generation immigrants, both of whom had a much larger percentage of children.

TABLE 4. *Population by age group, Cleveland, 1910*

| | | Percentages | | | |
	Total population	Native whites of native parentage	Native whites of foreign or mixed parentage	Foreign-born whites	Negroes
Under 5 years	11.1	14.1	18.6	.8	6.1
5–14 years	17.4	20.5	25.8	5.9	11.1
15–24 years	20.5	20.2	23.1	17.8	19.1
25–44 years	34.4	30.9	24.7	47.3	47.0
44–64 years	13.4	11.1	7.1	22.5	14.0
Over 64 years	3.0	2.8	0.6	5.9	2.4

SOURCE: U.S. *Thirteenth Census, 1910, Population* (Washington, 1913), I, 465.

[3] George Edmund Haynes, "Conditions among Negroes in the Cities," *Annals of the American Academy of Political and Social Science*, 49 (September 1913), 105–8; George Edmund Haynes, *The Negro at Work in New York City*, Columbia University Studies in History, Economics, and Public Law, vol. 49, no. 3 (New York, 1913), 27–32. See also the valuable discussion in Gilbert Osofsky, *Harlem: The Making of a Ghetto* (New York, 1966), 18–28.

About six out of every ten Negroes living in Cleveland in 1900 originated in states other than Ohio. (See Table 5.) Existing transportation
lines predetermined which states would contribute most to this flow of
migrants. The Baltimore and Ohio Railroad connected the city to the
southeastern seaboard, and the tier of states south of Pennsylvania
proved to be the point of departure for most black migrants who came
to Cleveland before World War I. More black residents of Cleveland

TABLE 5. *Area of birth of nonwhite residents of Cleveland, 1900*

Area of birth	Number per state	Percentage
Ohio	2,296	38.4
Middle West outside Ohio	370	6.2
Northeast	590	9.8
Upper South and Border	2,137	35.6
Lower South	300	6.0
West	17	0.3
Not specified or born abroad	153	2.6
Total	5,863	100.0

SOURCE: U.S. *Twelfth Census, 1900, Population* (Washington, 1902), 706–27.
The figures were obtained by adding the statistics from Tables 31 and 32 of the
census materials and subtracting the totals from Table 30.
NOTE: *Middle West:* Michigan, Ohio, Indiana, Illinois, Iowa, Kansas, Wisconsin,
Minnesota, Nebraska, North and South Dakota; *Northeast:* New England states,
Pennsylvania, New York, New Jersey; *Upper South and Border:* Virginia, Kentucky,
Tennessee, North Carolina, Maryland, West Virginia, District of Columbia, Missouri,
Oklahoma, Delaware; *Lower South:* Georgia, South Carolina, Alabama, Mississippi,
Louisiana, Texas, Florida, Arkansas; *West:* all other states.

were born in Virginia than any other state except Ohio, and Maryland
and North Carolina also contributed their share. A number of rail lines
linked Cleveland, via Cincinnati, to Kentucky and Tennessee, and both
of those states sent sizable groups of Negroes to Cleveland. A smaller
but still significant number (about 10 percent) came from the Northeast,
especially the adjacent state of Pennsylvania and nearby New York. The
Lower South was not yet an important source of migration; only 6 percent of the Negroes living in Cleveland in 1900 had been born in that
region.[4]

Although a majority of the city's black population in 1900 had migrated from other states, a large minority (38.4 percent) had been born

[4] On the influence of transportation lines on migration, see Lilian Brandt, "The
Make-Up of Negro City Groups," *Charities*, 15 (October 7, 1905), 8. Chicago experienced a much larger influx of migrants from the Deep South than did Cleveland
before World War I. In 1900, 17 percent of Chicago's black population had originated in the Deep South. Allan H. Spear, *Black Chicago: The Making of a Negro
Ghetto, 1890–1920* (Chicago, 1967), 13.

in Ohio; and most of these had probably been born in Cleveland. By 1910 this figure had declined only slightly to 35.7 percent. Compared with the black communities of New York, Chicago, Cincinnati, and elsewhere, Cleveland's Afro-American population was more stable prior to World War I and contained a considerably higher proportion of individuals who had been born and reared in the North.[5]

In the late nineteenth century, most of the black newcomers to the city settled in the Central Avenue district, one of the oldest areas of the city and a district in which some blacks had lived since before the Civil War. By 1910, however, the area of settlement had expanded. Migrants now began to move into the area to the north between Central and Euclid avenues and to the south and east along Scovill and Woodland avenues. At that time the major portion of the black community lived within an area circumscribed on the north by Euclid and the wealthy residential section beyond it (from which Negroes were excluded for economic as well as racial reasons); on the south and west by the Cuyahoga River with its industrial zone, a natural boundary which would serve in the years ahead to limit the Negro population to the eastern section of the city; and on the east by East 55th Street, a major north-south thoroughfare. This area, then, constituted the nucleus of what would become Cleveland's first black ghetto.[6]

Blacks were not totally restricted to this area, but when they lived in other sections of the city they were more likely to settle near each other than to spread evenly throughout a neighborhood. Three such black "enclaves" existed before World War I.[7] One, a lower-class neighborhood of dilapidated structures, stretched along Hamilton Avenue between East 9th and East 14th streets. Close to the industrial section and the docks,

---

[5] In 1910, 19.3 percent of Chicago's Negroes were born in the state of residence. Comparative figures for other large cities are: Boston, 29.2; New York, 29.4; Philadelphia, 35.1; Pittsburgh, 34.4; Cincinnati, 28.4; Detroit, 32.2. U.S. Bureau of the Census, *Negroes in the United States, 1920–1932* (Washington, 1935), 32. The 1910 census does not give a breakdown of the Cleveland population by state of birth. The only data available for that year is for the Ohio Negro population as a whole, as listed in Appendix II.

[6] Howard W. Green, comp., *Population Characteristics by Census Tracts, Cleveland, 1930* (Cleveland, 1931), 231–32.

[7] In using the term "enclave" to describe areas of settlement outside the formative ghetto, I have followed the lead of other scholars. In particular, see Spear, *Black Chicago*, 11–17, and August Meier and Elliott Rudwick, *From Plantation to Ghetto*, rev. ed. (New York, 1970), 215. However, "enclave" connotes a compactness or density which these black sections often did not have. Like the main region of black settlement, these smaller areas of black population often exhibited an amorphous quality, with blacks tending to cluster on certain streets but still remaining, to a large extent, residentially integrated.

it was the least desirable neighborhood for blacks to live in. In three other areas outside the Central Avenue district middle-class Negroes had established themselves in small numbers. One such area lay slightly east of the intersection of Carnegie Avenue and East 105th Street, between Cedar and Euclid. Another small group of elite Negroes lived in the new middle-class Hough Avenue development north of Euclid; but they resided almost entirely in the less-exclusive area north of Hough between East 84th and East 95th streets. The third and smallest enclave lay along Kinsman Road in the southeast section of the city.[8]

The fact that most blacks lived within fairly well defined areas of the city at this time, however, does not mean that a black ghetto existed in Cleveland. Beyond the Central Avenue district and the three enclaves already mentioned, Negroes were spread throughout the eastern part of the city (very few blacks resided on the West Side) in small groups or single families. An analysis of 1910 census tract data reveals that of 155 tracts, all but 17 contained some Negro residents. Twenty-four tracts were at least 1 percent black, and no tract was more than 25 percent black. Even in the growing Negro section on Central and Scovill avenues, Negroes were still in the minority and lived in close proximity to an ever-increasing immigrant population, composed primarily of Italians and Russian Jews, who also sought refuge in that crowded and aging section of the city. "We have no 'LITTLE AFRICA' in Cleveland," Robert Drake, a Negro clerk, boasted in 1915. "There is not a single street in this city that is inhabited by nothing but Negroes."[9]

Nevertheless, despite the fact that few of the sections of the city were totally white and none were all-Negro prior to the World War I migration, the trend toward increasing segregation of the black population had already begun. As Cleveland's black community expanded in the early twentieth century, it did so primarily by filling in areas already distinguishable as "Negro sections." An analysis of population statistics by wards for 1900 and 1910 indicates that 17.8 percent of the black population in 1900 lived in wards which were less than 0.5 percent black; in 1910 only 6.4 percent lived in such wards. Furthermore, in 1900 41.8 percent of Cleveland's Negroes lived in wards which were greater than 5 percent black, while by 1910 this figure had risen to 62.3 percent. By then one-third of the city's Negroes lived in the Twelfth Ward, while in

[8] Green, comp., *Population Characteristics by Census Tracts*, 231–32; interview with Dr. William P. Saunders, August 6, 1972.
[9] Robert I. Drake, "The Negro in Cleveland," Cleveland *Advocate*, September 18, 1915. See Table 14 in Chapter 7.

1900 no two wards combined could claim more than 27 percent of the total Negro population.[10]

In order to properly assess the significance of this trend, it is necessary to take a longer view and to compare the residential distribution of blacks with that of other groups. To do this, indexes of dissimilarity (a basic measurement of segregation between any two groups in the population, ranging from 0 to 100) for a number of ethnic and racial groups in Cleveland were calculated from ward data available for 1870 and 1910. These calculations demonstrate that the late-nineteenth- and early-twentieth-century trend toward residential segregation was not limited to blacks. Between 1870 and 1910 the index for Negroes v. all native whites (a category that includes native-born of foreign or mixed parentage as well as those of native parentage) rose from 49 to 61, while that of Negroes v. the foreign-born increased from 52 to 66. During the same period, however, the index for native whites v. the foreign-born also rose, from 13 to 36. Furthermore, this last statistic obscures a much higher degree of segregation among specific immigrant groups. No data on individual ethnic groups are available for 1870, but in 1910 Cleveland's Italians were considerably more segregated from the dominant native-white element than were blacks, and the city's Hungarian, Russian, and Romanian immigrant communities also displayed a fairly high degree of spatial isolation.[11]

Other "new immigrant" groups, such as the Poles, Slavs, and Croatians, also tended to cluster in a few areas; but unlike the Italians and Romanians, they were slightly more segregated from blacks than from the dominant native-white element or the older immigrant groups. The Polish neighborhoods along Broadway Avenue lay well to the south of the major area of black settlement; the Slavs and Hungarians along Kinsman Road and Woodland Avenue were well to the east; and the Polish and Croatian areas along Superior and St. Clair avenues were far to the north of Central Avenue. The older Italian neighborhoods along Mayfield and Woodhill roads, on the border between Cleveland and its east-

[10] U.S. *Twelfth Census, 1900, Population* (Washington, 1902), 672–73; U.S. Bureau of the Census, *Negro Population in the United States, 1790–1915* (Washington, 1918), 107.

[11] For a discussion of the index of dissimilarity, see Karl Taeuber and Alma Taeuber, *Negroes in Cities: Residential Segregation and Neighborhood Change* (Chicago, 1965), 235–38. After the completion of this study I learned that a number of the indexes that I had computed for Cleveland for 1910 and 1920 had already been tabulated by Stanley Lieberson; see the statistical appendix to his study *Ethnic Patterns in American Cities* (Glencoe, Ill., 1963), 213. Since there are occasional discrepancies in our respective data, I have retained my own figures.

TABLE 6. *Index of dissimilarity, selected immigrant groups with native whites and Negroes, Cleveland, 1910*

	Native whites[a]	Negroes
Italians	76	66
Germans	21	74
English	17	57
Hungarians	45	72
Irish	28	67
Russians	52	62
Romanians	65	54
Swedes	40	65
All foreign-born	36	66

SOURCE: U.S. Census Bureau, *Thirteenth Census, 1910* (Washington, 1912), I, 427.

[a] Computed by adding together the categories "native white—native parentage" and "native white—foreign or mixed parentage" for each ward before calculating the index.

ern surburbs, were also well removed from the black community. These ethnic communities were not homogenous, but they did occupy fairly distinct sections of the city; relatively few of the new immigrants lived outside these areas. Thus, in one sense, the trend of increasing segregation of blacks was part of a general urban phenomenon of the prewar decades. The half-century before 1920 was, in the phrase of one historian, the age of "the segregated city," and it would indeed have been surprising if blacks had not shared the same experience that other urban groups were undergoing.[12]

[12] Eleanor E. Ledbetter, *The Slovaks of Cleveland, With Some General Information on the Race* (Cleveland, 1918), 11; Eleanor E. Ledbetter, *The Jugoslavs of Cleveland, With a Brief Sketch of their Historical and Political Backgrounds* (Cleveland [1918]), 13, 21; Green, comp., *Population Characteristics by Census Tracts*, 23, 219–29; Josef J. Barton, "Immigration and Social Mobility in an American City: Studies of Three Ethnic Groups in Cleveland, 1890–1950 (Ph.D. dissertation, University of Michigan, 1971); Warner, *The Urban Wilderness*, 85–112. See Table 14 in Chapter 7 for segregation indexes for Poles, Czechoslovakians, and Yugoslavians for 1920. No data are available on these groups for 1910.

Recently, historians who have studied ethnic segregation patterns in detail have emphasized the rapid geographic mobility of immigrants, the instability of ghettos and the lack of complete ethnic homogeneity in sections of cities supposedly dominated by one ethnic group. See Humbert Nelli, *The Italians in Chicago, 1880–1930: A Study in Ethnic Mobility* (New York, 1970), 22–54, and especially Howard P. Chudacoff, *Mobile Americans: Residential and Social Mobility in Omaha, 1880–1920* (New York, 1972), 35–83. While I am in general agreement with these authors that the monolithic quality of immigrant districts has been overstressed in the past, I think it would be a mistake to go too far in the opposite direction in emphasizing the instability of ethnic neighborhoods. Though never uniform or homogeneous, immigrant neighborhoods in *major* cities during the 1880–1920 period were an

Yet the context of urban change does not entirely explain the situation that blacks found themselves in. There were some forbidding signs indicating that the black urban experience was destined to be different from all other groups. There was a striking divergence, for example, between the residency patterns of blacks and those of Irish and German immigrants, even though the black community was older than either of these two groups. By 1910 only a few predominantly Irish neighborhoods survived in the city, primarily along Detroit Road on the West Side and in the area between Union Street and Miles Avenue to the southeast. With those exceptions, the Irish were well distributed throughout the city, as indicated by their relatively low index of dissimilarity, 28. The Germans were even more dispersed, and, although they tended more often to reside on the West Side than the East Side, no good-sized "German sections" existed on the eve of World War I. What is surprising about the residential assimilation of these two groups is that it occurred despite the fact that both continued to supplement their populations with immigrants from abroad during the prewar years. The "new immigration" from eastern and southern Europe was proportionately smaller in Cleveland than elsewhere in the North, and in 1910 the German-born continued to be the city's largest immigrant group, with a population of 41,406; the Irish remained fourth (exceeded by the Russians and the Hungarians) with 11,316. Thus the divergent patterns of residential distribution between blacks on the one hand and the Irish and, especially, the Germans on the other cannot be ascribed to the fact that the black community was burdened with a constantly increasing horde of newcomers, making assimilation difficult and resulting in segregation, whereas the Germans and Irish were relieved of this burden and could as a result assimilate their numbers more easily into the general life of the community. Although Cleveland's black community was growing during the late nineteenth and early twentieth centuries, its rate of increase was hardly exceptional compared with other groups. With the exception of the 1890s, in fact, the city's total population outstripped the growth rate of its black community for every ten-year period between 1860 and 1910. Cleveland's black population, while exanding absolutely, declined relatively from 1.9 to 1.2 percent of the city's total population between 1860

important factor in shaping the urban milieu. Badly needed are broad, comparative studies that will trace the residential development of a *variety* of ethnic groups in several different types of cities over a prolonged period of time; the present approach too often overgeneralizes from the experience of a single ethnic group in a single city.

and 1890; by 1910 this figure had increased only slightly to 1.5 percent.[13]
One cause of the widening gap between the residency patterns of Negroes and certain ethnic groups was the economic discrimination that
blacks suffered at the time. This limited the size of the black middle
class and made it impossible for many blacks to take part in the general
exodus to newer parts of the city. The occupational difference between
German and Irish immigrants and blacks (as will be explained in a later
chapter) was not great enough to account for the huge discrepancy in
residency patterns, however. A more significant cause was the growing
reluctance of white property-holders outside the Central Avenue district
to sell to blacks. Growing white opposition to black families moving into
their neighborhoods is difficult to document in Cleveland for the prewar
period because, unlike Chicago, there was no evidence of violent action
aimed at driving black families out of predominantly white sections of
the city. Rather the strategy appeared to be one of selling to "whites
only," thereby preventing any further integration of the black population in outlying residential districts. Census statistics for 1900 and 1910
indicate that the number of black families living in such areas remained
virtually unchanged during the first decade of the twentieth century;
thus the slowly increasing black middle class was forced more and more
to settle near Central Avenue. Whether the reluctance to sell to blacks
was due to a fear of deteriorating property values or was just another
aspect of the racism of the times (if, indeed, the two can be separated)
is impossible to document; the ultimate motivation of these whites
eludes the historian in this instance. What is clear is that, on the eve of
the "Great Migration" of 1916–19, racial discrimination in property
sales had become widespread in Cleveland. There was a "noticeable
tendency" toward the use of restrictive covenants, and in 1916 one
prominent black Clevelander complained that such discrimination had
become unofficial policy among members of the Cleveland Real Estate
Board. There were some desirable neighborhoods, he claimed, where
realtors would not sell or rent to Negroes, "no matter how much money
we have to pay for the desired property."[14]

[13] U.S. *Thirteenth Census, 1910, Population* (Washington, 1912), I, 427. See
Table 1 in Chapter 1 for full information on population growth during the 1860–
1910 period.
[14] Untitled description (dated April 25, 1914) of the formation of the Cleveland
branch of the National Association for the Advancement of Colored People, by
Harry E. Davis, NAACP branch files (Container G157), Papers of the National
Association for the Advancement of Colored People (referred to hereafter as
NAACP Papers), Manuscript Division, Library of Congress; George A. Myers to
F. H. Goff, January 17, 1916, George A. Myers Papers, Ohio Historical Society. On

In a very unspectacular way, such a policy helped push Cleveland's black community one step further down the road to the ghetto. It forced the city's black newcomers to settle increasingly within a rather circumscribed area; and although this area was very far from being all-Negro in composition, it was nevertheless one of the oldest in the city and suffered from over a half-century of constant use. "The quality of shelter occupied by the vast majority of Negroes in the North," Robert C. Weaver has said in describing the prewar era, "was generally similar to that occupied by other low-income families." As in the case of residential segregation, however, the comparison with poorer immigrant groups could be carried only so far, because black housing "was usually in the least desirable segments of the low-income areas, and often commanded higher rents than comparable shelter for whites." Cleveland's Central Avenue district and the black section on Hamilton Avenue fitted this description well. Four census tracts in the Central-Scovill area, housing altogether about one-half of Cleveland's Negro population in 1910, were among the most crowded in the city. Their densities ranged from forty-eight to eighty-two inhabitants per acre, while that of Cleveland as a whole was only thirteen per acre. Upon arriving in the city in 1905, Jane Edna Hunter, a nurse who later founded the local Phillis Wheatley Society, soon encountered the experience undoubtedly shared by most Negro migrants who came to Cleveland: "the despairing search for decent lodgings—up one dingy street and down another, ending with the acceptance of the least disreputable room we encountered." The small minority of Negro families who owned homes outside the Central Avenue district frequently refused, because of middle-class pretensions, to take in roomers; and newcomers invariably found themselves "restricted to the unsightly, run-down sections of the city where houses rented for

the earlier and more violent opposition to residential integration in Chicago, see Spear, *Black Chicago*, 20–23, and William M. Tuttle, Jr., *Race Riot: Chicago in the Red Summer of 1919* (New York, 1970), 160–61. At this time housing discrimination against middle-class Negroes in Philadelphia was also on the rise, but in Boston opposition to blacks moving into "better" white neighborhoods apparently remained fairly light. See W. E. B. Du Bois, *The Philadelphia Negro* (Philadelphia, 1899), 348–49; John T. Emlen, "The Movement for the Betterment of the Negro in Philadelphia," *Annals of the American Academy of Political and Social Science*, 49 (September 1913), 88; W. E. B. Du Bois, "The Black North," *New York Times Magazine*, December 8, 1901; John Daniels, *In Freedom's Birthplace: A Study of the Boston Negroes* (Boston, 1914), 151–52. It should be noted that pre–World War I housing discrimination did not affect Cleveland's small Negro elite nearly as much as it did the black middle and lower class. Most members of this elite were of fair complexion and many had close social or business relationships with whites; this may help to account for white acceptance of them in some neighborhoods. See Chapter 5 for a fuller discussion of this group.

as little as fifteen dollars a month and the landlady, who secured two roomers at one dollar and a quarter [per week], could realize two-thirds of her rent." Under these circumstances, a "small, low-roofed, poorly furnished room" was rapidly becoming standard fare for many Cleveland Negroes.[15]

The existence of vice districts in close proximity to black residential sections further hampered Negroes in their efforts to find decent housing in Cleveland. As early as 1905 Hamilton Avenue was well known as an area of gambling houses, "dives," and brothels, many of which were, according to Jane Hunter, engaged in "wholesale organized traffic in black flesh." During the next ten years, a second, larger red-light district developed, this time in the vicinity of East 30th and Central, in the very heart of the developing black community. By the eve of the war time migration, the editor of the Cleveland Gazette, a Negro weekly, noted with dismay the proliferation of "speakeasies, gambling, and questionable houses" in that decaying section of the city, catering in a most democratic manner to whites and blacks, immigrants and the native-born alike.[16]

The development of vice districts in or near predominantly Negro neighborhoods was a phenomenon that Cleveland shared with many northern cities. New York had its Tenderloin district, Columbus its "Badlands," Detroit its "Heights" area, and each catered to the same kind of disreputable clientele. Although this phenomenon has not received systematic study from historians, it appears that the association of blacks with vice amounted to a kind of self-fulfilling prophecy on the part of the white population. In the late nineteenth century many whites, in accordance with the stereotypes then in vogue, conceived of blacks as prone to loose morals and illicit (if often humorous) behavior. Yet the predominantly white police forces of cities, responding to the pressures of white public opinion, often refused to allow red-light districts to develop anywhere except in or near a black neighborhood. "In more than one city," said R. R. Wright, Jr., surveying Negro housing in the North in 1908, "the distinctively Negro neighborhood is the same as, or next to, that district which seems, by consent of civil authorities, to be given up to vice." In New York, Chicago, and Philadelphia, where more than one red-light district existed, vice areas could also be found in immigrant neighbor-

---

[15] Robert C. Weaver, The Negro Ghetto (New York, 1948), 21; Howard W. Green, comp., Population by Census Tracts, Cleveland and Vicinity, with Street Index (Cleveland, 1931), 7–8; Jane Edna Hunter, A Nickel and a Prayer (Cleveland, 1940), 70–85. The tracts described are I–2, I–3, H–7, and H–9.

[16] Hunter, A Nickel and a Prayer, 68–69, 124; Cleveland Gazette, April 1, 1916.

hoods. But taking the North as a whole, and considering the small size of the black population of most northern cities at this time, it is clear that the police were far more prone to allow vice in or near black neighborhoods than in white sections.[17]

Occasionally a few civic-minded individuals, white as well as black, attempted to eliminate some of these unsavory aspects of urban life, but the resultant reforms were usually ineffectual or short-lived. In 1908 a number of prominent black leaders mounted a campaign against vice and crime on Central Avenue; but their original enthusiasm soon withered in the face of an uninterested community, and the movement for reform died. A few years later a more serious reform effort arose, only to meet the same fate. In 1911 and 1912 a number of prohibitionists and members of the clergy had launched a drive to curtail the activities of the numerous dance halls and saloons in Cleveland's lower-class neighborhoods. These establishments served as social centers in the immigrant and black communities, but many of them were also undoubtedly fronts for various kinds of illegal activity, especially gambling and prostitution; they were often the scene of raucous arguments, drunken brawls, and general disorder. It was while this reform movement was gaining ground that a particularly brutal murder occurred on Central Avenue. Incensed by this outrage, black leaders called a mass meeting to protest the lack of police protection in the black sections of the city. The meeting was well attended and a committee was formed to meet with Mayor Newton D. Baker, who agreed to crack down on the saloons. The city's dance halls also came under scrutiny. After an investigation by a committee headed by the progressive Twelfth Ward councilman Daniel E. Morgan, the city council passed an ordinance which allowed the mayor to license dance halls, impose a curfew on dances, and appoint a dance-hall inspector to enforce the regulations.

The entire effort for reform, however, soon came to nought. Baker did order the police to close several saloons, but this had little effect. The dance-hall ordinance also had no noticeable impact on the situation and soon became a dead letter; within a few years it had been largely nullified by pressure exerted by local musicians who were fearful of a cutback in their employment if the regulations were strictly enforced. At

[17] Du Bois, *The Philadelphia Negro*, 314; R. R. Wright, Jr., "Recent Improvement in Housing among Negroes in the North," *Southern Workman*, 37 (November 1908), 602 (emphasis added). See also J. S. Himes, "Forty Years of Negro Life in Columbus, Ohio," *Journal of Negro History*, 27 (April 1942), 140; David M. Katzman, *Before the Ghetto: Black Detroit in the Nineteenth Century* (Urbana, Ill., 1973), 172; Osofsky, *Harlem*, 14–15; Spear, *Black Chicago*, 25; Zane L. Miller, *Boss Cox's Cincinnati* (New York, 1968), 11.

the same time Morgan, who had received the Republican party's nomination for city solicitor and planned a further move against gambling
and prostitution in the city, was defeated in the next election. His successor in city council, Thomas W. Fleming, was too closely allied with
the notorious black racketeer Albert D. ("Starlight") Boyd to consider
mounting a campaign against organized vice. In retrospect, however, it
would appear that the whole campaign against the saloons and dance
halls had a basic flaw that would have made its success difficult under
any circumstances. In attempting to curtail these institutions, the city's
white leaders offered no alternatives to a black community that suffered
from a lack of public recreational facilities and was increasingly being
excluded from such private facilities as the YMCA and amusement parks.
Nor were the police or civic leaders particularly eager to drive vice from
Negro neighborhoods, when they realized that red-light districts might
spring up again in white areas. If, on the eve of the Great Migration,
Central Avenue's reputation as an "open," "loose" section of the city
seemed secure, most of the blame must be laid at the doorstep of the
city's white population.[18]

With eighty-five hundred Negro inhabitants in 1910, Cleveland looked
rather insignificant besides the "black metropolises" of Chicago (forty-
four thousand Negroes), Philadelphia (eighty-four thousand) and New
York (ninety-two thousand). In Cleveland, blacks were much less
segregated than in Chicago, which in 1910 had four census tracts that
were over 50 percent Negro, or New York, which had many predominantly Negro neighborhoods and which was in the process of transform-
ing Harlem from an upper-middle-class white community to a black
ghetto. Nevertheless, the same dramatic forces of urban change, black
migration, and discrimination in housing that were creating Chicago's
South Side black belt and New York's Harlem were at work in the
Forest City. Although no ghetto existed, the groundwork for future concentration had been laid. A definite trend toward the segregation of the
city's black population was evident, and about 80 percent of black Cleveland resided within four well-defined areas of settlement. Most significant was the emergence of the Central Avenue district as a potential
black belt. By 1915, this area, with its cheap lodging houses, deteriorating

18 Cleveland *Leader*, February 19, 1912; Cleveland *Gazette*, February 24, March
9, 16, May 11, 1912, September 15, 22, 1917; Frederick Rex, "Municipal Dance
Halls," *National Civic Review*, 4 (1915), 413–19; Hunter, *A Nickel and a Prayer*,
68–69, 131–32; Thomas F. Campbell, *Daniel E. Morgan, 1877–1949: The Good
Citizen in Politics* (Cleveland, 1966), 19, 35, 37, 41. The careers of Fleming and
Boyd are examined in detail in Chapter 6.

homes, and vice conditions, housed a majority of the Negro population under conditions that were decidedly inferior to that of most of the city's residential sections.[19]

Although almost all cities exhibited some increase in the residential segregation of blacks in the late nineteenth and early twentieth centuries, it is important to note that there was still, in 1910, great variation in the spatial distribution of blacks in American cities. If the development of ghettos proceeded at a faster pace in New York, Philadelphia, and Chicago than in Cleveland, it occurred at a slower rate in western cities like Omaha, Minneapolis, and Los Angeles and in most southern cities. This slower development in some cities was due not to a more liberal racial atmosphere (this was hardly true of southern cities) but to their divergence from the pattern of urban change that was affecting the industrial centers of the East and Midwest. The western cities were small, rapidly growing metropolises that in many ways resembled the Cleveland and Chicago of a half-century before. High levels of geographic mobility, combined with excessive population turnover and unstable housing markets, kept the black populations of these cities fairly well dispersed at the turn of the century. Southern cities were also small but, with few exceptions, they were not rapidly growing; urban growth in the South lagged far behind that of the rest of the country during the 1860–1910 period. It is true that even in the antebellum period, small sections inhabited almost exclusively by free Negroes had existed in Charleston and other southern cities; but at that time most blacks in the urban South—whether slave or free—lived in alleys behind the residences of the whites whose servants they were, or in shacks nearby. The languishing economy and slow growth of these cities between the Civil War and World War I had the effect of freezing this earlier pattern of racial intermingling in residency patterns and retarding the growth of the ghetto. Thus, in 1910, even though blacks in southern cities comprised a much larger proportion of the total urban population, they remained much more dispersed than in the North.[20]

[19] Spear, *Black Chicago*, 145; Osofsky, *Harlem*, 12, 105–23. Chicago also had a much higher percentage of census tracts from which blacks were excluded entirely. Ninety-four of 431 tracts (or 21.8 percent) in Chicago, as opposed to only 17 of 155 tracts (10.9 percent) in Cleveland, were completely white in 1910. Spear, *Black Chicago*, 17; Green, comp., *Population Characteristics by Census Tracts*, 160–62.

[20] Richard C. Wade, *Slavery in the Cities: The South, 1820–1860* (New York, 1964), 273–80; C. Vann Woodward, *Origins of the New South, 1877–1913* (Baton Rouge, La., 1951), 139; Blaine Brownell, "Urbanization in the South: A Unique Experience?" *Mississippi Quarterly*, 26 (September 1973), 116. The effects of rapid population turnover in Omaha in the late nineteenth and early twentieth centuries are illustrated in Chudacoff, *Mobile Americans*; on Los Angeles, see Lawrence B. De

While it would be incorrect to state that the pattern of residency of Cleveland blacks in the prewar years was typical, it would be fair to say that it lay at or near the middle of the spectrum when conditions in various cities are compared. The ghetto was in its formative stage, but it had not yet taken shape. This was but one aspect of black life that was in transition.

Graaf, "The City of Black Angels: Emergence of the Los Angeles Ghetto, 1890–1930," *Pacific Historical Review*, 39 (August 1970), 328–29. In 1910, Los Angeles had an extraordinarily low segregation index (for Negroes v. native whites) of 29, and in Minneapolis, Portland, and San Francisco the index was under 40. These statistics, as well as the general conclusions of this paragraph, are drawn from an in-progress study by the author of the residential segregation patterns of immigrants and blacks in thirty cities between 1870 and 1930.

CHAPTER 3

The Eclipse of Equality: Racial Discrimination

The period of the late nineteenth and early twentieth centuries was marked by what one historian has called "the betrayal of the Negro." In the South, the end of Reconstruction brought the return of white supremacy and the slow but steady disfranchisement and segregation of the black population, and a string of Republican administrations in Washington left the freedmen to fend for themselves in an increasingly hostile environment. The Supreme Court abetted this process in a series of decisions, beginning with the civil rights cases of 1883, which declared unconstitutional the Civil Rights Act of 1875, and culminating in *Plessy* v. *Ferguson* (1896), which established the "separate but equal" doctrine for public facilities. In a number of states blacks struggled vigorously against these trends, and as late as 1906 they boycotted streetcars in Savannah, Georgia, in an attempt to prevent the segregation of passengers by race. But in the end all such tactics were doomed to failure, and the victory of Jim Crow was assured for decades to come.[1]

[1] Of the many studies of the growth of racism between 1865 and 1915, I have found most useful Rayford W. Logan, *The Betrayal of the Negro: From Rutherford B. Hayes to Woodrow Wilson* (New York, 1965), chs. 6, 9, 10, 11, 13; C. Vann Woodward, *The Strange Career of Jim Crow*, 2d rev. ed. (New York, 1966), ch. 3; John Higham, *Strangers in the Land: Patterns of American Nativism, 1860–1925* (New Brunswick, N.J., 1955), chs. 4–7; Barton J. Bernstein, "*Plessy v. Ferguson*: Conservative Sociological Jurisprudence," *Journal of Negro History*, 48 (July 1963), 196–205; I. A. Newby, *Jim Crow's Defense: Anti-Negro Thought in America, 1900–1930* (Baton Rouge, 1965), part I; George M. Frederickson, *The Black Image in the White Mind: The Debate on Afro-American Character and Destiny* (New York, 1971), 256–319; and John S. Haller, *Outcasts from Evolution: Scientific Attitudes of Racial Inferiority, 1859–1900* (Urbana, Ill., 1971).

Historians who have studied race relations between the Civil War and World War I have for the most part focused on events in the South. Yet shifts in public opinion on the race question during this period were actually national rather than sectional in nature. During the quarter-century following the war, race relations were extraordinarily fluid in *both* sections. Interracial violence and discrimination in schools and public accommodations declined substantially in many parts of the North, and a number of northern states (beginning with New York in 1874) passed civil rights acts.

This favorable climate of opinion gradually faded, however. As memories of the war dimmed, so too did sympathy for the former slaves, and instead the late nineteenth century witnessed the growth of racial stereotypes and the emergence of a new "scientific" racism whose appeal transcended sectional boundaries. The new racism pictured the Negro as inferior to the white man in most respects (physical endurance and musical ability usually excepted) and morally deficient; in 1910 a leading sociologist categorized the black race as "improvident, extravagant, lazy . . . , easily adaptable, imitative, lacking initiative, dishonest and untruthful, with little principle of honor or conception of right and virtue, superstitious, over-religious, suspicious and incapable of a comprehension of faith in mankind." With such ideas in the ascendancy, it is not surprising that the mass of white opinion in the North began to look less favorably on the struggle for equal rights. In the early years of the twentieth century, "institutional racism" was on the rise throughout the North, and discrimination in restaurants, theaters, and other places of public accommodation was increasing in most northern cities. In 1908 Ray Stannard Baker reported that in every large northern city he visited, "both white and colored people told me that race feeling and discrimination were rapidly increasing: that more and more difficult problems were constantly arising." As lynchings continued apace in the South, friction between Afro-Americans and whites outside the states of the old Confederacy erupted in race riots in New York in 1900 and Springfield, Illinois, in 1908, presaging the more terrible violence of the World War I era. "The Negro Problem," W. E. B. Du Bois noted laconically in 1901, "is not the sole property of the South."[2]

---

[2] Howard W. Odum, *Social and Mental Traits of the Negro*, Columbia Studies in History, Economics, and Public Law, vol. 37, no. 3 (New York, 1910), 274; Ray Stannard Baker, *Following the Color Line: American Negro Citizenship in the Progressive Era* (New York, 1908), 111; W. E. B. Du Bois, "The Black North," *New York Times Magazine*, November 17, 1901. On racial violence in the North before World War I, see James Crouthemal, "The Springfield Race Riot of 1908," *Journal of Negro History*, 45 (July 1960), 164–81; Gilbert Osofsky, *Harlem: The*

As in the case of residential segregation, however, the growth of discrimination in public facilities was by no means uniform throughout the North. Conditions varied considerably from one area to another and ranged along a continuum from Cass County, Michigan, where a sizable group of black settlers shared governmental power and lived in integrated harmony with their white neighbors, to cities like Evansville, East St. Louis, and other "northern border" towns, where the forces of segregation and discrimination were so strong that the pattern of race relations closely resembled that of the South. Among large cities there were fewer extremes and less variation, but there were still important differences prior to World War I. Racial lines hardened most rapidly in such cities as Indianapolis and Chicago, where white hostility frequently led to violent clashes between the races. Cleveland and Boston, on the other hand, lay at the opposite end of the spectrum. In both cities the growth of racism, though quite evident, was more muted in its effects, and integrationist traditions remained influential much longer than elsewhere.[3]

Making of a Ghetto (New York, 1966), 46–52; William English Walling, "The Race War in the North," *Independent*, 45 (September 3, 1908), 529–34; Emma Lou Thornbrough, *The Negro in Indiana: A Study of a Minority* ([Indianapolis, Ind.] 1957), 277–87. Race riots, of course, were not restricted to the North. Two of the most violent racial conflicts of this period occurred in Wilmington, North Carolina in 1898 and in Atlanta in 1906. Charles Crowe, "Racial Massacre in Atlanta, September 22, 1906," *Journal of Negro History*, 54 (April 1969), 150–68; John Hope Franklin, *From Slavery to Freedom*, 3d ed. (New York, 1967), 341, 439–41.

[3] For information on race relations in cities outside the South prior to World War I, see St. Clair Drake and Horace R. Cayton, *Black Metropolis: A Study of Negro Life in a Northern City* (New York, 1945), I, 174–77; Allan H. Spear, *Black Chicago: The Making of a Negro Ghetto, 1890–1920* (Chicago, 1967), 11–50; Osofsky, *Harlem*, 35–52; W. E. B. Du Bois, *The Philadelphia Negro: A Social Study* (Philadelphia, 1899), 322–55; Mary White Ovington, *Half a Man: The Status of the Negro in New York* (New York, 1911), 209–16 and *passim*; John Daniels, *In Freedom's Birthplace: A Study of the Boston Negroes* (Boston, 1914), 111–15, 188–90, 406–411; Robert Austin Warner, *New Haven Negroes: A Social History* (New Haven, Conn., 1940), 160–81; Thornbrough, *The Negro in Indiana*, 255–76 and *passim*; J. S. Himes, "Forty Years of Negro Life in Columbus, Ohio," *Journal of Negro History*, 27 (April 1942), 134–35; Elliott Rudwick, *Race Riot at East St. Louis, July 2, 1917* (Carbondale, Ill., 1964), 6; Earl Spangler, *The Negro in Minnesota* (Minneapolis, Minn., 1961), 57–62, 91–92; Lawrence B. De Graaf, "The City of Black Angels: Emergence of the Los Angeles Ghetto, 1890–1930," *Pacific Historical Review*, 39 (August 1970), 329; Frank Quillin, *The Color Line in Ohio* (Ann Arbor, 1913), 88–165; David Gerber, "Ohio and the Color Line: Racial Discrimination and Negro Responses in a Northern State, 1860–1915" (Ph.D. dissertation, Princeton University, 1971), *passim*; Frank F. Lee, *Negro and White in Connecticut Town* (New York, 1961), 26–28. Racial conditions in Cass County, Michigan, are described in R. R. Wright, Jr., "Negro Governments in the North," *Southern Workman*, 37 (September 1908), 486–89, and George Hesslink, *Black Neighbors: Negroes in a Northern Rural Community* (Indianapolis, Ind., 1968), 59–61, 215. The information on northern black communities in Ray Stannard Baker's *Following*

There might be a major city with more harmonious race relations than Cleveland, Robert I. Drake conceded half seriously in 1915, but he hastened to add that "doubtless no such place exists." Noted Drake with undisguised pride, "We have no such marked and blighting discrimination in Ohio's [largest] metropolis, as our people have to contend with in other cities. . . ." He acknowledged that blacks in Cleveland had "some troubles" with racism, but on the whole he concluded that "we have more privileges and a greater freedom of opportunity than is accorded our people in any other city on American soil." Such views more accurately reflected the middle-class Negro's perception of race relations than that of the average black resident of the city; and even for the black middle class, conditions were becoming less tolerable with each passing year. Yet, comparatively speaking, Drake was correct in his assessment of Cleveland's racial scene. The smaller size of the city's black population made it less conspicuous than elsewhere; the higher proportion of Cleveland blacks born or raised in the North made it easier for them to be assimilated into the general life of the community. Equally if not more important was the city's nineteenth-century integrationist heritage. Traditional sympathy for the cause of Negro rights, though often amounting to little more than paternalism by the beginning of the twentieth century, continued to influence the attitudes and actions of a segment of Cleveland's old-line white Protestant element. This group was, of course, rapidly declining as a percentage of the total population, but it continued to dominate the political, financial, and social life of the community to a large extent, and this helped to retard the growth of discrimination to some degree.[4]

The posture of the white press on the race issue, though far from ideal, also helped keep down racial tensions in Cleveland. The Progressive era was a period of widespread and sometimes violent Negrophobia among white journalists. But while other white newspapers in the northern and border states (such as the Cincinnati *Enquirer*, the Washington *Star*, and the St. Louis *Globe-Democrat*) inflamed racial hatreds with lurid stories of lynchings and black criminal activity, Cleveland's two major dailies for the most part adopted a policy of ignoring the Negro. Since the Cleveland *Leader* remained a Republican newspaper and the Cleveland *Plain Dealer* an avowedly Democratic

---

the *Color Line*, though sometimes useful, must be used with caution. Baker by no means systematically surveyed black life in the North, and his analysis was often based on a superficial impression of local conditions.

  [4] Robert I. Drake, "The Negro in Cleveland," Cleveland *Advocate*, September 18, 1915.

organ, the two rivals continued to dispute national issues that touched upon the Negro question. As late as 1915, for example, the *Leader* editorially attacked the disfranchisement of blacks in the South and urged the enforcement of the Fourteenth Amendment to limit southern congressional power. When it came to *local* race relations, however, both papers gradually put aside the contentiousness of an earlier day in favor of a mutual desire to avoid the problem. On most occasions the white press paid little attention to the city's black community.[5]

These factors enabled Cleveland to avoid the more virulent forms of racism that infected many other cities during the period between about 1890 and 1915. No lynchings or even near-lynchings marred the city's history during these years, and although Central Avenue was sometimes the scene of drunken brawls, no clash remotely resembling a race riot transpired at this time.

In more subtle ways, however, the racial egalitarianism that had been so prominent an aspect of nineteenth-century Cleveland was beginning to weaken. With increasing momentum during the prewar years, a pattern of discrimination was becoming established in many areas of public service. This pattern was not yet a rigid one, and the practices of businesses outside the Central Avenue district varied widely. A number of exclusive downtown restaurants and hotels (including the prestigious Hollenden and Statler establishments) which had opened their doors, several decades before the Great Migration, to the city's light-skinned Negro elite continued their policy of serving anyone who could afford their exorbitant prices—regardless of race. Cleveland's City Club, a popular gathering place for businessmen and politicians, welcomed successful Negroes like the barber George Myers from its inception in 1912; by 1919 nine black men were members.[6] The exclusive Hippodrome Theater and the Opera House were open to members of both races. Such liberal policies, however, did not always extend to other parts of the city, and Negroes with less than middle incomes found it increasingly difficult to obtain adequate accommodations. Many restaurants refused to serve Negroes altogether, and a number of theaters attempted to segregate black patrons in the balcony; the increasing number of small black hotels and lodging houses on Central Avenue testified to the discrimination that blacks were beginning to encounter in similar white institutions.

[5] Cleveland *Leader*, June 23, 1915; Logan, *Betrayal of the Negro*, 195–241; Gerber, "Ohio and the Color Line," 469–71, 490.

[6] Helen M. Chesnutt, *Charles Waddell Chesnutt: Pioneer of the Color Line* (Chapel Hill, N.C., 1952), 294; Cleveland *Advocate*, April 1, 1916; R. H. Terrell to George A. Myers, April 14, 1916, George A. Myers Papers, Ohio Historical Society; *Crisis*, 19 (December 1919), 86.

Only through the painful process of trial and error could blacks discover which establishments were open to both races on a nondiscriminatory basis.[7]

Far more blatant than the exclusion of blacks from some hotels and restaurants was the discrimination they faced in the use of recreation areas. As was true of most cities, Cleveland had no parks anywhere near the main district of black settlement. "Playgrounds in Negro neighborhoods," George Edmund Haynes reported in a survey of Negro urban life in 1913, "are so rare as to excite curiosity. . . ." Private recreational facilities were also off-bounds to the black community most of the time. In 1896 the editor of the *Gazette* was surprised to learn that blacks were being excluded from the dance hall at Euclid Beach Park, but within fifteen years this policy had become the rule rather than the exception in all of the city's well-known amusement parks. Luna Park, a favorite entertainment center for Clevelanders, adopted the procedure around 1910 of allowing Negroes into the park only on designated Jim Crow days—almost all of the time the park was for whites only. Even on Jim Crow days, the management refused to allow Negroes to use the bathing facilities. The ruse they used to achieve this end became almost comical in its transparency after awhile. "Everything worked at the park on those days except the swimming pool," an old black resident explained several decades later. "The pool always 'happened' to be out of order on that day."[8]

Before 1900 blacks had participated in the programs and facilities of the Cleveland Young Men's Christian Association, but by 1910 there were signs of growing white hostility to Negro membership in the Y. In 1914 Charles W. Chesnutt, one of the city's most prominent colored residents, noted in a letter to a leading white citizen that those branches of the YMCA and YWCA which did not openly exclude blacks did "not welcome them with open arms." Chesnutt was apparently unaware that blacks had recently been barred entirely by the local YWCA; and by 1915 the YMCA had adopted a similar whites-only policy. This trend

[7] Drake, "The Negro in Cleveland." For examples of discrimination in theaters, see Cleveland *Gazette*, March 21, 1903, September 10, October 15, 1904, October 6, 1906, February 1, April 18, 1908, April 12, 1911, November 14, 1914, January 30, August 14, 1915. For discrimination in restaurants, see Cleveland *Journal*, May 9, 1908; Cleveland *Gazette*, April 12, 1911, January 30, 1915, August 14, 1915; George A. Myers to F. H. Goff, January 17, 1916, Myers Papers.

[8] George Edmund Haynes, "Conditions among Negroes in the Cities," *Annals of the American Academy of Political and Social Science*, 49 (September 1913), 117; Cleveland *Gazette*, July 4, 1896, October 20, 1913, February 14, 1914, July 31, 1915, August 11, 1917; Perry B. Jackson quoted in Julian Krawcheck, "Society Barred Negroes—They Formed Own Groups," Cleveland *Press*, May 30, 1963.

of discrimination was partially responsible for the formation of the all-Negro Phillis Wheatley home for girls in 1912 and later resulted in the opening of a YMCA on Cedar Avenue designed primarily for Negroes. Recreational facilities in the black community remained inadequate for many years, however.[9]

None of the exclusionary policies of theaters, hotels, or amusement parks was legal. Ohio had passed a Civil Rights Act in 1884 which, when amended in 1894, clearly prohibited discrimination in public facilities on the basis of race. The law provided that all persons "shall be entitled to the full and equal enjoyment of the accommodations, advantages, facilities, and privileges of inns, restaurants, eating houses, barber shops, public conveyances on land and water, theaters and all other places of public accommodation or amusement. . . ." Violations could result in fines up to five hundred dollars and jail terms of thirty to ninety days, in addition to damages awarded the party discriminated against.[10]

From time to time blacks used this law to initiate suits against discriminatory managers and proprietors, but the time was past when Cleveland's black community could expect almost automatic vindication in the courts. Blacks were probably somewhat more successful in Cleveland than elsewhere in bringing civil-rights suits. But no clear-cut victory for equality emerged as a result of such activity, and discrimination, in fact, seemed to be gaining ground in the years just before the Great Migration. There were several reasons for this lack of success. First, many Negroes had neither the time nor the inclination to take a case to court. When two black attorneys were denied service in a Cleveland restaurant in 1915, they quickly brought suit against the manager and won the case. The average Negro, confronted with a similar situation, would be more likely to leave with a shrug and seek out a more hospitable place to eat. Nor was it always easy to obtain convictions in civil-rights cases. In 1901, for example, a Negro brought suit against a Cleveland bowling alley proprietor who kept Negroes out of his establishment, only to have the case dismissed when the court decided "there was no cause for action." Judges sometimes interpreted the law so narrowly that they allowed blatant examples of discrimination to go unpunished, and appeals to higher courts—even to the State Supreme Court—did not guarantee the plaintiff success. Finally, there was the hard fact that most

---

[9] Cleveland *Journal*, October 6, 20, 1906; Cleveland *Gazette*, February 4, 1911, February 14, 1914; Chesnutt, *Charles Waddell Chesnutt*, 261. The formation of the Phillis Wheatley home is discussed in Chapter 6.

[10] Franklin Johnson, *The Development of State Legislation Concerning the Free Negro* (New York, 1918), 164, 166.

blacks simply did not have the necessary funds to carry out legal action. For those who did, a civil-rights suit was still a risky venture. "When we look back over the court decisions," one observer wrote in 1913, "and see the failures of the colored people to get damages, as provided in the equal rights law of the State, see the amount of litigation necessary, and consider how unable the negroes generally are to bear the expense of going to law, there can be but one conclusion arrived at; and that is that equal rights in Ohio for blacks and the whites is a myth."[11]

If black Clevelanders encountered discrimination in some public accommodations during the prewar years, however, there were other areas of public service where racism was noticeably less evident. There is no indication, for example, that any of the city's hospitals either excluded or attempted to segregate black patients prior to 1915. Complete documentation is not available, but it is clear that two major institutions, Huron Road Hospital and the Catholic St. Alexis Hospital, were open to both races on a nondiscriminatory basis during the years just preceding the Great Migration, and other hospitals were probably also integrated. The first change in this policy to be noted in the black press occurred in 1915, when Women's Hospital on East 107th Street instituted a new procedure of admitting black patients only on Saturday. The institution's directors not very successfully tried to hide its real motives by claiming that they were establishing a special "clinic" for black patents, rather than trying to restrict black use of the facilities. This change in policy came as a rude shock to those members of the black middle class who had come to take much of Cleveland's integrationist heritage for granted. "What does this mean?" one black woman asked. "Are we to arrange to get sick on Saturday only or is it possible that we are to be exempted from privileges enjoyed by every other nation or nationality?" Such incredulity would, within but a few short years, turn to cynicism as one medical institution after another adopted some kind of racist policy toward black patients.[12]

If institutions generally accepted black patients on an equal basis before 1915, however, white physicians and hospital administrators were united in their opposition to the admission of black doctors and nurses to hospital staffs. Prior to 1919, when Dr. Charles Garvin joined Lakeside Hospital, no black physician served on the staff of any Cleveland hospi-

---

[11] Cleveland *Gazette*, August 14, 1915; Cleveland *Advocate*, August 14, September 4, 1915; Quillin, *The Color Line in Ohio*, 118–19, 120.

[12] Chesnutt, *Charles Waddell Chesnutt*, 238; Jane Edna Hunter, *A Nickel and a Prayer* (Cleveland, 1940), 73; Cleveland *Advocate*, July 24, 1915, November 11, 1916.

tal. Black nurses also experienced the sting of racial prejudice. When Jane Edna Hunter arrived in Cleveland in 1905, she repeatedly met rebuffs in her effort to find suitable employment. One physician bluntly told her "to go back South—that white doctors did not employ 'nigger' nurses." Prospective Negro physicians and nurses also found it difficult to finish their training in the Cleveland area, since as late as 1930 no hospital would admit Negroes to internships or nurses' training programs. Nor were these discriminatory policies restricted to private institutions. City Hospital, a tax-supported facility, did not integrate its staff and training programs until 1931—and only then because the city manager ordered it to do so over the protests of white physicians.[13]

To a much greater extent than hospitals, Cleveland's educational facilities were able to avoid the racist trend that was affecting other areas of urban life. In the city's public school system the nineteenth-century tradition of racial equality remained intact to a remarkable degree. The public schools had been thoroughly integrated since the 1840s, and this policy seemed to retain the support of most citizens, black and white, during the Progressive era. In 1887 the *Gazette* proudly announced that in "Cleveland, Ohio, the white citizens do not feel themselves at all disgraced by their children associating with colored children in the same school room. . . ." There is no evidence that these values changed much during the next twenty-five years. Before World War I, there was no attempt to segregate black students in separate schools or classrooms (a procedure that was prohibited by law in Ohio but nonetheless occurred to some extent in Cincinnati, Columbus, and other cities). No racial violence significant enough to be noted in either the black or the white press occurred in Cleveland schools during these years; and compared to Chicago, where "there were frequent instances of discrimination and interracial friction after 1890," public education generally exuded an air of racial harmony.[14]

This philosophy of integration extended to the teaching staffs as well as the students. Negro teachers (there were four on the payroll as early as 1888) were fully integrated within the school system. In 1896 the

---

[13] Quillin, *The Color Line in Ohio*, 155; Russell H. Davis, *Memorable Negroes in Cleveland's Past* (Cleveland, 1969), 56; Hunter, *A Nickel and a Prayer*, 70–71; Mercy Hospital Association of Cleveland, *Does Cleveland Need a Negro-Manned Hospital?* (n.p. [1927], pamphlet); Thomas F. Campbell, *Daniel E. Morgan: The Good Citizen in Politics* (Cleveland, 1966), 115–17; Charles H. Garvin, "Pioneering in Cleveland," *The Women's Voice*, I (September 1939), 14–15 (copy in Charles Herbert Garvin Papers, Western Reserve Historical Society).

[14] Cleveland *Gazette*, October 29, 1887; Drake, "The Negro in Cleveland," Cleveland *Advocate*, September 18, 1915; Spear, *Black Chicago*, 44.

Gazette noted that black instructors were frequently placed in charge of all-white classes. Despite the steadily increasing size of the black population, this policy remained in effect during the years before the Great Migration (and even for a while after it). In 1911 the city's black teachers were located in nine different schools in widely scattered sections of the city, and four years later the *Advocate*, a black weekly, reported that in most cases "not more than one or two Colored teachers are assigned to any one school. There is absolutely no tendency or inclination on the part of the school authorities to segregate them." The result was that only a few of the city's Negro instructors had "even a few Afro-American pupils in the rooms over which they preside[d]." Nor were black teachers in Cleveland restricted to employment in elementary schools—a practice that was common in many cities. Two black teachers were on the staff of Central High School during the prewar years. Helen Chesnutt, an instructor of Latin, was hired in 1910, and Cora Fields, a music teacher, joined the staff in 1915.[15]

In spite of these liberal policies, black students did not always receive equal treatment in the schools. When the daughters of Charles Chesnutt began their final year at Central High School they soon discovered that even light-skinned Negroes with middle-class upbringings were not immune to the more subtle aspects of racial prejudice. "When the Senior Class was organized, and its activities under way, they realized with shock and confusion that they were considered different from their classmates; they were being gently but firmly set apart, and had become self-conscious about it." And although the Board of Education adopted no policies of segregation, it sometimes assisted the formation of racist attitudes by authorizing textbooks portraying the Negro in a stereotyped or prejudiced manner. It was discovered in 1913 and again in 1916 that a number of elementary schools were using a reader which employed the obnoxious term "darkies" in describing Negroes. Such problems were indeed minor compared with those that blacks encountered in schools in many other cities, but they were prophetic of the much greater difficulties that the future would hold.[16]

[15] Cleveland *Gazette*, March 3, 1888, May 16, 1896, September 16, 1911, February 28, 1914; Frank U. Quillin, "The Negro in Cleveland, Ohio," *Independent*, 72 (March 7, 1912), 519; Chesnutt, *Charles Waddell Chesnutt*, 276; Cleveland *Advocate*, May 15, 1915.

[16] Chesnutt, *Charles Waddell Chesnutt*, 75; Cleveland *Gazette*, December 20, 1913; Cleveland *Advocate*, February 5, 1916. (It is likely that texts containing racial slurs continued to be used in many schools until fairly recently. The author, who attended a Cleveland elementary school in the 1950s, vividly recalls a reader in which the word "nigger" was used.)

Prior to World War I, the schools were also integrated in Boston, New Haven,

With the possible exception of Boston, Cleveland was unsurpassed in the opportunity it afforded blacks to attend college. Nearby Oberlin College, of course, had a long tradition of integrated education, and a number of Cleveland Negroes took advantage of its proximity to attend classes there. Western Reserve University, which produced most of the city's black teachers, graduated its first black student in 1892; by 1910 a dozen more blacks had received degrees. The University's professional schools of law and medicine were also open to Negroes, and one of the city's first Negro dentists graduated from Western Reserve's School of Dentistry in 1903. (There may have been some effort to exclude blacks from certain training programs through various subterfuges, but these do not seem to have been successful. One of Western Reserve's first

---

and probably throughout most of New England (Daniels, *In Freedom's Birthplace*, 185; Warner, *New Haven Negroes*, 174–75). In other states, conditions varied widely from one locality to another. In northern Ohio blacks and whites generally attended the same schools and received fairly equal treatment. In the central and southern parts of the state, however, there was a good deal of hostility to interracial education, and local boards of education often set up segregated or quasi-segregated facilities. Similar differences between northern and southern Illinois developed during this period, but blacks in Chicago never attained the equality of treatment common in Cleveland's schools. In Indiana, where discrimination of all kinds was more widespread than elsewhere in the North, separate schools were everywhere more the rule than the exception. In Indianapolis and Gary, however, some blacks attended integrated elementary schools, and these cities did not establish separate black high schools until after the Great Migration. In Michigan there was no geographic pattern, but segregated facilities did exist in some localities outside of Detroit in the late nineteenth century. In Philadelphia the 1881 state law abolishing separate schools was to some extent evaded through subterfuges. In 1911 less than one-quarter of that city's black elementary-school pupils were attending separate schools; but most of the other black students were concentrated in a fairly small number of schools, and a pattern of de facto segregation was beginning to emerge as a result of the growth of the ghetto. See Mame Charlotte Mason, "The Policy of Segregation of the Negro in the Public Schools of Ohio, Indiana, and Illinois" (M.A. thesis, University of Chicago, 1917), 14–60; Himes, "Forty Years of Negro Life in Columbus, Ohio," 138–39; David Gerber, "Education, Expediency, and Ideology: Race and Politics in the Desegregation of Ohio Public Schools in the Late Nineteenth Century," *Journal of Ethnic Studies*, 1 (Fall 1973), 1–31; Michael W. Homel, "The Negro in the Chicago Public Schools, 1910–1941" (Ph.D. dissertation, University of Chicago, 1971), 1–21; Thornbrough, *The Negro in Indiana*, 332–37, 341–43; Emma Lou Thornbrough, "Segregation in Indiana during the Klan Era of the 1920's," *Mississippi Valley Historical Review*, 47 (March 1961), 600, 604; David M. Katzman, *Before the Ghetto: Black Detroit in the Nineteenth Century* (Urbana, Ill., 1973), 90; Du Bois, *The Philadelphia Negro*, 88–89, 349–50; Howard W. Odum, "Negro Children in the Public Schools of Philadelphia," *Annals of the American Academy of Political and Social Science*, 49 (September 1913), 45. August Meier and Elliott Rudwick, "Negro Boycotts of Jim Crow Schools in the North, 1897–1925," *Integrated Education*, 5 (August–September 1967), 57–68, has useful information on conditions in Alton, Illinois; East Orange, New Jersey; and Dayton and Springfield, Ohio.

medical students, for example, complained that the University refused to allow him to register for a course in clinical medicine because they feared the hostile reactions of white patients to a Negro doctor. The Cleveland branch of the National Association for the Advancement of Colored People investigated the case, however, and "failed to find convincing proof of actual discrimination." In any case, within a few years the student had received his degree and was practicing medicine in the city.) Most other specialized schools in the Cleveland area had no qualms about accepting Negroes. The Cleveland University of Medicine and Surgery and the Spencerian Business College admitted blacks on a nondiscriminatory basis by the end of the 1890s; and Union College of Law, which had accepted blacks as early as 1870, remained integrated in the early twentieth century. Blacks who wanted preparation for teaching without going through a four-year college course had no difficulty in obtaining the necessary training. The Cleveland Normal Training School graduated several Negroes during the prewar years, and in 1915 the *Advocate* reported that a "score or so of the school girls" at nearby, recently established Kent State Normal School (now Kent State University) were Negroes.[17]

Cleveland's continuing tradition of integrated schools and colleges and its relative lack of interracial violence during the years before the wartime migration marked it as exceptional among northern cities. But in other ways it was becoming painfully evident, even to middle-class Negroes who were able to maintain good relations with whites, that blacks were being gradually set apart as a group distinct from, and inferior to, the rest of the population. Indicative of the changing racial attitudes of whites was the decline in black office-holding during the so-called Progressive era. During this period, the black population was still too small to elect black candidates without the help of white votes. Yet at one point in the 1890s, two blacks from Cleveland served simultaneously in the Ohio House of Representatives, and another black politician, John P. Green, was elected to the Ohio Senate from a district that was overwhelmingly white. After 1900, however, whites backed black candidates less often, and between 1910 and 1920 no Negro politician

[17] John P. Green, *Fact Stranger than Fiction: Seventy-Five Years of a Busy Life with Reminiscences of Many Great and Good Men* (Cleveland, 1920), 119; Thomas W. Fleming, "My Rise and Persecution" (manuscript autobiography, Western Reserve Historical Society [1932]), 20; Quillin, *The Color Line in Ohio*, 155; W. E. B. Du Bois, *The College-Bred Negro American*, Atlanta University Publications, no. 15 (Atlanta, 1910), 48; Davis, *Memorable Negroes*, 40; Chesnutt, *Charles Waddell Chesnutt*, 75, 165; Cleveland *Journal*, May 20, 27, 1905; Cleveland *Gazette*, March 7, 1914; Cleveland *Advocate*, May 15, July 3, 1915.

in Cleveland could garner enough white support to win election to the state legislature—although several tried and failed. The growing distaste of whites for black candidates was but one sign of the times. Segregated facilities, once a rare phenomenon, were in some areas of public service becoming more the rule than the exception.[18]

Nothing revealed the unfortunate consequences of this change in racial attitudes better than the 1908 Cleveland Convention of the National Education Association, which drew hundreds of black teachers to the city. Many of the blacks found it all but impossible to get hotel accommodations, and a number of white-run restaurants either turned them away altogether, overcharged them, or gave them bad service.[19] These visitors to the Forest City were discovering what native blacks already knew: racism was on the rise in Cleveland. Denied admittance to many hotels, restaurants, amusement parks, and theaters at the same time they were accepted as equals in the city's schools and colleges, members of Cleveland's black community looked to the future with a good deal of uncertainty.

[18] The careers of black politicians during this period are discussed in detail in Chapter 6.

[19] Cleveland *Plain Dealer*, May 3, 1908; Cleveland *Journal*, May 9, 16, 30, 1908; Cleveland *Gazette*, July 11, 1908.

CHAPTER 4

Occupational Decline

If integrated facilities were in decline by the early 1900s, so too were the economic opportunities that Afro-Americans had enjoyed in Cleveland during the mid-nineteenth century. As in the case of access to public accommodations, however, the changing status of black occupations during the decades before the World War I migration was complex and not uniform in all areas. To understand the significance of these trends it is necessary to place the changing black occupational structure in comparative context.

The transformation of urban America in the late nineteenth and early twentieth centuries was closely related to the economic changes that were occurring during these years. The half-century after 1865 was marked by massive industrialization, and the new firms producing steel, oil, rubber, machinery, and refrigerated meat seemed to demand an ever-increasing supply of laborers. Almost every indicator of economic change recorded dramatic growth. During these years, steel ingot production rose from twenty thousand to thirty million tons per year, while the total index of manufacturing output increased from 17 to 200. Everywhere in America, with the exception of most of the South, the "triumph of the industrial spirit" was much in evidence.[1]

For the most part, unfortunately, black workers did not participate very much in this new upsurge of industrial activity. In Cleveland in 1890, only three blacks were employed in the city's rapidly expanding steel industry, and virtually no black males worked as semiskilled oper-

[1] Edward Chase Kirkland, *Industry Comes of Age: Business, Labor, and Public Policy, 1860–1897* (New York, 1961), and Douglass C. North, *Growth and Welfare in the American Past: A New Economic History* (Englewood Cliffs, N.J., 1966), 149–64, survey the changing economy.

atives in factories. By 1910 this situation had improved to some extent; several hundred Afro-Americans had managed to find work in mills or foundries, and a handful had broken the racial barrier in the city's cigar, tobacco, and furniture industries. Despite these gains, however, black workers continued to have far fewer jobs in manufacturing than their percentage of the total work force warranted. What jobs they were able to obtain in industry were almost all in the unskilled labor category; only a handful attained skilled or even semiskilled positions in factories prior to the Great Migration. With some variations, this was probably true of all northern cities. Black employment in factories was higher in Cleveland than in Chicago or, especially, New York, and considerably lower in Cleveland than in Philadelphia; but the variation among these cities was not dramatic.[2]

Why, given the booming industrial economy of Cleveland, Chicago, and other cities, did blacks find jobs in manufacturing difficult to obtain? Several factors were responsible. Employers were often reluctant to hire black workers because they shared the belief, common to many whites, that Negroes were particularly suited to agricultural employment and were therefore "inherently unfitted for industrial work." Whites felt this lack of adaptability was particularly true of those blacks who had recently migrated from the South, and as a result some manufacturers "refused even to give the Negro a trial because they considered his unfitness to be an established fact." It was true, of course, that many southern migrants lacked the skills necessary for employment in industry and the trades. Few, however, were able to acquire this knowledge in the North, since apprenticeship training was usually restricted to whites. In Cleveland, of seventeen hundred men enrolled in apprenticeship programs in 1910, only seven were Negroes. Second, no economic necessity compelled employers to hire blacks until the outbreak of hostilities in 1914 sharply reduced the stream of European immigrants that had previously provided American manufacturers with an abundant supply of cheap labor. Only during World War I would northern industrialists begin to realize the value of the Negro as an "industrial reserve." Finally, many trade unions affiliated with the American Federation of Labor refused to accept black members. Only nine AFL unions openly prohibited Negro membership through clauses in their constitutions, but others ac-

[2] U.S. *Eleventh Census, 1890* (Washington, 1893), II, 654–55; U.S. *Thirteenth Census, 1910* (Washington, 1912), IV, 548–50. Cleveland, with 22 percent of its employed black males engaged in manufacturing in 1910, stood midway between the black communities of New York (14 percent in manufacturing) and Pittsburgh (29 percent in manufacturing). Louise Venable Kennedy, *The Negro Peasant Turns Cityward* (New York, 1930), 75.

complished the same purpose by excluding Negroes from the initiation
ritual; still others, although they had no national policy of exclusion,
allowed locals to bar Negroes if they saw fit, or to segregate black members in subordinate Jim Crow locals. Since before the 1930s few unskilled
workers were unionized, these policies of the AFL did not prevent many
blacks from entering industry at the lower occupational levels. They did,
however, prevent most black workers from moving into the better paying
skilled jobs in factories.[3]

In Cleveland, union policies, both national and local, effectively kept
most eligible Negroes out of the trade union movement. The Boiler-
makers' Union, the International Association of Machinists, and the
Plumbers' and Steamfitters' Union had a national policy of excluding
blacks. Other union locals in the city, such as the Metal Polishers and
the Paperhangers, barred Negroes on their own initiative. In 1896 a
group of whites refused to join a Cooks' union being organized by the
Knights of Labor when they learned it was to be an integrated organization. The Paperhangers' local, established at the turn of the century, had
no black members whatsoever during its first twenty-seven years; the
union's leaders explained that "a storm of protest" occurred whenever
the question of admitting a Negro came up. Some unions, anxious to
keep their Negro membership within the labor movement, but also intent
upon segregating them, set up special Jim Crow locals to achieve their
purpose. This occurred in two Cleveland locals with significant Negro
memberships: the Freight Handlers' Union and the Porters' Union (not
to be confused with A. Philip Randolph's Brotherhood of Sleeping Car
Porters). Black musicians, although they had been members of an
integrated union as late as 1888, also had become part of a separate,
segregated organization by the 1920s.[4]

[3] Kennedy, The Negro Peasant Turns Cityward, 114; Charles H. Wesley, Negro
Labor in the United States, 1850–1925: A Study in American Economic History
(New York, 1927), 238–39; U.S. Thirteenth Census, IV, 548; F. E. Wolfe, Admis-
sion to American Trade Unions, Johns Hopkins University Studies in Historical and
Political Science, series 30, no. 1 (Baltimore, Md., 1912), 118–21, 125–30; Sterling
D. Spero and Abram L. Harris, The Black Worker: The Negro and the Labor
Movement (New York, 1931), 149, 53–86; Bernard Mandel, "Samuel Gompers and
the Negro Workers, 1886–1914," Journal of Negro History, 40 (January 1955),
34–60.
[4] Spero and Harris, The Black Worker, 57, 59, 103; National Urban League,
Department of Research and Investigation, Negro Membership in American Labor
Unions (New York [1929]), 40, 45, 67; Cleveland Gazette, May 23, 1896, December
3, 1887; Wesley, Negro Labor in the United States, 269. Unfortunately, there is a
scarcity of information on Negro-white labor relations in Cleveland prior to 1930,
and it is often difficult to determine the exact date of the inception of a union's
discriminatory policy.

On one level, the exclusionary policies of these new unions can be viewed as simply another example of the general elitism of the AFL under the leadership of Samuel Gompers. The AFL had no interest in organizing unskilled workers, whether black or white, and their general approach to industrial questions and social issues was conservative. A more important cause of black exclusion, however, was related to the fact that many of the trade unionists, as well as the people that they served, were members of what Robert Wiebe has called "the new middle class" of the Progressive era. As a result of their newly arrived status, these groups were particularly anxious to gain respectability, and they were eager to dissociate themselves from a racial group that was becoming stereotyped by popular writers and scientists alike as ignorant, lazy, and immoral. Thus members of the Paperhangers' Union in Cleveland objected to Negroes out of a "fear of personal contact" and because they did not "desire the close association which would naturally be expected" of union men. The city's Parquet Floor Layers, on the other hand, resisted Negro membership because they feared a loss in trade from their upper-middle-class white clientele, who disapproved of having black workmen in their homes. In both cases the underlying rationale for black exclusion was a quest for respectability and status.[5]

At a more basic economic level, a major obstacle to a rapprochement between black and white workers was the use of blacks as strikebreakers. Employers who balked at hiring Negroes on a permanent basis were quite willing to use them to break strikes. This often placed Negro workers in a peculiar situation. Excluded from many unions because of white prejudice, they were sorely tempted to accept temporary employment at good wages when the opportunity presented itself. But by acting as strikebreakers they only confirmed the worst fears of the white unionists: that all blacks were potential scabs who, because of their servile inclinations, would never be able to sympathize with the cause of labor. Friction in the North between union members and black strikebreakers frequently resulted in violence and sometimes in lynchings and race riots.[6]

[5] National Urban League, *Negro Membership in American Labor Unions*, 45, 40; Robert Wiebe, *The Search for Order, 1877–1920* (New York, 1967), 111–32. The general conservatism of the AFL has been noted by many labor historians during the last decade. A useful overview is Michael Rogin, "Voluntarism: The Political Functions of an Anti-Political Doctrine," *Industrial and Labor Relations Review*, 15 (July 1962), 521–35.

[6] Spero and Harris, *The Black Worker*, 128–29; Logan, *The Betrayal of the Negro* (New York, 1965), 156–57. Two excellent case studies of the interrelationship between black workers, white unions, and management are Elliott M. Rudwick's *Race Riot at East St. Louis, July 2, 1917* (Carbondale, Ill., 1964), ch. 11, and Wil-

In Cleveland, labor disputes involving racial conflicts occurred at least as early as 1863, when the use of Negroes to replace striking longshoremen provoked a minor riot. During the next fifty years, intermittent racial violence—although less common than elsewhere—continued to plague the city's labor relations. The most serious example was the strike at the Brown Hoisting and Conveying Machine Company, which lasted several months during the summer of 1896. Although no general racial conflict occurred, the strikebreakers, many of whom were black, found it necessary to carry arms to protect themselves from hostile white strikers who milled about the plant and attempted to discourage the strikebreakers from entering. The use of black workers to break strikes sometimes resulted in the adoption of a union policy of exclusion where none had existed previously. The Cleveland Waiters' and Beverage Dispensers' Union barred Negroes after a number had "served as strikebreakers, defeating the union and retaining their jobs, working for less wages and longer hours." During and after the Great Migration this union continued to be a thorn in the side of the black community as its members harassed or attacked Negro waiters and attempted to drive them out of many downtown establishments altogether.[7]

"The greatest enemy of the Negro," said one black leader from Indiana in 1899, "is the trade unionism of the North." Whether unions were the "greatest enemy" of blacks as a whole may be doubted, but it is clear that they were a major cause behind the decline of the number of blacks in the skilled trades, thereby undercutting one of the most important elements of the black middle class of the nineteenth century. In 1870 fully 31.7 percent of all black males in Cleveland had been employed in skilled trades; by 1910 this figure had dropped sharply to 11.1 percent (Table 9).[8] As early as 1886 Jere A. Brown, a prominent

---

liam M. Tuttle, Jr.'s *Race Riot: Chicago in the Red Summer of 1919* (New York, 1970), 108–55.

[7] Spero and Harris, *The Black Worker*, 198; Cleveland *Plain Dealer*, July 1, 2, 3, August 4, 1896; Cleveland *Gazette*, July 25, 1896; Joseph A. Burns to John P. Green, October 18, 1896, John Patterson Green Papers, Western Reserve Historical Society. (Burns was one of the strikebreakers and had been arrested for carrying a concealed weapon.) On the racial conflict in the Waiters' Union, see the Cleveland *Gazette*, September 27, 1902; National Urban League, *Negro Membership in American Labor Unions*, 91; and Chapter 9.

[8] It should be noted that the printed censuses for 1870, 1890, and 1910 (the source for much of the occupational data in this chapter) did not list all occupations and that, in addition, some jobs listed were unclassifiable (see Appendix I). For these reasons, it seems likely that the numbers—of both blacks and whites—in the skilled trades were slightly larger than the figures listed in Tables 7 and 9. But it is improbable that more complete occupational data for these years would alter the general conclusions that are made in this paragraph.

TABLE 7. *Male occupational structure of Cleveland, by racial and ethnic group, 1890*

| | Occupational category | | | | | | | | | | | | |
| | Professional | | Proprietary | | Clerical | | Skilled | | Semiskilled | | Unskilled | | Domestic | |
	Number	Percentage	Number	Percentage	Number	Percentage	Number	Percentage	Number	Percentage	Number	Percentage	Number	Percentage
Colored[a]	10	0.8	20	1.6	34	2.8	189	15.3	15	1.2	318	25.7	392	31.7
Native whites of native parentage	879	5.0	2,140	12.2	4,061	23.1	3,926	22.3	1,076	6.1	2,023	11.5	224	1.3
Native whites of foreign or mixed parentage	313	1.5	1,631	8.0	3,278	16.1	5,686	27.9	2,317	11.4	3,800	18.6	145	0.7
Foreign-born whites	393	0.9	3,798	8.7	2,013	4.6	11,522	26.3	5,223	11.9	15,018	34.2	470	1.1
All workers	1,495	1.8	7,599	9.1	9,407	11.3	21,263	25.6	8,631	10.4	21,159	25.5	1,231	1.5
Germans	86	0.5	1,534	8.7	594	3.3	5,270	29.5	1,941	11.9	5,747	32.1	151	0.8
Irish	29	0.5	326	5.6	174	3.0	846	14.3	860	14.8	2,628	45.3	114	2.0
English	100	1.5	562	8.3	555	8.2	2,175	32.1	1,162	17.1	1,105	16.3	111	1.6
Swedes and Norwegians	3	0.9	16	4.8	5	1.5	55	16.3	53	15.7	162	48.1	12	3.6

SOURCE: U.S. *Eleventh Census, 1890* (Washington, 1893), II, 654–55.
[a] "Colored" includes a very few Chinese, Japanese, and Indians. In 1890, 14.8 percent of the male occupations in Cleveland were either unspecified by the Census Bureau or were unclassifiable. The unclassifiable occupations are listed in Appendix I.

TABLE 8. *Female occupational structure of Cleveland, by racial and ethnic group, 1890*

| | Occupational category | | | | | | | | | | | | |
| | Professional | | Proprietary | | Clerical | | Skilled | | Semiskilled | | Unskilled | | Domestic | |
	Num-ber	Percent-age	Num-ber	Percent-age	Num-ber	Percent-age	Num-ber	Percent-age	Num-ber	Percent-age	Num-ber	Percent-age	Num-ber	Percent-age
Colored[a]	9	2.6	12	3.5	2	0.6	3	0.9	62	18.0	4	1.2	243	70.6
Native whites of native parentage	448	11.6	130	3.4	600	15.8	99	2.4	1,078	27.9	53	1.4	1,185	30.6
Native whites of foreign or mixed parentage	478	6.1	76	1.0	1,114	14.3	513	6.6	2,934	37.7	153	2.0	2,005	25.7
Foreign-born whites	153	2.1	239	2.3	260	3.5	349	4.8	1,984	27.1	110	1.5	3,944	53.8
All workers	1,108	5.7	457	2.4	1,976	10.2	964	5.0	6,058	31.3	320	1.7	7,377	38.2
Germans	42	1.6	70	2.7	77	2.9	115	4.4	653	24.9	59	2.2	1,498	57.1
Irish	30	2.0	53	3.5	28	1.9	10	0.7	229	15.2	11	0.7	1,125	74.6
English	33	3.4	48	4.9	62	6.4	12	1.2	319	32.9	6	0.6	436	45.0
Swedes and Norwegians	—	—	—	—	—	—	—	—	5	6.8	—	—	69	93.2

SOURCE: U.S. *Eleventh Census, 1890*, II, 654–55.
[a] "Colored" includes a very few Chinese, Japanese, and Indians. In 1890, 5.5 percent of the female occupations in Cleveland were either unspecified by the Census Bureau or were unclassifiable. The unclassifiable occupations are listed in Appendix I.

black Clevelander, noted that many younger blacks were already losing interest in the skilled trades (Brown found only three black apprentices in the entire city) and preferred to enter occupations which entailed less friction with whites. The decline of blacks in the skilled trades, however, must be qualified in a number of ways. First, part of this decline can be traced to a general contraction in the proportion of *all* workers engaged in these trades during the decades preceding World War I. The employment of all males in skilled work in Cleveland declined from over 30 percent in 1870 to 26.2 percent in 1910. Second, the drop in black skilled employment was by no means uniform in all trades. Among the older trades that had been the mainstay of the nineteenth-century black middle class, the blacksmiths, shoemakers, and painters experienced a sharp decline in the proportion of blacks. But the proportion of blacks in the carpentry trade declined much more slowly, and the percentage of brickmasons who were black actually increased substantially between 1870 and 1910. In the newer or more specialized trades, the exclusion of Afro-Americans was almost complete. Prior to 1915, almost no blacks were employed as cabinetmakers, typesetters, bakers, tinsmiths, or electricians; the 1910 Census listed only five black plumbers in the entire city.[9]

Although detailed documentary evidence is often lacking, it appears that a similar distinction between "new" and "old" trades must be made in regard to union policies of excluding Negroes. There was a strong tendency among the newer trades (such as the paperhangers') to exclude blacks altogether. Among the more traditional skilled crafts the situation was more complex. By the 1870s, many white carpenters, masons, and others had developed a tradition of working with Negroes on a basis of relative equality; and when these workers formed unions at the end of the nineteenth century, they admitted a number of Negroes to their ranks. Since few younger blacks joined apprenticeship programs (either because they were excluded or because they sensed the hostility of the younger whites who were entering the labor movement at the time), the number of blacks who were members of these unions probably declined at a steady pace, through attrition, during the prewar years. On the eve of the Great Migration, however, one black Clevelander reported that the Carpenters', Brickmasons', Plasterers', and Lathers' Unions, among others, still had black members, and a visitor to the

<hr/>

[9] Emma Lou Thornbrough, *The Negro in Indiana: A Study of a Minority* ([Indianapolis,] 1957), 356; U.S. *Thirteenth Census, 1910*, IV, 549. The index of the relative concentration of blacks in various occupations is computed in Table 26 in Appendix II.

TABLE 9. Occupational structure of Cleveland, by racial and ethnic group, 1910

	Occupational category												
	Professional		Proprietary		Clerical		Skilled		Semiskilled		Unskilled		Domestic	
	Number	Percentage	Number	Percentage	Number	Percentage	Number	Percentage	Number	Percentage	Number	Percentage	Number	Percentage
Males														
Negroes	50	1.4	87	2.5	104	3.0	388	11.1	255	7.3	905	25.9	1,033	29.6
Native whites of native parentage	1,436	3.6	3,696	9.5	9,523	24.3	9,691	24.5	3,134	8.0	1,923	4.9	953	2.4
Native whites of foreign or mixed parentage	979	1.8	4,730	8.6	10,137	18.8	15,412	28.0	4,970	9.0	3,626	6.6	1,263	2.3
Foreign-born whites	611	0.6	8,349	8.7	4,438	4.6	25,125	26.1	7,848	8.2	19,792	20.6	1,546	1.6
All workers	3,077	1.6	16,877	8.7	24,218	12.5	50,818	26.2	16,209	8.4	26,345	13.6	4,858	2.5
Females														
Negroes	54	3.4	62	3.9	23	1.4	36	2.3	201	12.7	—	—	1,149	72.6
Native whites of native parentage	1,508	12.3	530	4.3	4,481	37.5	222	1.8	2,498	20.3	—	—	1,404	11.4
Native whites of foreign or mixed parentage	1,756	7.2	483	2.0	6,506	26.3	1,204	5.0	7,412	30.5	—	—	2,597	10.7
Foreign-born whites	529	3.2	943	5.7	1,337	8.0	561	3.7	4,219	25.3	—	—	6,832	41.0
All workers	3,847	7.0	2,018	3.7	12,347	22.6	2,023	3.7	13,732	25.1	—	—	11,987	21.9

SOURCE: U.S. *Thirteenth Census, 1910* (Washington, 1912), IV, 548–50.
NOTE: Totals include the category "Indians, Chinese, Japanese, and all others." In 1910, 26 percent of the male occupations and 16 percent of the female occupations in Cleveland were unspecified by the Census Bureau.

city noted that black union men were still able to "receive the same wages and work on the same jobs with the white men without any friction." Thus Cleveland's nineteenth-century heritage of equality continued, in these unions, to linger on until well into the twentieth century.[10]

The skilled trades were not the only "integrated" black occupations that receded in importance during the 1870–1915 period. Throughout most of the nineteenth century, Negro waiters (especially headwaiters) who worked in Cleveland's exclusive downtown establishments were often held in high esteem by both the Negro and white communities, and a few were considered members of the black leadership class. As early as the 1880s, however, some black waiters were discharged and replaced with whites, and this marked the beginning of the exodus of black waiters from the city's better hotels and restaurants. The decline was a gradual one, but by 1918 only two leading establishments continued to employ black waiters. A parallel trend occurred in the bar-

[10] Cleveland *Gazette*, February 20, 1886; Frank U. Quillin, *The Color Line in Ohio* (Ann Arbor, 1913), 155–56. A decline in numbers of blacks in the skilled trades was probably common throughout the North in the late nineteenth and early twentieth centuries; the pace of change varied considerably from city to city, however. Three factors appear to account for a slower decline in some cities: (1) a tradition of racial liberalism; (2) smaller size and consequently less advanced state of industrialization and economic specialization; (3) a smaller immigrant population. It was primarily the first factor which retarded the decline of black opportunity in Cleveland, New Haven, and perhaps a few other cities. In 1890 15.3 percent of Cleveland's Negro males were engaged in skilled work, and in New Haven the percentage in skilled jobs was 16.6. In most cities, however, the second and third factors (or, in many cases, a combination of the two) were much more important. Thus, despite the high level of racial discrimination evident in schools and public accommodations in medium-sized Midwest cities at the end of the nineteenth century, these communities often afforded blacks more opportunities in the skilled trades than did eastern cities, chiefly because they contained fewer immigrants to compete for these jobs. In 1890, for example, Columbus, Indianapolis, and Des Moines had higher proportions of black males in skilled work (13.8, 10.8, and 19.2 percent, respectively) than eastern cities like Boston (9.7 percent), New York (4.8 percent), and Paterson, N.J. (6.1 percent). Chicago was also below average, with 7.8 percent of its black males in skilled occupations in 1890. It is evident that blacks in New York suffered a much higher degree of economic discrimination at an earlier date than did their counterparts in most other cities. In 1908, one observer noted of New York that "even in the colored districts the cobblers are largely Italians, and the colored shoemakers drift into other things." See Helen A. Tucker, "Negro Craftsmen in New York," *Southern Workman*, 37 (January 1908), 99; Mary White Ovington, *Half a Man: The Status of the Negro in New York* (New York, 1911), 85–91, 94–98, 99n; Herman D. Bloch, *The Circle of Discrimination: An Economic and Social Study of the Black Man in New York* (New York, 1969), 89–96. The percentages listed above were calculated from data in U.S. *Eleventh Census, 1890*, II, 638, 650, 654, 662, 674, 700, 704, 708. The occupational classification system used is discussed in Appendix I.

bering trade. George Myers's large well-known barbershop in the Hollenden, which sometimes employed thirty barbers, continued to serve an exclusively white clientele until Myers's death in 1930—but this was exceptional. Although blacks continued, in ever-decreasing numbers, to enter the barbering trade during the prewar years, their proportionate share of this occupation fell off sharply. In 1870, 43 percent of the city's barbers were blacks; by 1890, this figure had slipped to 18 percent. In 1910 less than one of every ten barbers in Cleveland was black, and it is likely that many of these were serving Negroes rather than the more lucrative white clientele.[11]

The declining importance of black waiters and barbers and the gradual disappearance of black businesses that catered to a predominantly white clientele were common to all northern cities during the late nineteenth and early twentieth centuries. In smaller, less industrialized cities the process occurred at a much slower pace than the big centers of population, however. In Columbus, Evansville, Indianapolis, Des Moines, and Kansas City, Missouri, blacks were able to maintain their hold on the barbering trade much longer than elsewhere, because these cities did not attract the large immigrant work force that was responsible for driving blacks out of barbering in other cities. In the major urban centers the process occurred much more rapidly and in most cases was virtually completed by 1915. Surveying Negro businesses in New York in 1909, George Edmund Haynes found that only seven of fifty Negro barber shops in the city still served a predominantly white clientele, while only one Negro merchant in ten catered to a predominantly white trade. "The Negro barber is rapidly losing ground in this city," said W. E. B. Du Bois in analyzing Philadelphia's black community in the late 1890s; and although he found some black catering establishments "still prominent," Du Bois noted that "they do not by any means dominate the field, as [a generation ago]." Students of the race situation in Boston, Detroit, and elsewhere echoed these observations. Because of its integrationist traditions, Cleveland did not succumb to this trend as quickly as other cities its size; but there, as elsewhere, the process of occupational change was irreversible.[12]

[11] H. T. Eubanks to John P. Green, February 5, 1899, Green Papers; Cleveland *Advocate*, September 7, 1918; John Garraty, ed., *The Barber and the Historian: The Correspondence of George A. Myers and James Ford Rhodes, 1910–1923* (Columbus, Ohio, 1956), xxii–xxiii; U.S. *Ninth Census, 1870* (Washington, 1873), I, 784; Thomas Goliber, "Cuyahoga Blacks: A Social and Demographic Study, 1850–1880" (M.A. thesis, Kent State University, 1972), 78; U.S. *Eleventh Census, 1890*, II, 654; U.S. *Thirteenth Census, 1910*, IV, 549.

[12] George Edmund Haynes, *The Negro at Work in New York City*, Columbia

In discussing the class structure of black communities around 1900, August Meier has noted that a "growing antipathy on the part of whites toward trading with Negro businessmen and changes in technology and business organization" were chiefly responsible for the decline of black entrepreneurs who serve an elite white clientele. While this is true, it is important to add that the changing nature of urban society itself (not just the growth of the ghetto) and developments in the white upper class during the 1870–1920 period may also have facilitated the decline in number of these Negro entrepreneurs. At the end of the nineteenth century, white urban elites were beginning to set themselves apart from the rest of the society residentially (through suburbs or the development of areas within the city which served much the same function) and institutionally (through clubs, private schools, and other institutions). This self-segregation on the part of the white upper class helped break the paternalistic tie between themselves and the black elite, and it is likely that this break would have eventually occurred even if racial discrimination had not been on the rise at the time. Commenting on the deterioration of the Negro catering business in Philadelphia during the 1900–1930 period, two writers found the main cause to be the caterers' "loss of personal contact with the fashionable group whose first thought used to be for the Negro when 'service' of any kind was to be done. . . ." While racism contributed to this loss of contact, the self-consciousness of the white upper class and the increasing fragmentation of urban life also played an important role.[13]

University Studies in History, Economics and Public Law, vol. 49, no. 3 (New York, 1913), 125, 128–29; W. E. B. Du Bois, *The Philadelphia Negro: A Social Study* (Philadelphia, 1899), 115–16, 119; John Daniels, *In Freedom's Birthplace: A Study of the Boston Negroes* (Boston, 1914), 324; Allan Spear, *Black Chicago: The Making of a Negro Ghetto, 1890–1920* (Chicago, 1967), 111–12; Ovington, *Half a Man*, 107; David M. Katzman, *Before the Ghetto: Black Detroit in the Nineteenth Century* (Urbana, Ill., 1973), 116–17. In 1890, the percentage of the barbering trade controlled by blacks varied widely throughout the North. In some cities blacks had already been virtually eliminated from the trade. In New York, only 2.2 percent of all barbers were Afro-Americans, and in Paterson, N.J., Newark, Hartford, Chicago, and Boston, the figure ranged from 1.9 to 9.5 percent. In other cities (New Haven, Philadelphia, Pittsburgh, Cleveland, and Minneapolis) the position of black barbers was declining, but they still held between 12 and 18 percent of the trade. There were a number of communities, however, where black barbers still dominated the trade at the end of the nineteenth century. In 1890 blacks controlled between 30 and 40 percent of the barbering trade in Columbus, Ohio; Kansas City, Missouri; and Indianapolis and Evansville, Indiana. These figures were computed from data in U.S. *Eleventh Census, 1890*, II, *passim*.

[13] August Meier, "Negro Class Structure and Ideology in the Age of Booker T. Washington," *Phylon*, 23 (Fall 1963), 259; G. J. Fleming and Berenice D. Shelton, "Fine Foods of Philadelphia," *Crisis*, 45 (April 1938), 114; Clara A. Hardin, *The*

In addition, black entrepreneurs who served a predominantly white clientele were adversely affected by the status anxieties of nouveau riche whites who, around 1900, were challenging an older, more genteel group of wealthy individuals. In 1913, for example, blacks in Dayton complained of "the newly-rich and uncultured [white] families who were ready to take advantage of all artificial props to uphold their importance. To the negroes they could show no mercy." Thus urban change, the growth of special upper-class white institutions, and the nouveau riche character of a portion of the white elite all contributed to the decline of the older group of Negro entrepreneurs.[14]

As traditional areas of black employment receded in importance, Negroes who aspired to middle-class status increasingly found themselves limited to three options: they could become clerical workers, enter one of the professions, or start a small business that catered to a predominantly Negro clientele. Each of these paths had its pitfalls.

One of the most significant changes accompanying the growth of the American economy between the Civil War and World War I was the creation of a new, much enlarged group of clerical and managerial positions in business firms of all types. Much like the urban systems of which they formed so crucial a part, these businesses were becoming more specialized in function as well as larger in size, and they required not only an army of factory workers but a wide variety of white-collar employees as well. Few Negroes, however, were able to gain entrance to this new white-collar world. In Cleveland the number of black males employed in clerical positions increased from 1.7 percent in 1870 to 3.7 percent forty years later. During this same period, the proportion of black females in clerical work rose from zero to 1.4 percent. (see Table 9). These modest increases in white-collar employment, however, fell far short of those experienced by the city's white work force. The one substantial gain occurred in black male employment as clerks in offices; the proportionate share of blacks in this occupation (where 100 percent would equal parity) increased from 28 to 54 percent between 1890 and 1910. In other white-collar jobs improvement was negligible at best, and

Negroes of Philadelphia: The Cultural Adjustment of a Minority Group (Bryn Mawr, Pa., 1945), 26. On the development of the white urban elite, see E. Digby Balzell, *Philadelphia Gentlemen: The Making of a National Upper Class* (Glencoe, Ill., 1958); E. Digby Balzell, *The Protestant Establishment: Aristocracy and Caste in America* (New York, 1964), 109–42; Neil Harris, "Four Stages of Cultural Growth: The American City," in *History and the Role of the City in American Life*, Indiana Historical Society Lectures, 1971–72 (Indianapolis, Ind., 1972), 35–42.
14 Quillin, *The Color Line in Ohio*, 139.

the proportionate share of blacks ranged from 20 percent to an abysmally low 3 percent. (See Tables 26 and 27 in Appendix II.)

Perhaps because of the existence of standardized tests for some jobs in the federal or municipal government, blacks sometimes found more opportunity for white-collar employment in public service than in private enterprise. In 1915 several Cleveland Negroes were clerks in departments of the city government; two were government meat inspectors; and forty-two were postal clerks or carriers. These gains were significant for the black middle class, but even in public service blacks suffered the onus of racial discrimination. In some areas of municipal employment it was standard procedure to exclude Negroes. The fire department, for example, employed no blacks in 1910 and had probably always been totally white.The number of blacks serving on the police force was inadequate. Cleveland had employed black constables as early as the 1870s, but in 1910 blacks still had only one-half their rightful share of police positions. Nor did blacks in civil service jobs always rise in the ranks as rapidly as they should have. The case of Charles S. Smith, an Afro-American who placed fourth in the police examinations in 1897, is a good example. Because of his valued stenographic skills, Smith was immediately chosen to be the secretary to the chief of police. He had to remain in that position for twenty years, however, before his salary was raised from a patrolman's to that of a lieutenant. Despite the significant number of blacks who found employment in the post office, as late as 1930 few had risen to positions of authority. Finally, although Cleveland's black community could point with pride to those of the race who had obtained white-collar government employment, the fact was that most of the Negroes employed by the city were unskilled laborers, hired to do a variety of unappealing, low-paying tasks. As the editor of the *Gazette* caustically noted in 1916, most blacks in municipal employment were restricted to "spittoon cleaning, garbage hunting [hauling?], street-cleaning, truck driving, and other jobs of that kind," with little opportunity to rise to better positions.[15]

The status anxieties of those whites who had moved up from factory to clerical work undoubtedly played a major part in the difficulties

[15] Robert I. Drake, "The Negro in Cleveland," Cleveland *Advocate*, September 18, 1915; U.S. *Thirteenth Census, 1910*, IV, 549; Charles W. Chesnutt, "The Negro in Cleveland," *The Clevelander*, 5 (November 1930), 24; Cleveland *Leader*, March 8, 9, 1875; Cleveland *Gazette*, April 1, 1916, January 11, 1919; Cleveland *Press*, April 21, 1923, clipping in unnumbered Walter B. Wright Scrapbooks, Western Reserve Historical Society; interview with Russell and Rowena Jelliffe, September 1, 1971.

blacks encountered in entering white-collar employment. Another factor may have been related to the beginnings, during the Progressive era, of the preoccupation of American business with public relations and advertising techniques. The preponderance of native-born white women in department store jobs, one observer noted in 1909, was partially "due to the fact that many customers prefer to be served by [native-white] Americans. . . ." The mass market that the department stores catered to forced the stores to adopt a neutral image in dealing with the public, and this virtually eliminated Negroes (as well as many immigrants) from positions as sales clerks. The newer communications and transportation industries also tended to exclude blacks from jobs involving contact with the public. In 1905, there was only a single Negro telephone operator in New York, and other northern cities were no different in this regard. In 1900 Cleveland was one of three cities in the North that employed a few Afro-Americans as streetcar conductors, but within ten years the city's privately owned transportation companies had ended this policy of integration.[16]

For those Negroes who had the funds to obtain the necessary specialized training, the professions offered a surer path to success than did the clerical occupations. At the beginning of the twentieth century the increase in Negro populations in urban areas, combined with the refusal of most white professional men to accept Negro clients, led to a general increase in the number of black professionals. This trend was not uniform in all occupations. Blacks were over-represented in the poorly paid profession of the ministry, but they found the newer engineering fields completely closed to them; black journalists found little opportunity outside the small Negro weeklies that struggled to survive in many urban areas. In the traditional professions, black doctors did much better than black lawyers. Surveying Negro professionals as a whole, Kelly Miller noted that blacks were "crowding into" the medical profession, but were not entering the legal field nearly as fast; at the turn of the century there were two and one-half times as many blacks in medicine as in the law. In Philadelphia, W. E. B. Du Bois found black doctors successful.

---

[16] Elizabeth Beardsley Butler, *Saleswomen in Mercantile Stores* (New York, 1912), 144; Haynes, *The Negro at Work in New York City*, 76; James S. Stemons, "The Industrial Color-Line in the North," *Century Magazine*, 60 (July 1900), 478; *Cleveland Journal*, June 3, 17, 1905; U.S. *Thirteenth Census, 1910*, 549. See also John Daniels, "Industrial Conditions among Negro Men in Boston," *Charities*, 15 (October 7, 1905), 37. The anti-immigrant and anti-Negro aspect of department stores at the turn of the century is ignored by Daniel Boorstin, who calls the stores examples of "the democratization of luxury." Boorstin, *The Americans: The Democratic Experience* (New York, 1973), 101–12.

Lawyers, however, were "a partial failure" because "Negroes furnish little lucrative law business, and a Negro lawyer will seldom be employed by whites." On the other hand, the number of blacks in the teaching profession grew rapidly during this period. Many cities established separate schools for Negroes, and when they did so they usually hired Negro teachers to preside over the classes; the result was a gain for the black middle class, if a loss for the principle of integration.[17]

Opportunities in the professions were unusually good for black Clevelanders. In 1915 the black community could claim eight doctors, three dentists, two professionally trained nurses, a dozen lawyers, and thirty school teachers. These numbers may seem small, but proportionately (with the exception of the nurses) blacks did not lag very far behind the rest of the population. The number of black lawyers in Cleveland was quite exceptional, given the relatively small size of the city's black community. In 1910, St. Louis and Philadelphia had black populations that were many times the size of Cleveland's; yet all three cities had about the same number of black lawyers. The success of these professionals in Cleveland was due primarily to their unusually integrated practices. Although most northern cities had some black lawyers serving an integrated clientele, all of Cleveland's black lawyers were able to draw clients from both races. A majority, in fact, had more white clients than Negro in 1915. At that time many of Cleveland's black doctors also had integrated practices.[18]

At the same time that the black professionals were making steady—if uneven—progress, a new group of black businessmen was on the rise. In the South as well as the North the Negro merchants and entrepreneurs whose clientele was primarily white were disappearing during the twenty years prior to the World War I migration. They were gradually replaced by a different group of entrepreneurs—real estate dealers, undertakers, newspaper editors, insurance agents, bankers, and a plethora of small businessmen—who were dependent mostly upon the Negro market. Ironically, the deterioration of race relations at the end of the nineteenth century, as evidenced by discrimination in housing, the trend

[17] Kelly Miller, "Professional and Skilled Occupations," *Annals of the American Academy of Political and Social Science*, 49 (September 1913), 13, 17; Du Bois, *The Philadelphia Negro*, 114; Meier, "Negro Class Structure and Ideology in the Age of Booker T. Washington," 259–60.

[18] Robert I. Drake, "The Negro in Cleveland;" U.S. *Thirteenth Census, 1910*, IV, 549; Jane Edna Hunter, *A Nickel and a Prayer* (Cleveland, 1940), 87; William A. Crossland, *Industrial Conditions among Negroes in St. Louis*, Washington University Studies in Social Economics, vol. 1, no. 1 (St. Louis, Mo., 1914), 38; interview with Dr. William P. Saunders, August 6, 1972.

toward residential concentration, the refusal of white insurance companies to grant policies to Negroes, and the discrimination of white
banks in authorizing loans, made the development of this new class
possible.[19]

This new group of black entrepreneurs did not gain ascendancy over
the old as fast in Cleveland as elsewhere. The moderate size of the city's
black community made it more difficult for black businessmen to acquire
an economic base among their own race. On the other hand, the continued (though weakened) heritage of integration and the paternalistic
support by a segment of the white upper class allowed a number of black
businesses that dealt only with whites to survive and prosper longer than
their counterparts in cities like Chicago and Philadelphia. On the eve
of the Great Migration, a small group of Negro tailors, caterers, barbers,
and merchants continued to serve a predominantly white clientele. One
of the most successful of this older group was Jacob E. Reed, who for
many years operated a well-known downtown markethouse that specialized in fish, oysters, and other seafood products. Reed's business may
have declined somewhat with the passage of time, but as late as 1919
the aging merchant could still count "a number of the best families in
the city" as well as "the leading hotels and restaurants" among his
customers.[20]

If the older, white-oriented black businessmen were represented by
Reed, the younger generation of entrepreneurs with roots in the black
community was exemplified by S. Clayton Green. Green began his business career in 1902 when he patented a sofa bed and, together with
several other Negroes, established the Leonard Sofa Bed Company. The
energetic Green did not limit himself to this venture, however. He soon
invested in a laundry company and purchased a restaurant on Central
Avenue. Well aware of the fact that Negroes were often given unequal
treatment in white theaters, Green opened the first Negro-owned and

[19] W. E. B. Du Bois, *The Negro in Business*, Atlanta University Publications, no.
4 (Atlanta, 1899), 10; Robert A. Warner, *New Haven Negroes: A Social History*
(New Haven, Conn., 1940), 233–34; St. Clair Drake and Horace R. Cayton, *Black
Metropolis: A Study of Negro Life in a Northern City* (New York, 1945), 462–63;
Meier, "Negro Class Structure and Ideology in the Age of Booker T. Washington,"
260 (see especially Meier's footnote 3 for additional sources on the development of
black business). A useful overview is J. H. Harmon, Jr., "The Negro as a Local
Business Man," *Journal of Negro History*, 14 (April 1929), 121–43, especially
140–41.

[20] Clement Richardson et al., eds., *The National Cyclopedia of the Colored Race*
(Montgomery, Ala., 1919), I, 245. The slower development of elite suburbs in
Cleveland (Shaker Heights was not established until after World War I) may
also have helped businessmen like Reed retain their white clientele.

-operated theater in the city in 1911. The Alpha Theater, located at 32d and Central, was an excellent example of how the new breed of black businessmen could turn segregation and discrimination to their own advantage. A severe stroke in 1913 followed by his death less than two years later cut short Green's remarkable career; but he had succeeded in proving that blacks could be financially successful by relying upon the buying power of the black masses.[21]

Green and a fellow businessman with the intriguing name of Welcome T. Blue were the two most important black real-estate dealers in Cleveland before World War I. At the turn of the century Blue established the Acme Real Estate Company, an enterprise designed to build low-cost homes for blacks who were finding it increasingly difficult to purchase houses in the white real estate market. Within a few years, he and Green had organized the much larger Mohawk Realty Company; they purchased several homes and two apartment buildings and constructed the Clayton Building, a complex of stores, offices, and apartment suites located in the heart of the developing ghetto. Blue also attempted, with some success, to crack the suburban housing market for blacks. He purchased a good-sized tract of land at the end of one of the new streetcar lines, on the outskirts of the city, and by 1907 had managed to induce about one hundred Negroes to move into the development.[22]

These were not the only examples of black businesses that served the Negro market during the prewar years. Four black undertakers, including the very successful J. Walter Wills, established themselves during this period; and the increased size of the black population also made possible the existence of two black newspapers, the *Gazette* (founded in 1883) and the *Journal* (founded in 1903). These and other race enterprises instilled a feeling of race pride among the new group of black entrepreneurs. "Central Avenue," one black resident boasted in 1905, "has developed into a regular business street, and we are happy to state that many of those business houses are owned by colored people." "When one walks up Central Avenue with a visitor," the *Journal* noted the same

21 Frank U. Quillin, "The Negro in Cleveland, Ohio," *Independent*, 72 (March 7, 1912), 518; "New Leonard Sofa Bed Company," *Colored American Magazine*, 7 (March 1904), 210–11; Cleveland *Journal*, March 24, 1906; Cleveland *Gazette*, December 30, 1911, May 1, 1915; Russell H. Davis, *Memorable Negroes in Cleveland's Past* (Cleveland, 1969), 43. Both Green and Reed are discussed in greater detail in Chapter 6.

22 Cleveland *Gazette*, December 10, 1904; Cleveland *Journal*, April 28, 1906; Carrie W. Clifford, "Cleveland and Its Colored People," *Colored American Magazine*, 9 (July 1905), 372; Davis, *Memorable Negroes*, 43; David A. Gerber, "Ohio and the Color Line: Racial Discrimination and Negro Responses in a Northern State, 1860–1915" (Ph.D. dissertation, Princeton University, 1971), 409–10.

year, "it should make his heart glad to be able to point out the residence and office of four or five doctors, a dentist, several churches, three groceries, two funeral homes, one hotel, three restaurants, one jeweler, one shoemaker, several dressmakers, one milliner, one club house, bicycle manufacturer, one tailor, and other places of interest." The impressive variety of the black businesses mentioned, however, could not obscure the fact that they were small in number and frequently lacking in sufficient capital to make them profitable. S. Clayton Green's achievements were laudable, but they looked rather insignificant beside those of Chicago's Jesse Binga or any one of a number of black real-estate dealers in Harlem. No Negro insurance companies were active in Cleveland before the Great Migration, and it was not until 1921 that a black entrepreneur established the first Negro-owned bank in the city. That Negro-based businesses in Cleveland were increasing in number was incontestable; but it was also evident that this growth rate was considerably slower than that of larger black communities elsewhere in the North.[23]

Among black males, occupational declines in some areas during the prewar decades were frequently offset by gains in other areas. For black females, however, the period can only be described as one of sharp decline relative to the rest of the population. Between 1870 and 1910, the occupational structure of Cleveland's entire female work force underwent something of a revolution. The proportion of women in clerical work increased dramatically from 1.7 to 22.6 percent, and the number of women in the professions also rose substantially. At the same time the percentage of all working women engaged in domestic and personal service plunged drastically from 65.7 to 21.9 percent (see Tables 2 and 9). White women, especially the native-born, were escaping from domestic service employment in increasing numbers—and with good reason. The pay was low, averaging in 1900 only $3.23 per week plus room and board. For almost all domestics there was no hope of advancement to better-paying positions. The work was dull, repetitive, and seemingly endless, and many women especially disliked the irregular working hours, which often interfered with their personal independence. A workday of ten hours or more was by no means exceptional. Yet it was to these unrewarding, personal-service occupations that black women found themselves increasingly relegated. Between 1870 and 1910 there

[23] Clifford, "Cleveland and Its Colored People," 278–80; Cleveland *Journal,* May 6, 1905. From 1884 to 1896 the *Globe,* another Negro weekly, was also published in Cleveland. For discussions of black businessmen in Chicago and New York, see Spear, *Black Chicago,* 74–75, and Gilbert Osofsky, *Harlem: The Making of a Ghetto* (New York, 1966), 92–104.

was, to be sure, a sizable increase in the number of black women in the teaching profession and a small gain in the number of proprietors (mostly boarding-house and hotel keepers), clerks, and skilled workers. But most black women remained mired in the low-status, personal-service jobs.[24]

To properly assess the changing economic status of Negroes in Cleveland in the late nineteenth and early twentieth centuries, it is essential to compare the black occupational structure with that of other ethnic and racial groups. To do so, occupational data for three other groups (native whites of native parentage, native whites of foreign or mixed parentage, and foreign-born whites) were tabulated for 1890 and 1910; statistics for four representative immigrant groups (German, Irish, English, and Scandinavian) were available only for 1890. On the basis of this information, occupational indexes were then calculated for each group.[25]

Looking first at the male work force, it is evident that there was a sharp decline in black occupational status during the period 1870–90. The occupational index for the *total* work force also declined during these years of heavy industrialization, but the slippage was much less pronounced for the total than for black workers alone. (See Table 10.)

Although matching data are not available, it is likely that during the twenty years after 1870 male Negroes in Cleveland lost ground to all other groups in the economy, including the relatively depressed Irish immigrants. The 1870 printed census does not give a breakdown of occupations by sex. By computing indexes for the total work force (males *and* females) for 1890, however, it is possible to make a general comparison with the 1870 data. (See Table 11.)

It is clear from these data that, overall, blacks suffered a much greater occupational decline during this period than the Irish immigrants did. The most important differences between these two groups were in the

[24] Lucy Maynard Salmon, *Domestic Service*, 2d ed. (New York, 1901), 96, 140–50. Despite the current emphasis on the important role played by women in the black social structure, scholars have displayed very little interest in tracing historical trends in black female occupations; nor has there been any effort to compare the status of black women with that of native whites and various immigrant groups. Though they do not necessarily reflect the occupational standing of black women in all northern cities at the time, two useful contemporary studies are Ovington, *Half a Man*, ch. 6, and Lilian Brandt, "The Make-Up of Negro City Groups," *Charities*, 15 (October 7, 1905), 10–11.

[25] It should be noted that the occupations are ranked from 1 (high) to 7 (low); hence any decline in the occupational index indicates an *improvement* in a given group's occupational standing. Changes in the index over a period of time, of course, tell us nothing at all about the occupational mobility of specific individuals who are members of the group being studied. Rather, the index measures *aggregate mobility*—changes in the mean occupational level of the group as a whole.

TABLE 10. *Occupational indexes by racial and ethnic group, Cleveland, 1870–1910*

	1870	1890	1910
Males			
Negroes	510	569	568
Native whites of native parentage	NA	364	362
Native whites of foreign or mixed parentage	NA	417	383
Foreign-born whites	NA	474	443
All workers	422	433	412
Germans	NA	466	NA
Irish	NA	512	NA
English	NA	430	NA
Swedes and Norwegians	NA	519	NA
Females			
Negroes	618	622	609
Native whites of native parentage	NA	461	367
Native whites of foreign or mixed parentage	NA	491	413
Foreign-born whites	NA	582	540
All workers	617	523	447
Germans	NA	595	NA
Irish	NA	629	NA
English	NA	550	NA
Swedes and Norwegians	NA	686	NA

SOURCE: Tables 3, 7, 8, and 9.
NOTE: NA indicates information not available.

TABLE 11. *Occupational indexes for total work force, Negroes and selected immigrant groups, Cleveland, 1870 and 1890*

	1870	1890	Change, 1870–90
Negroes	531	581	−50
Germans	459	483	−24
Irish	528	536	− 8
English (for 1870, English and Welsh)	447	445	+ 2

SOURCE: Tables 2, 7, and 8.

areas of domestic service employment, skilled labor, and the semiskilled occupations. In the lowest occupational category the proportion of black workers almost doubled between 1870 and 1890, while for the Irish there was very little change. (See Table 12.) Both Negroes and Irish immi-

TABLE 12. *Occupational structure of total work force, Negroes and Irish immigrants, Cleveland, 1870 and 1890*

	Profes-sional	Propri-etary	Clerical	Skilled	Semi-skilled	Unskilled	Domestic service
Negroes							
1870	1.3%	3.2%	0.7%	26.2%	16.8%	25.9%	22.9%
1890	1.2	2.0	2.3	12.1	4.9	20.4	40.2
Irish							
1870	0.7	3.1	1.7	16.9	11.6	19.8	15.8
1890	0.8	5.2	2.8	11.7	14.9	36.1	16.9

SOURCE: Tables 2, 7, and 8.

grants lost ground in the skilled trades, but the decline was far greater for the former than the latter. Finally, while the Irish were making some gains in the proprietary and semiskilled occupations, the percentage of blacks in these areas was falling off.[26]

Between 1890 and 1910 the structure of black occupations stabilized; the occupational index remained virtually unchanged during this period. *Relatively*, however, the gap between black workers and the rest of the population continued to widen. In 1910 the difference in occupational status between Afro-Americans on the one hand and foreign-born whites and native whites of foreign or mixed parentage (second-generation immigrants) on the other, was greater than it had ever been before or would be after. In several ways, of course, the immigrant and black labor forces had a good deal in common. Both were underrepresented in the professions and in clerical work and overrepresented in unskilled labor. Unlike the blacks, however, foreign-born males did not have three-tenths of their work force trapped in low-paying service jobs. Equally significant was the fact that immigrants were able to maintain their position in the skilled crafts, while black artisans steadily lost ground. In the area of small businesses, the foreign-born were phenomenally successful. Undoubtedly as a result of the economic base which the large ethnic communites provided, immigrants owned or operated nearly 60 percent of Cleveland's nine thousand retail stores in 1910; only twenty-eight of the city's retail dealers were black. As a group, second-generation immigrants and native whites of native parentage also easily surpassed the Negroes in the number of proprietorships and skilled

[26] For a thorough discussion of the occupational differential between Irish and black males in late nineteenth-century Boston, see Stephan Thernstrom, *The Other Bostonians: Poverty and Progress in the American Metropolis, 1880–1970* (Cambridge, 1973), 190–94.

tradesmen. In addition, they were able to gain access to many white-collar jobs which were beyond the reach of immigrants and blacks alike.[27]

For Negro women the period between 1870 and World War I was one of economic stagnation. The occupational index of Negro females rose only slightly, from 618 to 609, during this period, while that of all female workers climbed dramatically from 617 to 447. Among native whites, in fact, the occupational status of women was beginning to approach that of men, although women continued to be paid far less than men for comparable work.[28] Unlike their husbands, immigrant women continued to be occupationally depressed. Irish, Scandinavian, and German women, like the blacks, found it difficult to obtain positions outside of domestic service. Between 1890 and 1910 this changed somewhat, as the percentage of the foreign-born in clerical work improved; but the over-all occupational gap between immigrant and Negro women remained insignificant.

An analysis of occupational structure alone, however, does obscure one important aspect of the black employment picture: compared with the immigrant population, a much higher proportion of black women now found it necessary to work. The percentage of women who worked outside the home increased substantially among all groups at the end of the nineteenth century, but census data reveals that by 1900 this trend was more firmly established among Negro than white women. In that year 36.5 percent of all black females sixteen years of age and older were employed; only 16.8 percent of Cleveland's foreign-born women and 23.4 percent of all women in the city were wage-earners. Even more significant was the proportion of women of different age-groups who were employed. During their early adult years (ages sixteen to twenty-four), both first- and second-generation immigrant women were *more* likely than blacks to be employed outside the home. After marriage, however, most white women (especially immigrants) quit their jobs and devoted their time solely to raising children. For black women, given the increasing occupational discrimination against their husbands, this was often a luxury that they simply could not afford, and the proportion of black women who worked did not decline much with advancing age.

---

[27] U.S. *Thirteenth Census, 1910*, IV, 549. See also Table 9. Unfortunately, the 1910 census does not give a breakdown of occupations by specific ethnic groups. In all likelihood the occupational standing of recently arrived Polish and Italian immigrants was lower than that of older, more established immigrant groups.

[28] In many industrial occupations at the turn of the century, the wages of women were about one half of that of men doing comparable work. Edith Abbott, *Women in Industry: A Study in American Economic History* (New York, 1910), 305–13.

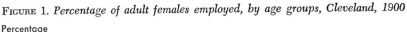

F<small>IGURE</small> 1. *Percentage of adult females employed, by age groups, Cleveland, 1900*

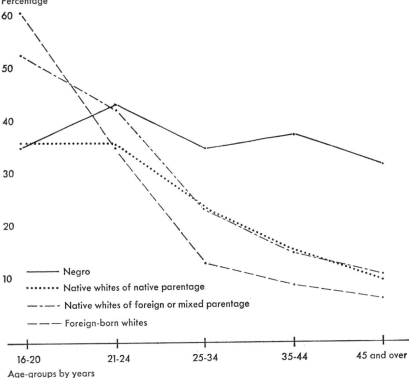

Percentage

——— Negro

········ Native whites of native parentage

—·—·— Native whites of foreign or mixed parentage

——— Foreign-born whites

16-20   21-24   25-34   35-44   45 and over

Age-groups by years

S<small>OURCE</small>: U.S. Bureau of the Census, *Statistics of Women at Work, 1900* (Washington, 1907), 48–50.

Tragically, a pattern had been set that was to remain virtually unaltered for decades to come.

Given the deteriorating occupational standing of blacks in Cleveland, it should come as no surprise that property ownership was becoming less widespread in the black community. Undoubtedly the *aggregate* amount of property owned by Negroes in Cleveland increased during the years between the Civil War and World War I. The growth of property ownership, however, did not keep pace with the increase of the black population. In 1860 a substantial minority of black Clevelanders—33.5 percent —owned real estate. By 1890 the percentage of Afro-Americans owning their own homes (a figure that probably only slightly underestimates total property ownership) had slipped to 14.8. By 1910 only 10.9 percent of the blacks owned homes. The proportion of whites in the city owning homes was three times as large.[29]

In 1910, property holding among blacks in Cleveland still exceeded that of blacks in most other large cities. Excluding the Lake Erie metropolis, black home-ownership rates in the nation's ten largest cities ranged from 2.4 percent in New York to 6.4 percent in Chicago.[30] But the gap was closing. While in Chicago and the eastern seaboard cities black home-ownership increased slightly between 1890 and 1910, in Cleveland the opposite trend was clearly in evidence.

[29] Thomas Goliber, "Cuyahoga Blacks: A Social and Demographic Study" (M.A. thesis, Kent State University, 1972), 101; U.S. Bureau of the Census, *Negro Population in the United States, 1790–1915* (Washington, 1918), 473; U.S. Bureau of the Census, *Report on Farms and Homes: Proprietorship and Indebtedness* (Washington, 1896), 582, 598. The percentages listed are for heads of households, not individuals. Most immigrant groups had considerably higher rates of home ownership than did Negroes. See Table 28 in Appendix II and (for data on a slightly later period, 1910–30), Josef J. Barton, "Immigration and Social Mobility in an American City: Studies of Three Ethnic Groups in Cleveland, 1890–1950" (Ph.D. dissertation, University of Michigan, 1971), 191.

[30] U.S. Bureau of the Census, *Negro Population in the United States, 1790–1915*, 473. It should be pointed out that black home-ownership rates in the smaller cities of the North and West were frequently much higher than in the large metropolises.

CHAPTER 5

Class and Culture in the Black Community

In his classic study, *The Philadelphia Negro* (1899), W. E. B. Du Bois noted that it was all too common for whites to view the city's black community as "one practically homogeneous mass." And yet, Du Bois concluded, if his study "emphasized any one fact it is that wide variation in the antecedents, wealth, intelligence and general efficiency have already been differentiated within this group." Actually, in Philadelphia, Boston, and other eastern-seaboard cities (as well as in the free Negro communities of New Orleans, Charleston, and other southern cities) a well-developed class structure was evident among blacks as early as the 1830s. In Cleveland prior to the Civil War, however, only an embryonic black class structure existed. The black community at that time was roughly divided into two broad groups: unskilled laborers on the one hand; skilled artisans, together with a few professionals and businessmen, on the other.[1]

The steady growth of Cleveland's black population at the end of the nineteenth century allowed social and economic differentiation within the black community to develop to a much greater extent. Because there

---

[1] W. E. B. Du Bois, *The Philadelphia Negro: A Social Study* (Philadelphia, 1899), 309–10. In analyzing the class structure of Cleveland's black community before World War I, I have been guided by Du Bois's study of Philadelphia and by the discussion of black Detroit in David M. Katzman's *Before the Ghetto: Black Detroit in the Nineteenth Century* (Urbana, Ill., 1973), 135–74. Though more sociological than historical, and dealing with a later period, St. Clair Drake and Horace R. Cayton's *Black Metropolis: A Study of Negro Life in a Northern City* (New York, 1945) is indispensable to an understanding of the social structure and cultural values of any black community.

were no Negroes who were, by white standards, even moderately wealthy, to an outside observer it often appeared that these class lines were rather unimportant. Yet to the black community, the differences between the upper, middle, and lower strata were becoming fairly well-defined. Class lines were not rigid, but in a number of ways variations in the quality of life were becoming evident. In the churches they attended, in the clubs they joined, in the neighborhoods they resided in, in the education they acquired and the occupations they held—in all of these and other ways as well black Clevelanders were differentiating themselves from their fellows and developing diverse life-styles.

The institution that most clearly reflected this trend was the black church. Church membership was perhaps the most important indicator of status in the black community because, as one scholar observed in 1913, it was often "the only institution which the Negro may call his own. . . . A new church may be built, a new pastor installed, new members received and all the machinery of the church set in motion without even consulting any white person. In a word, the church is the Negro's own institution, developing according to his own standards, and more nearly than anything else represents the real life of the race." During Cleveland's early history, few blacks had the opportunity to participate in this communal activity of church building, since most attended integrated congregations. The city's first black church, St. John's AME (African Methodist Episcopal), founded in 1830, grew slowly for twenty-five years. Beginning in the 1860s, however, more blacks became interested in setting up their own churches. By 1890 St. John's had increased its membership substantially, and blacks had organized four more churches: Shiloh Baptist, Cory ME (Methodist Episcopal), St. James AME, and Mt. Zion Congregational. The latter, an offshoot of predominantly white Plymouth Church, was founded in 1864 with an initial membership of about twenty. Whether the Negroes who founded Mt. Zion left Plymouth Church of their own accord or were forced out is unclear, but the incident marked the beginning of a reversal of the policy of integrated churches that had been common in Cleveland during the antebellum period. Racism, coupled with the dispersal of many native whites to newer parts of the city (and the building of new churches far removed from the major black residential areas), led to a steady decline in the number of blacks attending predominantly white congregations. By the beginning of the twentieth century, among the city's "white" churches only the Catholics still consistently accepted blacks on a basis of equality. A few elite Negroes from old, prominent families continued to attend white Episcopal and Methodist congregations, but this phenomenon became increasingly rare with the passage of time.[2]

Despite the existence of five black churches, many Negroes did not become regular church members before the 1890s. In 1894, one minister estimated that less than 40 percent of the black residents of Cleveland were regular church members. "Here is a great field of labor," he admonished his fellow pastors, "and . . . heroic efforts ought to be put forth with a view of winning this vast multitude to Christ." During the next twenty-five years, many religiously minded blacks heeded this advice. As the black population expanded, the number, diversity, and scope of activity of the black churches steadily increased. "There is not an Afro-American church in the city," the Cleveland *Journal* reported in 1903, "that is not contemplating improvements of some kind within the next year." By the eve of the wartime migration, there were seventeen black congregations in the city.[3]

Of these churches, only two were recognizably elite institutions. After two decades of slow growth, Mt. Zion Congregational expanded in membership and became, in the 1890s, the most prestigious of the black congregations. After the turn of the century its position was partially usurped by a new church, St. Andrew's Episcopal. To some extent, prior to about 1915, these churches reflected the division in the black upper and middle classes[4] between an older group of blacks whose occupations

[2] J. J. Watson, "Churches and Religious Conditions," *Annals of the American Academy of Political and Social Science* (September 1913), 120; William Ganson Rose, *Cleveland: The Making of a City* (Cleveland, 1950), 124, 325; John P. Green, *Fact Stranger than Fiction: Seventy-Five Years of a Busy Life with Reminiscences of Many Great and Good Men* (Cleveland, 1920), 96; Helen M. Chesnutt, *Charles Waddell Chesnutt: Pioneer of the Color Line* (Chapel Hill, N.C., 1952), 52. Of all northern cities, only Boston had a significant number of integrated churches after 1900. Although many separate black churches existed there, John Daniels observed in 1914 that "a considerable minority" of Boston's Negroes attended "white" churches. Most integrated congregations were Episcopal or Catholic, but some Negroes were also members of Christian Science churches and the then popular Swedenborgian and Spiritualist sects. Daniels noted, however, that "the general tendency at present is toward a distinct decrease in Negro attendance at white churches." John Daniels, *In Freedom's Birthplace: A Study of the Boston Negroes* (Boston, 1914), 226, 227–35, 237.

[3] Form letter from Alexander Moore to Cleveland ministers, 1894, reproduced in *Antioch Missionary Baptist Church Golden Jubilee, 1893–1943* (n.p. [1943?]), 3; Cleveland *Gazette*, July 4, August 1, 1896; Cleveland *Journal*, April 25, 1903; church notices in the *Gazette* and the Cleveland *Advocate*, 1916.

[4] In reference to the black community, the terms "upper class" and "middle class" do not have the same connotations that they have for whites. There were no black equivalents to the Swaseys, Mathers, and others who made sections of Euclid Avenue into an exclusive "millionaire's row" at the turn of the century. If the family of Charles W. Chesnutt (discussed later in this chapter) was typical, then the

had entailed considerable contact with whites of similar or higher social status, and a newer group of businessmen, politicians, and professionals, who had their economic roots in the emerging ghetto. Neither church was interested in accepting working-class Negroes as members, and most recent migrants from the South would have found the staid, dignified services that both provided rather uninviting. St. Andrew's, however, was smaller and more of a "social" church than its rival, and its membership for the most part was restricted to "old elite" families. Two of its founding members were John P. Green and Jacob Reed, men who were well known in the white as well as the black community and who were at the very top of the black social hierarchy. Mt. Zion was larger, less snobbish, and more inclusive in its membership. There was, to be sure, an older element in the church that closely resembled that of St. Andrew's, and Mt. Zion's membership rolls contained such prominent names as William ("Prince") Hunley, for many years a headwaiter in an exclusive white restaurant, and Jere Brown. By 1915, however, the church had accepted many of the new middle class as congregants and had even admitted to membership Thomas Fleming, Cleveland's leading black politician but also a man who was known to be allied with Central Avenue vice racketeer Albert D. Boyd. Thus Mt. Zion's congregation contained a representative cross section of the black elite, as well as a number of individuals whose social status was somewhat below that of the elite.[5]

It was not Mt. Zion or St. Andrew's, however, but the Baptist and AME churches which experienced the largest gains in membership during the prewar years. Between 1890 and 1915 seven new Baptist churches (Antioch, Emmanuel, Gethsemane, Sterling, Avery, Mt. Haven, and Triedstone), one AME congregation (Harris AME), one AME Zion church (St. Paul's), and one Colored Methodist Episcopal church (Lane

---

black upper class in Cleveland lived a life that resembled middle- or upper-middle-class white society. However, in the context of the black social structure, Negroes like Chesnutt were considerably better off than the average, middle-class Negro clerk or small businessman, and therefore the terms "upper class" or "elite" are appropriate designations for this group. As in the case of the white economic structure, of course, the division of the black community into upper, middle, and lower (or working) classes is somewhat arbitrary, since income levels and other measurements of class standing exist along a continuum. The tripartite division is used chiefly as an analytical convenience.

5 Clement Richardson et al., eds., *The National Cyclopedia of the Colored Race* (Montgomery, Ala., 1919), I, 245, 356; interview with Dr. William P. Saunders, August 6, 1972. Much of the basic information on black churches was obtained by scanning notices of church affairs and lists of trustees in the black press during this period.

Memorial) were founded. All of these churches grew in size during this period, but Antioch Baptist soon outstripped its rivals. Founded in 1893, Antioch underwent a dynamic era of expansion during the pastorate of Horace C. Bailey, its minister from the turn of the century to the mid-1920s. By 1905 the congregation had outgrown its original home, and found it necessary to construct a new church edifice, at a cost of $16,000. Ten years later Antioch had become the largest and most important black church in the city.[6]

Some of the well-to-do Negro elite belonged to the Baptist and AME congregations—George Myers, for example, attended St. John's—but for the most part it was the rank and file of the black community, the broad middle and working classes, that filled the pews of these churches each Sunday. As a result, these congregations (especially those of the Baptist denomination) generally reflected the religious aspirations of the typical urban black. "The Baptist minister," Du Bois explained, "is the elected chairman of a pure democracy, who, if he can command a large enough following, becomes a virtual dictator; he thus has the chance to be a wise leader or a demagogue, or, as in many cases, a little of both." The Baptist minister knew that, in order to hold his following and increase it, something more was needed than the decorous, formal ceremonies of St. Andrew's. In most cases, the message that he delivered to his congregation each week was no less conservative in its social import than the sermons that the pastors of St. Andrew's or Mt. Zion gave. Shiloh's minister lectured a black youth group on the doctrine of success through self-help ("Confidence, and How to Get It"), while Cory's pastor reminded his flock that woman was "the Conservator of Purity." It is unlikely that the Negro elite would have disapproved of such topics. It was the highly emotional form, not the content, of the typical Baptist sermon that the black upper class found distasteful. The average black man or woman enjoyed the singing, chanting, and enthusiasm that accompanied the Baptist rituals, and expected the sermon to be the emotional climax to the service. When Shiloh's minister "held the audience spellbound with his explanation of the divine truths," he could be sure that his church would be packed to overflowing the following Sunday.[7]

Undoubtedly as a result of their mass following, the Baptist churches tended to be involved to a greater extent than the elite churches in welfare work in the black community. Antioch, for example, sponsored boys'

[6] *Antioch Missionary Baptist Church Golden Jubilee*, 1–5.

[7] Richardson et al., eds., *National Cyclopedia of the Colored Race*, I, 279; Du Bois, *The Philadelphia Negro*, 112; Cleveland *Advocate*, June 2, 9, 1917, October 21, 1916.

clubs, girls' clubs, and a number of choral groups; the church also purchased—at a time when the need was very great—two houses adjacent to
the church, which were converted into small recreation centers for
neighborhood youth. Other black churches did not have the funds to
carry out similar activities, but most allowed what facilities they had to
be used for lodge meetings and political gatherings. At least one church,
Shiloh, aided its membership by organizing a mutual benefit society. The
church's Afro-American Benevolent Society provided its members with
life insurance and sick benefits at a time when most white insurance companies would not sell policies to working-class Negroes.[8]

Although membership lists are lacking, it is safe to conclude that there
was some class differentiation among even the Baptist and AME congregations. Mount Haven Baptist, located at East 37th and Cedar, and
Lane Memorial AME, at East 31st and Cedar, were both several blocks
from Central Avenue (where most of the black churches made their
home), and these churches probably had a larger proportion of middle-
class congregants than Gethsemane Baptist, which stood in the heart of
the slum district at East 22d and Scovill. Prior to 1915, the only church
that can be identified as having a strictly lower-class membership was
Lake City Spiritualist Church. Situated in a storefront on Central Avenue
near East 28th Street, Lake City was a precursor of a number of small,
fundamentalist sects that would flourish in Cleveland after the wartime
migration. The church probably appealed mostly to recent arrivals from
the South, and because of its smaller size it offered its congregants a degree of emotional involvement and personal participation that the larger
black churches could not match.[9]

Next to the churches, the fraternal lodges were the most important
focus of group activity in the black community. Negro participation in
these institutions dated to 1787, when the first black Masonic lodge was
formed in Boston. It was not until after the Civil War, however, that
lodges (white as well as Negro) grew rapidly in number and became an
important social phenomenon. The lodges served a variety of purposes.
Like some of the churches, they often functioned as mutual benefit societies, paying a small weekly stipend to members who became ill and
helping to pay funeral costs and support the widows of those who died.
Of equal importance were the social functions of the lodges. As Rowland
Berthoff has pointed out, the imposing rituals and colorful regalia of the

---

[8] *Antioch Missionary Baptist Church Golden Jubilee*, 5; Cleveland *Advocate*,
February 24, August 25, 1917.

[9] On the Lake City Spiritualist Church, see Cleveland *Advocate*, June 26, 1915,
December 30, 1916.

lodges, combined with the opportunity for social intercourse that they provided, helped restore a sense of community participation to what was becoming an increasingly atomized society.[10]

In almost every instance, the sense of community that the lodges fostered, however, did not extend beyond the color line, and almost all of these organizations were either all-black or all-white. Cleveland was quite exceptional in having, during the 1870s and 1880s, two Negroes, both light-skinned, who were members of white Masonic lodges. The first, Dr. Leonidas Wilson, was a dentist whose social and professional life was completely integrated; in fact, "most of his association was with white people." The second, John H. Hope, was on such good terms with his fellow Masons that he served at one time as Master of his lodge. By the turn of the century, however, these individuals had either died or moved away, and thereafter all the lodges of the city became segregated institutions.[11]

The most important black fraternal orders in Cleveland were the Masons, Odd Fellows, Elks, True Reformers, United Brethren, Knights of Pythias, Mysterious Ten, and Good Samaritans. There was some class differentiation among the lodges, but unlike the churches, there is no evidence that specific fraternal orders restricted their membership to the middle or upper classes. There was some tendency for the Negro elite, however, to gravitate toward three fraternal orders: the Masons, the Odd Fellows, and the Elks. Jere Brown was for many years an enthusiastic Mason, and he held a number of important positions in the order, eventually becoming Grand Master of the Ohio Lodge. George Myers was also a leading Mason, serving for a while as Master of his lodge; he also joined the Elks and rose to become Exalted Ruler of Cuyahoga Lodge No. 95. Jacob Reed surpassed both Brown and Myers in his enthusiasm for fraternal societies. He was not only an Elk and a 33d degree Mason, but became a member of the Odd Fellows and served as treasurer of his lodge for eight years. The fact that the Masons, Odd Fellows, and Elks were the oldest black lodges in Cleveland may account for the dominance of older, elite Negroes in these three fraternal orders. The Masons were the oldest Afro-American lodge in the city, dating back to at least the Civil War era, and the Odd Fellows and Elks were also well established by the 1880s. Thus blacks who wished to join lodges before

[10] Rowland Berthoff, *An Unsettled People: Social Order and Disorder in American History* (New York, 1971), 270–74; Edward Nelson Palmer, "Negro Secret Societies," *Social Forces,* 20 (December 1944), 207–12.

[11] Harry E. Davis, *A History of Freemasonry among Negroes* (Cleveland, 1946), 178–79.

about 1890 had very little choice in the matter. The True Reformers, Mysterious Ten, Good Samaritans, and other lodges were not founded in Cleveland until the 1890s. Unfortunately, no membership lists from these organizations have survived, but it seems likely that, compared to the older lodges, a larger percentage of their membership was drawn from the lower strata of the black social structure. They received less mention in the black press, and, since many of these more recent fraternal societies were originally founded in the South, the Cleveland lodges probably attracted a large number of recent migrants from that region.[12]

From the foregoing discussion of churches and lodges, it is evident that the black elite was becoming increasingly associated with certain institutions. Yet these institutional affiliations were but part of a broad nexus of socioeconomic relationships and cultural values that distinguished the Negro upper class from the rest of the Negro community.

At the end of the 1890s, Cleveland's Negro population was still dominated by a small upper class composed mostly of merchants and small entrepreneurs, skilled craftsmen, barbers who owned their own shops, headwaiters in exclusive establishments, and a few doctors, lawyers, and other professionals. Occasionally, a well-known clerical worker or mail carrier might also be considered a member of the elite. Most of this group, if they had not been born in Cleveland, were long-standing members of the community. A number had well-established businesses and had managed to accumulate considerable property—often through wise investments in real estate. Income varied widely within the elite; but at a time when the average factory worker was earning between $500 and $700 a year, most of this group was probably making between $1,500 and $3,000 a year. (A few individuals like George Myers, John P. Green, and Jacob Reed probably had incomes exceeding $3,000.) Almost without exception, members of the black upper class owned their own homes.[13]

[12] *Ibid.*, 177; lodge notices in the Cleveland *Gazette*, 1890–1910, and Cleveland *Journal*, 1903–1910; Richardson et al., eds., *National Cyclopedia of the Colored Race*, I, 245, 279; Russell H. Davis, *Memorable Negroes in Cleveland's Past* (Cleveland, 1969), 25. The first black Odd Fellows lodge in Cleveland was founded in 1856, and in that year the first mention is made in the press of an already existing black Masonic lodge. Cleveland *Leader*, September 11, 1856, June 10, 1868.

[13] There is no specific data on the incomes of the black elite in Cleveland at this time. In 1911, Mary White Ovington estimated the income of the average upperclass Negro in New York at $2,000 to $4,000 a year, but at that time the black elite of Kansas City, Missouri, usually earned less than $1,500 per year. In St. Louis black professionals (excluding ministers, who were often poorly paid) averaged $1,200 to $1,800 annually, and a number of black businessmen earned $1,500 to $3,000 a year. Ovington, *Half a Man: The Status of the Negro in New York* (New York, 1911), 178; Asa E. Martin, *Our Negro Population: A Sociological Study of the*

This group of elite blacks had particularly good rapport with whites, and in many ways continued to live the kind of integrated existence that had been much more common in Cleveland a generation before. In all of their occupations, they either had white clientele or associated with whites in the course of their work. Many had gone to Central High School, and a number had attended Western Reserve University, Oberlin, or Union College of Law—all of which were integrated institutions. In observing a similarly successful group of Boston Negroes in 1914, John Daniels noted that they had close relationships with whites and lived in pleasant, middle-class areas far removed from the incipient ghetto. With some exceptions, this was also true of Cleveland's integrated Negro elite. Residentially, this group tended to live in predominantly white neighborhoods, and their homes were scattered throughout the East Side and even, occasionally, the West Side of the city. There is no evidence that, prior to 1915, they suffered much from the tightening black housing market. The gradual movement eastward of a number of these elite Negroes during the prewar years, in fact, caused the members of St. Andrew's to sell their old church edifice at East 22d and Prospect in 1915 and move to a new location at East 49th and Cedar. Thus many members of the old black upper class were moving away from Central Avenue at the very time when the majority of the black population was being confined to that thoroughfare and the surrounding area.[14]

Throughout the North, the older, partially integrated Negro elite felt the need to distinguish itself not only from the rank and file of the black community, but from the rising, ghetto-based black bourgeoisie that was challenging its leadership during the early years of the twentieth century. "In Philadelphia," said Ray Stannard Baker in 1905, "I hear of the old Philadelphia Negroes, in Indianapolis of the old Indianapolis families, in Boston a sharp distinction is drawn between the 'Boston Negroes' and the recent Southern importation. Even in Chicago, where there is nothing old, I found the same spirit." The same attitude was evident among members of Cleveland's old Negro elite, and it resulted in the

---

Negroes of Kansas City, Missouri (Kansas City, Mo., 1913), 50; William A. Crossland, *Industrial Conditions among Negroes in St. Louis*, Washington University Studies in Social Economics, vol. 1, no. 1 (St. Louis, Mo., 1914), 122 (Appendix C).

[14] Daniels, *In Freedom's Birthplace*, 39; Cleveland *Advocate*, July 17, 1915. Information on the housing patterns of upper- and middle-class blacks was obtained from the *City Directory*. In 1908 R. R. Wright, Jr., noted that, despite white hostility, there had been a gradual movement of elite blacks away from the main areas of black settlement in a number of cities. Wright, "Recent Improvement in Housing among Negroes in the North," *Southern Workman*, 37 (November 1908), 602–6.

creation of special institutions and organizations designed to perpetuate their social status. Affiliation with St. Andrew's was one important mark of an upper-class, "old Cleveland" family. Another was membership in certain clubs. The Social Circle (the name was changed to the Euchre Club in 1904) was a club of light-skinned, old-elite Negroes, including John P. Green, John H. Hope, George Myers, and the Chesnutt family. The club dated to 1869 and was, in the words of one of its members, "a very restricted group," which for many years disdained to socialize with the darker-skinned, less-educated members of the new elite. The Caterers' Club, formed in 1903 by George Myers and several other well-known barbers, waiters, and caterers, was also composed mostly of "old Cleveland" Negroes, at least during its early years. The downtown clubrooms of the organization soon became known as "a center for the social elite of the race," and the Caterers' annual banquet was one of the most important social events of the year in the black community.[15]

In many respects, the older Negro elite sought to emulate the lifestyle of the more affluent members of the white middle class. "He is ambitious," said Mary White Ovington of the typical elite New York Negro in 1911, "to be conventional in his manners, his customs, striving as far as possible to be like his neighbor—a distinctly American ambition." A similar impulse motivated Cleveland's Negro elite. They moved within a familiar world of church, lodge, and club. They entertained frequently, and they were only too eager to display for their friends the "evidences of taste and even luxury" that their homes reflected. To a greater degree than most of their race, members of the black upper class were able to broaden themselves through cultural activities and travel. Travel was particularly important to elite blacks, and a number of them purchased automobiles to indulge their passion for experiencing new sights. Jacob Reed became a member of the Cleveland Automobile Club (at the time a rather aristocratic organization), and the Cleveland *Advocate* observed that he could "frequently be seen at the wheel of his Peerless touring car enjoying his hobby of letting his many friends enjoy his hospitality." A favorite summer pastime of Reed and other upper-class Negroes was the "touring party." A number of families who owned cars would set out together to visit friends in a nearby city, picking a route that would allow

[15] Ray Stannard Baker, *Following the Color Line: American Negro Citizenship in the Progressive Era* (New York, 1908), 218; Chesnutt, *Charles Waddell Chesnutt*, 61, 185–90; Cleveland *Leader*, August 25, 1874; Julian Krawcheck, "Society Barred Negroes—They Formed Own Groups," Cleveland *Press*, May 30, 1963; Jane Edna Hunter, "Negroes in Cleveland" (undated manuscript, Jane Edna Hunter Papers, Western Reserve Historical Society), 4; interview with Dr. William P. Saunders, August 6, 1972; Cleveland *Advocate*, December 4, 1915.

them to drive leisurely through a scenic section of the countryside. A few members of the elite were able to visit Europe. With some financial assistance from John D. Rockefeller, John P. Green traveled extensively in England and Scotland in 1893; and his son, William R. Green, was successful enough in his law practice to be able to afford visits to England, Ireland, and France in 1907 and 1908.[16]

In their activities and associations, the family of Charles W. Chesnutt exhibited many aspects of the life-style of the integrated Negro elite. Although Chesnutt held a law degree, his main occupation was that of legal stenographer (he eventually owned his own firm), and both the public court system and a number of private corporations in Cleveland found his services invaluable. Chesnutt's broad educational and cultural background gave him an entrée to white society that most Negroes could not hope to attain. Chesnutt was one of the early Negro members of the Cleveland Chamber of Commerce and was, according to an observer of race relations in the city in 1912, "honored and esteemed by many of the leading white men of the city." He was particularly proud of being the first Negro admitted to the Rowfant Club, an exclusive literary group that met weekly. "Chesnutt enjoyed those Saturday nights at the Rowfant Club," his daughter Helen later recalled. "There he met, in delightful fellowship, some of the finest and most scholarly men of Cleveland."[17]

Few Afro-Americans in the city were better off financially than the Chesnutt family, and none had better rapport with whites of similar social standing. The Chesnutts lived a comfortable existence in an integrated, upper-middle-class neighborhood. They paid for dancing lessons for their daughters, owned an expensive touring car, and complained about their white immigrant servants because it "was hard to make them wear shoes or wash their hair." During the summer, the family usually escaped the heat of the city by spending at least a month at one of the resorts in rural northern Ohio. After 1915, Chesnutt often vacationed with Daniel Hale Williams (a prominent black physician from Chicago) at an exclusive black resort in Idlewild, Michigan. Ches-

[16] Ovington, *Half a Man,* 171; Robert I. Drake, "The Negro in Cleveland," Cleveland *Advocate,* September 18, 1915; *Advocate,* July 17, 1915; Green, *Fact Stranger than Fiction, passim;* Richardson, et al., eds., *National Cyclopedia of the Colored Race,* I, 280.
[17] Chesnutt, *Charles Waddell Chesnutt,* 183, 288–89, and *passim;* Frank U. Quillin, *The Color Line in Ohio: A History of Race Prejudice in a Typical Northern State* (Ann Arbor, 1913), 155. On the activities and early history of the Rowfant Club (founded in 1892), see Russell H. Anderson, *The Rowfant Club: A History* (Cleveland, 1955), 1–22. Other aspects of Chesnutt's career are discussed in Chapter 6.

nutt's children attended integrated Central High School, and he sent
two daughters, Helen and Ethel, to Smith College and his son Edwin to
Harvard and then Northwestern School of Dentistry. Chesnutt's wife,
Susan, was a member of numerous social clubs, some all-Negro and
others predominantly white. The family attended white Emmanuel
Episcopal Church, the members of which were, according to Helen
Chesnutt, "among Cleveland's finest people." As a member of the Wom-
en's Auxiliary and the Women's Guild, Susan Chesnutt played a prominent role in church affairs.[18]

Even among the upper class, the degree to which the Chesnutts were
accepted by white society was unusual; but in most respects their style
of life was shared by other members of the old Negro elite. Needless to
say, this privileged group did not often come in contact with the black
masses. Chesnutt, for example, was quite aware of changing racial conditions in the nation as a whole (his ideological point of view will be
discussed in the following chapter), but his actual experience with the
problems faced by the black lower class was minimal. When he was
asked by a white church group, in 1914, whether a proposed settlement
house in the Central Avenue area was feasible, Chesnutt found it necessary to "renew his acquaintance with that part of the city" before he
could give an opinion. "For several weeks he took walks along Central
Avenue studying the people," his daughter recalled. Chesnutt found the
customs of the lower class amusing: "This little research delighted him."
Other members of the elite found the black laboring classes less than
humorous. From time to time George Myers criticized the masses for
failing to live up to middle-class standards, and he was especially dis-
pleased by the "loud and boisterous conduct" of some Afro-Americans.
"The great masses of our people," the barber declared angrily in 1916,
"have little regard for their word and are utterly devoid of commercial
honor." Such sweeping and unfounded generalizations tell us little about
the values of the average black person; they speak volumes about the
perspective of some members of the Negro elite.[19]

At the beginning of the twentieth century the black upper class of

[18] Chesnutt, *Charles Waddell Chesnutt*, 41, 49, 64, 74–76, 148–49; *Year Book of
Emmanuel Parish, Cleveland, Ohio* (n.p. [1914]), 61, 78, 136; Helen Buckler,
Doctor Dan (Boston, 1954), 259. On the early history of the black resort town of
Idlewild, see Pehyun Wen, "Idlewild—A Negro Village in Lake County, Michigan"
(M.A. thesis, University of Chicago, 1972), 72–82.

[19] Chesnutt, *Charles Waddell Chesnutt*, 260–61; George Myers, " 'Courtesy'
and 'Politeness' As an Asset," Cleveland *Advocate*, March 11, 1916; George Myers,
"Lest We Forget," *ibid.*, October 21, 1916. See also Du Bois, *The Philadelphia
Negro*, 316–17.

Cleveland was undergoing a gradual but steady transformation. The number, as well as the importance, of Negro businesses and professions which catered to a predominantly white clientele was declining. Black headwaiters, barber shop owners, and skilled artisans faced increasing competition from whites, especially immigrants. The smaller number of barbers serving whites was compensated for by an increase in barbers who catered to an all-Negro trade, but these individuals did not have the prestige of their predecessors. Depending upon the trade, the number of Negroes in the skilled trades did not always decline during this period. With the rise of predominantly white trade unions, however, many black artisans found themselves excluded from jobs in public buildings and white-owned establishments, and by 1920 blacks no longer looked upon the skilled crafts as elite occupations.

As the prestige of many older elite occupations fell off, a new black elite, consisting of real estate dealers, undertakers, and businessmen and politicians who relied mostly upon black patronage, began to challenge the older upper class for the leadership of the black community. In Chicago the new elite had clearly gained ascendancy by 1915; in Cleveland (and probably in other smaller black communities in the North as well) the situation was more complex. On the one hand, because of integrationist traditions and the continuing paternalistic support of some whites, the old elite was able to retain influence and prestige a good deal longer, both in the black community and among whites. Crucial in this regard was the role of black professionals. Unlike some other cities, Cleveland's black lawyers and doctors often continued to have integrated practices, even after the wartime migration; and the city's black teachers were thoroughly integrated in 1915. Thus until at least the 1920s, Cleveland's black professionals—unlike those of Chicago or Philadelphia—must be identified mostly as members of the old elite. (However, the position of black lawyers with integrated practices who sought political office by appealing to the black masses is, admittedly, ambiguous, and each case must be studied individually.) On the other hand, the new elite developed less rapidly in Cleveland because the city's smaller, less concentrated black population simply could not support as many Negro business enterprises; and successful black entrepreneurs like S. Clayton Green sometimes tried to cultivate the white as well as the Negro market. By 1915 the new elite was gaining in prestige and power, but it had by no means superseded its older rival.[20]

[20] On the changing nature of the black elite in Cleveland, see Hunter, "Negroes in Cleveland," 2–4, and Charles W. Chesnutt, "The Negro in Cleveland," *The Clevelander*, 5 (November 1930), 3, 26–27. The more rapid transformation of the

On the whole, a good deal less is known about the group affiliations and life-style of the new elite than the old, but even this points up an important fact about the new upper class: its members were not as well educated or as articulate as their predecessors. Unlike the old elite, few of this newer group of successful blacks were born or raised in Cleveland. They usually came from states outside Ohio (though not always from the South) and often arrived in Cleveland during the 1890s or early 1900s. In median income, the new and old elite were probably about equal, although the wealthiest figures among the newer group (S. Clayton Green and Albert D. Boyd) undoubtedly had the highest incomes in the black community before World War I.[21]

Some members of the ascendant elite were only too willing to manipulate the black masses for economic gain or political power, and they were eager to acquire homes, expensive cars, and other material symbols of success. But for the most part, blacks of the new upper class were less prone than those of the old to separate themselves from others of their race. Many had too much in common with average, working-class Negroes to feel snobbish toward them. Garrett A. Morgan, the black inventor and hair-products manufacturer, had no interest in "culture" or formal education (he failed to graduate from high school) and was proud that he had "accomplished so much without the learning of books." Unlike the old elite, the new upper-class blacks did not affiliate mainly with one church; instead they attended a variety of AME or Baptist churches or Mt. Zion Congregational. They usually resided fairly close

---

elite in Chicago is surveyed in Allan H. Spear, *Black Chicago: The Making of a Negro Ghetto, 1890–1920* (Chicago, 1967), 71–84, 192. On the phenomenon in other cities, see August Meier, "Negro Class Structure and Ideology in the Age of Booker T. Washington," *Phylon*, 23 (Fall 1963), 258–66, and Katzman, *Before the Ghetto*, 164–66. E. Franklin Frazier, in his *Black Bourgeoisie: The Rise of a New Middle Class* (New York, 1957) referred to the new elite as "a new middle class." I have preferred to use the term *new elite*, however, when referring to those ghetto-based black businessmen, politicians, and professionals whose income and prestige were substantially equal to that of their predecessors. The term *middle class* is used to designate individuals below the elite but above the working class.

It should be noted that not every successful Negro in Cleveland fitted neatly into either the "old" or "new" category. As will be explained in Chapter 6, some members of the new elite did not have their economic or political base solely in the black community; unlike the old upper class, however, these individuals almost never had anything but the most perfunctory social relationships with whites. There were also some individuals who, during the course of their careers, shifted from old-elite to new-elite occupations. Charles S. Weaver, for example, after migrating to Cleveland from North Carolina in the late nineteenth century, worked as a plasterer for thirty years before deciding to invest his savings in a billiard parlor and barber shop on Central Avenue. Cleveland *Advocate*, February 24, 1917.

[21] The activities of Green and Boyd are discussed in Chapters 4 and 6.

to Central Avenue (although seldom on the street itself), and their associations with whites tended to be far less frequent and more formal than those of the old upper class. The nonreligious voluntary organizations of the new elite also indicated less aloofness from the black lower class. The Cleveland Association of Colored Men, founded in 1908, was primarily a new elite organization, and it inaugurated some charitable projects in the black community. Both the new and old elite supported the Home for Aged Colored People, but it was Sarah Green and Letitia Fleming, the wives of S. Clayton Green and Thomas Fleming, who put in the most time and effort on that philanthropic project.[22]

Altogether, the black elite constituted perhaps 4 percent of the black community. Below it rested a considerably larger group—about 20 percent—that can be categorized as middle class. This group included teachers, most of the artisans, clerical workers, salaried employees, and a number of small businessmen. A few of the factory operatives might also have been in this class, especially if their wives worked. Financially, the middle-class black citizen was much better off than the average black resident of the city, and the yearly income of this group probably averaged between $900 and $1,200 at the turn of the century. Though economically quite restricted compared to the elite, members of the black middle class were nevertheless (as W. E. B. Du Bois put it) "comfortable" or in "good circumstances." Although few could purchase automobiles, some were able to own their own homes.[23]

In their occupations, a number of middle-class blacks (notably the clerks) associated with whites, but very few established social relationships with members of the dominant race. Although they had none of the haughty disdain for the masses that characterized some of the elite, middle-class residents still sought ways of distinguishing themselves from the rank and file of the black community. Club life was one of the chief means of doing this. Each week, the city's black newspapers listed a large number of such voluntary associations. The Fortnightly Club, the Book and Thimble Club, the Pleasant Company Club, and the Minerva Club were but four examples of middle-class social organizations. A few of these clubs—such as the Dunbar Literary Society of Shiloh Baptist Church—were intellectually or culturally oriented, but most were designed purely for social or recreational purposes. This was true as well

[22] Morgan, quoted in Cleveland *Advocate*, March 4, 1916.
[23] Du Bois, *The Philadelphia Negro*, 171. John Daniels estimated in 1914 that the black middle class comprised about 18 percent of the black population of Boston. Daniels, *In Freedom's Birthplace*, 178. Comparative data are lacking, but it is likely that the black middle class in Cleveland and Boston at that time was somewhat larger than in most other cities.

of the associations of college-educated Negroes (which included some of the elite as well as the middle class), such as Alpha Kappa Alpha sorority and the alumni association of Howard University, which had established chapters in Cleveland before 1915. When entertaining, the middle class could not hope to duplicate the frequent and sometimes costly affairs of the well-to-do, but the social gatherings of this group were no less refined or respectable. A typical example of one of the favorite middle-class social events, the "lawn party," was described by the *Advocate* in 1916:

> Mr. and Mrs. Fred D. Clark gave one of the prettiest lawn parties that it has been the good fortune of Cleveland's young folk to attend for quite some time. The affair was in honor of Miss Margaret Harper and Mr. Edward Hood and took place at the Clark residence on E. 36th Street. About twenty-five people attended. The yard was beautifully decorated and . . . Japanese lanterns furnished illumination for the guests gathered about picturesquely arranged tables, playing games and chatting. Beautiful strains of Hawaiian music furnished by Copeland's string orchestra finally caused the guests to lose interest in their games and conversations and helped prove that a lawn makes an ideal ballroom floor. A very delightful luncheon ended the festivities of the evening.[24]

In their racial ideologies, individual members of the black middle class often disagreed to a considerable extent. Above and beyond these differences, however, there was a rather remarkable consensus on certain other values. These values were reflected most clearly in news articles and editorials of Cleveland's black newspapers—especially the *Advocate*, a weekly founded in 1914 which is perhaps the best source of middle-class opinion just prior to the Great Migration. The black middle class firmly believed, in the words of one of its members, in the power of *"character, culture, and cash."* Such people all believed to some extent that the growth of racism could be attributed partially to black failure to adhere to white bourgeois standards of economic individualism, self-denial, and "good taste." What young blacks needed to do, one Negro wrote in the *Advocate*, was to "devote more of their time to literary societies, musical clubs, debating societies and sewing circles, as was true twenty-five years ago [1892], and less to pool playing, dancing, and playing and other virtue-robbing pleasures. . . ." He assured the black lower class that if they would only "stop their mad rush for pleasure and give more attention to the serious side of life; if they will prepare themselves, perhaps the pendulum, for us in the North, will

24 Cleveland *Advocate*, July 8, 1916.

swing back, and the privileges we once enjoyed . . . will be restored." A 1915 *Advocate* editorial, entitled "Thinking Black," pinpointed the cultural perspective of the black middle class even better. The editorial criticized Afro-Americans with a "chip on their shoulder":

They are oversensitive about the color of their skin and go around complaining eternally over their hard lot. The world has no room for GRUMBLERS. The spirit of the day is to "laugh and the world laughs with you." You may be born with a color that rivals ebony. That is no reason why you cannot put your shoulder to the wheel and push away; spread sunshine around you; whatever you undertake to do, *Do It With Your Might*. Cultivate good habits. BE EFFICIENT and greet the world with a smile. Don't think black—nor act black. Every slight, every seeming insult, every failure which some one of us meet is attributed directly to the color of our skins. We never think of our *Inefficiency*, *Inconstancy*, lack of initiative or numerous other faults which are everywhere apparent to students of the race problem.

We do not deny that in many instances the baneful color prejudice exerts its influences against us, but what we do contend is that in a number of cases where we meet with setbacks, disappointments and failures, our own *Inefficiency* and *Lack of Perseverance* are to blame. Let us one and all think "the color of snow." We have been thinking black for a long while. Let us try the alternative and in conjunction with our change of thought be prepared to play the game EFFICIENTLY AND WELL.[25]

Besides being an excellent example of the "strive and succeed" ethic, this statement revealed quite clearly in its rhetoric the aversion of many middle-class Negroes to black skin color. Every week Cleveland's black newspapers carried large advertisements for such items as Palmer's High Brown Face Powder ("The original and best face powder for dark skin— smooth as velvet"), Ford's Royal White Skin Lotion ("Makes the skin look whiter as it is put on"), and Ford's Hair Pomade ("Makes harsh, kinky hair softer, more pliable, easier to comb, and put up in any style the length will permit"), not to mention the products of Cleveland's own Morgan Hair Refining Company; and one can presume that such goods were sold primarily to the black bourgeoisie and that portion of the black lower that identified with the "white" conception of beauty. Not surprisingly, prior to World War I middle-class Negroes generally disassociated themselves from African traditions. From time to time the *Advocate* included a small section called "Jungle Jottings" that satirized African life and made fun of its supposedly common habits of polygamy and cannibalism. When a Zulu student addressed a mass meeting in

25 *Ibid.*, September 18, 1915, October 17, 1915, November 13, 1915.

Cleveland in 1917, the *Advocate* described him as something of an oddi-
ty, having been "born in the benighted land of Africa, among his own
savage people." The newspaper assured its readers, however, that "when
he has completed his education here at Ohio State University he will
return to his native land to diffuse civilization and education."[26]

To the average, dark-skinned Negro, the constant idealization of white
culture in the black press must have led to consternation and a good deal
of frustration—and it may have helped lay the groundwork for Marcus
Garvey and his philosophy of blackness, which would burst upon the
scene in the 1920s. Undoubtedly, there was a portion of the black lower
class that looked to the middle class for guidance and standards and
sought to emulate, to some degree, the bourgeois life-style. About one of
every fifteen Negro families with incomes below the middle-class level
(a conservative estimate) was able to own its own home in Cleveland in
1910, and a considerably larger proportion of this class could rent houses.
For these families, the attainment of a middle-class life-style was not
impossible, although many years of hard work, saving, and a measure
of luck was needed to reach the goal.[27]

[26] *Ibid.*, October 21, 1916, October 20, 1917. For examples of advertisements,
see *ibid.*, February 26, 1916; almost any issue of the black newspaper carried
similar messages from the producers of hair and skin products. Stereotyped views of
Africa were common among black leaders and the black elite in general in the
United States prior to 1915. This was especially true of black newspaper editors,
and one historian has noted that in the late nineteenth century "positive images of
Africa were relatively rare exceptions to the usual unfavorable presentation in
the black press" (Walter L. Williams, "Black Journalism's Opinions about Africa
during the Late Nineteenth Century," *Phylon*, 34, September 1973, 234). Much of
the black middle and upper classes probably gave little thought to Africa at this
time. "The [educated] colored man in New York," said Mary White Ovington in
1911, "has no associations with his ancient African home, no African traditions, no
folk lore" (Ovington, *Half a Man*, 171). It should be noted, however, that as early
as the 1890s a small minority of the race was beginning to take a more active
interest in the study of African history and culture. Although the subject has not
been analyzed in any systematic way, it appears that black interest in Africa was
centered chiefly in eastern cities. The development of segregated areas there prior
to 1915 facilitated a new consciousness of race which in turn made blacks much
more susceptible to identification with (or, at least, interest in) Africa. The lack of
any similar interest among blacks in Cleveland, on the other hand, may be traced
to the slower growth of the ghetto there and to the lack of contact with African
immigrants in an inland city. For perceptive comments on black attitudes toward
Africa, see August Meier, *Negro Thought in America, 1880–1915: Racial Ideologies
in the Age of Booker T. Washington* (Ann Arbor, 1963), 260–70, 313n, and Louis
Harlan, "Booker T. Washington and the White Man's Burden," *American Historical
Review*, 71 (January, 1966), 441–67.

[27] Property holding among the black lower class is a phenomenon which deserves
detailed study. In his study of Irish laborers, *Poverty and Progress: Social Mobility
in a Nineteenth Century City* (Cambridge, 1964), 115–65, Stephan Thernstrom

A clear majority of the black residents of the city, however, were too close to the bottom of the economic ladder to entertain such ambitions. It was not unusual for black unskilled laborers (especially those doing heavy construction work) to earn fairly good wages—fifteen dollars a week or more. This type of work, however, tended to be seasonal or sporadic; in 1890, fully 10 percent of Cleveland's unskilled laborers were unemployed for three to six months of the year. Black men who held positions as servants, janitors, chauffeurs, and porters in railroad and business establishments earned steadier wages—but most still brought home only five hundred dollars or less per year, and their jobs held out scant hope for advancement to better positions and higher wages. As a result, in many lower-class black families it was necessary for the wife to supplement the husband's income by going to work as a domestic. Any woman who became a domestic immediately lost caste, because of the long hours, low pay, and servile demeanor that the job required. "Not only are social advantages denied the domestic employee," one student noted in 1900, "but the badge of social inferiority is put upon her in characters as unchangeable as are the spots of a leopard." Yet three out of every ten black women in the city were then consigned, by economic necessity, to such a position.[28]

The life-style of typical members of the black lower class is difficult to reconstruct because, unlike their social betters, they left behind few documents from which the historian can piece together their day-to-day existence. This much is clear: their lives were a good deal simpler than those of the middle and upper classes because they had fewer options. The average black worker did not worry about where he would spend

---

demonstrated the importance of property acquisition as a means of upward mobility for urban workers. While far less significant in black communities, "property mobility" occurred there too. Property ownership was much more common among the black middle and upper classes than among the laborers at the beginning of the twentieth century, but there was always a certain proportion of the working class who were able to own their own homes. In Chicago in 1902, 193 of 505 black property owners were unskilled laborers or servants. In Boston, 43 percent of all black property holders in 1914 were from the two lowest occupational categories; and in that same year a spot check of 197 black home owners in Kansas City, Missouri, revealed that 134 were laborers, porters, teamsters, or servants of one type or another. See Monroe N. Work, "Negro Real Estate Holders of Chicago" (M.A. thesis, University of Chicago, 1903), 23–24; Daniels, *In Freedom's Birthplace*, 385; Martin, *Our Negro Population*, 37; and Lawrence B. De Graaf, "The City of Black Angels: Emergence of the Los Angeles Ghetto, 1890–1930," *Pacific Historical Review*, 39 (August 1970), 326.

[28] U.S. *Eleventh Census, 1890* (Washington, 1893), II, 654–55; Lucy Salmon, *Domestic Service*, 2d ed. (New York, 1901), 147n, 151–66. On the salaries of the working and servant classes, see Ovington, *Half a Man*, 83–85; Crossland, *Industrial Conditions among Negroes in St. Louis*, 123.

his vacation because he rarely had a vacation; nor was he in doubt about where to take up his residence, since the cheap lodging houses and tenements on or near Central Avenue were the only types of housing that fit his pocketbook. While the social life of the elite and middle strata of the black community revolved around a plethora of voluntary associations, that of the lower class was more likely to focus on a single institution: the church. The recreational pastimes of the lower class also tended to be simple and unadorned. For a ten-cent admission fee, blacks could (after 1912), attend either of two Central Avenue moving-picture houses. For the most part, these establishments featured Charlie Chaplin, Frank Keenan, and other white movie stars—although an occasional film like "The Black Box," a fifteen-week serial about the capture of a white man by a King Kong-like monster, must have proved a welcome addition to the standard fare. At slightly higher prices, the Grand Central Theater at East 36th and Central featured such vaudeville acts as Payne and Payne, Billy Maxey, Lovejoy and Douvenoir, and the Fairfax Company. Occasionally, special entertainment events in the black community drew a mass audience. Black singers such as Anita Patti Brown ("Nature's Goddess of Soul Expression") or Cleveland's own Rachel Walker (billed as "the race's greatest singer") were particularly popular, not only because they carried forward an important indigenous black cultural tradition, but because they served as role models of success to black lower-class youth. In the 1920s the black jazz musicians and bluesmen who performed in the city's cabarets and nightclubs would serve a similar function.[29]

Unfortunately, the static, depressed occupational structure of black Cleveland during the prewar years offered little hope to young Afro-Americans who sought to better their lot. Cleveland's black middle class was larger than that of most cities, but it remained much smaller than the white middle class; and the opportunity for lower-class black youth to rise higher than their parents was not very great. On the basis of the scattered evidence that is available, it would appear that most members of the middle class were born in the North or had parents who had already attained middle-class positions (or both). Relatively rare was the career of Robert I. Drake, who was born in impoverished circumstances in rural Kentucky, worked his way through school, came North, attended Oberlin College, and in 1909 managed to obtain a clerkship in Cleveland's city hall. Prior to World War I, most young blacks who migrated

[29] Cleveland *Advocate*, June 19, October 16, 1915, September 7, 21, October 5, 1918.

from the South remained what their parents had been—unskilled laborers or servants.[30]

"One can see the colored youth gazing wistfully through the office window at the clerk, whose business reaches across bewildering continents," said Mary White Ovington in 1911, "knowing as he does that the employment he may find in that office will be emptying the white man's waste paper basket." Such a situation inevitably bred dissatisfaction, frustration, and despondency among those who experienced it, and it is not surprising that a deviant subculture involving gambling, excessive drinking, and sexual promiscuity began to emerge among a portion of the black lower class. This subculture had always existed to some extent in Cleveland's black community, but as a permanent factor it developed much later in the Forest City than in New York or Philadelphia. Its appearance coincided not only with declining black economic status but with the trend toward ghettoization that black Cleveland experienced in the late nineteenth and early twentieth centuries. By 1915 Central Avenue had become known as a vice district, and more than a few blacks made money through illegal means. In effect, a large number simply dropped out of an economic system they knew to be stacked against them. To middle-class blacks as well as whites, the life-style of what the *Advocate* called the "sidewalk loafer" was incomprehensible. "He only works," the paper editorialized in 1915, "for the wherewithal to buy a gaudy creation of the tailor's art, some six-for-a-quarter so-called Havana's, and a rakish bowler, which he dons with the inevitable tilt. With this necessary equipment . . . he is then at peace with the world." Whether such an individual was indeed "at peace with the world" may be doubted. As Elliot Liebow has explained (in a discussion applicable to the past as well as the present), the black "streetcorner man" lives perpetually "in a sea of want." Unlike the middle-class person who accuses him of being excessively "present-oriented," he usually does not "have a surplus of resources, either economic or psychological. Gratification of hunger and the desire for simple creature comforts cannot be long deferred. Neither can support for one's flagging self-esteem. Living on the edge of both economic and psychological subsistence, the streetcorner man is obliged to expend all his resources on maintaining himself from moment to moment."[31]

---

[30] *Ibid.*, May 19, 1917.
[31] Ovington, *Half a Man*, 86; Cleveland *Advocate*, June 5, 1915; Elliot Liebow, *Tally's Corner: A Study of Negro Streetcorner Men* (New York, 1967), 65. Although the mode of existence of the streetcorner man, then, is a deviant one in terms of the

"Do you not see the need of the cultivation of your intellect," the *Advocate* admonished the "sidewalk loafer" at the end of its editorial, "to fit you for the duties of your future life? Bid your beloved sidewalks good-bye, and start out on the road to self-advancement."[32] It is unlikely that the man with the fashionable bowler read this advice; if he did, he certainly must have found it amusing. To most of the black lower class, the "duties" of the future promised to be no more complicated than those of the present: they included the necessity of staying alive and the hope of squeezing as much happiness as possible out of a rather narrow existence. The percentage of blacks who saw life in these terms would rise and fall, depending on economic conditions in the black community. But as long as racism remained, the culture of poverty that it helped produce would continue to be a disturbing part of black life in the city.

---

dominant societal norms, it is still functionally suited to his socioeconomic circumstances. Behavior that seems irrational to the middle-class observer may appear eminently reasonable to the slum dweller. For a discussion of the "provincial morality" of slum neighborhoods in general, see Gerald D. Suttles's excellent study, *The Social Order of the Slum: Ethnicity and Territory in the Inner City* (Chicago, 1968), 4–9, 223–34, and *passim*.

[32] Cleveland *Advocate*, June 5, 1915.

CHAPTER 6

Leadership, Politics, and Institutions

At the beginning of the twentieth century many black Americans were divided over what course to pursue in response to the increase in segregation, discrimination, and white hostility throughout the nation and to the loss of basic political rights in the South. With the ascendancy to national prominence of Booker T. Washington after 1895, Negro leaders were increasingly divided into two opposing camps. One group —easily the larger of the two—favored the approach of Washington. The headmaster of Tuskegee played down the importance of political rights and protest activities; he often flattered the white South in conciliatory language, and consistently stressed the theme of black self-help through racial solidarity. Although behind the scenes Washington sometimes fought segregation and disfranchisement in the South, in public he urged black acquiescence in these measures as a practical means of harmonizing race relations. The Tuskegean insisted that Negroes could only gain full citizenship rights after they had demonstrated the familiar nineteenth-century virtues of hard work, thrift, and the accumulation of wealth. It might take the black man decades to raise himself up in the eyes of the white community, but when he did, Washington concluded optimistically, "he will not have to seek privileges [equal rights], they will be freely conferred upon him." Not all black leaders accepted this view. Another group, which coalesced for a while around W. E. B. Du Bois but found its most consistent champion in Boston editor William Monroe Trotter, continued to emphasize the need for agitation for political and civil rights. Comprised mostly of northerners, this group looked forward hopefully to the day when Afro-Americans would be fully integrated into American society on a basis of equality, and they usually considered any attempt at segregation or racial separatism to be a shameful betrayal of American democratic principles. It is important to note that—unlike the black nationalists of a later generation—this group did not associate the advocacy of separate black schools and supportive institutions with militancy; on the contrary, they viewed any move toward black separatism as an accommodation to racism. "The colored man," said one Boston Negro of this persuasion, "must not draw the [color] line himself if he doesn't want the white man to do it. He must demand and insist constantly upon his rights as an American citizen."[1]

Not all black leaders, of course, identified themselves with one position or the other. Many (including even one of the two chief protagonists, Du Bois) held inconsistent views on specific issues or changed their allegiance over the course of time. Yet in spite of this, it was an indisputable fact that, in the words of journalist Ray Stannard Baker, "two great Negro parties" had emerged and were contending for the leadership of the black race. Although much research on black leadership at the local level remains to be done, it appears that in most northern cities the changing nature of the black elite accentuated this ideological struggle at the beginning of the twentieth century. In Chicago and Boston (and probably elsewhere as well), the old elite of the black community usually opposed the "accommodationist" philosophy of Booker T. Washington and his followers. Most members of this older group worked in occupations which entailed close contact with whites, had been educated in integrated institutions, and had developed personal relationships with whites of similar economic standing. Under these circumstances, they cleaved naturally to an integrationist outlook and usually resisted any attempt to establish all-Negro institutions. The new class of rising black businessmen, however, frequently took the opposite stance. Less educated than the old elite and having economic roots in the black community, this newer group favored the philosophy of the Tuskegeean and approved of segregated institutions as a practical way

[1] Booker T. Washington, *The Future of the American Negro* (Boston, 1899), in August Meier, Elliott Rudwick, and Francis L. Broderick, eds., *Black Protest Thought in the Twentieth Century*, rev. ed. (Indianapolis, Ind., 1971), 13; Ray Stannard Baker, *Following the Color Line: American Negro Citizenship in the Progressive Era* (New York, 1908), 216–32 *passim*. The subject of black ideologies is dealt with most thoroughly in August Meier, *Negro Thought in America, 1880–1915: Racial Ideologies in the Age of Booker T. Washington* (Ann Arbor, 1963), and I have relied heavily on this volume for background knowledge of black thought in the Progressive era. The best study of Washington is Louis Harlan, *Booker T. Washington: The Making of a Black Leader, 1856–1901* (New York, 1973), the first of a projected two-volume biography.

of advancing the race. By 1910 these two groups were vying for the leadership of black communities in the North and were in sharp conflict over such issues as the creation of all-Negro YMCAs and social centers.[2]

Cleveland did not follow this pattern in every respect. In particular, the ideological struggle between the new and old elites that emerged so dramatically in Chicago was somewhat muted in tone in Cleveland. One factor which contributed to this was the relative smallness of Cleveland's black population before 1915. Ideological conflict in Boston or Chicago usually developed over the formation (or proposed formation) of an institution or organization sponsored and maintained primarily by the black community. But in Cleveland—as in many northern cities—the Negro population before the Great Migration was not large enough to support many race enterprises. Thus, the issues around which ideological conflict could develop arose less frequently. Generally speaking, the ideological appeal of the Washington doctrine of self-help and racial solidarity was weaker in Cleveland than in larger black communities because the development of the ghetto and of segregated facilities progressed more slowly there. The integrationism of the old elite seemed, as late as 1910, still to be a workable philosophy; and the very ambiguity of Cleveland's racial atmosphere—compared to the blatant racism of the South—gave hope that the rising tide of discrimination might yet be halted or even reversed.

To relate Cleveland's tradition of racial fairness to the tenacity of the old elite on the one hand and the slow growth of black institutions on the other, however, is to oversimplify the development of black leadership, ideologies, and institutions during these years. For a more thorough understanding of these matters, one must analyze the personalities of the leading spokesmen of the black community. Knowledge of the careers and philosophies of these individuals, of their perceptions of their own status as well as that of other blacks, is a necessary prerequisite to a comprehensive understanding of the development of black Cleveland.

[2] Baker, *Following the Color Line*, 224; John Daniels, *In Freedom's Birthplace: A Study of the Boston Negroes* (Boston, 1914), 118–31; Meier, *Negro Thought in America*, 151–57; Allan H. Spear, *Black Chicago: The Making of a Negro Ghetto, 1890–1920* (Chicago, 1967), 51–54, 71–72. It should be noted at the outset that not all members of the old elite were chronologically older than members of the new elite. The term "old elite" is used to identify a social and ideological grouping in the black community. As time went along, this group did indeed become composed mostly of older individuals, but—at least prior to 1915—a number of younger blacks also fit this category.

I

At the end of the 1890s almost all of the acknowledged leaders of Cleveland's black community were drawn from the old elite. For the most part, this group of leaders shared a common racial ideology: they were *conservative integrationists* whose fondest hopes were to preserve as much as possible of the old order of relative equality that was beginning to deteriorate at the end of the nineteenth century. Not all of these leaders were totally consistent in their ideology, and a few were beginning to back away from their commitment to integrationism during the years just preceding the Great Migration; but the dominant thrust of their thinking remained unaltered. It was in the area of *tactics* (that is, the implementation of their ideology) that the greatest disagreement existed among the old elite. Historians of black thought during the Progressive era have been too prone to identify integrationism with the "radical" tactics of protest and agitation. In some national civil rights organizations—the Niagara Movement, for example—such a conjunction of belief and action is indeed evident, but a study of black leadership at the local level reveals that leading black integrationists did not always favor vigorous protest as a means of redressing black grievances. During the decades before World War I, tactics among Cleveland's integrationist leadership ranged along a spectrum from those who opposed any kind of agitation to those who favored strong and immediate protest against every form of racial discrimination. By 1915, however, the latter were fewer in number and less influential than those who favored a more moderate approach to the problems of race.[3] The discussion which follows will begin with the most conservative black leaders and progress to those of more militant persuasion.

In his 1908 study, *Following the Color Line*, Ray Stannard Baker noted that "in some Northern cities some of the ablest Negroes will have nothing to do with the masses of their own people or with racial movements; they hold themselves aloof, asserting that there is no color line,

---

[3] It is the author's belief that, in studying trends in black leadership, one must be careful to distinguish ideology from tactics. To a greater extent, perhaps, than their white counterparts, black leaders have been subject to indecision and conflicting pressures. It is essential, then, in analyzing their role, to discriminate between rhetoric and action. Although I am greatly indebted to Allan Spear for his elucidation of a typology of local black leadership during the Progressive era, I cannot agree with his assessment that "most of Chicago's old established [black] leaders retained their commitment to the equal rights ideology and rejected compromise" during the years prior to the Great Migration (Spear, *Black Chicago*, 65). Admittedly, black leadership was more aggressive in Chicago than in most other cities; but by failing to differentiate ideology from tactics, Spear paints the old elite as too uniformly militant.

and if there is, there should not be. Their associations and their business are largely with white people and they cling passionately to the fuller life." This statement is an excellent description of Jacob Reed and Walter B. Wright, two older black leaders who, though nominal integrationists, were completely disinclined to join with other Negroes in fighting the growth of segregation. In an age which worshiped material success above all else, Reed represented the black version of the Horatio Alger myth. Born in Harrisburg, Pennsylvania, in 1852, Reed started with very little. After coming to Cleveland in the late 1880s, he worked briefly as a waiter and then as a streetcar conductor before becoming a partner in a downtown fish market. (In 1915 Reed bought out his associate.) Reed's business was eminently successful, and by 1919 he had accumulated $30,000 in property and was reputed to own a "palatial home." Reed had close associations with a number of whites (even his business partner was white) and at the same time maintained his ties with upper- and middle-class blacks through his lodge and church affiliations. Safe within this biracial world, Reed did not feel compelled to help blacks below him in the social scale maintain their rights and privileges, and he seemed oblivious to the fact that the lot of the average black man was increasingly distant from his own.[4]

Walter B. Wright was another important member of the black upper class who displayed little interest in changing racial conditions that did not affect him personally. For a Negro living at the end of the nineteenth century, Wright's career was quite exceptional. Born in Virginia in 1852, Wright moved with his family to Columbus, Ohio, at the close of the Civil War. There he had the extraordinary good luck, in 1873, of entering the service of R. D. Caldwell, a Cleveland-based official of a subsidiary of the Nickel Plate Railroad. The ambitious Caldwell rose rapidly through the railroad's hierarchy and in 1894 became the president of Nickel Plate. Because of his close association with Caldwell, Wright's own career followed a similar upward path. Starting as a mere porter, he first received a clerkship and then, gaining the confidence of his mentor, became Caldwell's private secretary.[5]

As Caldwell's private secretary, Wright held a position of trust and authority shared by few Negroes of his day. In the course of his assign-

---

[4] Baker, *Following the Color Line*, 228–29; Cleveland *Plain Dealer*, October 14, 1900; Cleveland *Journal*, March 28, 1903; Clement Richardson et al., eds., *The National Cyclopedia of the Colored Race* (Montgomery, Ala., 1919), I, 245.

[5] Zanesville *Courier*, September 14, 1894; Columbus *Dispatch*, September 17, 1894; Cleveland *Plain Dealer*, July 24, 1897; Cleveland *Gazette*, January 26, 1901 (clippings in unnumbered Walter B. Wright Scrapbooks, Western Reserve Historical Society).

ments he communicated frequently and socialized freely with numerous white railroad officials. Wright's wedding in 1893 was a thoroughly integrated posh affair, attended by Caldwell and a number of his white subordinates as well as most of the upper crust of the black community. Few Negroes enjoyed such social privileges or were able to rise as high in the white-collar ranks as Wright, and the secretary's prestige among both Negroes and whites remained high as a result. Yet Wright seemed to identify much more with the power-oriented world of his mentor than the increasingly powerless world of the average black citizen. The scrapbooks he left behind are filled with clippings on the rivalry of railroads, the stunning achievements of the transcontinentals, and the meteoric career of Caldwell—whom Wright increasingly idolized; they reveal little interest in the deteriorating status of blacks. Wright was theoretically an integrationist. With the exception of his opposition to the creation of an all-Negro YMCA in 1911, however, he took no apparent interest in the growing problems of the black community in Cleveland, and his name is not associated with any of the racial advancement organizations which came into existence after 1910.[6]

A much more important figure than Wright was John Patterson Green, the most successful black politician among the old elite. Described as a "self-made man" by the Cleveland *Leader* in 1902, Green had every reason to believe the accolade to be true. Born in North Carolina of free, mixed parentage, Green came to Cleveland at the age of twelve in 1857. After graduating from Central High School and Union College of Law, he entered upon a career as a lawyer. At the same time he commenced a life-long interest in Republican politics. In 1873 he was elected a justice of the peace, an office which at that time entailed both judicial and police powers, and he served in that capacity for nine years. After losing in a disputed election in 1877, Green won election to the lower house of the state legislature in 1881 and again in 1889. Finally, in 1891 Green became the first (and only) northern Negro to be elected to a state senate in the nineteenth century. This achievement was indicative of the liberal racial attitude prevailing in Cleveland at that time: most of the voters in Green's district were white. Green did not seek reelection in 1893; but although he served only two years in the Ohio Senate, his prestige and influence among blacks throughout the North increased dramatically because of this accomplishment.[7]

---

[6] Cleveland *Globe*, April 25, 1891 (clipping in Wright Scrapbooks); Cleveland *Gazette*, April 25, 1891; Cleveland *Plain Dealer*, October 14, 1900, February 1, 1911.

[7] John P. Green, *Fact Stranger than Fiction: Seventy-Five Years of a Busy Life*

From his prominent position, Green could have become an important leader in the Negro's fight for equality. Instead he came to believe that militant protest was both unnecessary and unwise. In some ways Green's views were similar to those of Booker T. Washington. In 1890 Green seemed to presage the theme of Washington's Atlanta Address when he told an audience that Negroes were ostracized in America not because of the color of their skin but "because they are poor." The path to racial equality, he stated, was essentially through the classic American virtues of thrift and perseverance. "With better fortunes," he told his black brethren, "we shall attain power, and our status will be elevated." Evidently Green did not have a close relationship with Washington, but he counted as friends three Negro editors, E. E. Cooper, George L. Knox, and Cyrus F. Adams, who usually supported the Tuskegeean in their editorials.[8]

It should be not be thought, however, that Green was in agreement with all aspects of Washington's racial philosophy. His own life style was too integrated and the racial situation in Cleveland was too fluid to allow a complete acceptance of the accommodationism preached by Washington. In 1893, while serving in the state senate, Green helped defeat a bill which would have made the segregation of Negroes in separate schools much easier in most Ohio communities. Yet at the same time he approved of the expansion of Wilberforce University, an AME school that received substantial state funds, even though that facility was clearly designed for blacks alone. Since very few members of the old elite opposed the expansion of Wilberforce, Green's stand on that particular issue did not mean that he was changing his mind about the value of integrated institutions in general. Nevertheless, after 1900 Green showed little interest in fighting the trend toward segregation and separate institutions in Cleveland.[9]

Regardless of his ideological position on specific issues, the hallmark of Green's approach to any question involving blacks was his extreme caution. In his private occupation as an attorney, Green sometimes defended Negroes who were victims of discrimination. In 1897 he was even

---

with Reminiscences of Many Great and Good Men (Cleveland, 1920), 1–192 *passim*; Cleveland *Leader*, October 30, 1902.

[8] *Ibid.*, January 24, 1890; Cleveland *Leader and Morning Herald*, August 15, 1890 (clippings in John Patterson Green Papers, Western Reserve Historical Society); E. E. Cooper to John P. Green, November 25, 1896; George L. Knox to Green, March 31, 1897; C. F. Adams to Green, March 6, 1897, Green Papers. On Cooper, Knox, and Adams, see Meier, *Negro Thought in America*, 230–36.

[9] Green, *Fact Stranger than Fiction*, 186, 187–88; Cleveland *Herald*, March 31, 1894; Cleveland *Commercial Gazette*, March 31, 1894 (clippings in Green Papers).

willing to travel to Charleston, West Virginia, to defend a black servant who had been unjustly charged with assault in what was an obvious case of self-defense. As a public figure, however, Green soon realized that successful Negro politicians placed loyalty to party above loyalty to race. In Ohio in the 1890s this meant supporting to the hilt the machine candidates of Republican boss Marcus Alonzo Hanna, regardless of their positions on important race issues. In 1896 Green worked hard for William McKinley, despite the fact that—as Rayford W. Logan has pointed out—"the Negro was almost completely forgotten" during the campaign. For his assistance in the election the president rewarded Green in 1897 with the newly created position of Postage Stamp Agent in Washington, at an annual salary of $2,500—a sinecure which the black politician managed to hold on to for nearly a decade. Thereafter, Green's loyalty to his mentor was unquestioning. Although he was quite aware of the increasing racism and disfranchisement of the Negro in the South (he received long descriptions of the deteriorating conditions in Louisiana from a black Republican there), Green followed the example of McKinley by remaining silent on those matters. He continued to support the president, even when McKinley declined to take action against southern lynch mobs or to back antilynching legislation in Congress. "I heard, occasionally," Green wrote many years later, "caustic criticisms of President McKinley's policy, with reference to the colored people, by colored men. But on such occasions, I always challenged those hostile statements, and endeavored to prove, to the face of the critic, the falsity of his assertions. . . ."[10]

Green's amicable position on race issues won him influential friends in Cleveland as well as in Washington. During his long life he was on favorable terms with literally dozens of prominent white politicians and businessmen; he even had a passing acquaintanceship with John D. Rockefeller. Green was the first Negro member of the Logos Club, an exclusive group that convened periodically to discuss "social questions" from an Olympian perspective. The wide circle of important people he knew in Cleveland is evidence of the continuing liberality of a portion of the city's white elite; but it also attests to the benign and compromising stance which Green took toward the growing problem of racial oppression. Although discrimination was increasing during the prewar

[10] Daniel W. Shaw to John P. Green, June 9, 1897; Shaw to Green, June 16, 1897; Harry Lott to Green, October 1, 1896; Lott to Green, October 14, 1896; Postal Department Form #32, dated August 2, 1897, Green Papers; Green, *Fact Stranger than Fiction*, 218–19, 269–70; Cleveland *Gazette*, July 8, 1905; Rayford W. Logan, *The Betrayal of the Negro: From Rutherford B. Hayes to Woodrow Wilson* (New York, 1965), 95.

years, Green failed to speak out against it, much less lead a fight to reverse the trend. With the passing years he preferred more and more to bask in the glory of his former accomplishments and to savor the privileged position he had attained. As he approached retirement, Green could convince himself that his achievements proved that success was still possible for members of either race, and he urged the younger generation to take heart from the example of his own upward mobility: "O, ye humble, struggling, ambitious American youth, both white and black! Reflect on these facts—ponder over them; take courage; and persistently, press onward and upward." This kind of advice may have had some validity in the 1860s, when Green was just embarking on his own career. In the much different racial atmosphere of the early 1900s, it only underscored his growing conservatism on race issues.[11]

More clearly than in Green's case, the career of another black leader, Jere A. Brown, illustrates the shift away from the militancy that had characterized Cleveland's antebellum black elite. Born in Pittsburgh in 1841, Brown attended an industrial school in Pennsylvania before coming to Cleveland in 1871. For a while he worked as a carpenter, but like Green he soon looked to politics as a means of upward mobility. His services to the Republicans earned him an appointment as a deputy sheriff in Cuyahoga County in 1877, and political pull may also have helped him get a position as a letter carrier (an elite occupation among Negroes at that time) four years later. He stayed in that occupation until 1885, when he was elected to the Ohio House of Representatives.[12]

During much of his earlier career, Brown exhibited a tendency toward radicalism, and he was much less hesitant than Green to engage in agitation for civil rights. "There is no influence that will be a greater lever to eradicate all prejudices that may exist," Brown stated in 1886, "than the influence of *education, organization, and agitation.* But no separate organizations can effect what we desire to accomplish; for as we are a component part of this great government, we *must* have accorded to us such treatment as other citizens have, which can only be attained by persistent agitation and intermingling." In 1887 Brown was largely responsible for getting the last of the black laws wiped off the statute books in Ohio, and three years later he supported the formation of the militant Afro-American League, a national protest organization.

[11] Green, *Fact Stranger than Fiction*, 206, 212–21, and *passim*; L. E. Holden to John P. Green, March 6, 1893, Green Papers.
[12] Green, *Fact Stranger than Fiction*, 181; Cleveland *Leader*, September 11, 1902 (clipping in Wright Scrapbooks); Cleveland *Gazette*, November 5, 1887; Russell H. Davis, *Memorable Negroes in Cleveland's Past* (Cleveland, 1969), 25.

But this mood gradually changed. Perhaps because of discouragement over the small success of the league, perhaps simply as a result of financial insecurity, Brown soon became more interested in the emoluments of partisan politics than the struggle to attain equal rights. Throughout the 1890s, he worked diligently for the GOP; and in turn he was rewarded with a variety of patronage posts. At one time or another during the decade he served as a customs inspector in Cleveland, clerk in the office of the Cuyahoga County auditor, and as a minor functionary in the Ohio State Insurance Department in Columbus. Few politicians—white or black—pursued the spoils of office as persistently as Brown. "Jere," the Cleveland *Gazette* noted sarcastically in 1897, "never forgets Jere, for race or anything else."[13]

Brown could find no fault with politics of the Hanna-McKinley variety. He described the election of Hanna to the U.S. Senate as "a great and glorious victory" and defended the policies of President McKinley against Negro critics. He applauded Green for standing by McKinley even when all others had (in his own words) "gone mad." Brown was quite specific in expecting to be rewarded for his loyalty. After the election of 1897 he requested that Green speak to "Uncle Mark" Hanna in his behalf. As Brown bluntly put it, "I want a Christmas present from them in some way or the other." Green used his influence to help Brown secure a minor position in the Internal Revenue Department the following year. A few years later, the former carpenter was back in Cleveland as an immigration inspector. He remained in Cleveland until his death in 1913.[14]

Although he never held political office, George A. Myers had more influence with prominent whites than either John P. Green or Jere Brown, and a white newspaper declared in 1900 that he was "without a doubt the most widely known colored man in Cleveland." Myers was born in Baltimore in 1859. His father, Isaac Myers, was a leader in the Baltimore black community and had established the Chesapeake Marine Railroad and Dry Dock Company, an all-Negro shipyard, when white carpenters refused to work with Negroes. Against the wishes of his

[13] Benjamin Arnett and Jere A. Brown, *The Black Laws* (n.p. [1886]); Cleveland *Leader*, January 24, 1890; Cleveland *Gazette*, February 20, 1886, October 3, 1896, November 6, 1897; Jere A. Brown to William R. Green, March, 1897, Green Papers; Brown to George A. Myers, January 7, 1893, George A. Myers Papers, Ohio State Historical Society; Davis, *Memorable Negroes in Cleveland's Past*, 25.

[14] Jere A. Brown to George A. Myers, July 11, 1894, Myers Papers; Brown to John P. Green, April 14, 1898; Brown to Green, January 21, 1899; Brown to Green, December 14, 1897; Brown to Green, April 7, 1898, Green Papers; Cleveland *Leader*, September 11, 1902; Columbus *Standard*, February 4, 1905 (clippings in Wright Scrapbooks); Cleveland *Journal*, August 27, 1904.

father, the younger Myers took up barbering as a trade, and when he came to Cleveland in 1879 he quickly found employment in the Weddell House barber shop. Nine years later, with financial assistance from some of the white friends he had made in the intervening period, he became the owner of the barber shop in the then new Hollenden Hotel, one of the city's most exclusive establishments. Myers's barber shop, which catered almost entirely to whites, soon became known as a gathering place for local politicians and visiting dignitaries. One result was that Myers developed close relationships with a number of famous people; he was a personal friend of James Ford Rhodes, Newton D. Baker, and, most important, Marcus A. Hanna.[15]

Myers's friendship with Hanna soon led the barber into increasing involvement in Republican politics. As a delegate to the 1892 Republican National Convention, he was instrumental in swaying a number of key votes which helped the Hanna-McKinley group gain control of the party in Ohio. Thereafter Myers worked diligently among Negroes throughout the state on behalf of the Hanna machine. "We are Hanna men, tried and true," he wrote to John P. Green in 1897, and he proved it by bribing a black legislator to insure the election of his chief to the U.S. Senate the following year. However, politics did not serve for Myers (as it did for Green) as a path to economic success. The barber later confided to James Ford Rhodes that Hanna and McKinley "repeatedly offered and desired to take care of me politically," but he always declined because his barber shop "was far more remunerative than any position" they could offer. Myers steadfastly maintained that he desired only to be an "armor-bearer" for the Republicans, and like Walter Wright he seemed to gain a certain amount of satisfaction in just being close to those who wielded vast power.[16]

Myers had a greater awareness of deteriorating racial conditions in

[15] Cleveland *Plain Dealer*, October 14, 1900; Charles H. Wesley, *Negro Labor in the United States, 1850–1925: A Study in American Economic History* (New York, 1927), 173; Meier, *Negro Thought in America*, 298; Richardson et al., eds., *National Cyclopedia of the Colored Race*, I, 279; untitled biographical sketch of Myers by John P. Green, in Myers Papers; John A. Garraty, ed., *The Barber and the Historian: The Correspondence of George A. Myers and James A. Rhodes, 1910–1923* (Columbus, 1956), xv–xvi.

[16] George A. Myers to John P. Green, December 19, 1897, Green Papers; Myers to Nahum D. Brascher, June 23, 1905; D. C. Westenhaver to Myers, May 22, 1916; first draft of Myers letter to James Ford Rhodes, March 4, 1920, Myers Papers; Garraty, ed., *The Barber and the Historian*, xiv, 106–7, 146; Henry E. Siebert IV, "George A. Myers: Ohio Negro Leader and Political Ally of Marcus A. Hanna" (senior thesis, Princeton University, 1963), 43–55, 70. Although Myers sought no political office for himself, he did attempt to obtain positions for his friends and consequently was enmeshed in the patronage game for a number of years.

Cleveland than did most of the Negro elite. In a letter to Rhodes, Myers reminded the historian that "intense color prejudice, race discrimination, and persecution" still existed everywhere in the United States. "You cannot fully appreciate this because you have never been discriminated against. I do not perhaps feel it so much as some by reason of a wide and beneficial acquaintance, but it has been brought home to me on many occasions." Commenting on the crime rate in the black community, Myers bluntly told a Cleveland judge that white racism was a cause that could not be overlooked. "While I do not," he said, "condone crime (all criminals look alike to me), the negro, morally and otherwise, is what the white man has made him through the denial of justice. . . . The negro asks no special favor by reason of being a negro, only an equal opportunity in all things."[17]

Myers disagreed sharply with those Cleveland Negroes who felt that the proper black response to increasing discrimination was the creation of their own institutions. The barber was on friendly terms with Booker T. Washington and approved of much of the Tuskegeean's program for the South. But he found the concept of separate black institutions inappropriate to the northern racial atmosphere, and in 1914 he candidly told Washington that "Segregation here [Cleveland] of any kind to me is a step backward. . . ." In line with this belief Myers came out against the creation of an all-Negro YMCA in 1911 and also opposed the Phillis Wheatley home for black girls when it was founded two years later. Myers seldom committed himself publicly on racial matters, however, and he seemed content on some occasions to vent his discouragement through the medium of his personal correspondence. He took no part in the formation or operation of the Cleveland branches of the NAACP, the Urban League, or any other race organization. Before 1920, Myers's only prolonged public struggle against racial discrimination was on an issue which decidedly involved his own self-interest; for over a decade he fought vigorously against the passage of a bill which would have placed the barbering trade firmly in the hands of the state's all-white barber colleges. He did, however, act behind the scenes on several occasions in an effort to ameliorate racial conditions. He used his influence with editors of the Cleveland *Plain Dealer* to keep the objectionable terms "negress" and "darkey" out of that paper, and he sought to enlist the aid of prominent whites to ban the showing of a racist film in the city in 1917.[18]

---

[17] George A. Myers to George S. Adams, October 4, 1926, Myers Papers; Garraty, ed., *The Barber and the Historian*, 78.

[18] George A. Myers to Booker T. Washington, July 20, 1914; Emmett J. Scott to

Several factors were responsible for Myers's shying away from any active, organized struggle against discrimination. First, it is probable that too great a militancy on Myers's part would have upset his social relationship with many of the whites (especially white politicians) who patronized his barber shop and thus have undercut his economic base of support. Myers's reticence can also be traced to certain ambiguities that are evident in his thought. The barber seemed to oscillate between the idea that discrimination was caused by white racism and the contradictory notion that blacks were often responsible for their own difficulties. His own prosperity coupled with the success of the black middle class in Cleveland convinced Myers that the black lower class was not worth fighting for unless it changed its ways. He attacked the lower-class churches for their "propensity to emotionalism, a heritage of slavery days," and told his fellow Negroes that part of the cause of rising discrimination was their own "clannish" habits. "Cease crying about discrimination," he exclaimed impatiently, "and confounding it with a LACK OF INITIATIVE." Myers was certain as well that "concentration, courtesy and efficiency is the trinity that will break down every barrier of race prejudice in the industrial world."[19]

Myers, July 15 [1905?]; W. B. Gongwer to Myers, February 5, 1917; Myers to Frank S. Harmon, August 23, 1923, Myers Papers; Garraty, ed., *The Barber and the Historian*, xx. For Myers's relationship with Washington, see *ibid.*, 37; Booker T. Washington to George A. Myers, March 1, 1893; Washington to Myers, July 15, 1914; Myers to Washington, July 20, 1914; Emmett J. Scott to Myers, July 15 [1905?]; Scott to Myers, June 3, 1915; Scott to Myers, March 16, 1916, Myers Papers; George A. Myers, "A Tribute to My Lost Friend," Cleveland *Advocate*, November 20, 1915. On Myers and the barber bill, see Myers to John P. Green, February 11, 1904, Green Papers; William H. Clifford to Myers, February 25, 1898; Ralph Tyler to Myers, July 3, 1905, Myers Papers; "Colored Men Aroused Against Middleswart Barber Bill," Columbus *Dispatch*, February 5, 1902 (clipping in Myers Papers); *H. B. No. 40: A Bill to Establish a Board of Examiners for Barbers* (Columbus [1910]).

[19] George Myers, "Religious Unity is Present Need," Cleveland *Advocate*, June 26, 1915; Myers, "A Tribute to My Lost Friend," *ibid.*, November 20, 1915; Myers, "Our Lack of Initiative," *ibid.*, June 15, 1918; Myers, address before the Caterers' Association, *ibid.*, December 4, 1915. Many of the articles Myers wrote for the *Advocate* illustrate great mental confusion and a perplexing tendency simultaneously to blame and praise certain trends in black life. In "Religious Unity is Present Need," for example, Myers first praised the black church as "the one place where discrimination and race prejudice never enter," only harshly to attack the "emotionalism" of the church in the next sentence. Contradiction and inconsistency were also common in the thought of other black leaders prior to the wartime migration, and this phenomenon presents continuing problems for the historian trying to discern ideological divisions in the black community. This tendency to lapse into inconsistency seems particularly noticeable during periods of deteriorating race relations (such as the Progressive era), and it is probably related to the frustration of black leaders who are asked to put forth "solutions" to racial problems for which no

However frustrated Myers became over the deteriorating racial climate of the day, he continued to eschew militant protest. Other blacks, he felt, could achieve acceptance in the same slow, laborious way he had. He agreed with the Bookerites that "the Negro's progress must hinge upon his economic well being." "What we need most," said Myers in 1915, "is to enter business. How can this be done? Just the same as the other races of peoples have started from humble beginnings and buil[t] up." Myers opposed the Tuskegee emphasis on ghetto-based, Negro-supported businesses, however, and he refused to take part in Washington's National Negro Business League. "Many of our people in business and practicing the professions," the barber complained, "seek to make color an asset. This should not be. . . . Don't be a *colored* business man. Don't be a *colored* professional man. It's an admission of inferiority." Instead he urged black entrepreneurs to seek out customers among whites as well as blacks and to advertise more widely. Yet the end result envisioned by Myers was the same as that optimistically predicted by Washington: the acceptance of blacks as equals without the need for organized struggle against racism. "With education and proper moral and religious influences made possible by economic betterment," Myers concluded, the Afro-American would "soon learn to feel himself a man among men and take his place with other people."[20]

If George Myers was well known in Cleveland, Charles Waddell Chesnutt, another prominent Negro leader, was able to achieve a national reputation during his lifetime. Chesnutt was born in Cleveland in 1858. but he spent most of his early years in North Carolina. At the behest of his mother, Chesnutt received a thorough training in both the liberal arts and the more practical subject of stenography. In the liberal, post-Reconstruction atmosphere of North Carolina, he was able to put his education to good use, and at the extraordinarily young age of twenty-two he became the principal of the Fayetteville State Normal School. Chesnutt soon sensed, however, that the future of an educated Negro in the South was limited and uncertain, and in 1884 he and his family, after a brief stay in New York, returned to Cleveland permanently.[21]

one alternative seems workable. See Mary White Ovington, *Half a Man: The Status of the Negro in New York* (New York, 1911), 185; Gunnar Myrdal, *An American Dilemma* (New York, 1944), II, 782; Meier, *Negro Thought in America*, 168–70.

[20] George Myers, "Envy is Race's Scourge," Cleveland *Advocate*, January 29, 1916; Myers, " 'Be Superlative,' " *ibid.*, July 3, 1915.

[21] Helen M. Chesnutt, *Charles Waddell Chesnutt: Pioneer of the Color Line* (Chapel Hill, N.C., 1952), 1–37.

An unusually talented individual, Chesnutt engaged himself successfully in a variety of occupations during his career. He worked primarily as a court stenographer, but in 1887 he passed his bar exams with a very high score and for a while practiced as an attorney as well. In the meantime, Chesnutt was developing his talent as a writer, and by 1901 he had acquired a considerable reputation with the publication of three novels (*The Conjure Woman, The House Behind the Cedars,* and *The Marrow of Tradition*) and dozens of short stories, including several which appeared in the prestigious *Atlantic Monthly.* This literary reputation gave Chesnutt an entrée to white society, and he soon moved as easily among the city's white elite as among its black upper class. When, in 1887, a white philanthropist offered to help finance a move to Europe, Chesnutt declined. "He felt," his daughter related, "that success in his own country against terrific odds would be worth more than success in a foreign country. He would wait and see whether someday, perhaps, in the city of his birth, the time would come when he would be treated as a scholar and a gentleman." By 1900 Chesnutt could feel, with some satisfaction, that he had achieved his goal.[22]

Chesnutt was articulate and much more vocal than Myers in his advocacy of equal rights for Negroes. Although he was on good terms with Booker T. Washington (they corresponded at length, and two of Chesnutt's children worked at Tuskegee for a while), Chesnutt was diametrically opposed to Washington's doctrines of economic self-help and racial solidarity, and to his deprecation of political rights and protest activities. In supporting the passage of the Lodge Federal Elections Bill in 1890, the Cleveland author stated that "the ever-lengthening record of Southern wrongs and insults . . . calls for whatever there is of patriotism, of justice, of fair play in the American people, to cry 'hands off' and give the Negro a show, not five years hence, or a generation hence, but now, while he is still alive, and can appreciate it. . . ." Chesnutt criticized Washington for his emphasis on industrial education for blacks, rebuked him for "always dwelling upon the weakness of the Negro race," and thought that the Tuskegeean's policy of cultivating the good will of progressive southerners was futile as long as "the white South insists upon judging the Negroes as a class." During the first decade of the twentieth century, Chesnutt was in close contact with W. E. B. Du Bois, Monroe Trotter, and other leaders of the opposition to Tuskegee, and he enthusiastically endorsed the formation of the National Negro Committee (later renamed the National Association for the Ad-

[22] *Ibid.,* 41; Cleveland *Journal,* August 22, 1903.

vancement of Colored People) and agreed to speak at its second annual
conference in 1910.[23]

For the most part, however, Chesnutt refused to become too deeply
involved in the projects and activities of the anti-Bookerites. Perhaps
because he considered parts of the Tuskegee educational program useful
to southern Negroes, he declined to join the struggle for leadership of
the race. Furthermore, it is interesting to note that most of Chesnutt's
criticisms on the race question were directed at conditions in the South;
he had little to say about mounting discrimination in the North. Only
occasionally did Chesnutt enter the fight for equal rights in Cleveland.
He used his influence with Newton D. Baker to help defeat an Ohio
anti-intermarriage bill in 1913, and two years later he fought to have
the racist film "The Birth of a Nation" banned from the state. But at no
time, apparently, did Chesnutt ever offer his legal services in any of the
civil rights suits that were filed in Cleveland during his lifetime. After
the Great Migration, the Negro author would become active in a number
of racial advancement organizations; prior to 1915, however, he tended
to remain aloof from such enterprises.[24]

Although Chesnutt was aware of the developing ghetto on Central
Avenue, he seldom came in contact with the people who lived there and
rather easily took the attitude of the patrician toward them. The lack of
anti-Negro violence in Cleveland compared with his native South, the
liberality of his white friends, and his own exceptional economic status
made it difficult for Chesnutt to fully understand the increasing discrimination that most Negroes were facing during the prewar years.
Nowhere was this attitude better revealed than in a letter Chesnutt
wrote to a friend in Fayetteville in 1916. After listing the exclusive,
predominantly white organizations of which he was a member, the
author went to explain that "it is needless to say that it is not wealth

[23] Chesnutt, Charles Waddell Chesnutt, 54; Charles W. Chesnutt to W. E. B. Du
Bois, November 21, 1910, Charles Waddell Chesnutt Papers, Fisk University; Charles
W. Chesnutt to Booker T. Washington, August 11, 1903; Chesnutt to Carrie W.
Clifford, October 15, 1908; Chesnutt to Wendell P. Stafford, June 25, 1909; Ches-
nutt to W. E. B. Du Bois, November 21, 1910; Chesnutt to William English Walling,
April 18, 1910, Chesnutt, Charles Waddell Chesnutt, 194–96, 230–32, 235, 240–42;
Stephen R. Fox, The Guardian of Boston: William Monroe Trotter (New York,
1971), 40, 57; Otto H. Olsen, Carpetbagger's Crusade: The Life of Albion Winegar
Tourgée (Baltimore, Md., 1965), 70, 350; Charles Flint Kellogg, NAACP: A History
of the National Association for the Advancement of Colored People (Baltimore,
Md., 1967), I, 26–27.

[24] Meier, Negro Thought in America, 243–44; Charles W. Chesnutt to Newton D.
Baker, April 3, 1913; Chesnutt to Gov. Frank B. Willis, November 23, 1915, Chesnutt, Charles Waddell Chesnutt, 257–58, 265–66.

or blood or birth that makes me acceptable in such company." Chesnutt continued:

> One of my daughters is a member of the College Club, composed of alumnae of the better colleges and universities. Indeed in this liberal and progressive Northern city we get most of the things which make life worth living, and this in spite of the fact that every one knows our origin. . . . In the North, race prejudice is rather a personal than a community matter, and a man is not regarded as striking at the foundations of society if he sees fit to extend a social courtesy to a person of color.[25]

Chesnutt's thought was complex, and it is not easy to summarize it briefly. From time to time he exhibited a rare degree of self-awareness. It was possible for him to fictionally satirize the "Blue Vein Society" northern Negro elite and criticize the "cultivated white Negroes who are always bewailing their fate and cursing the drop of black blood which 'taints'—I hate the word, it implies corruption—their otherwise pure race." Yet Chesnutt moved in "blue vein" elite circles himself; and though he never sought to "pass" (conceivably, he could have done so), he did adopt a life style that cut him off, both culturally and physically, from the vast majority of black Clevelanders. In his optimistic belief that northern racial prejudice was more "a personal than a community matter," Chesnutt revealed the central thrust of his thinking on the race question before the Great Migration. Individual blacks could overcome the disabilities of their color by adopting the culture and values of the white middle class. In a speech entitled "Race Prejudice: Its Causes and Its Cure," given in Boston in 1905, Chesnutt theorized that since a prime cause of racism was differences between the races, the main solution would be the obliteration of as many of these differences as possible. (In the long run, he felt, amalgamation through intermarriage would be necessary.) Chesnutt countered the popular theory of racial solidarity with the concept of the melting pot. Only one standard of human development could be allowed, and the author did not try to hide his preference for the traditional values and norms of the American middle class. Chesnutt was not so naïve as to believe this process of cul-

[25] Charles W. Chesnutt to E. J. Lilly, October 16, 1916, Chesnutt Papers, Fisk University. On the idea that the race problem was primarily southern rather than national, see Chesnutt to F. D. Crumpacker, May 9, 1902, *ibid.*, and Chesnutt, "The Disfranchisement of the Negro," in Booker T. Washington et al., *The Negro Problem* (New York, 1903), 106–7, 119–20. (Two collections of Chesnutt manuscripts are used in this study. Those at Fisk University are cited hereafter as Chesnutt Papers, Fisk; those at the Western Reserve Historical Society as Chesnutt Papers, WRHS.)

tural assimilation would transform race relations overnight, and by 1906 he had reached the conclusion that in the South equality would "be deferred for many a day." But at that time Chesnutt was much more hopeful about conditions in the North, especially in liberal cities like Cleveland and Boston. His own career gave him confidence that racial integration and the complete acceptance of blacks as equals, however gradually these changes might be achieved, were still possible in the United States.[26]

Not all black leaders in Cleveland were content to accept a gradualist solution to the problems of racism and discrimination. Several black lawyers were prominent in the agitation for civil rights. The most notable of these was Charles S. Sutton, a black attorney who began practicing in Cleveland around 1905. Sutton was responsible for bringing a number of discrimination suits to trial, and on two occasions he won substantial settlements for his clients. "Charley Sutton," a friend commented in 1915, "believes that the Negro should continue to fight for every right guaranteed him by the United States Constitution until the last vestige of prejudicial vapor resting upon the splendid prerogatives of American manhood has forever passed away." Little is known about Sutton's background, but there is little doubt that, prior to 1917, he was the leading civil rights attorney in the city.[27]

It was in Harry C. Smith, however, that the protest tradition lived on in its purest and most militant form. Born in West Virginia in 1863, Smith came to Cleveland at an early age and remained there until his death in 1941. After graduating from Central High School in 1882, Smith established the *Gazette*, a Negro weekly. The *Gazette*, one of the better black newspapers of its day, soon became the principal organ for the dissemination of Smith's political and ideological views, and throughout the years it retained an uncompromising integrationist stance unequaled by any other race paper, with the possible exception of the Boston *Guardian*.[28]

[26] Charles W. Chesnutt to George W. Cable, June 5, 1890, Chesnutt, *Charles W. Chesnutt*, 57–59; Chesnutt, "Race Prejudice: Its Causes and Its Cure," manuscript in Chesnutt Papers, Fisk; Chesnutt to Booker T. Washington, October 9, 1906, *ibid.* A good example of the fictional satirization of the Negro "blue vein" elite is Chesnutt's story, "The Wife of His Youth," in *The Wife of His Youth and Other Stories of the Color Line* (Boston, 1899), 1–24.

[27] Robert I. Drake, "The Negro in Cleveland," Cleveland *Advocate*, September 18, 1915.

[28] William J. Simmons, *Men of Mark: Eminent, Progressive, and Rising* (Cleveland, 1887), 194–96; I. Garland Penn, *The Afro-American Press and Its Editors* Springfield, Mass., 1891), 281–83.

From the very first issue of the *Gazette* in 1883, Smith attacked segregation, discrimination, and racial prejudice in all its forms; and he was equally as critical of self-segregation by Negroes in the name of racial solidarity. Fearing that all-Negro institutions would be an "opening wedge to segregation and jim-crow schools," Smith led the fight against the creation of the black Phillis Wheatley home and opposed movements for separate recreational facilities and penal institutions for Negroes. Smith saved his most trenchant invective for those who advocated separate schools. The *Gazette* editor rejected the theory, advanced by some middle-class blacks, that segregated schools would produce more jobs for black teachers; the Cleveland experience, he declared, proved that wherever integrated schools existed, it was also possible to have integrated teaching staffs. For Smith, however, the main value of integrated schools was not economic; he considered them to be "the greatest, most powerful and successful engine for the destruction of prejudice than can be secured, in that they commence with the child of five or six years giving him the association [with persons of the opposite race] . . . that is calculated to eradicate . . . baneful prejudice. . . ." In fighting discrimination, Smith advocated three different methods of attack: political action to end public policies of discrimination; legal action against businesses clearly covered by the Ohio Civil Rights Act of 1894 (which Smith helped pass while serving in the state legislature), and Negro boycotts of other discriminatory businesses. With rather amazing consistency Smith kept the single goal of equal justice and opportunity for all Americans, regardless of their race, firmly in mind throughout his entire career.[29]

Except for his advocacy of Negro support of Negro businesses and an occasional editorial reference to the value of Negro history, Smith was scarcely affected by the increasingly popular doctrines of "race pride," economic self-help, and racial separatism. (He viewed racial solidarity only as a temporary expedient in the fight against discrimination and segregation.) Instead, the editor continually attacked what he called the "doctrine of surrender" enunciated by the followers of Booker T. Washington—he was one of the first to criticize the Atlanta Address—and called for more "sane radical" leaders like Monroe Trotter. Smith spared no words in denouncing the accommodationists. Commenting on the annual Tuskegee Conference in 1917, he lashed out at the con-

[29] Cleveland *Gazette*, September 25, 1915, January 17, 1914, May 16, 1896; Jane Edna Hunter, *A Nickel and a Prayer* (Cleveland, 1940), 94; Meier, *Negro Thought in America*, 48.

servatives' "truckling and shameful betrayal of the best interests of the race. . . . It goes without saying, our people will ignore the paid servants of southern oppression." To counteract the Tuskegee philosophy during a period of deteriorating race relations, Smith advocated the formation of national protest organizations. He was one of the founders of the short-lived Afro-American League in 1890, and throughout the following decade was a prominent ally of Albion W. Tourgée in his unsuccessful fight to outlaw Jim Crow railroad facilities in the South. Smith was one of twenty-nine militant black leaders from across the country who took part in the anti-Bookerite Niagara Movement of 1905. In 1910 he became a member of the NAACP's select Committee of One Hundred shortly after the organization was established.[30]

Like several other members of the older leadership group in Cleveland's black community, Smith became involved in Republican politics. During the 1880s the editor of the *Gazette*, although somewhat skeptical of the blandishments of the Republicans, loyally backed the party; in return he received the patronage post of deputy state inspector of oils in 1885. A persuasive orator, Smith was elected three times to the Ohio General Assembly (serving during the years 1894–98 and 1900–1902) and helped enact the Anti-Mob Violence Act of 1896 as well as the Civil Rights Act.[31]

During the 1890s, however, Smith picked the wrong side in the political battle that was shaping up in the Ohio Republican party. He broke with the Hanna machine and found himself increasingly alienated from the main sources of political power. At the same time, Smith's attacks on those Negroes who supported Hanna drove a wedge between himself and much of the old elite in Cleveland. He twice attempted to organize anti-Hanna Negro Republican groups, but failed both times. In 1898 Jere Brown reassured John P. Green that the local Hanna-McKinley organization was "sufficiently united to meet and defeat the little Gaz[ette] man at every turn." Wrote Charles W. Chesnutt to Green, "Poor Smith is neither a prophet nor the son of a prophet, and from the

[30] Cleveland *Gazette*, December 7, 1895, May 2, 1914, January 31, 1914, February 14, 28, 1920, January 27, 1917, January 18, 1890; Cleveland *Leader*, January 24, 1890; Elliott M. Rudwick, "The Niagara Movement," *Journal of Negro History*, 42 (July 1957), 179; National Association for the Advancement of Colored People, *First Annual Report, January 1, 1911* (n.p. [1911]), n.p.; Kellogg, *NAACP*, I, 48–49; Olsen, *Carpetbagger's Crusade*, 325.

[31] Cleveland *Leader*, September 12, 1899; "Harry C. Smith" (clippings in Wright Scrapbooks); Cleveland *Gazette*, May 9, 1896; Simmons, *Men of Mark*, 197; Leslie H. Fishel, Jr., "The Negro in Northern Politics, 1870–1900," *Mississippi Valley Historical Review*, 42 (December 1955), 477.

present indications, he will long have difficulty in making any number of people believe that he is." Smith's reelection to a third term in 1899 improved his political stature briefly, but after 1902 his influence in Cleveland's Negro community appreciably diminished. A friend of Green's remarked in 1904 that "from all accounts, Harry Smith is dead politically," and by then the editor was fairly well isolated from most of the city's black leadership.[32]

Once Smith had broken with the black Hanna Republicans, he moved toward a more independent brand of politics. As early as 1896 Smith had urged black voters to judge candidates on the basis of their attitude toward the needs of Afro-Americans, only to add quickly that "outside of the republican party our hopes are dead." But in 1902 the editor helped found the Interstate League of Independent Colored Voters, a midwest Negro organization which advocated political independence from the Republicans as well as a variety of municipal reforms. By the end of the decade Smith had become completely disenchanted with the GOP, and he was particularly infuriated by Theodore Roosevelt's handling of the Brownsville affair. He urged blacks to register their protest against Republican policies by voting against Taft in 1908, and the following year he endorsed a Negro Democrat for local office and refused to support the Republican mayoral candidate. Smith's movement toward political independence ended, however, with Woodrow Wilson's administration, and by 1916 he had returned to the Republican party.[33]

Few race leaders at the turn of the century were as vigorous as Smith in the struggle for equality, and none could match the editor's ideological consistency. In spite his dynamism, however, the militant editor lacked two essential qualities of leadership: the ability to compromise and the capacity to delegate authority. He exposed his egotism and con-

[32] Jere A. Brown to John P. Green, March 13, 1898; Charles W. Chesnutt to Green, December 7, 1897; J. L. Todd to Green, March 6, 1904; George A. Myers to Green, July 26, 1904, Green Papers. On the rift between Smith and the rest of Cleveland's black leadership, see also Thomas W. Fleming, "My Rise and Persecution" (manuscript autobiography, Western Reserve Historical Society [1932]), 18–19; James Taylor to John P. Green, January 14, 1897; E. E. Cooper to Green, November 25, 1898, Green Papers; correspondence of Ralph A. Tyler and George Myers, 1897–1900, Myers Papers; Siebert, "George A. Myers," 64.

[33] Cleveland *Gazette*, August 22, 1896, October 31, 1908, May 15, September 11, 1909; Detroit *Free Press*, October 24, 1902 (clipping in Walter L. Brown Papers, Western Reserve Historical Society); Cleveland *Journal*, October 24, 31, 1909; *Platform and Constitution Adopted at the Second Annual Conference of the Interstate League of Independent Colored Voters* [Cleveland, 1903]; Ann J. Lane, *The Brownsville Affair: National Crisis and Black Reaction* (Port Washington, N.Y., 1971), 82.

tentiousness in the pages of the *Gazette* by continually referring to himself as "the Hon. Harry C. Smith" long after he had ceased to hold office, by quoting flattering copy from other race papers, and by carrying on personal vendettas against individuals whom he disliked.[34] Jere Brown not unjustly described Smith as "little big head" and related that the editor imagined himself "as large as any statesman the world has ever produced." These unfortunate traits made it difficult for Smith to work with race organizations, even those which he had personally helped create, and it separated him further from a Negro elite which would not have wished, under any circumstances, to take the militant stance that the editor demanded. Smith's personality became less palatable to the voters as well: he ran for a fourth term in the state legislature in 1914 but lost in the primary. After the Great Migration, the shrill voice of the *Gazette* continued, as insistent as ever—but fewer and fewer bothered to listen.[35]

For all his militancy, Smith usually remained within the Republican fold. It remained for Walter L. Brown to become the first prominent Cleveland Negro to actively and consistently support the Democratic party. Brown grew up in Tennessee and attended Knoxville College; he served as a deputy sheriff and justice of the peace in Hamilton County before migrating to Cleveland in 1893. After arriving in the Forest City, Brown pursued an erratic career. For a while he was a house painter, then a streetcar motorman, later a city employee and part-time lawyer. During the 1890s, Brown became enmeshed in Republican politics and served for a while on the executive committee of the county organization of black Republicans. A firm integrationist, Brown attacked those Negroes who "would have us as a race build up more separation than the whites have yet thought of," and he twice brought suits against discriminatory business establishments in the city. One is not sur-

[34] At least part of Smith's later dislike for Thomas W. Fleming, for example, can be traced to Fleming's establishment of a competitive race paper, the *Journal*, in 1903. (See Cleveland *Journal*, October 3, 10, 17, 24, 1907.) Smith, of course, was not the only black leader of the Progressive era who too easily fell into a stance of carping criticism of other prominent blacks. As Nancy J. Weiss has pointed out, rivalry and envy affected black leaders at both the national and local levels and often hindered the progress of race organizations. A chief cause of this spirit of contentiousness, Gunnar Myrdal noted in 1944, is the fact that "power and prestige are scarce commodities in the Negro community," and the struggle for leadership is consequently often intense. Nancy J. Weiss, "From Black Separatism to Interracial Cooperation: The Origins of Organized Efforts for Racial Advancement, 1890–1920," in Barton J. Bernstein and Allan J. Matusow, eds., *Twentieth-Century America: Recent Interpretations*, 2d ed. (New York, 1972), 64–65; Myrdal, *An American Dilemma*, II, 775.

[35] Cleveland *Gazette*, August 15, 1914.

prised to find that Brown once shared a law office with Charles Sutton.[36]

Perhaps because of his strong integrationist stance, perhaps because he found the path to success within the local GOP blocked by men like George Myers and John P. Green, Brown gradually withdrew his allegiance from the Republicans. In 1897 he was known as a straight "party man"; within five years, however, he had deserted the party regulars and had allied himself with the rebellious Smith. In the fall of 1902 he became one of the founders of the Interstate League of Independent Colored Voters. Finally, Brown broke completely with the GOP, formed a black Democratic club to support Mayor Tom L. Johnson, and became the club's first president.[37]

During the next ten years, Brown worked assiduously for the Democrats, and Johnson awarded him for his initiative by giving him a job with the city as a brick and cement inspector. But if Brown hoped to build a power base in Cleveland within the Democratic party, his move was badly timed. The policy of segregation in federal departments adopted by Woodrow Wilson's administration kept most black voters securely in the Republican ranks; and locally the tide also ran strongly against the Democracy after Johnson's last term as mayor ended in 1909. Brown narrowly missed election as a justice of the peace in 1910 and failed to win election to the state legislature six years later. His consolation during Newton D. Baker's term as mayor (1911–15) was a clerkship in the street-cleaning department.[38]

Undoubtedly, Brown's failure to advance politically played a part in the next strange turn in his career: his active involvement in the Spiritualist Church, an emotionally charged religious sect that became popular with ghetto dwellers during the Great Migration. By 1914 Brown had become deeply engrossed in the Spiritualist movement, and the following year he was ordained a minister and established the first Spiritualist congregation in Cleveland, the Lake City Church. Brown continued to

[36] Cleveland *News*, February 5, 1909 (clipping in Brown Papers); Cleveland *Gazette*, August 11, 1906, January 30, May 15, 1909; Walter L. Brown to George A. Myers, October 5, 189[7]; Brown to Myers, October 6, 1897, Myers Papers. A business card in the Brown Papers identifies Brown and Sutton as partners.

[37] Detroit *Free Press*, October 24, 1903; Cleveland *Leader*, October 27, 1903 (clippings in Brown Papers); Cleveland *Gazette*, May 31, October 25, 1902; Cleveland *Plain Dealer*, October 27, 1903; *Platform and Constitution Adopted at the Second Annual Conference of the Interstate League of Independent Colored Voters* [Cleveland?, 1903], 1–6.

[38] Cleveland *Gazette*, May 15, November 6, 1909; Cleveland *Plain Dealer*, February 1, 1909, December 17, 1912, August 9, 1916; William J. Finley to Walter L. Brown, September 22, 1908; William Davis to Brown, October 19, 1908, Brown Papers.

maintain an active interest in Democratic politics, but after World War I religion became his major preoccupation.[39]

Most of the older leadership group in Cleveland's black community shared a number of characteristics. They had migrated from the Upper South but had spent most of their lives in Cleveland; they had close business and social relationships with whites, had attended integrated schools and had lived in integrated neighborhoods; they had risen to a much higher socioeconomic position than their parents.

This common pattern of career and life-style made these individuals natural proponents of integration. Between 1900 and 1915, however, some members of this older leadership group were modifying their ideological stance and making concessions to the Washington doctrine of self-help and racial solidarity. This trend was evident even in so firm an integrationist as Chesnutt, who just prior to the wartime migration was beginning to qualify his previous hard-line opposition to separate black institutions. In 1914 Chesnutt agreed to support a social settlement on Central Avenue only if it was to be a biracial facility; but he was aware that, because of its location, the settlement might become all-Negro in the future. Chesnutt also gave a nodding approval to the Phillis Wheatley home shortly after it was founded and wrote to a white philanthropist that he found it "well conducted and serving a very useful purpose." This change in attitude was important, because it showed that at least some members of the old elite were seeing beyond their own life-styles to the extent that they recognized the usefulness and even the necessity (given the trend of increasing residential segregation) of some separate race institutions to aid the masses of blacks living in the city. After the Great Migration, the need for these institutions would become even more evident, and very few black leaders would continue to oppose them on principle.[40]

[39] Sandusky (Ohio) *Register*, September 13, 1914 (clipping in Brown Papers); Cleveland *Advocate*, June 26, 1915, March 25, December 30, 1916; Walter L. Brown to the Board of Trustees of the NSA [National Spiritualist Association?], September 4, 1915, Brown Papers. A scrapbook Brown left behind is filled with newspaper accounts, stories, poems, and so on, relating to the Spiritualists.

[40] Charles W. Chesnutt to A. T. Hills, February 18, 1914, Chesnutt Papers, Fisk. Apparently the old elite in Boston was undergoing a similar shift toward accommodationism at this time. John Daniels noted in 1914 that "a majority of the Negroes who were formerly in the forefront of the equal-rights agitation have substantially modified their views. . . . Most of the earlier leaders in that agitation no longer take part in it with their pristine vehemence, and have grown to be at least tolerant of the prevailing [accommodationist] attitude. Some, while not abandoning their belief in the importance of constant activity by the Negro to safeguard his rights, have become convinced that tactics less precipitate and more conciliatory

This shift in thought among some of the older leadership group was accompanied by a growing ambivalence toward Booker T. Washington. When Chesnutt visited Tuskegee in 1901, he was "impressed" and "realized for the first time what a really great work Washington was doing for the Negroes in the black belt." Subsequently, in an exchange of correspondence with Monroe Trotter, Chesnutt told the editor that although he strongly opposed Washington's general philosophy and admired the *Guardian's* editorial stand, he could not "see my way to adopt the extreme position you have taken. His school has accomplished a great deal of good; I have been there and seen it. I am willing to approve the good, and when I disagree with him to preach the opposite doctrine strenuously." George Myers and Walter Wright also, upon occasion, expressed a certain admiration for Washington, even though their integrated way of life and general faith in integrated institutions gave them little cause to favor Washington's program. There are several possible explanations for this ambivalence. First, it is clear that the Tuskegeean's emphasis on the accumulation of property and economic mobility as a key to progress for the race struck a responsive chord with these black leaders, despite the fact that racial solidarity played no part in their rise from obscurity to relative affluence. Second, it is possible that the great disparity between their own socioeconomic condition and that of most blacks (especially those in the South) softened their attitude toward Washington. "In a social system which forces Negroes to think of themselves *first* as Negroes and only second as Americans," sociologist St. Clair Drake notes, "a problem of 'double identification' is posed for those who are partially integrated. Guilt feelings sometimes arise over the charge hurled by others that they are 'running away from the Race.'" Some of the Negro elite must have realized that few black Americans enjoyed the opportunities they had in Cleveland. The resulting sensitivity about their own fortunate position might well have precluded an open attack on Washington and instead have inculcated a grudging admiration for a man who, after all, was struggling in the South against much harsher circumstances than they had to deal with in Cleveland.[41]

Clearly the most important cause of the ambivalence of these black

---

in character are better adapted to that purpose, and have at the same time openly committed themselves to the substance of Washington's position." Daniels, *In Freedom's Birthplace*, 128. If accurate, this observation is yet another example of the close parallel in the development of the black communities of Cleveland and Boston.

[41] Charles W. Chesnutt, "A Visit to Tuskegee," Cleveland *Leader*, March 31, 1901; Chesnutt, *Charles Waddell Chesnutt*, 159, 192; St. Clair Drake, "The Social and Economic Status of the Negro in the United States," in Talcott Parsons and Kenneth B. Clark, eds., *The Negro American* (Boston, 1967), 35.

leaders, however, was the changing racial climate of the times. As discrimination became more noticeable in Cleveland (even if it did not touch the elite very much) and as the racial caste system crystallized in the South, they began to see some validity in the racial advancement program of Booker T. Washington. They seldom abandoned the philosophy of integration and equal rights as an *ideal*, but for some it was becoming clear that—especially in the South—this ideal was not going to be realized in the foreseeable future. Under these circumstances, it is not surprising that sensitive individuals like Chesnutt were uncertain and confused as they confronted an extraordinarily difficult racial situation.

In their tactical approach to the problems of racism and discrimination, the integrationist leaders of the black community became steadily more conservative during the prewar years. Although a distinct minority carried forth the protest tradition of an earlier day, most of these black leaders were not very forceful in their approach to the question of racism, and some sought to avoid the issue of discrimination altogether.

One cause of this lack of militancy was the close relationship of some members of the old elite to the Republican party. Between 1890 and 1915 Ohioans were particularly prominent in national politics, and the steady flow of patronage into the Buckeye State made several Cleveland Negroes intensely loyal to the GOP. Men like John P. Green and Jere Brown were aware that their upward economic and social mobility depended upon the success of the Republicans. They realized that it was not through militancy but through the cultivation of amicable relationships with leading whites that they had been able to maintain their privileged position; and as the GOP grew more conservative, so did they.[42]

A second and more important factor was the awareness among the older leadership group of their superior position in the social order compared to other blacks and the generally superior status of race relations in Cleveland compared to other parts of the country. In his sociological study *Protest and Prejudice*, Gary T. Marx notes that a lack of exposure to "southern values" is usually conducive to increased militancy among blacks. But many members of the old elite in Cleveland *had* been exposed to such values: they either had been brought up in the South, had visited there, or had kept in contact with other Negroes who lived in the South. Comparing that region with Cleveland, it is not surprising that

[42] The favorable position of Ohio blacks, especially during the 1890s, often occasioned envy among black office-seekers in other states. "Are you Ohio people going to take all the good things Major McKinley has to give," T. Thomas Fortune asked John P. Green after the Republican victory of 1896, "or are you going to give us poor devils in New York a chance?" Fortune to Green, January 9, 1897, Green Papers.

they found little to complain about in the Forest City. On the whole, the old elite fought vigorously for civil rights only when they felt some cherished aspect of their own life-style threatened. Even such a basically conservative Negro as John P. Green battled to prevent the Ohio legislature from enacting a bill that probably would have ended Cleveland's tradition of integrated schools. But the old leadership group seldom found such defensive posturing necessary.[43]

The more successful members of the old leadership found themselves in a paradoxical situation. Interaction with whites and reliance on white economic support made these Negro leaders generally amenable to the philosophy of integration; but their very economic success made them cautious and conservative and placed limitations on their ability to defend and advance their own principles. Prominent Negroes like George Myers and Walter Wright might desire racial equality and an end to discrimination; but had they become militant race leaders they would have risked alienating themselves from the respectable white elite who were the key to their economic status and social prestige. Had Cleveland's white leaders been as supportive and as racially liberal as they had been during the Civil War era, the close relationship that these black leaders had with them would have presented no problems. At one time, whites had applauded—even encouraged—black leaders who spoke out and fought for equality. But the paternalism of a Mark Hanna was not the same as the egalitarianism of a Joshua Giddings, and it is quite unlikely that Myers's barbershop would have become such a famous gathering place for white politicos if its proprietor had become actively involved in the struggle for civil rights. Among the socially prominent leaders of the old elite, only Charles Chesnutt spoke out strongly from time to time on the question of racism. Perhaps Chesnutt's lack of involvement in the political scene gave him more freedom in this regard. Even Chesnutt, however, avoided becoming too closely involved with the radicals. Both he and, especially, George Myers preferred to act behind the scenes, dealing with influential white friends, when they attempted to eliminate some of the more blatant examples of racism in the city. By dealing with the white power structure in this manner, these black leaders accomplished some good, but their sphere of action in countering racial discrimination was also sharply curtailed as a result.

[43] Gary T. Marx, *Protest and Prejudice: A Study of Belief in the Black Community* (New York, 1967), 52, 76; Green, *Fact Stranger than Fiction*, 186–88; Cleveland *Gazette*, September 15, 1894. A similar point is made by Larry Cuban, "A Strategy for Racial Peace: Negro Leadership in Cleveland, 1900–1919," *Phylon*, 28 (Fall 1967), 299–310, and by Kelly Miller, "Negro Migration," Pittsburgh *Courier*, July 7, 1917 (clipping in Brown Papers).

It is interesting to note that the most militant of the integrationist leaders—Harry C. Smith, Charles Sutton, and Walter Brown—were not among the most socially prominent members of this group; and although they undoubtedly had many contacts with whites, they were not tied in a paternalistic manner to white patrons or a white employer. These individuals were free to speak out vigorously because their socioeconomic position was not threatened by doing so. Smith, for example, had little to lose by criticizing the Republican party, since he had already, by 1900, alienated himself from the main sources of power in the Ohio GOP.

II

After 1900 the leadership of men like Chesnutt, Myers, and Smith began to be challenged by a new group of black businessmen and politicians who relied primarily upon Negro patronage for their success. This new group of leaders tended to be less educated and less articulate than their predecessors; many of the new elite, in fact, left no record of their ideological or political beliefs. Their actions, however, spoke for them. The fact that they were self-made men who relied chiefly upon black patronage showed their implicit faith in Booker Washington's philosophy of economic self-help and racial solidarity. Even those blacks who disagreed with Washington on many issues could sympathize with the plight of Negro businessmen during a period of increasing white hostility. "Nicholas Davis," Harry C. Smith admonished his readers in 1911, "has a first-class bakery at 2905 Central Avenue. All who patronize him will attest this fact. Why not patronize an energetic, competent, and obliging member of the race, when he is in business? 'Help one another' should be our slogan." Such sentiments made the new elite possible.[44]

As in the case of Cleveland's old elite, leaders among the new elite were not always ideologically consistent. There was a strong *tendency* among the new elite to favor the accommodationist approach to racial problems, and many members of the new leadership group were unequivocal in their support of the Washington doctrine. Others were aware that the smaller size of Cleveland's black community made the self-help ideology less practicable than elsewhere, and they were unwilling to always support segregated institutions or to completely deprecate protest or agitation.

It was in the pages of the Cleveland *Journal*, a Negro weekly published between 1903 and 1912, that the ideology of the new elite was stated in its most conservative and pristine form; and the general temper

[44] Cleveland *Gazette*, January 7, 1911.

of the paper was at opposite extremes from the militant rhetoric of the *Gazette*. (The Cleveland *Advocate* also appealed to the new elite to some extent, but since the paper did not begin publishing until 1914, a discussion of its ideological position will be left to Chapter 11.) The *Journal* was established by three leaders among the new elite, Thomas Fleming, Welcome T. Blue, and Nahum D. Brascher. Throughout most of its existence the paper was edited by Brascher, a real estate and advertising man who was a strong supporter of the Tuskegee philosophy of racial solidarity and self-help. Brascher grew up in a small Indiana town. After attending college in Zanesville, Ohio, he migrated to Cleveland at the end of the 1890s and remained there until the end of the Great Migration period, when he moved to Chicago to become an editor of the Associated Negro Press. Under Brascher's guidance, the *Journal* soon became a popular advertising medium for local race businesses.[45]

The conservative temper of the *Journal* was evident in the slogan on its masthead: "Labor Conquers All Things." The paper featured appeals for self-help among Negroes and vignettes of black Horatio Algers who had, through hard work and perseverance, achieved economic success. "To become recognized as a factor in this great land," the *Journal* editorialized in 1903, the Afro-American "must . . . become thoroughly established in the commercial field; he must become a man of tact and ability. . . . [The Negro's] great fault has been in his lack of business tact and in his failure to keep up with the times." As might be expected, the *Journal* looked to Booker T. Washington for leadership. When Washington came to Cleveland in 1910, the paper applauded the philosophy of the "Wizard of Tuskegee" and condemned the "'slap back,' 'indignation' spirit" of Harry C. Smith and other militant integrationists.[46]

Many of the smaller black businessmen on Central Avenue probably subscribed without question to Washington's belief in building a "group economy" through black support of black businesses. The limited size of the city's Negro population, however, forced more ambitious black entrepreneurs to seek out white customers as well as black.

Garrett A. Morgan was one of the leading success stories among the new elite. Born in a small town in Kentucky in 1879, Morgan came to

[45] Cleveland *Gazette*, December 7, 1901, August 11, 1906; Cleveland *Journal*, May 9, September 12, 1903; Fleming, "My Rise and Persecution," 16; Cleveland *Advocate*, August 7, 1915; Chicago Commission on Race Relations, *The Negro in Chicago: A Study of Race Relations and a Race Riot* (Chicago, 1922), 563; David A. Gerber, "Ohio and the Color Line: Racial Discrimination and Negro Responses in a Northern State, 1860–1915," (Ph.D. dissertation, Princeton University, 1971), 292–93.
[46] Cleveland *Journal*, April 11, 1903, April 16, 23, 1910.

Cleveland in 1895 and began his career by sweeping floors in a factory at five dollars a week. He was eventually able to set himself up in a small clothing store on Central Avenue; by 1914 he had invested his profits from this enterprise in the far more lucrative business of manufacturing hair products and cosmetics for Negroes. Only part of Morgan's economic success, however, was based on the Negro market. Morgan was also an inventor (he designed one of the early prototypes of the automobile turn signal), and some of the items that his factory in Cleveland manufactured—such as a new type of safety helmet for firemen—clearly were not oriented toward the Negro market.[47]

The most successful legitimate businessman among the new elite was S. Clayton Green. Many of Green's enterprises, such as the Alpha Theater and various real estate ventures, were Negro-supported. But even Green sometimes found that the theory of racial solidarity, though good psychology, was bad economics. Two of Green's business undertakings, the People's Drug Store and the Clayton Grocery Store, both founded in 1906, folded within five years due to insufficient support from black customers. An incident involving Green in 1909 revealed the limitations of the self-help ideology in Cleveland's prewar black community. In what was surely one of the most unusual civil rights cases in the city's history, Walter L. Brown sued Green and his partner when a Central Avenue roller rink which they operated refused to admit Brown. Originally the rink had been planned as an all-Negro enterprise, but because of the lack of black patronage Green had tried to entice white customers by setting up "white only" nights twice a week. Brown eventually won the suit (the lawyers for the defense had lamely tried to prove that Brown did not know how to roller skate, and therefore was not entitled to admission!), but the mere establishment of such a strangely inverted Jim Crow policy showed that ultimately Green was less committed to racial solidarity than to the profitable business venture.[48]

Another prominent business leader among the new elite was J. Walter Wills. A native of southern Ohio, Wills came to Cleveland in 1899 after graduating from Antioch College. In 1904 he became a co-director of a Central Avenue funeral home. A few years later Wills and his sons erected their own funeral home, and by 1920 he had established himself as the city's leading Negro undertaker. Wills actively supported the theory that economic self-help was the key to black progress. In 1905 he founded the black Businessmen's League, a Cleveland affiliate

[47] Cleveland *Advocate*, July 24, 1915, March 4, 1916, June 9, 1917.
[48] Gerber, "Ohio and the Color Line," 411–12; Cleveland *Gazette*, January 30, May 15, 1909.

of Booker T. Washington's National Negro Business League, as a means of organizing black economic power in the community. "The Anglo-Saxon People will not refuse our money," Wills argued in defense of an early version of black capitalism, "but they will look upon us with contempt and ridicule when we continue to spend it with their own business firms and allow our own [businesses] to suffer."[49]

Unlike S. Clayton Green, whose chief pastime was devising new entrepreneurial schemes, Wills played a prominent role in Negro community life. He worked with church and charitable organizations and for several years was active in the Cleveland branch of the NAACP, the local affiliate of the Urban League, and other organizations. Perhaps because he was college-educated and had lived his entire life in the North, Wills was less conservative than some members of the new elite; several times he helped bring suits against Cleveland theaters which discriminated against Negroes. At the same time, however, Wills did not find it inconsistent to support the all-Negro Phillis Wheatley home.[50]

Members of the new elite, no less than the old, took an active interest in Republican politics; their strategy in pursuing public office, however, was quite different from their predecessors. In the late nineteenth century, black politicians like John P. Green, Jere Brown, Harry C. Smith, and others were able to win nomination and election to the state legislature because they represented certain factions in the Ohio Republican party. To some extent, of course, their election to office over Democratic opponents signified the extent of racial liberalism among Cleveland's white voters. But these black politicians would not even have won a place on the ballot unless they had been chosen by the white politicos who controlled the party nominating conventions. During the prewar years, however, two changes occurred that would, in the long run, transform black politics. First, increasing racial prejudice made black candidates less appealing to white voters. This fact alone might not have led to a precipitate decline in black office-holding, since whites might still have preferred to support black Republicans over white Democrats. But the substitution, beginning in 1907, of the direct primary for the convention system allowed white voters to exercise their prejudicial im-

---

[49] Cleveland *Journal*, March 25, 1905, July 28, 1906; Cleveland *Gazette*, November 27, 1909; Davis, *Memorable Negroes in Cleveland's Past*, 45.

[50] Cleveland *Gazette*, April 22, 1905, November 27, 1909; [Pamphlet Committee of the Cleveland Association of Colored Men,] *Summary of the Work Done by the Cleveland Association of Colored Men* (n.p. [1914]), n.p.; *Historical Sketch and Financial Report of the Cleveland Association of the Home for Aged Colored People . . . from July, 1893 to July, 1908* (n.p. [1908]), 7; Julian Krawcheck, "Society Barred Negroes—They Formed Own Groups," Cleveland *Press*, May 30, 1963.

pulses in the Republican primary, and often effectively prevented black candidates from even getting on the ballot in the November elections. (Between 1900 and 1920, H. T. Eubanks, a barbershop proprietor at a well-known hotel, was the only black Clevelander to win election to the state legislature. Eubanks was elected twice, serving during the years 1904–6 and 1908–10.) Under these circumstances, black politicians among the new elite turned to the task of building a secure political base within the developing ghetto, and their first successes would be in local politics rather than at the state level.[51]

One of the most persistent office-seekers among the new leadership was William R. Green, the elder son of John P. Green. Born in 1873, the younger Green attended Central High School, studied law with his father, and was admitted to the bar in 1894. Early in the twentieth century Green (and undoubtedly other members of the aspiring leadership group) chafed under the control which George Myers exercised over the city's black Republicans. He privately criticized Myers's "arrogant and important manner" and confided to his father in 1904, "I can, and I don't brag . . . influence ten votes to one for him." The death of Mark Hanna undercut Myers's political influence and opened the door to younger Negro politicians in Cleveland. Green's political career, however, proved as unsuccessful as his father's had been rewarding. He ran for a city council seat in 1909, for state representative in 1910 and 1912, and for municipal judge in 1927, and lost every contest, although he came close in the last effort. Like his father, Green was a cautious man; although he participated in several local race organizations, he consistently avoided identifying himself with the activist element in the black community.[52]

William Green divided his time between politics and the law. Thomas

---

[51] On the negative effects of the direct primary in Detroit, see David M. Katzman, *Before the Ghetto: Black Detroit in the Nineteenth Century* (Urbana, 1973), 203–4. The only other black Clevelander to win election as a state representative before 1920 was William H. Clifford, a lawyer who served two terms in the 1890s.

[52] Columbus *Vindicator* (undated clipping, c. 1898, in Myers Papers); William R. Green to John P. Green, February 6, 1904; Green to John P. Green, May 28, 1904; Theodore B. Green to John P. Green, September 12, 1909, Green Papers; Cleveland *Gazette*, November 12, 1910, August 8, 1914, February 17, 1923, May 21, November 27, 1927; *Summary of the Work Done by the Cleveland Association of Colored Men*, n.p. It is interesting to note that John P. Green's younger son, Theodore B. Green, who was also a lawyer, took much more interest in civil rights than either his father or brother. The younger Green took a strong stand against the creation of a black YMCA in 1911 and helped bring suits against discriminatory proprietors in Cleveland. His death in 1917 cut short a career of great promise. See Cleveland *Gazette*, February 1, April 18, 1908, October 15, 1910, January 21, February 4, 1911; Green, *Fact Stranger than Fiction*, 356.

W. Fleming, Green's chief competitor for many years, pursued political office more single-mindedly; and this may explain why he succeeded where Green failed. Like many members of the new elite, Fleming was proud of his lowly origins. Born in Mercer, Pennsylvania, in 1874, Fleming experienced severe poverty during his early years after his father deserted the family. The young Fleming was trained as a barber, and in 1892 quit school and journeyed to Cleveland, where he quickly found employment in a Euclid Avenue barber shop. Within two years Fleming and another black barber accumulated sufficient capital to set up their own shop. At the age of twenty-one, Fleming was already a successful businessman.[53]

Aware that barbering was no longer the path to upward mobility that it had once been for blacks, Fleming stayed in the trade for only a decade before taking a law degree and moving into the ranks of the professions. At the same time, he was slowly building a political base in the community. At first Fleming was a follower of Harry C. Smith, but he broke with the editor when Smith's "Progressive League" (a group of local Negro Republicans) opposed a Hanna candidate for state office in the mid-1890s. During the next twenty-five years Fleming was careful not to offend the white power structure; he worked assiduously to mobilize the black vote for the Republican party and received political favors and organizational support for his own candidacy in return. In 1903 he organized the Twelfth Ward Republican Club to "combine and solidify the Afro-American voters" living there and three years later founded the Attucks Republican Club, a citywide organization that soon became the Negro branch of the white Republican machine in Cleveland. Between 1903 and 1909, Fleming tried unsuccessfully to gain election to City Council; undoubtedly Democratic ascendancy during that period (Tom L. Johnson was mayor from 1901 to 1909) of the city's history was partly responsible for his failure. But in 1909, with the aid of Republican boss Maurice Maschke and with an enlarged black electorate behind him, Fleming became Cleveland's first black councilman. "It proved to me," Fleming said glowingly of the election, "that Cleveland, Ohio, was the Garden Spot for anyone who chose to rise, no matter what his nationality." The former barber failed to win reelection in 1911 and during the next four years, ironically, held Harry C. Smith's old patronage post as deputy state inspector of oils. In 1915 Fleming was once again elected to the council from the newly redrawn Eleventh Ward, and he served in that capacity until 1929.[54]

[53] Fleming, "My Rise and Persecution," chs. 1, 2.
[54] *Ibid.*, 10–38, 39, 42–100; Cleveland *Journal*, May 2, 1903, November 9, 1907,

Fleming's growing power in the black community was partly based on his control of the small amount of patronage that was allotted the black community by the Maschke machine. In 1916 he appointed seventy Negroes to replace whites as election officers in the Eleventh Ward and secured a number of positions for Negroes as clerks and assistant supervisors in several city departments. Fleming's rise, however, was not due solely to such traditional political methods; for his career was inextricably intertwined with that of the notorious black prostitution and gambling lord Albert D. ("Starlight") Boyd, who helped finance Fleming's campaigns and in turn received political favors from the black councilman.

Starlight Boyd (he reputedly derived his name from the large diamond ring he wore) was the greatest success story among the new black leaders who were coming into prominence in the early twentieth century. Because his success was based on illegitimate activities, however, Boyd was hardly recognized as a "leader" by polite Negro society. He was, in the phrase of Drake and Cayton, an "upper shady," a man whose underworld activities were acknowledged but deplored by the respectable middle and upper strata of the black community. Born in 1872 in a small town in rural Mississippi, Boyd left home while still in his teens and arrived in Cleveland, penniless and alone, in the late 1880s. For ten years he worked for a white Ontario Avenue hotel proprietor, first as a handyman, later as a bookkeeper and clerk. Boyd saved his money and invested in real estate that later became valuable, and this gave him the stake he needed to begin operations on Central Avenue. Although the figure was probably quite exaggerated, Boyd was reputed to have left an estate valued at $200,000 when he died in 1922.[55]

Few would have disagreed with Jane Edna Hunter's description of Boyd as "suave, impressive, impervious to shame, . . . gifted with the art of leadership, a born political henchman. . . ." During the first decade of the twentieth century, Boyd allied himself with Maurice Maschke, and the "Starlight Cafe," a Scovill Avenue saloon owned by the black racketeer, soon became the center of political activity in the black community. Fleming and Boyd soon joined forces. During the World War I era it was no secret that the city administration allowed vice to flourish in the Central Avenue district; and, as chairman of the committee over-

November 6, 1909; Cleveland *Gazette*, February 16, 1929. Fleming's later career is discussed in Chapter 11.

[55] Fleming, "My Rise and Persecution," 47–49; Cleveland *Plain Dealer*, November, 1922 (clipping in Scrapbook 1, Chester K. Gillespie Papers, Western Reserve Historical Society). See also St. Clair Drake and Horace R. Cayton, *Black Metropolis: A Study of Negro Life in a Northern City* (New York, 1945), 524–25, 546–50.

Charles Waddell Chesnutt

John P. Green

Harry C. Smith

Jere A. Brown

The staff of George A. Myers's Hollenden Hotel barber shop during the 1896 presidential campaign. Myers's large barber shop, considered one of the finest in the country, was in existence until his death in 1930.

Guests at the Fifth Annual Charity Ball of the Cleveland Association of Colored Men, January 26, 1914. The charity ball and the Caterers' Club annual banquet were the most important social events in Cleveland's black community.

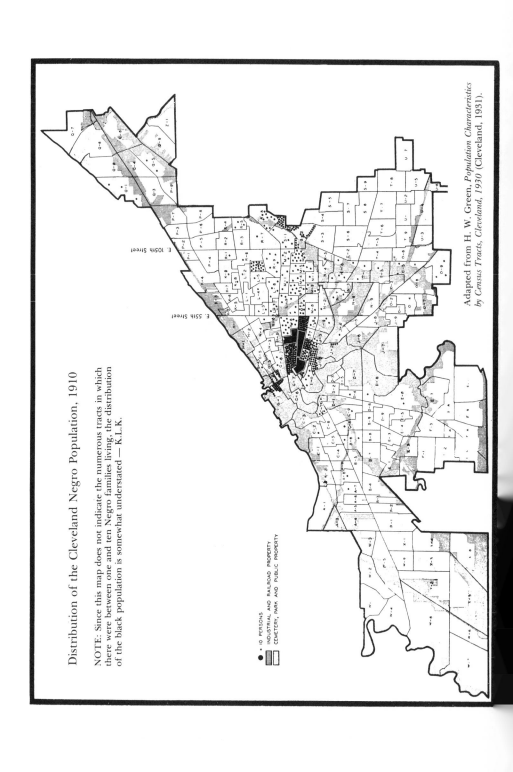

Distribution of the Cleveland Negro Population, 1910

NOTE: Since this map does not indicate the numerous tracts in which there were between one and ten Negro families living, the distribution of the black population is somewhat understated — K.L.K.

- • 10 PERSONS
- ▨ INDUSTRIAL AND RAILROAD PROPERTY
- ☐ CEMETERY, PARK AND PUBLIC PROPERTY

E. 105th Street

E. 55th Street

Adapted from H. W. Green, *Population Characteristics by Census Tracts, Cleveland, 1930* (Cleveland, 1931).

Distribution of the Cleveland Negro Population, 1930

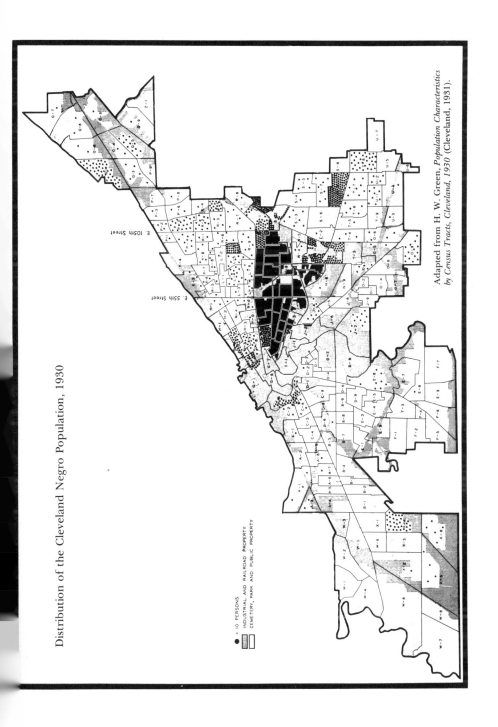

E. 105th Street

E. 55th Street

• = 10 PERSONS

INDUSTRIAL AND RAILROAD PROPERTY

CEMETERY, PARK AND PUBLIC PROPERTY

Adapted from H. W. Green, *Population Characteristics by Census Tracts, Cleveland, 1930* (Cleveland, 1931).

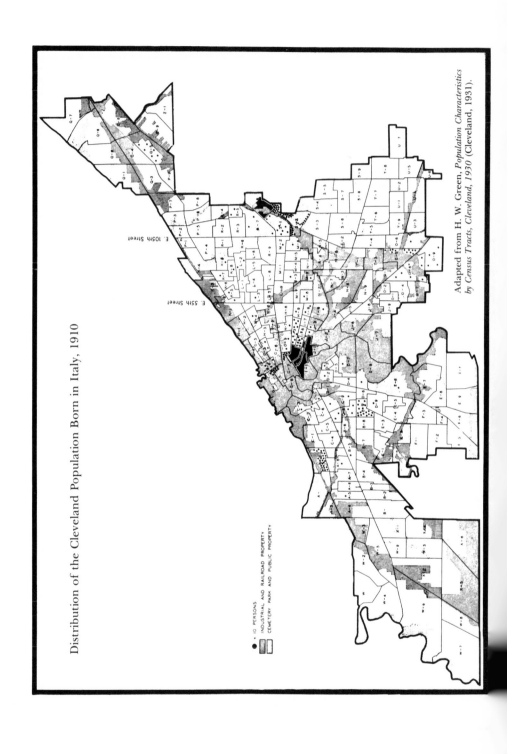

Distribution of the Cleveland Population Born in Italy, 1910

E. 105th Street

E. 55th Street

• = 10 PERSONS

INDUSTRIAL AND RAILROAD PROPERTY

CEMETERY PARK AND PUBLIC PROPERTY

Adapted from H. W. Green, *Population Characteristics by Census Tracts, Cleveland, 1930* (Cleveland, 1931).

Distribution of the Cleveland Population Born in Italy, 1930

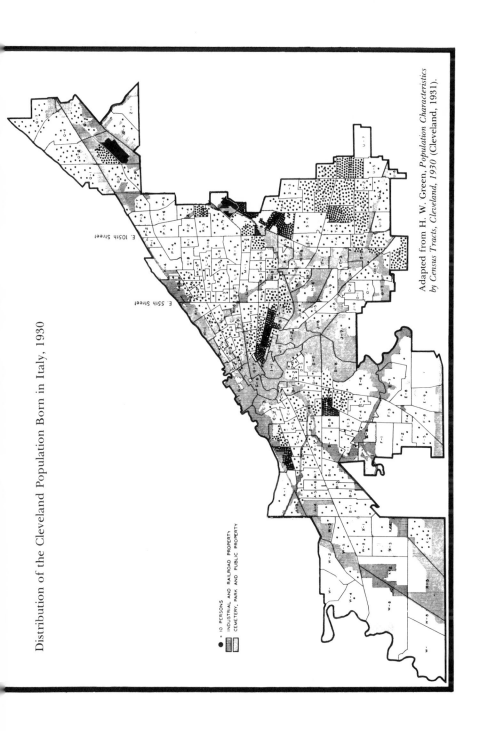

E. 105th Street

E. 55th Street

• = 10 PERSONS
INDUSTRIAL AND RAILROAD PROPERTY
CEMETERY, PARK AND PUBLIC PROPERTY

Adapted from H. W. Green, *Population Characteristics by Census Tracts, Cleveland, 1930* (Cleveland, 1931).

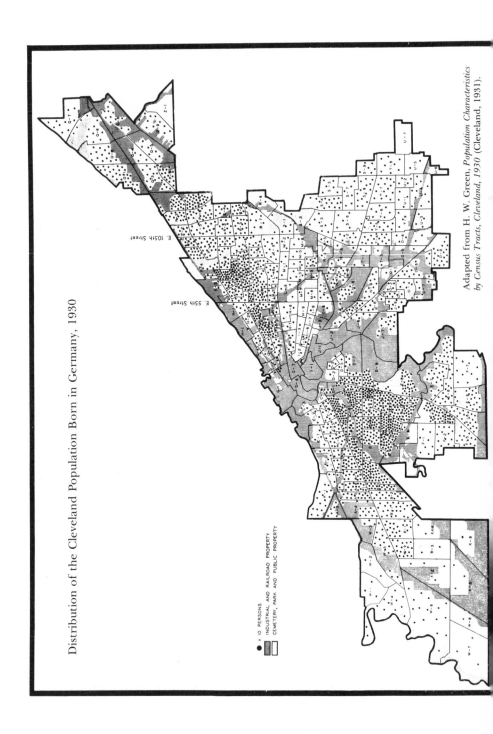

Distribution of the Cleveland Population Born in Germany, 1930

= 10 PERSONS
INDUSTRIAL AND RAILROAD PROPERTY
CEMETERY, PARK AND PUBLIC PROPERTY

E. 105th Street

E. 55th Street

Adapted from H. W. Green, *Population Characteristics by Census Tracts, Cleveland, 1930* (Cleveland, 1931).

seeing the police and fire departments, Councilman Fleming was in an ideal position to offer protection to some of Boyd's more unsavory "businesses." After Fleming and Boyd cemented their alliance, vice conditions in the developing black ghetto became more entrenched than ever. "New dives and brothels opened all around us," Jane Hunter later recalled, and "all attempt at concealment was abandoned. . . ."[56]

Too little is known about Starlight Boyd to assess his ideological position—although his wife's participation in the Phillis Wheatley Association and the committee that ran the Home for Aged Colored People and Boyd's financial support of these facilities would seem to indicate his general support of all-black institutions. Thomas Fleming, however, was an ardent admirer of Booker T. Washington, whom he described in his unpublished autobiography as "a great leader of his people." This accolade was appropriate, for no member of the new elite had better exemplified the Tuskegee philosophy of self-help and racial solidarity than had Fleming. He had risen from poverty to a position of power and relative affluence by mobilizing the black electorate behind him. Race pride and the promise of a share of the spoils of office were the issues which reelected Fleming seven consecutive times to the council. "Men of both races," the black councilman bragged in 1915, "thought it was impossible for a Negro to be elected to the city council from any ward. But the Negroes of the Eleventh ward have proved that it was not impossible."[57]

Fleming was a strong believer in the value of all-Negro institutions, and he was an early backer of the Phillis Wheatley Association. He viewed his own career as an example of what black unity could achieve. Yet his early successes were, in retrospect, indicative of the ambiguous position of the new elite during the prewar era. Fleming's original contacts with white politicians in Cleveland probably occurred as a result of his being in the barbering trade—an old-elite occupation that Fleming left only after he had used it to his own advantage. More important, Fleming's first elections in 1909 and 1915 were by no means the clear-cut victory for the principle of racial solidarity that Fleming later portrayed them as being. In 1909 the black councilman was elected to an at-

[56] Cleveland *Gazette*, November 27, 1909, June 8, 22, 1910; Fleming, "My Rise and Persecution," 47–49; Hunter, *A Nickel and a Prayer*, ch. 11.

[57] Fleming, "My Rise and Persecution," 42; Cleveland *Advocate*, November 13, 1915, January 22, March 11, 1916. Fleming was one of the founders of the Phillis Wheatley Association and at one time served as president of the Cleveland Association of Colored Men. Minutes of the Phillis Wheatley Association, February, 1913, Phillis Wheatley Association Papers; *Summary of the Work Done by the Cleveland Association of Colored Men*, n.p.

large seat with an electorate spread over several wards; he needed many white votes to win, and he would hardly have gotten them without the strong support of the white Republican machine. The 1915 election was more clearly the product of black unity, but even then the Eleventh Ward had more white voters than Negro, and Fleming profited from machine support and an excessive disunity among his white opponents in the primary. As in the case of S. Clayton Green, Fleming discovered that racial unity was necessary but not sufficient to his personal success.[58]

III

The limitations of the self-help ethic and the need to compromise it in practice was also evident in the movement to create Negro institutions in Cleveland.

With the exception of lodges and social clubs, the earliest example of an institution sponsored by Negroes for nonreligious purposes was the Cleveland Home for Aged Colored People. The idea for the home originated in 1893 with a group of Negro women, led by Eliza Bryant, an old resident of the city. It took this group three years to raise the necessary funds to purchase a house, but in 1896 the first indigent residents were admitted. With meager support from the black community, the CHACP remained a small and poorly financed institution during the first two decades of its existence. In 1908 the home had a balance of only $163 in its treasury; three years later the *Gazette* reported that the old folks' residence was in such poor repair that it was "almost falling down." The creation of a men's auxiliary and the assistance of the Cleveland Federation of Charity and Philanthropy helped the CHACP better meet its expenses, and in 1914 the trustees purchased a new, slightly larger building on Central Avenue; but at the end of the year they had been able to pay off only a tenth of the $15,000 mortgage.[59]

[58] For a further discussion of the role of individuals like Fleming in the black political subsystem, see Chapter 11 and Martin Kilson's valuable survey, "Political Change in the Negro Ghetto, 1900–1940's," in Nathan I. Huggins, Martin Kilson, and Daniel M. Fox, eds., *Key Issues in the Afro-American Experience* (New York, 1971), II, 167–92.

[59] Essie Brown to John P. Green, September 12, 1896, Green Papers; Cleveland *Journal*, April 25, 1903; W. E. B. Du Bois, ed., *Efforts for Social Betterment among Negro Americans*, Atlanta University Publications, no. 14 (Atlanta, 1909), 76; *Historical Sketch and Financial Report of the Cleveland Association of the Home for Aged Colored People*, 4–9; Cleveland *Gazette*, February 11, 1911, February 21, 1914; Cleveland Home for Aged Colored People, *Eighteenth Annual Report* (n.p., 1914), 3–4; Cleveland *Advocate*, November 6, 1918; "Official Records [of] the Men's Auxiliary to the Home for Aged Colored People, Cleveland, Ohio [1909–1918]" (notebook in Lethia C. Fleming Papers, Western Reserve Historical Society).

No member of the black community opposed the home for the aged. A plan to counter the growing discrimination in the Cleveland YMCA by creating an all-Negro branch, however, stirred up considerable controversy. The idea for an all-Negro Y was first advanced by Nahum Brascher in 1906, but it was not until 1910 that a movement for such an institution got firmly under way. Most of the new elite endorsed Brascher's proposal as a useful example of race solidarity and self-help, while the Old Guard almost to a man (with the notable exceptions of John P. Green and Jere Brown) protested the establishment of such an institution as a step down the road to segregation. Harry C. Smith, as might be expected, was particularly vocal in his criticism; he attacked the proponents of the black YMCA for attempting to build an institution from which they and their friends would gain jobs and prestige. Blacks, the editor insisted, should "be trying to wipe out color-lines, rather than be trying to multiply them." As it turned out, Smith had little to fear: in 1911 the YMCA movement died out. But its defeat—the boasting rhetoric of the *Gazette* notwithstanding—signified less a triumph for integrationism and the old leadership than a pragmatic facing of economic realities. Cleveland's black community was barely large enough to support a home for the elderly; in 1910 the creation of a second secular community organization was only a pipe dream in the minds of the new elite. New York's first Negro YMCA (there were three by 1915) dated to 1899, and in 1911 black Chicagoans quickly raised $65,000 toward the construction of what became "the largest and finest [YMCA] building for colored men in the United States." It would not be until after the Great Migration, however, that Cleveland's Negroes were able to create a similar, smaller facility of their own.[60]

During the prewar era, the only major secular institution created solely for Negroes was the Phillis Wheatley Association, a residence and job-training center for girls who had come to the city on their own or who were separated from their families for some other reason. The association was founded in 1912 by Jane Edna Hunter, a black professional nurse who was determined to find "ways and means of ameliorating the hard lot of homeless girls." Hunter was an admirer of Booker T. Washington and felt that a more self-sufficient black community was the

[60] Cleveland *Journal*, October 6, 1906, March 5, 1910; Cleveland *Plain Dealer*, February 1, 1911; Cleveland *Gazette*, March 9, 1910, January 21, February 4, 1911, February 14, 1914; Gilbert Osofsky, *Harlem: The Making of a Ghetto* (New York, 1966), 15; Channing H. Tobias, "The Colored Y.M.C.A.," *Crisis*, 9 (November 1914), 33, quoted in Spear, *Black Chicago*, 101. In 1914 a movement to establish an all-Negro children's home in Cleveland also failed. Cleveland *Gazette*, August 8, 1914.

answer to increasing white hostility. She viewed the struggle for integration as misguided:

> Too often, alas, has the Negro been misled by leaders of his own race. There are those false prophets who would persuade us that some day the Negro will be absorbed by the white race. What the Negro really desires is a change of industrial and economic status so that he may enjoy the privileges and culture that other men possess. By thorough and complete miscegenation we should lose our richest heritage. The Negro must continue to make his distinct contribution to the world—as a Negro.

The Phillis Wheatley Association met with opposition from one segment of the black community, and the ensuing dispute was one of the chief examples of ideological conflict between the old and new elite. Harry C. Smith was a vociferous opponent of the PWA (he once labeled it a "jim-crow hotel" for black girls) and continued to denounce it for years as the first step down the road to institutional segregation. The main opposition, however, came from "a small group of club women who, blessed with prosperity, had risen from the servant class and now regarded themselves as the arbiters and guardians of colored society." The aloofness of these members of the old upper class from the city's black masses and their unawareness of the increasing discrimination which the average Negro faced was evidenced by the naïve criticism of one of the "club women": ". . . we will not permit you, a Southerner," she said to Jane Hunter, "to start segregation in this city." Another elite black woman remarked in a similar patronizing vein: "We call on the white people, and the white people call on us. Now that the more intelligent of us have broken down the barriers between the races, you are trying to build them up again with your absurd Southern ideas for working girls."[61]

The founders of Phillis Wheatley gradually overcame these critics, converted most of the Negro ministers of the city to their side, and launched their enterprise. Financing the new organization was another matter. The PWA started with literally "a nickel and a prayer," and by 1914 Jane Hunter realized that white philanthropy would be a necessity if her dream was to become a reality. Henry A. Sherwin, the head of the Sherwin-Williams Paint Company, agreed to help finance Phillis Wheatley, but only on the condition that certain prominent white women

[61] Hunter, *A Nickel and a Prayer*, 84, 90–91, 94, 189; Cleveland *Gazette*, January 17, 1914, November 13, 1926. The association was named after Phillis Wheatley (1753?–84), who was brought from Africa to Boston as a slave in 1761, began writing poetry at the age of thirteen, and gained fame in America and England for her published work.

be named to the Board of Trustees. Jane Hunter found herself faced with a dilemma, however, when these women refused to serve unless they were allowed the right of choosing the Negro officers of the organization as well. "This," said Hunter, "created a delicate situation. I was faced with a choice between offending members of my own race who had given far more than they could actually afford, and yielding to influences which could give our organization a sound financial basis." Hunter reluctantly chose the latter. "It seemed necessary," she later related, "to sacrifice personal feelings for the sake of the cause."[62]

By 1916 170 girls were being housed yearly in Phillis Wheatley, and many more were using its facilities. To achieve this, however, Hunter had been forced to jettison the principle of black control of a community institution. Though billed as such by its black supporters, Phillis Wheatley was hardly an example of black self-sufficiency during its early years. The organization was almost entirely financed by whites. But more important was the fact that the direction of the institution at the beginning was strongly influenced by a group of upper-class white women who knew little about the needs and interests of recent southern migrants. In addition, some of these women probably had ulterior reasons for backing the organization. There was a direct relationship between the creation of Phillis Wheatley and the movement to exclude black girls from Cleveland's YWCA. Harry C. Smith claimed that the whites who supported the PWA did so to head off a movement to keep the local Y integrated. George Myers, in a less conspiratorial explanation, asserted that Phillis Wheatley was "fostered by a few misguided whites endeavoring to relieve their consciences of the discrimination by the YWCA against our women." In either case, one of the latent functions of Phillis Wheatley, with its facilities for lodging, board, and recreation, was to keep blacks out of the YWCA. It was certainly no coincidence that Mrs. Levi T. Schofield, the white woman who became the first president of the Board of Trustees of the PWA, was also head of the city's YWCA at the time when that organization began its discriminatory policy.[63]

Unlike the Phillis Wheatley Association, the Cleveland Association of Colored Men was a racial advancement organization that caused no dispute in the black community. The CACM, founded in 1908, was primarily sponsored by the new elite, although a few of the city's older

[62] Hunter, *A Nickel and a Prayer*, 99–100.
[63] *Ibid.*, 93–94, 104; Harry C. Smith, "Some 'Phillis Wheatley' History," Cleveland *Gazette*, May 14, 1927; *ibid.*, March 28, 1928; George A. Myers to Booker T. Washington, July 20, 1914, Myers Papers; minutes of the Phillis Wheatley Association, February 13, 1917, December 8, 1921, Phillis Wheatley Association Papers.

Negro leaders also took part. The popularity of the organization derived from the breadth of its activities: the CACM sponsored social events, inaugurated a lecture series, and launched several modest charitable projects in the black community. In addition, one of the avowed purposes of the organization was to take up the question "of discrimination in public places. . . ." At no time, however, did the CACM take a strong civil rights stance; typically, the association "investigated" cases of blatant discrimination but took little concrete action. This accommodationism is not surprising, since William Green and Thomas Fleming were the most prominent leaders of the CACM during its early years and the organization contributed to several of Booker T. Washington's Tuskegee projects. The rather conservative nature of the association was revealed in its policy of holding the major black social event of the year (ironically dubbed the "Emancipation Celebration") at the usually whites-only Luna Park, a policy that Harry C. Smith repeatedly criticized to no avail.[64]

IV

In Cleveland, as in other northern black communities, the growth of the black population in the late nineteenth and early twentieth centuries promoted a shift in black leadership and led to the development of black institutions. But in several ways these developments did not duplicate patterns established elsewhere. On Chicago's South Side, for example, ideological conflict often developed when the rising new black leadership attempted to establish all-Negro institutions. In Cleveland, however, fewer separate institutions were proposed because the black population was too small to support them. The smaller size of the black community, combined with the absence (before 1915) of a clearly defined ghetto, made the business-oriented new black leadership less predominant in Cleveland than in Chicago. This, coupled with the growing conservatism of some black integrationists, kept the ideological differences between the two groups from breaking into the open too often. Nevertheless, hostility between the old and new elites was increasing during the decade before the Great Migration as more and more blacks began to support the idea of separate institutions.[65]

Regardless of their positions on purely racial questions, most black

[64] *Summary of the Work Done by the Cleveland Association of Colored Men*, n.p.; Cuban, "A Strategy for Racial Peace," 305; Cleveland *Gazette*, July 31, 1915.
[65] For a discussion of ideological conflict among black leaders in Chicago, see Spear, *Black Chicago*, 52–54, 84–89, and chs. 3 and 4, *passim*.

leaders adhered to a basically conservative view of social change. Whether they opposed or favored the creation of a separate, "group" economy, both the old elite and its challengers firmly believed that the "strive and succeed" ethic and the doctrine of economic individualism were applicable to the black experience in the United States. These black leaders—and, for that matter, blacks in general—did not participate very much in the new organizational, bureaucratic society that was beginning to emerge during the Progressive era. For that reason and, perhaps, because many of the black elite had through various means risen from poverty to middle-class respectability, they retained a faith in individualism and the free-enterprise system that sometimes bordered on naïvete; and their economic conservatism was bolstered by the growing racism of many labor unions.

Because of its smaller size, Cleveland's black community remained more dependent on white institutions and white financial support than did the black communities of cities such as New York, Chicago, and Philadelphia. There was no equivalent in Cleveland to Chicago's Provident Hospital, for example. Philadelphia's black community also had its own hospital (Douglass Memorial, founded in 1895); and as early as 1896 its Home for Aged Colored Persons had an annual income of $20,000 and property valued at $400,000. A survey of black life in New York in 1901 found "a successful building association, a hospital, an orphan asylum, and a home for the aged, all entirely conducted by Negroes, and mainly supported by them." The institutional development of Cleveland's black community lagged behind these larger metropolises.[66]

The experience of blacks in Cleveland was far from being unique, however. Early in the twentieth century there were many moderate-sized or small black communities in the North. In 1910, Detroit's black population was only 5,700; Newark's was 9,500; New Haven's only 3,600. Paterson, New Jersey; Albany and Buffalo, New York; and Gary, Indiana, all had black populations under 2,000. Although detailed studies of black leadership and institutional development in these cities during the Progressive era are lacking, it is highly probable that in many cases the tradition of black dependency that developed in Cleveland at this time found expression there as well. Actually, even in larger black com-

[66] W. E. B. Du Bois, *The Philadelphia Negro: A Social Study* (Philadelphia, 1899), 230, 231–32; Elliott Rudwick, "A Brief History of the Mercy-Douglass Hospital in Philadelphia," *Journal of Negro Education,* 20 (Winter 1951), 50–53; W. E. B. Du Bois, "The Black North," *New York Times Magazine,* November 24, 1901; Ovington, *Half a Man,* 171–80; Osofsky, *Harlem,* 67; Spear, *Black Chicago,* 91–105.

munities like Chicago and Philadelphia, blacks were frequently unable to establish separate race institutions without at least some white assistance, and this assistance sometimes entailed white paternalistic involvement and hence a degree of white control. (This was especially true of the branches of the National Urban League, established in 1911; since the League did not gain prominence until after the wartime migration, however, a discussion of its role is left to a later chapter.) In the political sphere also, the patron-client relationship that developed between Cleveland's Republican machine and black councilman Thomas Fleming was duplicated in many cities of the North.[67] Only in the wake of the Great Migration, with the consolidation of the ghetto and intensification of racism that accompanied it, would a more independent and assertive black leadership begin to emerge.

[67] Population data taken from U.S. Bureau of the Census, *Negroes in the United States, 1920–1932* (Washington, 1935), 55.

PART III

A Ghetto Takes Shape, 1915-30

CHAPTER 7

The Great Migration and the Consolidation of the Ghetto

Blacks had been coming north in a slow but steady stream since the Civil War. There was little precedent, however, for the huge exodus of southern migrants that accompanied the World War I era. While war raged in Europe, the inhabitants of northern black communities were undergoing their own traumatic experience as their numbers were swelled by the arrival of hundreds of thousands of newcomers. Between 1910 and 1920, Cleveland's black population increased 308 percent, Detroit's rose 611 percent, and Chicago's increased 148 percent; other cities experienced substantial, if smaller, gains. These cities were suddenly faced with the difficult task of assimilating a large number of individuals who were, in most cases, uneducated and completely unaccustomed to urban surroundings. The responses of both the Negro and white communities to this problem helped shape and delimit the lives of northern Negroes for decades afterward.[1]

Like most mass movements, the causes of the Great Migration were many and varied. Dissatisfaction with race relations in the South undoubtedly played a part in motivating many Negroes to move. The violence of lynch mobs and the sharp discrimination in housing, schools, and the court systems in many southern communities were constant sources of grievance to blacks. The desire to "go North," however, involved more than an aversion to the racial prejudices of white southerners. In his invaluable 1932 study of black migrants from the South Caro-

---

[1] U.S. Bureau of the Census, *Negroes in the United States, 1920–1932* (Washington, 1935), 55 (Table 10).

lina Sea Islands, Clyde Vernon Kiser indicated that one of the chief underlying causes of black migration from the region was what we would now call a "generation gap." Despite poor economic conditions, few blacks left the Islands between 1865 and 1890. "The Islanders of that time," Kiser explained, "had little besides their former slave condition by which to judge their economic status." After 1890, however, younger black residents of the Islands who had been born after the Civil War had a different perspective. They often viewed their condition as one of social and economic stagnation rather than (as their fathers had) one of improved circumstances. One migrant who left the Islands in 1911 at the age of nineteen put it this way: "Young people grow up now and say, 'I want to get 'way from heah. No diggin' in the sile fo' me. Let other man do the diggin'. I'm through with farmin'.'" In a similar vein, another migrant stated her distaste for the monotonous routine of farm life: "Got tired living on Island. Too lonesome. Go to bed at six o'clock. Everything dead. No dances, no moving picture show, nothing to go to. . . . That's why people move more than anything else." Said another migrant, "Young folks just ain't satisfied to see so little and stay around on farm all their lives like old folks did."[2]

However important such underlying motivations were, it is unlikely that they would have resulted in the extensive movement of population that occurred between 1916 and 1919, had immediate and powerful economic factors not intervened. Immigration to the United States, which had reached a high point in 1914, fell off drastically during the next four years and with it the supply of cheap labor which American manufacturers depended upon. The labor shortage became particularly acute because of the sudden demands placed upon industries for the production of war materials. The need for workers in the North coincided with a period of economic depression in the South. Many southern Negroes, of course, had been reduced to virtual peonage by the crop-lien and tenant-farm system that was introduced during and after Reconstruction. But the spread of the boll weevil throughout the South, ruining thousands of acres of cotton, and a series of floods in the Gulf States in 1915 made the lot of black farmers particularly hard. It was under these unusual circumstances that northern manufacturers began to realize the value of the black labor force as an "industrial reserve." Putting aside their doubts about the adaptability of black workers, northern industrialists began to send labor agents south to induce Negroes to migrate. More than a few blacks accepted the inducement of

[2] Clyde Vernon Kiser, *Sea Island to City: A Study of St. Helena Islanders in Harlem and Other Urban Centers* (New York, 1931), 117, 131, 144.

free train tickets and the promise of good jobs when they reached their destination.[3]

After a while, the migration became self-generating as news of the better life in the North circulated through southern black communities. "For the first time in American history," one contemporary historian noted, "opportunities, large in number, in skilled as well as unskilled labor, were offered to Negro workmen." Northern Negro editors, gleeful over the inability of the white South to stop the migration, urged southern blacks to take advantage of the unusual economic situation. "To ask the colored people to remain" in the South, the editor of the *Gazette* exclaimed, "depending upon the people who have destroyed them in the past to aid them in the future, is sheer folly." Recent arrivals in the North wrote home to relatives telling of the high wages they were receiving. "We are making good money here," one newcomer to Cleveland wrote in 1917. Although wages in the South averaged between $1.10 and $1.25 per day in many instances, in Cleveland he could earn three times that amount—or more. He explained (in the semiliterate style typical of many immigrants), "I have made as hight at 7.50 per day and my wife $4 Sundays my sun 7.50 and my 2 oldes girls 1.25 but my regler weges is 3.60 fore 8 hours work." In February, 1917, the city employment Bureau in Cleveland was receiving an average of fifty to sixty letters a day from southern blacks seeking jobs. By spring hundreds of migrants were arriving each week, and the *Gazette* reported that newcomers were "vainly 'running the streets' in the Central Avenue vicinity, seeking rooms last week worse than ever before, two carloads more having arrived from the South, Sunday evening. . . ." The Cleveland *Advocate* caught the drama of the situation. "There is no mistaking what is going on," the paper editorialized at the end of April, "it is a REGULAR EXODUS. It is without head, tail, or leadership. Its greatest factor is MOMENTUM, and this is increasing, despite amazing efforts on the part of white southerners to stop it. People are leaving their homes and

[3] Charles H. Wesley, *Negro Labor in the United States, 1850–1925: A Study in American Economic History* (New York, 1927), 290–92; Louise Venable Kennedy, *The Negro Peasant Turns Cityward* (New York, 1930), 42–48; Emmett J. Scott, *Negro Migration during the War* (New York, 1920), 13–15 and *passim*; U.S. Department of Labor, Division of Negro Economics, *Negro Migration in 1916–17* (Washington, 1919), 17–18, 86–87; George Edmund Haynes, "Negroes Move North," *Survey*, 40 (May 4, 1918), 115–22; Chicago Commission on Race Relations, *The Negro in Chicago: A Study of Race Relations and a Race Riot* (Chicago, 1922), 80–84, 357–65; Roi Ottley and William J. Weatherby, eds., *The Negro in New York: An Informal Social History* (New York, 1969), 188. See also the recent study by Florette Henri, *Black Migration: Movement North, 1900–1920* (New York, 1975), 47–62.

everything about them, under cover of night, as though they were going on a day's journey—leaving forever." The Great Migration was under way.[4]

The annual number of migrants to Cleveland prior to 1916 was small compared to other northern cities, but during and after the war the Forest City became one of the principal destinations of Negroes leaving the South. The city's black population increased from 8,448 in 1910 to 34,451 in 1920, a gain of 26,003. It is likely that about three-quarters of this increase was due to migration from the South between 1916 and 1919. Thus the black community, which numbered no more than 12,000 in 1916, had to accommodate an increase of over 20,000 during a single three-year period. By March, 1919, this wave of migrants had temporarily slackened. A railroad office in Cleveland reported that the number of newcomers from the South had fallen off sharply and that some of the recent arrivals, unable to find work because of the postwar business slump, were returning to their native states.[5]

With the return of prosperity after 1920, migration quickly resumed. During the 1920s, Cleveland's black population more than doubled; by 1930 there were almost 72,000 Negroes living in the city (see Table 1). It is likely that over one-half of this new increase occurred between 1921 and 1924; the acceleration of business activity during those years brought a new wave of seventeen to twenty thousand blacks to the city. It is fair to say, then, that the twenties—especially the first half of the decade—in many ways represented a continuation, rather than a curtailment, of the crisis engendered by the Great Migration of 1916–19. Population growth did gradually diminish between 1920 and 1930, but the influx of migrants during that period was still so large that the assimilation of newcomers into the urban setting remained a continuing problem.[6]

[4] Wesley, *Negro Labor in the United States*, 282; Cleveland *Gazette*, February 10, April 21, 1917; Scott, *Negro Migration during the War*, 17; Emmett J. Scott, comp., "Additional Letters of Negro Migrants of 1916–1918," *Journal of Negro History*, 4 (October 1919), 460–61; minutes of the Board of the Negro Welfare Association, March 19, 1918, Cleveland Urban League Papers, Western Reserve Historical Society; Cleveland *Advocate*, April 28, 1917.

[5] Cleveland *Gazette*, March 15, 1919. There is no way to ascertain the exact number of migrants who came to the city during and immediately after the war. Allan Spear estimates that 50,000 of the approximately 61,000 Negroes who migrated to Chicago between 1910 and 1920 came during the 1916–20 period, and I have followed his analysis in computing figures for Cleveland. See Spear, *Black Chicago: The Making of a Negro Ghetto, 1890–1920* (Chicago, 1967), 140–41.

[6] This estimate is based on elementary school enrollment figures compiled in Howard W. Green, *A Study of the Movement of the Negro Population of Cleveland* (Cleveland, 1924), 1–5. In April, 1921, there were 5,078 Negro children in city

Before World War I a large minority of the city's black residents had been born and raised in Cleveland. This element of demographic stability was ruptured by the Great Migration, however, and between 1910 and 1920 the proportion of Cleveland Negroes born in Ohio fell precipitously from 35.7 to 16.9 percent. A shift in the origins of migrants was also evident. Before the war, most of the Afro-Americans who came to Ohio (no breakdown by city is available for 1920) from other states had been born in the Upper South or the border states, and less than 5 percent had listed the Deep South as their place of birth. During World War I, migrants from Kentucky and Tennessee continued to come to Ohio in substantial numbers, but over 50 percent of the increase in Ohio's Negro population between 1910 and 1920 was due to migration from the Deep South. (See Table 24 in Appendix II.) The data on migration into Ohio gives only a rough indication of the nativity of migrants to Cleveland between 1910 and 1920. The census statistics for 1930, however, which give a breakdown by city, indicate that the Ohio figures for 1920 accurately reflect the origins of black migrants to Cleveland during the war. In 1930, Cleveland had far more black migrants from Georgia and Alabama than from any other state outside Ohio.[7]

The new migration accelerated the process of residential segregation which had already begun in Cleveland before World War I. Between 1910 and 1920, the number of census tracts containing no Negroes at all rose from seventeen to thirty-eight. At the same time the migrants began to crowd into neighborhoods where Negroes had previously been only a minority of the population. In 1910 no census tract in the city was greater than 25 percent Negro, but ten years later ten tracts exceeded that figure, and two tracts had become more than 50 percent black (see Table 13). The pattern of increasing concentration of the

---

elementary schools; in October, 1923, there were 7,430, an increase of 2,352 during that two-and-one-half-year period. If these statistics reflect the growth of the Negro population as a whole, then it seems likely that the black community grew by about 50 percent during this period. Most of this growth can be attributed to migration into the city. The correlation between school statistics and the entire population, however, is of limited accuracy because there was some natural increase and, more important, because many of the migrants were single and hence did not bring children; it is probable, then, that the 50 percent figure is an underestimation of the amount of migration between 1921 and 1924. For a more detailed discussion of the use of such statistics, see Elliott M. Rudwick, *Race Riot at East St. Louis, July 2, 1917* (Carbondale, Ill., 1964), 163–65. On the general resurgence of migration in the early 1920s, see "Southern Negroes Again Moving," *Opportunity*, 1 (January 1923), 19, and "Negro Labor Moves Northward," *ibid.*, 1 (May 1923), 5–6.

[7] U.S. Bureau of the Census, *Negroes in the United States, 1920–1932*, 32, 34–37. (The title of this volume is somewhat misleading, since it contains some data for 1910 as well as later years.)

TABLE 13. *Distribution of Negroes by census tracts, Cleveland, 1910–30*

Percentage Negro[a]	Number of census tracts[b]		
	1910	1920	1930
None	17	38	47
1–2	114	92	100
2–5	9	11	11
5–10	8	10	7
10–20	5	6	6
20–30	1	6	5
30–50	0	5	4
Over 50	0	2	17

SOURCE: Howard W. Green, *Population Characteristics by Census Tracts, Cleveland, 1930* (Cleveland, 1931), 160–65.
[a] The percentages for several of the tracts are estimates, because the Census Bureau statistics for two or more tracts were sometimes combined.
[b] The number of tracts increased from 158 in 1910, to 185 in 1920, and to 208 in 1930.

black population in certain areas continued during the early 1920s. This is clearly revealed by enrollment figures for Cleveland elementary schools. Between April, 1921, and October, 1923, there was a gain in black enrollment of 2,352 students. Almost all of this increase (2,287 students, or 97.5 percent) occurred in schools which were already 5 percent or more black—in areas, in other words, where the black population had already gained a foothold. At the same time the number of all-white elementary schools increased from 17 to 30 (out of a total of 112), and several schools experienced substantial declines in black enrollment as Negro families moved out of predominantly white neighborhoods.[8]

During the Great Migration, the area west of East 55th Street between Euclid Avenue and the Cuyahoga River absorbed most of the new-comers; Census Tracts H-7, H-9, I-2 through I-8, J-1, and J-2 recorded the largest gains in Negro population between 1910 and 1920. At the same time, a smaller but still significant number of Negroes had crossed the East 55th Street boundary and were beginning to fill in areas where a few scattered black families (usually members of the elite) had settled before the war. The Negro enclaves to the north of Hough Avenue (Tract L-6) and to the east of East 105th Street (Tract S-2) grew slowly during the wartime migration. Few Afro-Americans moved into other parts of the city, despite the huge influx of migrants, and the West Side remained almost solidly white. Most significant, by 1917 a few all-Negro neighborhoods had begun to emerge in the Central Avenue district.

[8] Green, *A Study of the Movement of the Negro Population of Cleveland*, 1–5, 14.

Though only a few blocks in size at the time, these black areas were portents of future developments. Kelly Miller, visiting the city at the height of the wartime migration, observed that it was possible for an individual, by standing on the right street corner, to "imagine himself in the heart of Hayti or Liberia. The segregated sections are as sharply meted out as if cut by a knife." In the midst of a city that had once been proud of its integrationist tradition, a black ghetto was taking shape.[9]

The inexorable trend toward segregation continued throughout the 1920s as blacks moved into the area between Euclid and Woodland avenues in larger numbers. Enclaves of Russian immigrants (most of whom were probably Jewish) and Italians in that part of the city which had resisted Negro encroachment as late as 1920 now suddenly gave way. Tracts I-8 and I-9, for example, were almost 60 percent Russian in composition in 1920; ten years later Russian immigrants constituted less than 5 percent of both tracts. The Italian immigrants, who had shared the oldest sections of the city with Negroes for two decades, proved more tenacious; and as a result some neighborhoods near Central Avenue remained integrated even after 1920. Nevertheless, a significant exodus of Italians was also evident. In 1920 four tracts in the Central-Woodland area were, respectively, 61, 54, 48, and 41 percent Italian. By 1930 the proportion of Italian immigrants in these tracts ranged from 13 to 34 percent.[10]

Prior to World War I, the tendency toward residential segregation that was exhibited by Cleveland's black population was shared by several of the city's immigrant groups. Italian and Romanian immigrants were actually more segregated from the dominant native-white population than were Negroes in 1910, and Hungarians and Russians also tended to settle within fairly well restricted sections of the city. Although specific data on the population distribution of Polish, Czech,

[9] Kelly Miller, "Negro Migration," *Pittsburgh Courier*, July 7, 1917 (clipping in Brown Papers). See Tables 12 and 25 and maps between pp. 146 and 147.

[10] Howard W. Green, comp., *Population Characteristics by Census Tracts, Cleveland, 1930* (Cleveland, 1931), 23–27 (maps showing location of Russian and Italian immigrants, 1910–30), 216–23. As late as 1928, in surveying conditions in a number of northern cities, Thomas J. Woofter could state that "Almost without exception the groups which are most heavily mixed [residentially] with Negroes in the North are Jewish and Italian." Woofter et al., *Negro Problems in Cities* (Garden City, N.Y., 1928), 39. By that time, however, the physical separation of blacks from these white ethnic groups was already well under way. In 1930, in most northern cities, the segregation of Italian and Russian immigrants from blacks was almost as great as that of other ethnic groups. See the segregation indexes computed for nine cities by Stanley Lieberson in his *Ethnic Patterns in American Cities* (Glencoe, Ill., 1963), 209–18.

and Slavic immigrants do not exist for the period before 1920, it is likely that these groups also had a rather high degree of spatial isolation.[11]

Between 1910 and 1920 this demographic pattern underwent a subtle but significant change. The segregation of foreign-born whites from native whites, which had been increasing for several decades before World War I, now receded to some extent. The index of dissimilarity for native whites v. all foreign-born whites declined during this period from 36 to 31 (see Table 14). To be sure, several immigrant groups con-

TABLE 14. *Index of dissimilarity, selected immigrant groups with native whites and Negroes, 1920; and change in index, 1910–20*

| | Index, 1920 | | Change in index, 1910–20 | |
	Native whites	Negroes	Native whites	Negroes
Italians	52	50	−24	−16
Germans	19	78	− 2	+ 4
English	18	68	+ 1	+11
Hungarians	46	76	+ 1	+ 4
Irish	23	72	− 5	+ 5
Russians	45	46	− 7	−16
Romanians	54	48	−11	− 6
Swedes	35	72	− 5	+ 7
Poles	48	78	NA	NA
Czechoslovakians	45	81	NA	NA
Yugoslavians	56	84	NA	NA
All foreign-born whites	31	68	− 5	+ 2

SOURCE: U.S. Bureau of the Census, *Fourteenth Census, 1920, Population* (Washington, 1922), I, 801–2.
NOTE: NA indicates data not available.

tinued to have moderately high rates of segregation; and they would continue, for several decades to come, to live for the most part within fairly distinct (though not completely homogeneous) ethnic neighborhoods. But the declining segregation rates of the three ethnic groups which had been most isolated geographically before the war—the Italians, Romanians, and Russians—was a clear indication that even the poorer, more recent immigrant communities were beginning to undergo the process of residential dispersion that had already affected the Irish, German, and English populations of the city.

At the same time that the immigrant population of the city was becoming generally more dispersed, however, the black community was becoming ever more concentrated. Between 1910 and 1920, the index of

[11] See Chapter 2.

dissimilarity between Negroes and native whites increased from 61 to 70; the index for Negroes v. all foreign-born whites rose from 66 to 68. Although comparable data on residential segregation is lacking for 1930, it is clear that no diminuation of the trend toward the concentration of the black population of Cleveland occurred during the intervening ten years. When the black community expanded during the twenties, it did so not by diffusing throughout the city (as did the native whites, the Germans, the Irish, and the English) or by moving out to newer, smaller ethnic areas in better sections of the city (as did many Italians), but by filling in areas contiguous to the already existing black neighborhoods along Central and Scovill. On the eve of the Great Depression, at least 90 percent of the city's Afro-Americans lived within a region bounded by Euclid Avenue on the north, East 105th Street on the east, and Woodland Avenue to the south.[12]

Prior to World War I, suburban growth in Cuyahoga County had been rather slow. In fact, during the last three decades of the nineteenth century, Cleveland had continued to grow in size by annexing nearby towns and unincorporated areas. When voters in several suburbs rejected annexation proposals in the early 1900s, however, it signaled the rise of a new feeling of independence among suburbanites. During the 1920s, the suburbs encircling Cleveland, though still small in size compared to what they would become after 1945, expanded at a dynamic pace compared to the central city. While Cleveland's population during that decade increased only 11 percent, Cleveland Heights grew by 234 percent and Garfield Heights by 511 percent. Shaker Heights, one of the most rigorously planned suburbs in the nation, had a phenomenal growth rate of 1,000 percent. Few blacks were able to join this exodus from the metropolis. White hostility and an economic barrier (most of the early suburbanites were upper middle class or above) kept over 97 percent of Cuyahoga County's black population within Cleveland. In 1930, Charles W. Chesnutt reported that "only a few families not obviously Negroid" had been able to establish themselves in Shaker, Garfield, or

---

[12] Unfortunately, the size of the areal units available for measuring the index of dissimilarity changes drastically from 1920 (wards) to 1930 (census tracts); this change has some effect on the index and thus makes any direct comparison between 1920 and 1930 impossible. (See Karl Taeuber and Alma Taeuber, *Negroes in Cities: Residential Segregation and Neighborhood Change*, Chicago, 1965, 220–31, for a theoretical discussion.) It is clear, however, from the data and maps in Green, comp., *Population Characteristics by Census Tracts, Cleveland, 1930*, that there was some tendency toward dispersal among major white ethnic groups in the city during the 1920s. For a discussion of the dispersal and regrouping of the Italian population of Chicago after World War I, see Humbert Nelli, *The Italians in Chicago, 1880–1930: A Study in Ethnic Mobility* (New York, 1970), 204–11.

Cleveland Heights. At that time only fifteen Negro families altogether lived in those three communities. Ten Negro families resided in East Cleveland and six in nearby Euclid. Western suburbs proved even less hospitable to blacks; in 1930 Lakewood had but three black families and the rapidly growing community of Parma none at all.[13]

The increasing concentration of the black population exacerbated the housing problem faced by black Clevelanders. Even before the war, blacks had encountered difficulties in obtaining suitable lodging. During the Great Migration, however, the housing shortage in the black community reached crisis proportions. In the spring of 1917 the arrival of thousands of migrants was already having its effect. Harry C. Smith noted that the "local boarding and rooming houses are packed" with migrants, and complained that it was "distressing to meet daily numbers of these people almost begging to stop and house their families, even temporarily." In August, 1917, the secretary of the Cleveland Real Estate Board reported the need for an additional ten thousand housing units to take care of the newcomers, and the *Gazette* stated that many migrants were "living in old railroad cars, abandoned buildings, shacks, under tents. . . ." Landlords openly took advantage of this situation by charging black tenants higher rents than whites. "Our people," charged Smith in 1918, "are being asked EIGHT AND TEN DOLLARS A MONTH more rent for rooms and houses than white people, or our people, paid for the same a year ago. . . ." The local Urban League affiliate reported that one black family was paying almost one-third more for rent than white tenants occupying similar suites in the same building, and the *Advocate* declared angrily that, in the face of increased demand, owners were "raising their rents all the way from 25 to 75 percent. . . ." It was all too easy to take advantage of the uninitiated newcomers, and one Negro complained that "some landlords raise rents in houses occupied by white people to get rid of them, and then make a higher charge to colored tenants." A survey conducted by a committee of the Cleveland Chamber of Commerce in 1918 verified these claims. Negroes, the committee discovered, paid 65 percent more for comparable housing than did whites. The average monthly rent for white workers in the city was $13.12; the average for Negroes $22.50.[14]

---

[13] Charles W. Rawlings and Lyle E. Schaller, *Suburbanization of the Negro Population* (Cleveland, 1963), 1–2; Charles W. Chesnutt, "The Negro in Cleveland," *The Clevelander*, 5 (November 1930), 3; Charles N. Glaab and A. Theodore Brown, *A History of Urban America* (New York, 1967), 281; U.S. *Fifteenth Census, 1930, Population (Families)* (Washington, 1932), VI, 1046–49; interview with Russell Jelliffe, September 1, 1971.

[14] Cleveland *Gazette*, May 5, 12, August 18, 1917, May 11, August 17, 1918;

Some whites in areas close to the expanding ghetto were torn between their desire to resist the "Negro invasion" and the opportunity to make money by dividing their homes into kitchenette apartments and renting the "suites" to black migrants clamoring for a place to live. As one famous Negro resident of the city, Langston Hughes, sardonically put it, "the white neighborhoods resented Negroes moving closer and closer—but when the whites did give way, they gave way at very profitable rentals." The promise of monetary gain, however, did not always prove sufficient as a deterrent to white hostility. Few whites objected to blacks filling in the older areas of settlement on Central and Scovill avenues—a phenomenon that had been taking place at a slower rate even before the Great Migration. But when blacks began to move into all-white neighborhoods, white resistance, now accompanied sometimes by intimidation and violence, began to harden. Whites tried, of course, to exclude Negroes from neighborhoods through mutual understandings or restrictive covenants that denied (in theory) the owner of the house the right to sell to Afro-Americans. But if these methods failed, some whites were willing to adopt more drastic means to maintain the racial "purity" of their section of the city. In 1917 and 1919 gangs of whites attacked the homes of blacks on several occasions. In one case "windows were smashed with large stones, fence pickets torn off and the front porch smashed," in an effort by a white mob to convince a black family that they should leave the previously all-white neighborhood into which they had moved.[15]

White reaction was particularly hostile to those blacks who tried to establish themselves in the suburbs or in outlying sections of the city. When a black family attempted to occupy a home in Garfield Heights in 1924, they soon found their house surrounded by a mob of two hundred whites. A spokesman for the mob informed the occupants that they would have ten days to vacate; he returned a few days later and repeated the threat. When the purchaser, Arthur Hill, asked the mayor of Garfield Heights for protection, he received the response that the village could not afford to pay for police guards and that, furthermore, "colored people had no right to purchase such a nice home." The Cleveland

---

Cleveland *Plain Dealer*, August 4, 1917; Cleveland *Advocate*, August 18, 1917; Report of the Executive Secretary [of the Negro Welfare Association], May to August, [1918], April 9 to May 6 [1919], Cleveland Urban League Papers; Committee on Housing and Sanitation of the Cleveland Chamber of Commerce, *An Investigation of Housing Conditions of War Workers in Cleveland* (Cleveland, 1918), 12–15, 21.

[15] Langston Hughes, *The Big Sea* (New York, 1940), 27; Chesnutt, "The Negro in Cleveland," 3; Cleveland *Gazette*, September 8, 1917, July 5, 1919. The near-riots of 1917 and 1919 are discussed at greater length in Chapter 8.

branch of the NAACP intervened on Hill's behalf and attempted, for several months, to pressure the governor to investigate the case and provide protection for the Hill family. When this appeal also failed to bring about the desired result, the Hills decided to abandon their new home rather than face the continued threats of white mobs.[16]

When Dr. E. A. Bailey, a black physician, moved into a white neighborhood in the much more exclusive suburb of Shaker Heights, he encountered similar threats. Unlike Hill, Bailey refused to flee in the face of this intimidation. As a result, whites threw stones at his house, fired shots into it, and set his garage on fire. The mayor of Shaker Heights was somewhat more helpful than his counterpart in Garfield; he provided police protection almost immediately after the first incident of violence occurred. The Shaker Heights police, however, proved less than model law-enforcement officers. While guarding the Bailey home, they insisted on searching the black doctor and his family, as well as any visitors, whenever they entered or left the premises. Dr. Bailey was able to endure these harassments as well as the threats of some of his neighbors, but it took considerable personal sacrifice on his part to gain even the grudging toleration of the community in which he lived.[17]

Perhaps the most serious example of interracial conflict over housing occurred when Dr. Charles Garvin, one of the city's most prominent Negro residents, built a home in a neighborhood close to the border of Cleveland Heights. When whites learned in the fall of 1925 that the house was being constructed by a black man, they immediately circulated a handbill which warned blacks to stay out of their community or suffer the consequences of violent resistance:

> Be Sure to Read This.
>
> Certain niggers have recently blackmailed certain residents of the Cleveland Heights and other sections of the city. They are now trying to erect a house at 11114 Wade Park Avenue to blackmail us. But they will not. The residents of the Neighborhood will not give one cent to those blackmailers.

[16] "Resumé of Facts in Case of Intimidation of Mr. and Mrs. Arthur Hill" (typescript); James Weldon Johnson to Harry E. Davis, September 29, 1924; Davis to Johnson, October 1, 1924; Johnson to Davis, October 3, 1924; "Ohio Governor Fails to Assure Protection for Negro against Mob" (NAACP press release, October 24, 1924); Harry C. Smith to Herbert Selligmann [sic], November 1, 1924, Papers of the National Association for the Advancement of Colored People, branch files (Container G157), Manuscript Division, Library of Congress; *Crisis*, 29 (November 1924), 20.

[17] Clayborne George to Robert W. Bagnall, October 13, 1925; Bagnall to George, October 20, 1925, branch files, NAACP Papers; Cleveland *Gazette*, October 17, 1925; interview with Russell and Rowena Jelliffe, September 1, 1971.

Appoint your committees to oppose and eradicate this group of black gold diggers. Let them know we can duplicate [the] riots [that took place] in Tulsa, St. Louis, Chicago, and Baltimore.

Whites in the Wade Park development used every conceivable tactic in their attempt to keep Garvin out of the neighborhood. While the house was being built, they harrassed and threatened the workmen. Once construction was completed and the Garvins had occupied their new home, whites dynamited the house twice in an effort to force the black doctor to leave. The first bomb, luckily, only shattered a window, but the second did considerable damage to one section of the house.[18] Some of Garvin's friends, concerned for his own safety, urged him to move. "People are advising that he put up a 'For Sale' sign and *sell out,*" Garvin's sister, Mabel Clark, wrote to James Weldon Johnson shortly after the second bombing. But Garvin was determined to fight it out. As his sister told Johnson, "he has made a home for himself and will stay there[;] all he wants is to be let alone." During the summer of 1926, Garvin was anything but alone. Police officers were usually stationed outside his house; and when at one point they were temporarily withdrawn, a number of Garvin's friends (whites as well as Negroes) took on the burden of providing protection for the black doctor. This determined effort had, by the fall of 1926, broken the back of white resistance to Garvin's occupying his new home, and in March, 1927, Mrs. Clark could inform Johnson that "He and his family are living in their home, peacefully, and we are happy. . . ." But while the tactics of intimidation and violence again failed to achieve their purpose, the traumatic experience which the black doctor and his family went through must have given many Negroes second thoughts about moving into predominantly white sections of the city.[19]

[18] Harry E. Davis [to Walter White], February 5, 1926; White to Davis, February 6, 1926; Davis to White, February 8, 1926, Container G157, NAACP Papers; Cleveland *Plain Dealer*, July 7, 1926; President's Conference on Home Ownership and Home Building, *Negro Housing* (Washington, D.C., 1931), 46; Russell H. Davis, *Memorable Negroes in Cleveland's Past* (Cleveland, 1969), 57.

[19] Mabel Clark to James Weldon Johnson, July 12, 1926; Johnson to Clark, July 13, 1926; Walter White to Clayborne George, July 12, 1926; Harry E. Davis to James Weldon Johnson, July 15, 1926; George to White, July 20, 1926; Johnson to Davis, August 13, 1926; Mabel Clark to Johnson, March 24, 1927, branch files, NAACP Papers; interview with Russell Jelliffe, September 1, 1971 (Jelliffe was one of the individuals who helped guard Garvin's home). Though less publicized, Garvin's situation was in many ways similar to that of Dr. Ossian Sweet, a Detroit Negro who shot and killed a white man while defending his home against a mob in 1925. See David A. Levine, " 'Expecting the Barbarians': Race Relations and Social Control, Detroit, 1915–1925" (Ph.D. dissertation, University of Chicago, 1970), 247–98.

The mob action precipitated by the movement of individuals like Garvin into upper-middle-class areas of the city or suburbs was a clear indication that the integrated residency pattern of the black elite, so noticeable at the beginning of the century, was becoming impossible for all but a handful. Middle- and upper-class blacks were increasingly forced to live in predominantly black sections of the city, even if they had the money to purchase better homes in other neighborhoods. The group that was largely responsible for this was that segment of the native white population which had forsaken the central city for the suburbs. Once the bulwark of egalitarianism, this group now became increasingly hostile to blacks (and, indeed, all non-WASP groups) when it abandoned the urban milieu for the purified islands of suburban culture.[20]

However hostile they were to integration, it was not suburbanites who were chiefly responsible for the shaping of the black ghetto during the postwar years. The suburban housing market was simply too expensive for the vast majority of black Clevelanders. A much more important factor in containing and channeling the black population was the staunch resistance of certain urban ethnic groups. During the 1920s, the primary area of black expansion was to the east of the original area of settlement. Lying between East 55th and East 105th streets and bounded on the north by Euclid and on the south by Woodland Avenue, this area of the city had been occupied mostly by native Americans, British immigrants, and Russian Jews prior to 1920. Possibly because they had reached an economic stage where they were ready to move to better neighborhoods, these groups did not offer much resistance to the black influx, and by 1930 the area was about two-thirds black (although in some census tracts the proportion of Negroes was lower than this). Dispersion of the black population to the south and southeast of this area and the Central district, however, was checked by the immigrant

---

[20] It should not be thought, however, that all of the "old American" types in Cleveland became violently Negrophobic during the twenties. In fact, most of the enclaves of elite Negroes that continued to exist outside of the main ghetto at this time were located in sections of the city inhabited predominantly by native whites. It is clear that native whites became most hostile to blacks when they moved farthest away from the main black district. For an explanation of this seeming incongruity, see the informative discussion in Richard Sennett, *The Uses of Disorder* (New York, 1970), 3–84.

In some of the eastern suburbs during the post-World War I era there was a good deal of hostility to Jews as well as to blacks. Although anti-Semitism never resulted in violence, there was a concerted effort to keep Jews out of Shaker and Cleveland Heights. Throughout most of the twenties there was only one Jewish family in the entire city of Shaker Heights. Interview with Melvin Jay, September, 1974.

groups who resided there. To the south of the original black residential area, along Broadway, ethnic communities composed mostly of Poles and other Slavic-Americans halted the black population advance; to the southeast, Hungarians, Italians who had moved out from the Central district, and other ethnic groups put up resistance. When blacks tried to integrate the facilities at Woodland Hills Park, located slightly to the southeast of the principal black section of the city, it was members of these immigrant groups who fought against this change. Throughout the twenties the park remained a smouldering racial trouble spot.[21]

These resistant white groups were not the poorest of the ethnic population. A breakdown of the census tracts of Cleveland and four nearby suburbs by economic-tenths shows that, in 1930, these groups generally ranked from the 10th to the 30th percentile in yearly income—a few cuts above the most impoverished residents of the city. For the most part artisans, factory operatives, and small entrepreneurs, the inhabitants of these areas had acquired a modest level of middle-class respectability, as is evidenced by the moderate or high incidence of home ownership in the census tracts in question. It seems likely that these ethnic communities were composed of individuals highly prone to what social scientists have called "status anxieties." Having raised themselves above poverty, acquired a small home (with perhaps a large mortgage as well), and attained a modest level of income, they were fearful of association with any group bearing the stigma of low status. They naturally resisted the encroachment of a racial group that American society had designated as inferior. In so doing, they unthinkingly helped create a black ghetto.[22]

Prior to World War I, clearly defined black ghettos existed in only a few large northern cities—notably New York, Chicago, and Philadelphia.

[21] Cleveland Branch, NAACP, "Statement of Activities of the Branch for the Year ending Dec. 31 [1927]," Container G157, NAACP Papers; Green, comp., *Population Characteristics by Census Tracts, Cleveland, 1930*, 20–33 (maps); George A. Myers to Frank S. Harmon, August 23, 1923; Myers to Harmon, August 25, 1927; Myers to William R. Hopkins, August 9, 1927, George A. Myers Papers, Ohio Historical Society; interview with Dr. William P. Saunders, August 6, 1972. On ethnic hostility to black expansion in other cities, see Gilbert Osofsky, *Harlem: The Making of a Ghetto* (New York, 1966), 45–46, 81; St. Clair Drake and Horace R. Cayton, *Black Metropolis: A Study of Negro Life in a Northern City* (New York, 1945), 61–64, 180–82; Spear, *Black Chicago*, 201, 206, David M. Katzman, *Before the Ghetto: Black Detroit in the Nineteenth Century* (Urbana, Ill., 1973), 78, 101. Particularly valuable is the discussion in William M. Tuttle, Jr., *Race Riot: Chicago in the Red Summer of 1919* (New York, 1970), 156–83.

[22] Howard W. Green, *Nine Years of Relief, 1928–1937* (Cleveland, 1937), 45 (map showing economic divisions of Cleveland).

In Cleveland, Boston, and many other cities, there had been a definite trend of increasing segregation of the black population, but the process of ghetto development had not yet reached the point where all-black areas of significant size had emerged. In the wake of the Great Migration this diversity among black communities rapidly declined. The sudden influx of migrants accelerated trends that had been gathering force for several decades and caused the black ghetto in cities like Cleveland to consolidate sooner than would otherwise have been the case. By the eve of the Depression, the vast majority of urban centers outside the South had clearly defined black ghettos. Even Los Angeles, which in 1910 had had an extraordinarily low degree of residential segregation, now began to witness the beginnings of the Watts ghetto. The newer, more industrialized cities in the South also shared in this trend. Black sections in Birmingham, Tulsa, and Durham tended to develop on the outskirts of the city, rather than (as in the North) in the older central core. But they were no less segregated as a result.[23]

There were two exceptions to this trend. First, in a distinct minority of northern communities (mostly small or medium-sized cities), egalitarian traditions, slow population growth, the lack of urban transportation systems to facilitate geographic separation, or unstable housing patterns (due to a city's youthfulness) retarded the growth of ghettos. In Minneapolis in 1926, for example, not one but four general areas of

[23] Many of the conclusions presented here are based upon a study being made by the author of the growth of residential segregation in thirty cities for the period 1870–1930. For information on the consolidation and expansion of ghettos in specific cities after 1915, see J. S. Himes, "'Forty Years of Negro Life in Columbus, Ohio," *Journal of Negro History*, 27 (April 1942), 141–42; George Edmund Haynes, *Negro New-Comers in Detroit, Michigan: A Challenge to Christian Statesmanship* (New York, 1918), 8–10; A. L. Manley, "Where Negroes Live in Philadelphia," *Opportunity*, 1 (May 1923), 10–15; George W. Buckner, "'St. Louis Revives the Segregation Issue," *ibid.*, 1 (August 1923), 239; Woofter et al., *Negro Problems in Cities*, 37–111; Scott Nearing, *Black America* (New York, 1929), 107–26; E. Franklin Frazier, *The Negro Family in Chicago* (Chicago, 1932), 91–97; Drake and Cayton, *Black Metropolis*, 61–64, 77–83, 174–213; Emma Lou Thornbrough, "Segregation in Indiana during the Klan Era of the 1920's," *Mississippi Valley Historical Review*, 47 (March 1961), 595–97; Osofsky, *Harlem*, 127–49; Lawrence B. De Graaf, "The City of Black Angels: Emergence of the Los Angeles Ghetto, 1890–1930," *Pacific Historical Review*, 39 (August 1970), 345–50; Jerome Dowd, *The Negro in American Life* (New York, 1926), 96–97; Charles S. Johnson, *Patterns of Negro Segregation* (New York, 1943), ch. 1.

In the industrial cities of the South, it should be pointed out, the ghettos were less unified than in the North. In Birmingham in the 1920s, for example, most of the black population lived in residentially distinct neighborhoods, but these districts tended to be scattered over a much wider portion of the city than in the North. See Blaine A. Brownell, "Birmingham, Alabama: New South City in the 1920's,'" *Journal of Southern History*, 38 (February 1972), 28–29.

black settlement existed. Even those sections were not clearly defined, however, and blacks lived in many parts of the city. As late as 1940 Robert Warner could describe the residential pattern of New Haven blacks as "not distinct and clear cut. . . . There is no section, perhaps no street block, where white people do not also dwell; and every ward in the city has at least one Negro resident." The development of the ghetto in cities like Minneapolis and New Haven would be as much a product of the migration after World War II as that of earlier years.[24] The growth of ghettos was also retarded in a number of older southern cities. For example, while there was some increase in residential segregation in Charleston, South Carolina, and Savannah, Georgia, during the period between the wars, both of these cities failed to develop well-defined ghettos. Slow population growth, coupled with an extreme separation of the races in all other aspects of life, allowed the traditional pattern of white and black residential intermingling in Charleston, Savannah, New Orleans, Little Rock, and some other cities in the South to remain in effect until as late as the 1950s.[25]

These exceptions aside, black ghettos had become a permanent feature of the urban landscape by the eve of the Great Depression. By today's standards, of course, these ghettos appear rather moderate in size; since 1945, continued black migration to the cities has led to an enormous increase in the size of black districts in urban areas. Yet for the most part, this second phase of ghetto expansion simply repeated on a larger scale what had already ocurred prior to 1930. During the period since 1930 there have been significant changes in many areas of black life, including black occupational structure and access to public accommodations. There had been little change, however, in the degree of residential segregation that urban blacks have experienced.[26] Even before the post–World War II migration began, the physical isolation of black people in most cities had reached a high level.

[24] Abram L. Harris, *The Negro Population in Minneapolis: A Study of Race Relations* (Minneapolis, Minn. [1927]), 13–14; Robert Austin Warner, *New Haven Negroes: A Social History* (New Haven, 1940), 195. See also Charles S. Johnson, "The Negro Population of Waterbury, Connecticut," *Opportunity*, 1 (October 1923), 299, and Frank F. Lee, *Negro and White in Connecticut Town* (New York, 1961), 28–30.

[25] Charles L. Knight, *Negro Housing in Certain Virginia Cities* (Richmond, Va., 1927), 36; Taeuber and Taeuber, *Negroes in Cities*, 189–92; Johnson, *Patterns of Negro Segregation*, ch. 1; E. Franklin Frazier, *The Negro in the United States*, rev. ed. (New York, 1957), 237.

[26] See the segregation indexes computed for 1940, 1950, and 1960 in Taeuber and Taeuber, *Negroes in Cities*, 39–41.

CHAPTER 8

Racism at High Tide

The increasing residential segregation of urban blacks after 1915 was accompanied by an intensification of white hostility and a crystallization of the pattern of discrimination that had begun to take shape before the war. Both were in large part the result of what one historian has called the "flowering of racism" that occurred during the 1920s. To be sure, a few scholars were beginning to build a scientific critique of the racist theories that had been formulated at the turn of the century. But the average white person continued to believe in Negro inferiority; and as black sociologist Charles S. Johnson lamented in 1923, "False notions, if believed, . . . may control conduct as effectively as true ones." During and immediately after World War I, whites vented their fears and frustrations in a series of vicious race riots; the two worst riots alone, in East St. Louis and Chicago, were responsible for eighty-five deaths and over a thousand injuries. Although this type of extreme violence fell off sharply after 1919, lesser forms of white hostility did not. The white quest for racial purity found its embodiment in a rejuvenated Ku Klux Klan, an organization which directed its propaganda at Catholics and Jews as well as blacks. Founded in 1915, the new Klan was as much a northern as a southern phenomenon, and at least one-third of all Klansmen could be found in urban areas. By 1924 at least one million whites had joined the organization, and in several localities the Ku Klux Klan became a force to be reckoned with.[1]

[1] John Higham, *Strangers in the Land: Patterns of American Nativism, 1860–1925* (New York, 1963 ed.), 264–99; Herbert Adulphus Miller, "The Myth of Superiority," *Opportunity*, 1 (August 1923), 228–29; Charles S. Johnson, "Public Opinion and the Negro," *ibid.*, 1 (July 1923), 202; Kenneth T. Jackson, *The Ku Klux Klan in the City, 1915–1930* (New York, 1967), 236 and *passim*; William M.

Cleveland, a city more liberal than most, managed to avoid the racist excesses that plagued other communities. During the tense summers of 1917 and 1919, interracial violence did break out on several occasions, but these encounters did not, luckily, escalate into racial warfare. Nor was the Ku Klux Klan an important factor in Cleveland's racial scene. During the 1920s, a small local chapter was organized, but Klan membership in the city never exceeded two thousand (Chicago may have had fifty thousand Klansmen at one time), and local authorities remained hostile to the secret organization. But there was still a noticeable increase in race prejudice in the city after 1915. Before the war the Negro population of Cleveland was small and easily overlooked. By 1920 it could no longer be ignored. As black migrants entered the mills and foundries of the city, whites sometimes felt that their jobs were threatened. At the same time, the expansion of the ghetto made white home owners fearful for the value of their property and the stability of their neighborhoods. The result was a sharp rise in racial tension and an increase in institutional discrimination.[2]

The initial response of many whites to the Great Migration was one of fear. White journalists, who previously had for the most part avoided any discussion of the city's black community, now took a more hostile view of the race. In the spring of 1917 one white newspaper printed a scare article which warned Clevelanders of the "danger of the spread of small pox, hookworm, and other diseases prevalent in the South, as a result of the Negro influx." Throughout the year, two Cleveland newspapers, the *News* and the *Leader*, continued to stir dangerous emotions by allowing the terms "nigger" and "darkey" to appear in print. In 1919, a year of anti-Negro violence throughout the nation, these two papers fanned the flames of racial discord by publishing blatantly prejudiced articles. Both papers made derogatory remarks about the all-Negro 372d Regiment when it returned to Cleveland after the signing of the peace treaty. During the "red summer" of 1919, the *News*, a leading daily, printed a sensationalistic article on lynchings on the front page and blamed the racial disturbances that were spreading across the country on "the active and systematic proselyting [*sic*] done among the colored workers of the South by Bolshevists." Such copy was hardly designed to promote racial harmony.[3]

Tuttle, Jr., *Race Riot: Chicago in the Red Summer of 1919* (New York, 1970), 64; Elliott M. Rudwick, *Race Riot at East St. Louis, July 2, 1917* (Carbondale, Ill., 1964), 50, 52.

[2] On Klan membership in cities, see Jackson, *Ku Klux Klan in the City*, 236.

[3] Cleveland *Advocate*, December 30, 1916 (quoting the *News*); Cleveland *Lead-*

Mass circulation newspapers were not the only media that reflected (and influenced) the deepening antagonism toward blacks that surfaced during the war. The popularity of the racist films *The Nigger* and *The Birth of a Nation*, both of which came to the city in 1917, were signs of a growing anti-Negro sentiment among the white population. *The Nigger*, as described by the *Advocate*, contained "huge mob scenes and race riots" and was filled "with the crack of the white man's whip and the scream of the blacks. . . ." A cheap but gaudy production, it was the less popular of the two motion pictures. *The Birth of a Nation* was more invidious because of its high technical—if not moral—qualities. Produced by D. W. Griffith, *The Birth of a Nation* was quickly recognized as an outstanding example of the art of film-making. The subject matter of the film, however, was volatile; based on a caustically racist novel by Thomas Dixon, it portrayed Negroes as ignorant brutes and glorified the original Ku Klux Klan as the righteous upholders of white civilization in the South. *The Birth of a Nation* was eventually banned from Cleveland, but not before it had become a box-office hit in several theaters.[4]

White politicians, sensitive to the changing temperament of the electorate, equivocated on the issue of civil rights or dangerously played upon the racist emotions of voters for their own political advantage. In 1917 William Finley, the state chairman of the Democratic party in Ohio, attempted to gain support for the Democratic ticket by associating Republicans with the migration of southern Negroes that was then under way. Negroes were traditionally Republican, and Finley claimed that the Ohio GOP was assisting in the "colonization" of thousands of poor black migrants for the purpose of increasing the Republican vote. A similar claim, made against the Republicans of East St. Louis in 1916, was one of the underlying causes of the bloody race riot that occurred there the following year. Such racist propaganda was not limited to the party of Woodrow Wilson. In Cleveland the Republican successor to Mayor Newton D. Baker, Harry L. Davis, implied in a speech in 1917 that the Central Avenue area had developed into a vice district because Negroes were naturally degenerate. Davis steadfastly refused to appoint

---

er, April 17, 1917, March 2, 1919; Cleveland *Gazette*, January 20, June 2, 1917; March 8, 1919 (quoting the *News*).

4 Cleveland *Advocate*, April 14, 1917; Cleveland *Leader*, April 18, 1917; Cleveland *Plain Dealer*, April 8, 1917; Cleveland *Gazette*, April 14, 21, May 12, 1917. See also Thomas R. Cripps, "The Reaction of the Negro to the Motion Picture *Birth of a Nation*," *The Historian*, 25 (May 1963), 344–62, and Everett Carter, "Cultural History Written with Lightning: The Significance of *The Birth of a Nation*," *American Quarterly*, 12 (Fall 1960), 347–57.

Negro clerks to City Hall during his administration or to choose a Negro as an assistant police prosecutor or member of the mayor's Advisory War Board—despite the fact that one of the board's functions was to deal with the immediate problems resulting from the influx of black migrants during the war. In 1920, race once again became an election issue when several candidates for local office distributed racist literature claiming that blacks would not be satisfied until they could "dominate" Cleveland.[5]

Fears of black "domination" were more than simply false; they actually amounted to an inverted view of race relations in the city. Politically, blacks had gained little as a result of their consistent support of the Republican party. From 1915 to 1930 a string of Republican administrations in Cleveland refused, with few exceptions, to appoint Afro-Americans to anything but minor positions. In the area of municipal services, black neighborhoods were consistently shortchanged. In the Central and lower Woodland Avenue districts, recreational facilities were scarce, garbage and rubbish removal were often irregular, and the streetcars were notorious for their poor service and shoddy conditions—despite the fact that the Central line was one of the most profitable in the city. During the twenties, Cleveland adopted the city manager form of government (it was the largest metropolis to do so), yet the vaunted "efficiency" of this system of administration did not seem to work to the benefit of the black community.[6]

As far as police protection was concerned, black people could without contradiction say that they received both too little and too much. Throughout the postwar period no effort was made by City Hall to clean up the gambling and prostitution rackets on Central Avenue. The

[5] Cleveland *Gazette*, May 5, 19, 26, November 10, 1917, October 23, November 13, 20, 1920; Rudwick, *Race Riot at East St. Louis*, ch. 2. Not all white politicians lapsed into racist demagoguery, of course, and there were a few who remained consistent supporters of equal rights. Two racial liberals on the City Council in the 1920s were Peter Witt and F. W. Walz; both supported the integration of City Hospital when that issue arose at the end of the decade. Congressman Henry I. Emerson, of the East Side 22d Congressional District, was also a strong advocate of equality. Emerson was a firm supporter of the National Association for the Advancement of Colored People. "He has stood 'right' and voted 'right,'" the Cleveland NAACP Branch *Bulletin* stated in 1920, "on every race issue which was presented to congress during his first three terms." Among other actions, Emerson endorsed the federal anti-lynching bill and entered a resolution condemning the Washington race riot of 1919. Francis Young to Mary White Ovington, February 26, 1919, Container B-1, Papers of the National Association for the Advancement of Colored People, Manuscript Division, Library of Congress; Cleveland Branch *Bulletin*, 1 (August 1920), 1.

[6] Cleveland *Gazette*, January 13, February 24, March 17, 1917, October 12, 1918, October 15, 1927, March 31, 1928.

number of police assigned to black sections of the city was inadequate, and when the police received reports of crimes they were often slow to arrive on the scene. "It is only on rare occasions," complained Harry C. Smith, that "policemen are seen in 'the roaring third' [as whites called the Central area] and then as a rule, after some crime has already been committed." On the other hand, when police did enter the ghetto to make an arrest or to patrol the area, they often seemed unnecessarily brutal. In 1917 Smith noted that "flagrant and barbarous beating-up of Negroes" was an all too common occurrence with white officers. ". . . since the influx from the South," Smith reported a few years later, "there has been a growing tendency upon the part of the police, both public and private, to kill members of the race sought for committing crimes and misdemeanors." Police were "too quick to shoot" if the suspect was a Negro and were not overly concerned about harming bystanders if they had the misfortune of being black. Undoubtedly, part of the problem was the small number of black patrolmen; in 1919 only seven of the city's thirteen hundred police officers were Negroes, and eleven years later there were still only twelve blacks on the force.[7]

In 1919 a small incident symbolized the state of race relations in Cleveland in the wake of the Great Migration. With the city's tradition of fairness to blacks in mind, the NAACP in that year chose Cleveland as the site of its annual convention. "We were not in the cotton fields of Louisiana," Mary White Ovington wrote in retrospect, "but in the City of Cleveland of the State of Ohio, that had bred abolitionists, and started Oberlin." At the same time that Miss Ovington was exulting over the heritage of northern freedom, however, James Weldon Johnson, field secretary for the NAACP, was being refused service in a Cleveland restaurant because he was black. The irony of the situation was symptomatic of the continuing deterioration of the city's liberal racial climate during the postwar era: the abolitionist heritage of Cleveland's past was rapidly being supplanted by the reality of its discriminatory present.[8]

Nowhere was this increasing discrimination more evident than in the unequal treatment Negroes received in the city's restaurants, theaters,

[7] *Ibid.*, November 24, 1917, March 2, 1918, October 11, 1919, June 12, 1920; U.S. *Fifteenth Census, 1930, Population (Occupations)* (Washington, 1932), IV, 1286. For several years during the 1920s, black prisoners were segregated in the county jail. This policy ended in 1927, however, when racially liberal Edward J. Hanratty was elected sheriff. *Ibid.*, October 30, 1926, April 30, 1927. There was a sharp decline in the relative concentration of blacks in the police force between 1910 and 1930; see Table 26 in Appendix II.

[8] Mary White Ovington, *The Walls Came Tumbling Down* (New York, 1948), 171–72; Cleveland *Gazette*, April 27, 1919. Oberlin was not founded by Ohioans, as Ovington suggested, but by settlers from New England.

and other places of public accommodation. As the black population expanded out of its original area of settlement, white restaurant owners, like some white property owners, often tried to "hold the line" against the advancing black tide. They used a variety of tactics. Some simply refused Negroes altogether, and a few of these had the effrontery to place "white only" signs in their windows. Others discouraged black patrons by giving them poor service. Still others served Negroes but charged them higher prices; one Greek restaurant owner blandly informed a Negro customer that he would be glad to serve him but would have to charge him four times the regular price of a meal. Previously liberal downtown restaurants and hotels also began to exclude Afro-Americans more frequently, although they faced no threat of "invasion." Even prominent black visitors were not always able to find adequate hotel accommodations. When Robert R. Moton, Booker T. Washington's successor as head of the Tuskegee Institute, came to Cleveland in 1923 to address the Chamber of Commerce, officials at the Statler Hotel told him that they would be able to accommodate him only if he agreed to take his meals in his room. In a number of exclusive establishments, however, skin color remained an important factor in determining who would be admitted. Light-skinned Negroes could still eat at many of the city's better restaurants during the twenties, but Charles W. Chesnutt (who himself had a very fair complexion) noted in 1930 that he did not "know more than one place downtown where [he] could take for luncheon a dark-colored man." Not all of the increase in restaurant discrimination, it should be noted, was the result of a conscious policy of management. In many cases waiters and waitresses acted on their own initiative in refusing to serve Afro-Americans. The white Waiters' Union was one of Cleveland's most intensely racist labor organizations.[9]

Discriminatory practices were not limited to hotels and restaurants. Theaters often refused to admit Negroes, segregated them within the theater, seated them in the balcony, or charged them higher prices. Blacks could, of course, ride the city streetcars. But a local taxi company attempted to restrict its service to whites only, and by the end of the

[9] Cleveland *Gazette*, May 12, June 23, 1917, March 16, May 4, 1918, March 3, 1923, February 18 March 24 May 5, 26, 1928, August 31, 1929; Langston Hughes, *The Big Sea* (New York, 1940), 51; Cleveland *Herald*, September 11, 1926 (clipping in Scrapbook 1, Chester K. Gillespie Papers, Western Reserve Historical Society); [Charles White,] "Cleveland Branch of the N.A.A.C.P., Communication to Executive Committee, February 14, 1927," 1; "Brings Action against Two Restaurants for Segregation" (in 1929 folder); Harry E. Davis to Walter White, September 29, 1929, all in branch files (Containers G157 and G158), NAACP Papers; Charles W. Chesnutt, "The Negro in Cleveland," *The Clevelander*, 5 (November 1930), 24. For additional examples, see the discussion of NAACP activities in Chapter 11.

twenties the Greyhound Bus Company was making blacks sit in the back of buses traveling to the South.[10]

Racial lines also hardened in recreational facilities. Cleveland's two main amusement parks, Luna Park and Euclid Beach Park, continued their established policy of restricting the use of their facilities by blacks to a small number of days each summer. Social agencies involved in recreation frequently introduced a policy of segregation where none had existed before the war. "Some of the settlement houses," Jane Edna Hunter remarked, "alternate their camp periods, sending the Negro children out to the camp for one period and the white children for another." The YMCA restricted Negro participation in its activities to one branch on Cedar Avenue in the 1920s, and the YWCA continued its policy of excluding blacks altogether. Blacks also encountered a considerable amount of discrimination in public facilities. At the city beach nearest to the ghetto, Gordon Park, blacks were segregated, while they were excluded altogether from some other beaches. At the instigation of Thomas Fleming, the Negro councilman, the city did construct a bathhouse on Central in 1919 at a cost of $45,000. It was apparent, however, that the black community was being shortchanged when the city announced construction of a similar facility in the ethnic St. Clair Avenue area with a price tag of $125,000. Surveying the Central Avenue bathhouse shortly after it opened, the editor of the Gazette pronounced it "cheaply constructed." "*Anything*," he concluded, "seems good enough for *colored* people, as far as Fleming and the Davis Administration goes. . . ."[11]

As before the war, black Clevelanders achieved only partial success in forcing white establishments to end discriminatory practices. Negroes actually brought more civil rights suits in the 1920s than ever before, and they did force a number of white restaurants and downtown theaters to open their doors to black people. Those of the race who sought redress in the courts, however, were hindered in a number of ways. They continued to be stymied by narrow interpretations of the Ohio Civil Rights Law. In 1918, for example, a black man brought suit against an

[10] Cleveland *Call*, February 12, 1927 (clipping in Scrapbook 1, Gillespie Papers); Cleveland *Gazette*, May 5, 12, 1917, July 25, 1929; Julian Krawcheck, "Society Barred Negroes—They Formed Own Groups," Cleveland *Press*, May 30, 1963. A Negro who was refused service by the taxi company, however, brought suit against the firm in 1917 and won the case.

[11] Cleveland *Gazette*, March 10, 1917, August 17, 31, 1918, March 1, September 13, 1919, September 12, 1925, May 31, 1927, March 10, 1928, January 19, 1929, July 9, 1930; Chesnutt, "The Negro in Cleveland," 4; Jane Edna Hunter, "Negroes in Cleveland" (undated manuscript, Jane Edna Hunter Papers, Western Reserve Historical Society), 2.

Euclid Avenue restaurant owner who refused him service. The jury, however, ruled in favor of the proprietor, apparently on the ground that the black man "was not a bona fide patron but was merely there for the purpose of stirring up trouble." Such circuitous reasoning made "test cases" against discriminatory establishments difficult and in some instances rendered the Civil Rights Law null. Blacks encountered less hostility and prejudice from white judges and lawyers than from juries. "Juries are prejudiced," one black lawyer reported, "and if a personal injury case is worth $5,000 the jury would give a colored man, in my opinion, $2,000 or possible $2,500." One of the hindrances to equal justice in Cleveland was the fact that fewer Negroes served on juries than their percentage of the population would seem to warrant. Negroes complained that—whether by design or accident—too few of their race were called to jury duty and that many who were called were "excused." "Only ceaseless insistence on the enforcement of law," the black *Call and Post* editorialized in 1928, "will prevent the Ohio Civil Rights Statute from becoming a dead letter. . . ." Such continual vigilance, however, was bothersome, difficult, and often expensive; few blacks had sufficient time, funds, and tenacity to indulge in such tactics. As Charles Chesnutt laconically put it, "One does not care to have to bring a lawsuit or swear out a warrant every time one wants a sandwich or a cup of coffee."[12]

Cleveland's hospitals and schools also mirrored the rising tide of discrimination after 1915. Before the war, little noticeable discrimination was seen in hospital policies. During the Great Migration several hospitals adopted the procedure of segregating Negro and white patients in separate wards; during the next decade many other hospitals in the area followed suit. In addition, some medical institutions reserved only a designated number of beds for black patients. The number of spaces reserved was sometimes woefully inadequate. "These hospitals," a group of Negroes complained in 1927, "ask doctors on requesting admission of patients whether the patient is white or colored, and frequently the answer is: 'there are no colored beds vacant.'" At the peak of the wartime migration, one institution, Charity Hospital, belied its name by refusing to accept black patients who could not pay for their treatment

[12] Cleveland *Gazette*, April 21, May 12, 1917, July 27, 1918, July 26, 1919, February 18, May 26, 1928, March 9, 1929; Cleveland *Call and Post* [February, 1928], (clipping in Scrapbook 1, Gillespie Papers); Chesnutt, "The Negro in Cleveland," 4, 26. "Recently [civil rights cases] have met with poor results," the Cleveland *Herald* complained in 1926, "juries in most instances voting verdicts of 'Not Guilty' against white proprietors of restaurants." Cleveland *Herald*, September 11, 1926 (clipping in Scrapbook 1, Gillespie Papers).

in advance. Although there is no evidence that this policy became standard procedure in later years, while in force it was most disconcerting to black Clevelanders.[13]

The color bar against Negro doctors and nurses remained as firm in Cleveland hospitals as it had been before the war. Most Cleveland hospitals refused to allow Negro physicians on their staffs or to provide training programs for black interns. This eventually led to an unsuccessful attempt, by a group of black doctors, politicians, and businessmen, to establish an all-Negro hospital. But at the end of the twenties, there was still no hospital in the city which would accept Negro interns or nurse trainees. Only two hospitals had black doctors attached to their staffs.[14]

The changes that occurred in the policies of Cleveland's educational institutions as a result of the migration were more subtle. The city's public schools had been integrated for many decades and to a large extent they remained this way during and after the war. With the exception of the city's trade schools, which discouraged black attendance because of the exclusionary policies of many union apprenticeship programs, the schools and colleges of Cleveland remained open to both races on a nondiscriminatory basis.[15] During the peak month of the wartime migration, however, several school principals sought to establish segregated classes *within* their schools, and one head of an all-white school refused to accept a black teacher who had been assigned to his district. Yet there is no indication that either of these policies became accepted practice or amounted to anything more than a temporary aber-

13 Cleveland *Gazette*, November 10, 1917, December 21, 1918, November 26, 1926, January 12, 1929; George A. Myers to Msg. Joseph F. Smith, September 21, 1927; Joseph Smith to Myers, February 4, 1929; Harry C. Smith to Myers, August 17, 1929, George A. Myers Papers, Ohio Historical Society; Mercy Hospital Association of Cleveland, *Does Cleveland Need a Negro-Manned Hospital?* (n.p. [1927], pamphlet).

14 Cleveland *Gazette*, October 22, 1927; Chesnutt, "The Negro in Cleveland," 4; Henry C. Smith to George A. Myers, August 17, 1929; Smith to Myers, September 4, 1929 (two letters); Smith to Myers, September 11, 1929, Myers Papers; Mercy Hospital Association of Cleveland, *Does Cleveland Need a Negro-Manned Hospital?* On the controversy over the proposal to establish a black hospital, see Chapter 11.

15 Chesnutt, "The Negro in Cleveland," 3–4. Another partial exception was the city's business colleges, which, according to George Myers, only allowed Negroes to attend evening classes. George A. Myers, "Answer to Questionnaire from Chamber of Commerce Committee on Immigration and Emigration" (in 1926 correspondence, Myers Papers). In addition, Carter G. Woodson reported in 1934 that Western Reserve University was one of a number of northern institutions that "restrict the number of Negro nurses that might be admitted because of the racial difficulties encountered in providing for their field experience." Carter G. Woodson, *The Negro Professional Man and the Community* (n.p., 1934), 144.

ration. During the twenties black teachers not only increased steadily in numbers but remained fairly well integrated in the system. In 1929 eighty-four black instructors taught in forty-one different schools, most of them in predominantly white neighborhoods.[16]

Nevertheless, a subtle process of discrimination did begin to affect the public schools. Two of the city's technical high schools—Jane Addams Vocational School and the Cleveland Trade School—had no black students at all. The third, East Technical High School, although located in the heart of the ghetto, was only 4 percent black in 1929. As the ghetto consolidated and expanded during the twenties, some schools became predominantly Negro. On the eve of the Great Depression, 89 percent of Cleveland's black junior high school students were enrolled in only four (out of a total of twenty-three) schools; and fully 61 percent of all black senior high school students attended a single institution, Central High. In 1931 whites made up only about 3 percent of the student body at Central. The gradual development of segregation in the schools after World War I was, initially, a by-product of the shifting demographic patterns of the city; as blacks moved into neighborhoods in larger numbers, nearby schools naturally gained in black enrollment. By the early 1930s (it is difficult to determine exactly when the policy began), however, the Board of Education was beginning to reinforce and accelerate this trend through artificial means. In 1933 blacks complained that most black children on the East Side were being forced to attend Central High, even though many lived much nearer to other schools. A few years later, it was charged that white students who lived in the Central High district were permitted to transfer to other schools. This policy of selective transfers, which would continue

---

[16] Cleveland *Gazette*, April 21, May 5, September 22, 1917; Alonzo Gatskell Grace, "The Effect of Negro Migration on the Cleveland Public School System" (Ph.D. dissertation, Western Reserve University, 1932), 64–66. It should be noted, however, that Grace found that almost all of these black teachers (seventy-eight of eighty-four) were elementary school instructors. Despite this, the large number of black teachers and their relative integration within the school system made Cleveland truly exceptional compared to other northern cities at the end of the 1920s. In Pittsburgh and Omaha, for example, black students were integrated to about the same extent as in Cleveland, but school boards in both cities refused to hire *any* black teachers. Most northern cities hired black teachers, but they usually placed black instructors in charge of classes composed entirely or predominantly of Negro students. See Ira De A. Reid, *Social Conditions of the Negro in the Hill District of Pittsburgh* ([Pittsburgh,] 1930), 16; T. Earl Sullenger and J. Harvey Kerns, *The Negro in Omaha: A Social Study of Negro Development* (Omaha, Neb., 1931), 19; Hannibal G. Duncan, *The Changing Race Relationship in the Border and Northern States* (Philadelphia, 1922), 37–39; Emma Lou Thornbrough, "Segregation in Indiana during the Klan Era of the 1920's," *Mississippi Valley Historical Review*, 47 (March 1961), 600.

for several decades, often placed a considerable hardship on students, since it sometimes forced them to attend a school that was several streetcar lines away from their home. Ironically, in the 1960s and 1970s, whites would vigorously oppose the busing of children for the purpose of creating racial balance in the schools, whereas over thirty years earlier, the Board of Education had already established a program of busing (or its equivalent), not for the purpose of ending segregation but as a means of furthering it.[17]

As schools became predominantly Negro, their curricula often changed from an emphasis on liberal arts to a stressing of skills of a more mundane nature. The changes that occurred at Kennard Junior High School during the twenties are a good example of this process. In 1924 the school's student body was 31 percent Negro in composition; in 1930, as a result of the white exodus from neighborhoods near the school, Negroes constituted 60 percent of the students. As the racial balance of the school shifted, administrators gradually altered the curriculum. They dropped foreign languages altogether; intensified course offerings in certain types of industrial work; cut back on the number of available electives, and placed more emphasis on "sewing, cooking, manual training, foundry work, and sheet metal [work]." In Central High School the same transformation was occurring. In 1933 the Cleveland branch of the NAACP discovered that over half the tenth-grade students at Central were receiving no training in mathematics at all. Most of the home economics courses at the school emphasized laundry work, and such electives as Spanish, German, bookkeeping, and stenography (standard fare in other high schools) had been dropped from the curriculum. These changes in course offerings undoubtedly lowered the expectations of black students and oriented them, at an early age, toward lower-paying, less prestigious occupations. Once a powerful force for equality and integration, the public schools had by 1935 become yet another factor leading to two separate but unequal worlds of race.[18]

With the growth of prejudice evident in so many aspects of life in

[17] Grace, "The Effect of Negro Migration on the Cleveland Public School System," 20–23; Willard C. Richan, *Racial Isolation in the Cleveland Public Schools* (Cleveland, 1967), 33; interview with Russell and Rowena Jelliffe, September 1, 1971. It was also during the 1930s that the policy of placing black teachers in predominantly white schools came to an end. By 1944 most black teachers in Cleveland taught in the ghetto. Christopher G. Wye, "Midwest Ghetto: Patterns of Negro Life and Thought in Cleveland, Ohio, 1929–1945" (Ph.D. dissertation, Kent State University, 1973), 56–57.

[18] Grace, "The Effect of Negro Migration on the Cleveland Public School System," 84–86; Richan, *Racial Isolation in the Cleveland Public Schools*, 33–36.

Cleveland after 1915, it was almost inevitable that violent encounters between blacks and whites would occur. Before the war, the city had been relatively free of interracial violence; but now whites were more willing to use intimidation, mob action, and even terrorism in the face of an assumed threat to their homes and jobs.

It was during the tense summers of 1917 and 1919 that anti-Negro violence in Cleveland reached a peak. Several times lynchings or a race riot seemed imminent but miraculously failed to materialize. In June, 1917, two incidents occurred within the span of a single week. The first took place in the predominantly white neighborhood near East 71st Street, far from the main area of black settlement. The trouble began when a white woman began to complain loudly that a Negro had insulted her. A crowd of whites soon gathered and started to harass and then to chase the black man, who sought refuge in a nearby house. By the time a patrol wagon arrived on the scene, a menacing crowd of two hundred whites had gathered and were preparing to storm the house, capture its black occupant, and lynch him. Only the somewhat belated appearance of the police prevented bloodshed. Less than a week later, a near riot occurred in the lower Central Avenue district. No one seemed to know how the trouble began, but by the time the police were summoned "scores of Negroes and foreigners were fighting with fists, clubs, and stones." After these two outbursts of racial hostility, Harry C. Smith feared that a major clash between blacks and whites was imminent. Not one to mince words, he urged his readers to "purchase a regular army riot gun and plenty of ammunition" for self-defense.[19]

In the summer of 1919, anti-Negro violence again flared up in Cleveland. This time the attackers directed their fury at children rather than adults. On three separate occasions mobs of white men and boys stoned groups of black youngsters. The first incident occurred when a group of black children were riding a streetcar through a white neighborhood; the second and third while parties of black youths were swimming in one of the local park lakes, a recreation spot some distance from the ghetto and usually not frequented by Negroes. Luckily, in none of the incidents were there any serious injuries. For many weeks afterward, however, the racial atmosphere of the city was taut with fear. Commenting on the two occurrences at the park lakes, the editor of the *Gazette* cautioned his readers that "this is just what started the Chicago riot" and again urged black Clevelanders to prepare to defend themselves. Fortunately, Smith's premonition proved to be without founda-

[19] Cleveland *Gazette*, June 9, 16, 1917.

tion, and the "red summer" of 1919 ended without a major racial confrontation in Cleveland.[20]

Given the intensification of racial prejudice and the propensity of some whites to resort to violence against Negroes, why did no race riot take place in Cleveland during the migration years? A comparison with Chicago—which did experience a violent race riot in 1919—shows that a number of factors must be taken into account. First, Cleveland's industries were far more diversified than Chicago's. In Chicago the stockyards served as a focal point of racial hostility between black and white workers; in the Lake Erie metropolis no such focal point existed. In addition, Cleveland was fortunate in that its black steel workers were almost completely unionized during the crucial year 1919. By refusing to act as strikebreakers, blacks in Cleveland temporarily undercut a major source of racial strife. The residential pattern of black settlement in the city also was important in preventing a riot. In Chicago, black workers found it necessary to pass through hostile ethnic neighborhoods on their way to work; this made them easy prey for white mobs. In Cleveland, however, as the black ghetto consolidated after 1915 it abutted the main industrial district, and most blacks could go to and from work without straying very far from the predominantly black (or at least integrated) sections of the city. Despite the hostility of white ethnic groups, blacks in Cleveland had considerably more opportunity for expansion than the hemmed-in South Side black belt of Chicago. The streets directly to the east of the original area of Negro settlement were occupied primarily by Russian Jews, British immigrants, and native white Americans. Though far from unprejudiced, most of these whites were not anti-Negro in the violent, defensive manner of suburbanites and those ethnic groups living to the south and southeast of the ghetto; and when black expansion became a necessity after 1915, they were willing to allow the peaceful movement of Negroes into their neighborhoods. The existence of this "escape valve" reduced the possibility of contested neighborhoods and lessened tensions in the city during a critical period of race relations.[21]

Finally, in assessing the differences between the two cities one cannot underestimate the effects of the slower development of the ghetto in Cleveland. In Chicago, the black belt had taken shape by 1910 (perhaps earlier), and on the eve of the wartime migration a gulf had opened

[20] *Ibid.*, July 5, August 2, 16, 1919.

[21] On Chicago, see Chicago Commission on Race Relations, *The Negro in Chicago: A Study of Race Relations and a Race Riot* (Chicago, 1922), *passim*; Allan H. Spear, *Black Chicago: The Making of a Negro Ghetto, 1890–1920* (Chicago, 1967), 159–64, 208–22; Tuttle, *Race Riot, passim*.

between the two races that has not yet, to this day, been bridged. Sociologists have noted that personal experience with Negroes is an important factor in shaping white racial attitudes, and that those who have the least contact with members of the opposite race often harbor the most intense prejudice. Conditions in Chicago before the riot nurtured such intolerance. There, says historian William Tuttle, Jr., "because of extreme residential segregation, there was a paucity of social interchange between the races. Consequently, there was a decided lack of interracial understanding. . . ." In spite of increasing evidences of racism in Cleveland during the prewar years, the city's black community was not nearly as isolated as was Chicago's in 1915; the existence of integrated schools and neighborhoods kept open crucial lines of communication between the races and helped check the racial paranoia that resulted in a bloodbath in Chicago.[22]

By the end of the 1920s, however, most of these lines of communication had been effectively closed. With the new racism in public facilities and the increasing ghettoization of the black population more evident with each passing year, Cleveland was coming to resemble other metropolises in its prejudicial treatment of black citizens. This fact was a painful one for older black residents of the city to accept. "Time was," said George Myers despairingly in 1928, "that Cleveland was the freest from race prejudice and the fairest city in the United States not excepting Freedom's birthplace Boston. Today we have only two unrestricted privileges left, the Ballot and the Public Schools." The same year, the Negro *Call and Post* editorialized: "Daily it becomes more apparent that the virus of southern race prejudice is bearing its malignant fruit in this cosmopolitan city of Cleveland. With amazing rapidity it is spreading through the very arteries of this city—once famous for its liberality to minority groups."[23]

The comparison of Cleveland with the South was apt, and it pinpointed an important national trend. Among whites, something of a consensus in favor of racial separation emerged in the postwar era. "There seems to be a concerted effort," Robert W. Bagnall, the NAACP's director of branches, wrote in 1925, "to force segregation on Negroes

---

[22] Tuttle, Jr., *Race Riot*, 103. On the importance of personal experience with members of the opposite race in shaping personal attitudes and attenuating racial antagonisms, see Morris L. Haimowitz, "The Development and Change of Ethnic Hostility" (Ph.D. dissertation, University of Chicago, 1951), 110–24.

[23] George A. Myers to William R. Hopkins, February 6, 1928, Myers Papers; Cleveland *Call and Post* [February, 1928] (clipping in Scrapbook 1, Gillespie Papers).

all over [the United States]. . . ." The "Southern Way," remarks C. Vann
Woodward in his discussion of racial discrimination in the twenties,
"was spreading as the American Way in race relations." Nevertheless,
while the distance between North and South on the race question had
narrowed, essential differences still remained. Blacks, as George Myers
pointed out, retained the right to vote in the northern states, and in
Cleveland they would soon use their increased numbers as a political
tool to gain concessions from city government. Furthermore, the separation of the races never became as complete in Cleveland as it did in many
of the southern states. No system of "racial etiquette" took root in the
North in the twenties—there were no Jim Crow streetcars, Jim Crow
drinking fountains, or Jim Crow bibles for witnesses in court, and northern blacks were not required by custom to constantly show deference to
whites in day-to-day contacts between the races.[24]

Why did Cleveland not become like Atlanta, Charleston, and Mobile,
where the principle of segregation was applied rigidly, dogmatically,
to almost every facet of life? The question is not one that can be answered
with absolute certainty, but two important factors, at least, must be
taken into account. First, a portion of the white community continued
to adhere to the tradition of tolerance and egalitarianism that at one
time had been dominant. Influential white liberals included Russell
Jelliffe, codirector of the interracial settlement house that would later
become known as Karamu House, and Charles F. Thwing, president of
Western Reserve University. Both were active in the NAACP, and Jelliffe served on a number of interracial committees during the 1920s.
Although it is clear that Thwing and Jelliffe were not representative of
most whites, they did speak for a constituency that was able to exercise
some restraint on the growth of segregation and intolerance in the city.[25]

Perhaps a more important factor that has been neglected was the
nature of urban life in the North. The intricate subtleties of the race
system common throughout most of the South simply could not be
adapted to life in huge, industrialized, impersonal northern cities such
as Cleveland. Beyond a certain point in urban development, the separa-

[24] Robert W. Bagnall to Clayborne George [President of Cleveland NAACP],
October 20, 1925, branch files (Container G157), NAACP Papers, Manuscript
Division, Library of Congress; C. Vann Woodward, The Strange Career of Jim
Crow, 2d rev. ed. (New York, 1966), 115 and 111–18 passim; Bertram W. Doyle,
The Etiquette of Race Relations in the South (Chicago, 1937), 136–59; Jerome
Dowd, The Negro in American Life (New York, 1926), 41.

[25] Information from interviews. On Thwing's active support of the NAACP, see
also Senator Harold Burton to Charles F. Thwing, September 1, 1913; Oswald
Garrison Villard to Thwing, September 13, 1913, Container C403, NAACP Papers;
and Cleveland Gazette, April 14, 1917.

tion of the races in public and private facilities becomes inefficient, expensive, and dysfunctional to the operation of a modern industrial metropolis; by 1920, Cleveland, Chicago, and other large northern cities had long since passed that point. Paradoxically, however, the same dynamic urban growth that made segregated streetcars and certain aspects of racial etiquette almost impossible also rendered them largely unnecessary. In contrast to the South, where in many cities the growth of ghettos was retarded, in the North blacks were rapidly becoming residentially isolated from the rest of the population. Thus in northern cities informal contacts between the races in daily life were becoming less and less frequent. Because most blacks now lived in a circumscribed section of the city, there was less need for the formal establishment of separate streetcars, schools, and so on: de facto segregation, resulting from the growth of the black ghetto, was accomplishing in many instances the same end.

CHAPTER 9

Occupations in Flux: The Industrial Breakthrough

Despite the increasing segregation and discrimination that confronted blacks in Cleveland after 1915, thousands of migrants came to the city and became permanent residents. They were drawn there—as they were to other northern cities—by the lure of economic opportunity. Before World War I, almost a third of the city's employed Negro men were engaged in domestic or personal service occupations and only 22 percent worked in manufacturing. During the Great Migration the occupational status of Cleveland's Negro workers underwent a considerable transformation. By 1920, almost two-thirds of the city's black males worked in industrial occupations, while only 12 percent were now engaged in domestic or personal service. During the next ten years, the percentage in industrial work fell off slightly, and the proportion in service occupations rose to 16 percent; but this reversal was quite moderate compared to the gains that had been made during the war years.[1]

Most of the new job openings were in the area of unskilled labor (over half of all black males were in this category in 1920), but blacks made significant gains in semiskilled and skilled factory work as well. The pressing needs of manufacturers during the wartime crisis broke down the color barrier in Cleveland's heavy industries. In 1923 an official of the city's National Malleable Casting Company stated his approval of the performance of black employees in a wide variety of positions. "We have [black] molders, core makers, chippers, fitters, locomotive crane

[1] Louise Venable Kennedy, *The Negro Peasant Turns Cityward* (New York, 1930), 75; U.S. *Fourteenth Census, 1920* (Washington, 1922), IV, 1084–86; U.S. *Fifteenth Census, 1930* (Washington, 1932), IV, 1285–87.

operators, melting furnace operators, general foremen, foremen, assistant foremen, clerks, timekeepers[;] in fact, there is no work in our shop that they cannot do and do well, if properly supervised." A survey of local firms the following year revealed that twelve large foundries employed labor that ranged from 10 to 60 percent Negro in composition. In all but one of the plants some Afro-Americans had advanced to semiskilled and skilled positions, and a few had become foremen. Many of the migrants earned double or triple the wages they had received in the South. A 1918 study of over one thousand Cleveland workers revealed that the growing discrimination in other areas of life was not reflected in wage scales; white and black workers in similar industries received essentially the same pay, which averaged about $20 a week.[2]

At the opposite end of the occupational scale, the increase in black population after 1915 created a larger clientele for some Negroes in the professions and stimulated the further development of black business. "For the first time in the history of the city," the *Advocate* proclaimed in 1917, "the Average Business and Professional Man is making real money. He is able to meet his obligations promptly and to lay something aside for the proverbial 'rainy day.'" With a few exceptions, the increase in black professionals kept pace with the growth rate of the black community. The largest gains were in the teaching field; the number of black public school teachers increased eightfold between 1910 and 1930. The number of black clergymen and dentists expanded equally as fast during these years. The number of Negro physicians increased at a more moderate rate, and movement of blacks into the legal profession slowed considerably. The less dramatic expansion in law and medicine was probably due to the changing racial climate of the city. Prior to World War I, both black doctors and, especially, black lawyers often were able to draw clients from both races. In the wake of the Great Migration this situation gradually changed. For several years after his arrival in Cleveland in 1917, Dr. William P. Saunders, a Negro physician, had as many white patients as Negro; by the end of the 1920s, however, his clientele was becoming almost exclusively Negro. Although as late as the early 1930s a few black lawyers and physicians still had integrated practices, the consolidation of the ghetto and the intensification of racial prejudice that accompanied the postwar era made this much less likely

[2] John B. Abell, "The Negro in Industry," *Trade Winds* (March 1924), 20; J. O. Houze, "Negro Labor and the Industries," *Opportunity*, 1 (January 1923), 21; Committee on Housing and Sanitation of the Cleveland Chamber of Commerce, *An Investigation of Housing Conditions of War Workers in Cleveland* (Cleveland, 1918), 28.

than before. Increasingly, the clientele of these professionals was limited to members of their own race.[3]

The trend toward increasing reliance on black patronage was also evident among Negro businessmen. Between 1910 and 1930, the number of black retail dealers in Cleveland increased almost tenfold. Most of these enterprises were relatively small, ghetto-based enterprises; the Negro tailors, barbers, and caterers who serviced an all-white, elite clientele were rapidly becoming obsolete. A survey of black businesses made in 1929 found 215 stores in the black community. Each was usually owned by a single proprietor, and altogether they employed only 161 full-time and 34 part-time employees. Food stores, restaurants, and lunch counters accounted for over one half of all black businesses; a variety of drug stores, cigar stands, candy shops, clothing and jewelry stores, ice houses, coal yards, and automotive repair shops and parts dealerships made up the remainder. Black businesses had increased dramatically in number as a result of the migration, but they continued to be inadequately financed. Unable to compete with the lower prices, wider selection of goods, and expensive advertising campaigns of the large white firms and chain stores, black businessmen depended almost exclusively on the ghetto trade for their livelihood.[4]

In spite of these handicaps, a number of black businessmen managed to establish profitable enterprises. The tightening housing market for blacks proved a boon for real estate dealers. During the severe housing shortage of the Great Migration period, Thomas Fleming, Welcome Blue, Nahum Brascher, and several other prominent blacks formed the Cleveland Realty, Housing, and Investment Company for the purpose of buying up Central Avenue properties. By the winter of 1917–18, the company owned almost every apartment building on East 40th Street between Central and Scovill, and was still expanding. These black real

[3] Cleveland *Advocate*, January 13, 1917; U.S. Census Bureau occupational data, 1910–30; interview with Dr. William P. Saunders, August 6, 1972. It should be noted, however, that while there was strong tendency for black professionals to rely upon the patronage of their own race to a great extent, many black doctors, lawyers, and dentists managed to retain some white clients. This was especially true of the lawyers. At the beginning of the 1930s, there was still one Negro lawyer in Cleveland whose practice was 50 percent white, and some others had a "considerable" number of white clients. This state of affairs also prevailed in New York, Chicago, Detroit, and throughout New England, and Negro lawyers in these areas were perhaps the members of their race most integrated in society at this time. For a discussion of the clientele of black professionals in different parts of the country, see Carter G. Woodson, *The Negro Professional Man and the Community* (n.p., 1934), 98–103, 171–73, 237–39.

[4] U.S. Bureau of the Census, *Negroes in the United States, 1920–1932* (Washington, 1935), 522.

estate dealers, like their white counterparts, attempted to squeeze the most economic gain out of the wartime emergency. The *Gazette* complained that after the company gained control of properties, it proceeded to overcharge the new black tenants, "boosting the rents from three to seven and ten dollars a month above what the 'rooms' were renting for up to the time they secured control of them." Such activities among black entrepreneurs were not, of course, unique to Cleveland. In New York at the turn of the century Philip A. Payton, Jr. organized the Afro-American Realty Company and was responsible for opening up a number of apartment buidings in Harlem to Negro tenants for the first time; and although the Afro-American Realty Company folded in 1908, Payton and other black entrepreneurs who succeeded him reaped small fortunes as a by-product of housing discrimination against blacks. For Payton, as for black real estate men in Cleveland, segregation sometimes could be profitable.[5]

Other black businessmen capitalized on the existence of the ghetto in non-exploitative ways. By the end of the 1920s there were ten Negro undertaking establishments in the city. Of these, J. Walter Wills's "House of Wills" remained by far the most prominent. Aware that the shift of the black population eastward could mean losing clientele to his competitors, Wills sold his Central Avenue funeral home in 1925 and invested in a much larger building on East 55th Street. By then Wills was well on his way to becoming one of the richest Negro funeral directors in Ohio, and he enjoyed the respect of both the black community and white leaders in the city.[6]

Less well known among whites, but equally successful, was the young black entrepreneur Alonzo Wright. Born in Tennessee, Wright had only an eighth-grade education when he came to Cleveland in 1917. After working for a while in a downtown garage as a parking attendant, Wright was befriended by a Standard Oil Company executive who helped him obtain the franchise for the first Standard service station located in a predominantly black neighborhood. Through innovations in customer service (Wright was among the first to institute free tire and radiator checks and windshield cleaning as a regular procedure), he made this station a success; and when Standard built gas stations in other black neighborhoods during the following decade, the company

[5] Cleveland *Gazette*, April 28, 1917, September 7, 1918; Cleveland *Advocate*, March 31, April 21, December 8, 1917; Gilbert Osofsky, *Harlem: The Making of a Ghetto* (New York, 1966), ch. 7.

[6] Charles W. Chesnutt, "The Negro in Cleveland," *The Clevelander*, 5 (November 1930), 4; Russell H. Davis, *Memorable Negroes in Cleveland's Past* (Cleveland, 1969), 45.

found it both natural and profitable to lease the new franchises to Wright. By the early 1930s, the black entrepreneur had acquired a chain of seven service stations.[7]

If the expanding ghetto created an economic base for a businessman like Wright, it also enlarged the opportunities for black journalists. Although a number of black newspapers were founded in Cleveland before World War I, only the *Journal*, which published continuously for nine years, managed to compete successfully against the *Gazette*, the city's oldest race paper. After the *Journal* folded in 1912, its place was taken two years later by the *Advocate*, a moderate weekly edited by an articulate West Indian immigrant, Ormand Forte. For several years the *Advocate* appeared quite successful, but by 1922 it too had folded. Undoubtedly this failure was the result of competition from two additional race papers, the *Call* (founded in 1920 by Garrett Morgan) and the *Post* (published by Norman McGhee and Herbert S. Chauncey). Undaunted, Forte established in 1924 yet another black weekly, the *Herald*. The black population of the city, however, was simply not large enough to support three or four newspapers. By the end of the decade, the *Herald* had ceased publication, and the two remaining competitors of the *Gazette* had wisely merged to form the *Call and Post*. The *Call and Post* would soon outdistance its older rival and become, during the following decade, the leading race paper in Cleveland.[8]

The most successful businessman in Cleveland's postwar black community was Herbert Chauncey. Born in Georgia, Chauncey migrated to Cleveland before the war. While working in the postal service, he studied law and soon was able to pass the bar exam and open his own law office. In 1921 with the assistance of George Hinton and several other black entrepreneurs, Chauncey opened the first Negro-owned and -operated bank in the city, the Empire Savings and Loan Company. "The company grew," a Negro resident later recalled, "because it was the one banking institution that was willing to finance home buying for Negroes without discrimination." By 1926 Empire Savings had succeeded to the point where it was able to open a branch office. Chauncey

---

[7] Chesnutt, "The Negro in Cleveland," 4; interview with Dr. William P. Saunders, August 6, 1972.

[8] Biographical statement and newspaper clipping relating to Ormand Forte, Western Reserve Historical Society; interview with Norman McGhee, September 3, 1971. According to Harry C. Smith (Cleveland *Gazette*, May 29, 1920), at one time or another prior to 1920, sixteen black newspapers had competed with the *Gazette*. If this was true—Smith was given to exaggeration in comparing his newspaper to others—then most of the *Gazette's* competitors must have been very short-lived, for no clippings or record of their existence seems to have survived.

was similar to his predecessor, S. Clayton Green, in the diversity of his activities. Besides the *Post* and Empire Savings, the black entrepreneur also established a real estate company and one of the first black life insurance companies in Cleveland. Unfortunately, like Green, Chauncey did not live to see his many projects come to fruition. After his untimely death in 1930, Chauncey's enterprises quickly collapsed in the wake of the Great Depression.[9]

The chief difference between Chauncey and S. Clayton Green was the degree of white involvement in, and patronage of, their business enterprises. Green found it necessary to widen his financial base by appealing, in some of his entrepreneurial schemes, to white customers. The increased size of Cleveland's black population after 1915, however, made it possible for Chauncey to build up successful businesses without relying even partially upon white patronage. With the exception of Empire Savings, in which a few whites had savings accounts, *all* of Chauncey's projects were committed exclusively to the Negro market.

Despite notable advances in industrial work and moderate gains for some blacks in business and the professions, the postwar economic achievement of Cleveland's black community was still deficient in a number of respects. Perhaps the most notable failure was the small change which occurred in the economic status of black women. As a result of the wartime labor shortage, black women in cities throughout the North were able, for the first time in many instances, to obtain jobs as semiskilled operatives in manufacturing. Blacks who optimistically saw this as the beginning of "a new day for the colored woman worker," however, were mistaken. After 1918, most of the black women in manufacturing lost their jobs to returning soldiers; and by 1930 the overwhelming majority of employed Negro women were still engaged in domestic or personal service. As charwomen, laundresses, and house servants, these women continued to occupy the lowest rungs of the occupational ladder.[10]

[9] Cleveland *Gazette*, January 15, 1921, November 10, 1923, September 18, 1926, November 5, 1927; Davis, *Memorable Negroes in Cleveland's Past*, 53. In addition to banking and insurance, another area of black entrepreneurial involvement in the 1920s was sports promotion. A number of black businessmen were responsible for organizing a black baseball team in Cleveland early in the decade. The Cleveland Stars were managed by George Tate, a black baseball star who had attended Oberlin College. Interview with Dr. William Saunders, August 6, 1972; Cleveland *Gazette*, March 18, 1922.

[10] For an example of the ill-founded optimism over wartime employment of black women in industry, see [Joint Committee on Employment of Colored Women in New York and Brooklyn,] *A New Day for the Colored Woman Worker: A Study of Colored Women in Industry in New York City* (n.p., 1919), *passim*.

Another deficiency in the black economic structure was the lack of improvement in white-collar employment. The percentage of the black work force engaged in clerical work changed very little between 1910 and 1930. In most cases white businesses steadfastly refused to hire Negro clerks. When a Euclid Avenue department store hired two Negro saleswomen in 1919 and placed them "conspicuously" at the front of the store, it was an item worthy of mention in the Negro press. As during the prewar era, only a handful of blacks gained positions as book-keepers, cashiers, or stenographers. Throughout the 1920s, the East Ohio Gas Company and the Ohio Bell Telephone Company refused to employ Negroes "in anything but the humblest positions," and the small number of clerical jobs opening up in black businesses could not possibly counter the effects of the exclusionary policies of such giant firms.[11]

In the area of public service, Negroes did register some gains. The dramatic increase in black population after 1915, coupled with the consolidation of the ghetto, made the election of a Negro to the state leg-islature once again possible. Councilman Thomas Fleming helped a number of blacks acquire positions as clerks or assistants to department heads in city government. However, most Afro-Americans employed by the city or county occupied low-level positions. The highest Negro ap-pointments before 1928 were those of assistant county prosecutor in 1918 and assistant city police prosecutor six years later. Some city agen-cies, such as the fire department, continued to exclude blacks after the Great Migration, and it was small consolation that the city's garbage collection unit was manned and supervised mostly by blacks by 1930.[12]

Animosity between black workers and white labor unions continued to hinder black economic progress after 1915. At the annual convention of the American Federation of Labor in 1916 the Cleveland Federation expressed the fear, shared by many unionists, that a large-scale migra-tion of southern Negroes to the North might seriously threaten the labor movement there. By then, the fears of white laborers that blacks were antilabor had almost become (like so many other racial fears) a self-fulfilling prophecy. Many Afro-Americans had come to associate the labor movement with discrimination and mob violence, and more than a few looked to their employers, rather than their white fellow workers, for protection and an equal opportunity to work. To be sure, an impor-tant exception to this pattern of interracial hostility between black and

[11] Cleveland *Gazette*, February 1, 1919; Chesnutt, "The Negro in Cleveland," 4. For occupational data, see Tables 15 and 16.

[12] Thomas W. Fleming, "My Rise and Persecution" (manuscript autobiography [1932] in Western Reserve Historical Society), 54–55; Chesnutt, "The Negro in Cleveland," 4.

white workers occurred in the Cleveland steel industries during World War I. The Amalgamated Association of Iron and Steel Workers local actively recruited black workers during the war, and one result was that Cleveland became one of the very few cities where black workers solidly backed the Great Steel Strike of 1919. After 1920, however, the Amalgamated rapidly declined as an organization, and the general conservatism and racism of the AFL led to a neglect of the black worker. This, coupled with the immigrant steelworkers' increasing "feeling of antagonism and dislike" toward blacks, fueled black hostility to unions. A survey conducted among seventy-five Cleveland firms in 1924 reported that black workers were "loyal to their northern employers to the best of their ability. Scarcely has there been a complaint against these people," the study noted, "on the ground of their being trouble makers. . . . They come here understanding the American Language and having a knowledge of our basic ideals. They do not bring with them any of the communistic or socialistic spirit to be found among some immigrants from certain portions of Europe."[13]

Ironically, evidences of interracial solidarity during the steel strike of 1919 did not lead unionists in other industries or trades to change their attitude toward blacks. During the Great Migration, one Ohio AFL spokesman bluntly stated that integrated locals were not in the best interests of labor. Southern black migrants, he claimed, did not make good union men because they did not understand the necessity for a "sustained effort" by labor organizations against manufacturers. Black workers rarely had an opportunity to vindicate themselves of this charge. The policy of excluding blacks from union membership, widespread before 1916, came close to being universal in the craft unions during the 1920s. Only in a few of the more traditional skilled trades, such as masonry, did a small group of older black workers continue to maintain union ties. Younger blacks were kept out of the unions by being denied the opportunity to gain the skills requisite for union membership. "The trade schools conducted by the Board of Education," Charles Chesnutt explained in 1930, "are so tied up by rules and regulations, largely dictated by the labor unions, that it is difficult for a Negro boy to acquire a trade in them." The Negro youth, Chesnutt continued,

cannot study unless he secures in advance the promise of a job where he can do practical work on part time during his studies, or where he

[13] Sterling D. Spero and Abram L. Harris, *The Black Worker: The Negro and the Labor Movement* (New York, 1931), 102, 257–61; Abell, "The Negro in Industry," 17; Houze, "Negro Labor and the Industries," 21, 22; David Brody, *Labor in Crisis: The Steel Strike of 1919* (Philadelphia, 1965), 162.

will be permanently employed at the end of his course. The difficulty in placing them has caused the officials to discourage the attendance of Negro students. A colored youth can take elementary training in the East Technical High School, but practical training in many trades can only be acquired in factories which discourage or limit the number of apprentices and especially Negro apprenticeships.

By such devious means blacks were effectively excluded from the skilled trades for decades to come.[14]

Perhaps the most severe example of white antagonism toward black workers was that of the Waiters' Union. In 1917 white waiters, many of whom were Greek immigrants, went on strike in an attempt to force black waiters out of their jobs. Violence erupted between the two groups and one Negro was severely beaten. Within a year, these tactics proved partially successful; white waiters forced the managers of three Cleveland hotels to fire their black waiters and replace them with whites. By 1929, "jobs as hotel help had practically vanished" for blacks. Black waiters gained partial revenge in 1930 when they served as strikebreakers against the now completely white Waiters' Union. Once again violence broke out between the two groups, and for a while the police found it necessary to place an armed guard at the home of the leader of the strikebreakers. The black waiters gained no lasting benefit from their retaliation, however. When the strike was finally settled in 1931, the whites were allowed to return to the jobs, and the black waiters were once again dismissed from their positions in the hotels. Nothing had changed.[15]

In the face of such blatant racism, it is not surprising that black leaders had small regard for labor unions. The opposition of prominent Negroes, in 1928, to the Shipstead anti-injunction bill was indicative of a long-standing distrust of organized labor. Two influential Cleveland Negroes, Charles Chesnutt and Harry E. Davis, appeared before the Senate Judiciary Committee to oppose the bill, claiming that any restriction on the power of the courts to limit union activities would have a damaging effect on the black labor force. If black workers were going

[14] Cleveland *Gazette*, March 24, May 12, 1917, February 22, 1919; George A. Myers, "Answer to Questionnaire from Chamber of Commerce Committee on Immigration and Emigration," in 1926 correspondence; George A. Myers to Clayborne George, November 29, 1926, George A. Myers Papers, Ohio Historical Society; Chesnutt, "The Negro in Cleveland," 3–4. See also F. Ray Marshall and Vernon M. Briggs, Jr., *The Negro and Apprenticeship* (Baltimore, Md., 1967), 102.

[15] Chesnutt, "The Negro in Cleveland," 27; Cleveland *Gazette*, November 3, 1917, September 21, 28, 1918, August 16, 30, 1930; interview with Russell and Rowena Jelliffe, September 1, 1971.

to be denied the protection of union membership, Davis told the Committee, there was only one place where they could have their "employment rights" protected: the courts. "For all practical purposes the proposed bill would take away this right from the group of independent workers for whom I am speaking and it would mean their subjection to a state of economic serfdom." When white unionists simultaneously denied Negroes membership and vilified them for becoming strikebreakers, black citizens had ample reason to question the utility of the labor movement. They had little to lose by favoring the open shop.[16]

How did the changes in black occupational structure wrought by the Great Migration compare to the pattern of job-holding of other groups? To answer this question, occupational data for native whites and foreign-born whites for 1920 and 1930 were tabulated and transformed into occupational indexes, using the same procedure followed in analyzing the 1870, 1890, and 1910 census data. Unfortunately, no data on specific immigrant groups are available after 1890, and for 1930 the category "native whites" is not broken down into second-generation immigrants and native whites of native parentage. As a result, the comparative analysis must be somewhat less detailed than for other years.

Considering first the male work force, it is evident that the 1910–20 decade was one of moderate occupational improvement for Cleveland Negroes. These changes occurred mostly at the lower levels of the occupational hierarchy, but this does not make them less significant as a result. The percentage of blacks employed in domestic or personal service fell sharply from 29.6 to 12.2; the proportion in unskilled labor rose dramatically, and the percentage in semiskilled and skilled work also improved. The overall occupational index for black males moved up from 568 to 549.[17] (See Tables 15 and 17.)

The increased wartime demand for unskilled and semiskilled factory labor also affected native whites and the foreign-born. Between 1910 and 1920, the percentage of all male workers engaged in unskilled labor rose from 13.6 to 20.2; the percentage in semiskilled labor increased from 8.4 to 16.6. Unlike the employment impact on blacks, however, the impact of this trend on the overall occupational status of white groups in the economy was negative. Because their occupational status in 1910 was fairly high, the movement of some native whites and immigrants

[16] Spero and Harris, *The Black Worker*, 139; *A Bill to Amend the Judicial Code . . .*, Hearings before the Senate Subcommittee of the Committee on the Judiciary on S. 1482, 70th Cong., 1st sess. (1928), 603–14. For a general survey of the strained relationship between organized labor and black workers in the 1920s, see Spero and Harris, *The Black Worker*, 87–315 *passim*.

[17] The occupational index is discussed in Appendix I.

TABLE 15. *Occupational structure of Cleveland, by racial and ethnic group, 1920*

	Professional		Proprietary		Clerical		Skilled		Semiskilled		Unskilled		Domestic	
	Number	Percentage	Number	Percentage	Number	Percentage	Number	Percentage	Number	Percentage	Number	Percentage	Number	Percentage
Males														
Negroes	212	1.3	217	1.4	406	2.7	2,194	14.6	1,785	11.9	7,953	53.0	1,830	12.2
Native whites of native parentage	4,629	7.0	5,636	8.5	16,047	24.3	20,998	31.8	9,629	14.6	4,656	7.1	1,196	1.8
Native whites of foreign or mixed parentage	3,115	4.3	5,726	8.0	15,027	20.9	24,278	33.8	12,958	18.0	6,603	9.2	1,222	1.7
Foreign-born whites	2,103	1.7	9,416	7.8	7,251	6.0	38,404	31.8	20,878	17.3	36,009	29.8	2,541	2.1
All workers	10,065	3.7	21,014	7.7	38,760	14.2	86,164	31.5	45,377	16.6	55,230	20.2	6,854	2.5
Females														
Negroes	150	2.9	164	3.2	191	3.7	151	2.9	888	17.4	176	3.5	3,223	63.0
Native whites of native parentage	3,585	15.8	718	3.2	11,958	53.0	350	1.5	3,846	17.0	153	0.7	1,458	6.4
Native whites of foreign or mixed parentage	2,574	9.2	625	2.2	13,852	49.3	767	2.7	7,434	26.5	302	1.1	1,963	7.0
Foreign-born whites	733	4.1	915	5.2	3,551	20.1	470	2.7	6,253	35.3	667	3.8	4,531	25.6
All workers	7,042	9.6	2,422	3.3	29,552	40.2	1,738	2.4	18,421	25.0	1,298	1.8	11,178	14.8

Occupational category

SOURCE: U.S. *Fourteenth Census, 1920* (Washington, 1922), IV, 1084–87.
NOTE: Totals include the additional category "Indians, Chinese, Japanese, and all others." In 1920, 3.6 percent of the male occupations and 2.9 percent of the female occupations in Cleveland were unspecified by the Census Bureau.

TABLE 16. *Occupational structure of Cleveland, by racial and ethnic group, 1930*

	Occupational category													
	Professional		Proprietary		Clerical		Skilled		Semiskilled		Unskilled		Domestic	
	Number	Percentage	Number	Percentage	Number	Percentage	Number	Percentage	Number	Percentage	Number	Percentage	Number	Percentage
Males														
Negroes	630	2.5	537	2.1	899	3.6	2,783	11.1	3,848	15.3	11,255	44.7	4,108	16.3
Native whites	9,949	6.2	11,654	7.3	36,807	23.0	42,609	26.6	33,749	21.1	14,394	9.0	3,832	2.4
Foreign-born whites	2,774	2.5	9,263	8.4	8,206	7.4	31,870	29.0	21,354	19.4	27,285	24.9	4,221	3.8
All workers	13,365	4.5	21,626	7.3	45,947	15.5	77,624	26.2	59,035	20.0	53,469	18.1	12,369	4.2
Females														
Negroes	297	2.7	291	2.7	282	2.6	292	2.7	1,714	15.6	99	0.9	7,665	69.8
Native whites	10,285	15.0	1,360	2.0	31,288	45.5	1,319	1.9	14,797	21.5	553	0.8	6,639	9.7
Foreign-born whites	1,215	6.3	849	4.4	3,927	20.4	277	1.4	6,135	31.9	283	1.5	5,785	30.1
All workers	11,801	11.9	2,514	2.5	35,499	35.9	1,888	1.9	22,662	22.9	935	0.9	20,094	20.3

SOURCE: U.S. *Fifteenth Census, 1930* (Washington, 1932), IV, 1285–88.
NOTE: Totals include the additional category "other races." "Native whites" includes all whites born in the United States, whether of native, foreign, or mixed parentage. In 1930, 4.2 percent of the male occupations and 3.7 percent of the female occupations in Cleveland were unspecified by the Census Bureau.

TABLE 17. Occupational indexes, Cleveland, 1920–30

	1920	Change, 1910–20	1930	Change, 1920–30
Males				
Negroes	549	+19	546	+ 3
Native whites of native parentage	371	− 9	NA	NA
Native whites of foreign or mixed parentage	392	− 9	NA	NA
All native whites	383	− 9	386	− 3
Foreign-born whites	459	−16	451	+ 8
All workers	425	−13	426	− 1
Females				
Negroes	601	+ 8	618	−17
Native whites of native parentage	330	+37	NA	NA
Native whites of foreign or mixed parentage	368	+45	NA	NA
All native whites	351	+47	356	− 5
Foreign-born whites	479	+61	479	NC
All workers	397	+50	410	−13

SOURCE: Tables 10, 15, and 16.
NOTE: As discussed in Appendix I, the occupational categories upon which the occupational index is based are ranked from 1 (high) to 7 (low). Thus a change in the index for a given group from a higher to a lower number indicates an improvement in occupational status, and is denoted with a plus (+) sign. NA indicates data not available. NC indicates no change.

into semiskilled and unskilled work tended to depress the white occupational index. The index for all native whites dropped from 374 to 383; for foreign-born whites it fell from 443 to 459; for all male workers, from 412 to 425. Thus between 1910 and 1920, black males gained occupationally in both an absolute *and* a relative sense, when their progress is compared with the moderate downward trends of other groups. The steady occupational decline that blacks experienced in the late nineteenth and early twentieth centuries had finally been halted, and the large economic gap between white and black workers had been shortened to some extent.[18]

[18] It must be emphasized again that changes in the occupational index measure *group* mobility and tell us nothing at all about the mobility of particular individuals within a given group. Thus we cannot know, on the basis of the occupational index, whether certain elements of the black, native white, or immigrant populations were advancing (or declining) occupationally faster than others. Despite this limitation,

During the 1920s, the occupational index for black males improved only to a negligible degree. The proportion of blacks in domestic service increased slightly, but this was offset by gains in the semiskilled, proprietary, and professional categories. (See Table 16.) The occupational index for native whites continued to decline during this period (probably because of the migration of unskilled southern whites to the city after World War I), while the index for foreign-born whites improved. In neither case, however, was the change very significant, and in general the postwar decade was marked by exceptional occupational stability for all groups in the economy.[19]

As in the decades before 1910, the trend in female occupations during the 1910–30 period did not parallel that of the male half of the population. During the war there was some upgrading of the occupations of black women. About one out of every seven Negro domestics took factory jobs, and the percentage of black clerical workers advanced from 1.4 to 3.7 percent. The occupational index for black women advanced from 609 to 601. Relative to other racial and ethnic groups, however, the position of Negroes continued the precipitous decline that had begun in the 1870s. White women continued, in even greater numbers than before the war, to move into clerical and professional work. Between 1910 and 1920 the proportion of all employed women in clerical work increased from 22.6 to 40.2 percent; fully one-half of native white women held white-collar jobs at the close of the decade. The occupational index for all employed women rose from 447 to 397. Equally significant was the gap in occupational status which began to open up between Negroes and the foreign-born. Prior to World War I, the position of black women was not unique, since a large proportion of immigrant women were also mired in low-paying domestic work. But between 1910 and 1920 foreign-born women began for the first time to obtain white-collar employment in sizable numbers, and at the same time the proportion of immigrant females working as domestics fell from 41 to 25.6 percent. While the occupational status of Negro women moved slowly upward, the index for foreign-born women jumped from 540 to 479.

---

the index is still a useful index of changes in the job structure—especially for the period after 1900, for which there is insufficient information to draw conclusions on the occupational mobility of specific individuals or families.

[19] It is likely, of course, that the occupational standing of native whites of New England stock was much higher than that of southern white migrants who had recently moved to the city. The anomalous rise in the occupational index of the foreign-born during the 1920–30 period may have been caused by the implementation of the Quota Act of 1924, which sharply reduced the influx of impoverished, occupationally depressed immigrants from southern and eastern Europe.

For women as well as men the 1920s was a period of occupational stability. The gradual upgrading of women's occupations that had occurred during the previous half-century now came to an end, and a slight trend in the opposite direction set in. The proportion of the total female work force in clerical positions slipped to 35.9 percent, and their overall occupational index dropped from 397 to 410. Black women also experienced a postwar occupational slump, but its significance was much more profound. The minor gains that they had made during and before the war were now completely wiped out, and the percentage of black women in domestic service returned to the high level it had reached in 1910. In 1930, the occupational status of Negro women was not much different from what it had been in 1870.[20]

In spite of all this, the economic status of Cleveland's black community in the postwar period cannot be summarized in negative terms. In 1930, males comprised approximately seven-tenths of all Negro workers in the city, and *their* occupational status had measurably improved since the Great Migration, even if that of Negro women had not.

Unfortunately, as blacks would all too soon discover, improvements in occupational status did not always entail job security. Accurate unemployment figures for the 1920s are not available, but it would appear that, in Cleveland, black workers—despite their loyalty to their employers and incipient distrust of labor unions—were too often "the last to be hired and the first to be fired." The problem of unemployment was not very serious during the early 1920s, when the mills and factories of the city were reaching new heights of productivity and were constantly in need of new workers. In 1924 the Cleveland Urban League affiliate was able

[20] The slight improvement in occupational opportunity for black women during the war masked the important fact that, in 1920, blacks made up a much higher *proportion* of all domestic service workers than they had in 1910. In 1910 only 9 percent of Cleveland's female domestic servants were Negro, but a decade later this figure had risen to 30 percent. This change was also common to other cities in the North, and in cities like Philadelphia, Indianapolis, and Kansas City, Missouri, the proportion of blacks in domestic service jobs rose to over 50 percent. This change was due less to the influx of blacks into these jobs than to an exodus of whites out of them. A study of eleven northern cities (using only slightly different occupational criteria than I have adopted) by the Census Bureau in 1929 showed that the total number of female servants actually declined between 1910 and 1920 from 238,002 to 187,894, while the number of black servants increased from 43,778 to 57,807. Given the large influx of migrants from the South, this black increase was rather moderate; nevertheless, the proportion of all servants who were black rose from 18.4 to 30.8 percent. Joseph A. Hill, *Women in Gainful Occupations, 1870–1920*, Census Monographs no. 9 (Washington, 1929), 115. The restriction on immigration from abroad after 1924 accelerated the black domination of the domestic occupations, gradually making northern cities, in this respect, more and more similar to the South.

to place almost three-fourths of its job applicants; three years later, it was still able to find employment for 60 percent of the blacks who came to its agency. Beginning in 1928, however, a serious black unemployment problem began to emerge. The Urban League reported that only 30 percent of its job applicants obtained employment; more ominous, one League official noted that in some factories "the colored worker was the first to go" when a layoff occurred. In 1930, as the city began to feel the effects of the Depression, the heaviest concentration of the jobless was in the Negro district west of East 55th Street. It was no coincidence that, five years later, the greatest concentration of relief cases would be located in this same area.[21]

[21] Annual Report of the Negro Welfare Association for 1924; Annual Report, June–October 1927; minutes of the Board of Trustees of the Negro Welfare Association, December 8, 1927, February 9, November 30, 1928, all in Cleveland Urban League Papers; Department of Industrial Relations of the National Urban League, *Unemployment Status of Negroes: A Compilation of Facts and Figures Respecting Unemployment among Negroes in One Hundred and Six Cities* (New York, 1931), 36; Howard W. Green, *Nine Years of Relief in Cleveland, 1928–1937* (Cleveland, 1937), 26–27, 59. The problems of black employment in Cleveland during the Great Depression are surveyed thoroughly by Christopher G. Wye in "The New Deal and the Negro Community: Toward a Broader Conceptualization," *Journal of American History*, 59 (December 1972), 621–39.

CHAPTER 10

Progress and Poverty
in the Black Community

The consolidation and expansion of the black ghetto in Cleveland had contradictory effects on the social and cultural life of the black community. On the one hand, it intensified the stratification of the black population along class lines that had begun before the Great Migration. More than ever, the particular church that a black family attended and the neighborhood they lived in indicated their socioeconomic status in the community, and after 1915 the divisions between upper, middle, and lower strata generally became more clear cut. On the other hand, the growth of the ghetto and the increase in white prejudice that followed in the wake of the migration fostered a growing sense of unity among Negroes, while a new middle-class interest in African and Afro-American folk traditions helped bridge the cultural gap between the average Negro and the black bourgeoisie, to some extent.

After World War I, the fraternal orders that had played so important a part in the social life of the black community declined in both numbers and significance. The gradual decline of the lodges, which would continue during and after the Depression of the 1930s, has not been studied much by historians, but it is likely that the factors involved were mostly nonracial in character and affected white fraternal orders as much as black. At the end of the nineteenth century, lodges served a number of social and economic purposes: they offered members a convenient place for entertainment and socializing and at the same time provided valuable life insurance and health benefits. Between roughly 1915 and 1945, however, the development of radio, motion pictures, and the automobile helped undermine many of the social functions of the lodges, while the growth of insurance firms rendered the fraternal benefit programs less valuable. It is probable that the black lodges declined less rapidly than the white orders. Because they had less economic and geographic mobility than their white counterparts, working-class blacks in particular continued to find the lodges useful as all-purpose social and recreational centers. But even for the black working class, the fraternal orders were no longer the central institutions they once had been.[1]

In contrast to the lodges, the black church entered a period of dynamic change as a result of the Great Migration. The prewar trend toward an increasing number and diversity of black religious institutions accelerated rapidly during the two decades after 1915. A few years before the onset of the migration, there were only 17 black churches in Cleveland. By the winter of 1918, there were 44; by 1921, 78; by 1933, over 140. The Baptists remained the largest single denomination, claiming fourteen thousand of the city's twenty-two thousand Negro church members in 1921. Antioch Baptist Church grew steadily during the migration and remained the largest black congregation in the city; by 1925 its membership reached one thousand.[2]

Conspicuous among the new churches were the numerous storefront congregations of the Holiness and Spiritualist sects and the poorer Baptists. In the 1920s, lower Central and Scovill avenues were dotted with the makeshift edifices of these congregations. These churches, with their personalized, informal services and fervid religious emotionalism, appealed to many of the lower-class Negro migrants from the South. Some

[1] For a useful discussion of the decline of the fraternal orders in the new urban environment of the 1920s, see Robert S. Lynd and Helen M. Lynd, *Middletown: A Study in Modern American Culture* (New York, 1929), 277, 304–8. On the growth of Negro insurance companies, which dated to the turn of the century, see August Meier, *Negro Thought in America, 1880–1915: Racial Ideologies in the Age of Booker T. Washington* (Ann Arbor, Mich., 1963), 141–46, and Walter B. Weare, *Black Business in the New South: A Social History of the North Carolina Mutual Life Insurance Company* (Urbana, Ill., 1973).

[2] Report of the Executive Secretary [of the Negro Welfare Association for the period September–October, 1918], Cleveland Urban League Papers, Western Reserve Historical Society; The Cleveland Foundation, *The Cleveland Year Book, 1921* (Cleveland, 1921), 294; *The Baptist Answer in 1924–25: Being the 95th Annual Report of the Cleveland Baptist Association* (Cleveland, 1925), 26; Julian Krawcheck, "Negro Tide from South Swelled City's Problems," Cleveland *Press*, May 31, 1963. Useful studies of the religious life of black Americans in general include Benjamin E. Mays and Joseph W. Nicholson, *The Negro's Church* (New York, 1933); Arthur H. Fauset, *Black Gods of the Metropolis: Negro Religious Cults of the Urban North* (Philadelphia, 1944); and Seth M. Scheiner, "The Negro Church and the Northern City, 1890–1930," in William G. Shade and Roy C. Herrenkohl, eds., *Seven on Black: Reflections on the Negro Experience in America* (Philadelphia, 1969), 92–116.

of these new churches were able to preserve the congregations of southern communities almost intact. For example, one black minister, Charles
C. Ailer, came to Cleveland from Alabama with his congregation and
founded Zion Hill Baptist Church. This type of institutional "transplant-
ing" gave a measure of continuity to the lives of southern migrants, and
helped smooth the path of their adjustment to urban society.[3]

At first, many of the new black churches were unable to find permanent quarters. An Urban League survey of 1918 showed that all but
one of the black churches founded between 1916 and 1918 were holding
services in rented buildings. For the larger congregations, however, this
problem was solved with the passage of time. As the Afro-American
population gradually moved eastward, it often engulfed areas where
white congregations had, many years before, erected churches. White
churches usually held out for a while, but when most of their membership had moved to the suburbs or to outlying districts of the city they
invariably sold the church edifices and relocated far from the ghetto. In
1927 the white First Baptist Church, an institution which had at one time
personified the spirit of integrationism in Cleveland, symbolized the
changing pattern of race relations in the city when it sold its Prospect
Avenue building to a black church and moved out of the city. A member
noted later that the Prospect Avenue location "was suited neither to a
mission church nor to a membership who were gradually moving eastward to Cleveland Heights." In most cases it was unnecessary for Negro
congregations to construct new churches; they usually bought the buildings of white congregations who were only too willing to sell at a
reasonable price. In 1920 alone thirteen white congregations sold their
buildings to black churches.[4]

[3] Krawcheck, "Negro Tide from South Swelled City's Problems." The growth of
black churches during the postwar era probably obscures a gradual decline in
church attendance among some of the migrants—notably younger black males.
Though conducted during a later period, Frank T. Cherry's study of black migrants
in Chicago after 1945 is probably indicative of the changing pattern of religious
behavior that an earlier generation of newcomers underwent. Surveying a selected
group of migrants, Cherry found that 98 percent had attended church in the South,
but only 76 percent did so after having lived in Chicago for several years. This
decline was due almost solely to the changing attitudes of young blacks; only 59
percent of the young males interviewed reported that they still attended church.
Frank T. Cherry, "Southern In-Migrant Negroes in North Lawndale, Chicago,
1949–59: A Study of Internal Migration and Adjustment" (Ph.D. dissertation, University of Chicago, 1965), 121. For suggestive earlier comments on this phenomenon,
see Charles S. Johnson, "The New Frontage on American Life," in Alain Locke, ed.,
The New Negro (New York, 1925), 286, and St. Clair Drake and Horace R. Cayton,
Black Metropolis: A Study of Negro Life in a Northern City (New York, 1945),
650–53.
[4] Report of the Executive Secretary, 1918, Cleveland Urban League Papers; His-

The expansion of black religious activity during the migration years was primarily a lower- and middle-class phenomenon. Before World War I, there had been only two elite churches, Mt. Zion Congregational and St. Andrew's Episcopal; both were moderate in size compared to the larger Baptist churches, and St. Andrew's was quite select in its membership, which consisted of old-elite, light-skinned Negroes. After 1915 both of these churches expanded in size, and a third elite church, St. Mark's Presbyterian, was founded in 1918. Neither Mt. Zion nor St. Mark's was limited to old-elite families, and in the face of their competition St. Andrew's was also forced to open its doors to respectable members of the new business and professional classes in the black community. By 1922 St. Andrew's had almost four hundred communicants, and it remained the most prestigious black church in the city.[5]

Even more so than before the war, there were few integrated congregations in Cleveland. Most white Protestant churches took little interest in the city's enlarged black population and discouraged even the most respectable Negroes from joining their congregations. The Chesnutt family, which continued to attend a white Episcopal church, was virtually the only exception to this rule. In addition, the Catholic Church, which had previously made an effort to assimilate blacks into the activities of the Church, now reversed its policy in 1922 and set up a separate parish for blacks, Our Lady of the Blessed Sacrament.[6]

Prior to the Great Migration, there was a good deal of residential intermixing among classes in the black community. The average black family lived on or near Central Avenue; but many middle-class and even elite Negroes also resided close to that thoroughfare. Only the completely integrated old elite of the black community lived in neighborhoods far removed from the main area of black settlement. After 1915, this changed. The expansion of the black community and the tightening of the housing market altered this pattern to a considerable extent, and one's place of residency became a more accurate indicator of an individual's status in the black community.

In the wake of the Great Migration, as E. Franklin Frazier pointed out

---

tory of the First Baptist Church of Greater Cleveland, 1833–1933 (Cleveland [1935]), 62; The Cleveland Foundation, *The Cleveland Year Book, 1921,* 294; George A. Myers to Bishop J. H. Jones, September 8, 1922, George A. Myers Papers, Ohio Historical Society.

[5] George F. Bragg, *History of the Afro-American Group of the Episcopal Church* (Baltimore, Md., 1922), 239; interview with Dr. William P. Saunders, August 6, 1972.

[6] Cleveland *Gazette,* April 15, 1922; John T. Gillard, *The Catholic Church and the American Negro* (Baltimore, Md., 1929), 74–75.

in his classic study, *The Negro Family in Chicago*, upper- and middle-class blacks, as well as the more successful whites, fled the inner city and its impoverished masses. The result was "segregation by class" within the black community. In Chicago at the end of the 1920s, the economic status of residents of the Black Belt rose as one traversed from north to south. The poorest Negroes lived in the northernmost, oldest section of the ghetto, while the elite resided in the extreme southern part of the Black Belt. Frazier divided Chicago's South Side into seven socioeconomic "zones," which he differentiated by employing a number of variables for the measurement of income and status. Unfortunately, not all of the kinds of data which Frazier had at his command are available for Cleveland, but enough information exists to show that Cleveland's black community was also segregated residentially by economic class. I have used four variables to determine the economic status of different sections of the black community: home ownership, ownership of radios,[7] Negro illiteracy, and the percentage of individuals engaged in selected middle- and upper-class occupations. In each case, since there are no data available for earlier years, census-tract figures for 1930 were used. An area of high economic status would tend to have a low illiteracy rate but would register higher (relative to other predominantly Negro tracts) in the other three categories. Higher illiteracy rates would also indicate a greater concentration of recent arrivals from the South.[8]

These four measurements of economic status reveal that Cleveland's Afro-American population was stratified along an east-west axis at the end of the 1920s. It was possible to identify four zones in the black belt. (See Tables 18 and 19.) The zones, which correspond roughly to a series of concentric rings, contained neighborhoods of progressively higher economic status as one moved outward (primarily eastward) from the lower Central district. Zone 1, consisting of the area west of East 40th Street, was the oldest residential section of the Negro community. This

[7] In the 1920s, radios were usually fairly expensive items, and thus the ownership of radios can be used as a rough measure of economic status. In Cleveland in 1930, 22.8 percent of all black families, 37.9 percent of the foreign-born white families, and 62.5 percent of the native-white families owned radios. U.S. *Fifteenth Census, 1930, Population (Families)* (Washington, 1932), VI, 70.

[8] See E. Franklin Frazier, *The Negro Family in Chicago* (Chicago, 1932), ch. 6; for class differentiation in Harlem, see E. Franklin Frazier, "Negro Harlem: An Ecological Study," *American Journal of Sociology*, 43 (July 1937), 72–88. In analyzing class differentiation within the Cleveland ghetto, the most accurate indicator is the rate of illiteracy. The other three indicators are not broken down by race for each tract and hence are most useful, for the present purpose, in evaluating tracts where the black population constituted a high proportion of the total population.

area was filled with crowded and deteriorating lodging houses, had a high incidence of crime, and was close to the soot and noise of the industrial district and the docks. It contained the highest illiteracy rates and the lowest percentage of home ownership of any black section. Most blacks living in this area had recently migrated from the South, and few

TABLE 18. *Economic status of Cleveland Negroes by selected census tracts, 1930*

Census tract	Percentage Negro	Percentage of total families owning homes	Percentage of total families owning radios	Percentage of Negroes illiterate
Zone 1				
G-2	9	4	12	10.8
G-5	6	13	12	9.2
I-2	37	12	12	7.9
I-4	29	6	3	15.7
I-5	26	14	9	8.4
I-6	53	13	6	9.5
I-7	76	6	9	8.5
J-2	49	12	7	12.7
J-3	49	10	11	11.2
Zone 2				
H-9	89	6	19	5.6
I-8	76	6	17	7.3
I-9	82	10	10	6.7
Zone 3				
L-9	71	6	33	2.5
M-3	81	20	35	2.0
M-7	91	4	17	1.3
M-8	78	26	19	6.9
M-9	33	12	28	6.1
N-2	57	19	26	3.9
N-7	31	22	35	1.9
Zone 4				
L-6	9	21	60	3.9
M-4	76	26	44	0.9
M-5	70	34	40	1.3
M-6	81	26	31	0.9
S-2	19	28	41	1.2
S-8	14	28	43	0.7

SOURCE: Green, *Population Characteristics by Census Tracts, Cleveland, 1930* (Cleveland, 1931), 58, 60, 160–62.

NOTE: The figures in the second and third columns must be used with caution if the census tract in question contains less than about 70 percent Negro residents. It is probable, however, that whites and blacks in most tracts were of comparable economic status.

TABLE 19. *Percentage of residents of predominantly Negro census tracts engaged in selected occupations, 1930*

Census tract	Percentage Negro	Percentage engaged in professional, semiprofessional, or postal service
Zone 1		
I-7	76	0.6
Zone 2		
H-9	89	2.2
I-8	76	2.2
I-9	82	1.4
Zone 3		
L-9	71	3.0
M-3	81	3.8
M-7	91	1.9
M-8	78	1.8
Zone 4		
M-4	76	6.8
M-5	70	5.2
M-6	81	6.0

SOURCE: Green, *Population Characteristics By Census Tracts, Cleveland, 1930*, 189–92.

were engaged in professional, semiprofessional, or postal service occupations.[9]

As one moved eastward, illiteracy rates dropped and the number of residents owning their own homes and employed in middle- or upper-class professions increased. Zone 2 stretched approximately from East 40th to East 55th streets; as late as 1920 it was populated mostly by immigrants, but by 1930 it had become overwhelmingly Negro. Although less crowded and further removed from the industrial section than the lower Central area, this section was also deteriorating rapidly and beginning to take on the characteristics of a slum. Very few members of the black middle or upper classes lived in this area. One of the few who did so was Thomas Fleming, who was compelled to live there because of the residency requirement for his councilmanic seat. But even Fleming tried

[9] The census-tract data for 1930 do not give a further breakdown for the "professional and semi-professional service" category. On the characteristics of Zone 1, see also R. B. Navin, William D. Peattie, et al., *An Analysis of a Slum Area in Cleveland, Prepared for the Cleveland Metropolitan Housing Authority* (Cleveland, 1934), *passim*, and Gordon H. Simpson, comp., *Economic Survey of Housing in Districts of the City of Cleveland Occupied Largely by Colored People* (Cleveland [1931]), 20–50.

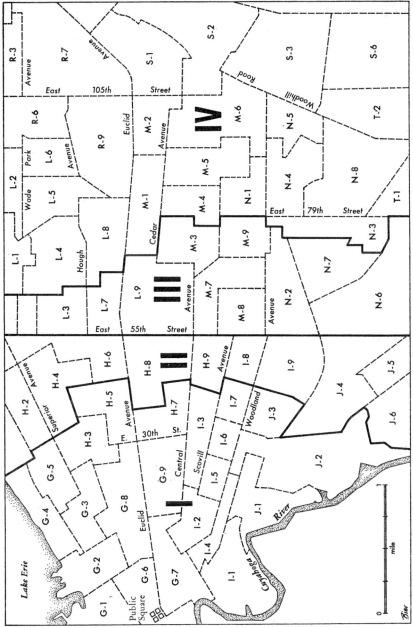

Map 2. Census Tracts and Socioeconomic Zones of Cleveland's East Side, 1930

to keep as far away from his constituency as possible, and in 1918 he moved into a new home on East 55th Street, on the very edge of the Eleventh Ward. Zone 3, from East 55th to East 79th streets, had a much higher incidence of home ownership and a substantially lower illiteracy than neighborhoods to the west. In 1930, the area between East 55th and East 65th (Tracts L-9 through M-8) was already making the transition to a working-class neighborhood, but the part of the zone stretching from East 65th to East 79th was solidly middle class.[10]

Only middle-class or elite Negroes lived in Zone 4, the area beyond East 79th Street. A pleasant residential section, it had only one-tenth of the illiteracy rate, and ten times the number of professionals, as Zone 1. Its population density was less than one-third that of the lower Central district. Included in Zone 4 were three small enclaves of elite Negroes outside of the main black belt. The two enclaves to the north of Hough Avenue near East 84th Street and to the east of East 105th Street had existed for several decades. The third lay along Kinsman Road (Tract S-8), well to the southeast of the central ghetto, and had come into being sometime prior to World War I. Residency in Zone 4 had once been limited almost exclusively to old-elite families who had close ties to the white community. After 1920, however, many businessmen and professionals who had offices or stores on Central Avenue now also resided far from the heart of the ghetto.[11]

The increasing "integration" of the new and old elites in patterns of residency and church affiliation signaled the decline of the once dominant group of light-skinned Negro entrepreneurs, barbers, and professionals who had catered to a predominantly white clientele. Although many teachers and professionals and a very small number of businessmen continued to maintain some social relationships with whites, this phenomenon was uncommon by 1930. Among the newer black businessmen there was no inclination to associate with whites, and as black lawyers and doctors found themselves increasingly restricted to a black clientele, they also had less occasion to socialize with the opposite race on an informal basis. Changing career ambitions among the children of the old elite and their propensity to intermarry with successful members

[10] Cleveland *Advocate*, October 19, 1918 (letter to the editor).
[11] Howard W. Green, comp., *Population by Census Tracts, Cleveland and Vicinity, with Street Index* (Cleveland, 1931), 7–9; Charles W. Chesnutt, "The Negro in Cleveland," *The Clevelander*, 5 (November 1930), 3; Simpson, comp., *Economic Survey of Housing*, 98–120, 157–70; interview with Dr. William P. Saunders, August 6, 1972. Much of the information on the residency of businessmen and professionals was obtained from newspaper reports and from the Cleveland *City Directory*.

of the new elite also helped undermine divisions between the two groups. Edwin Chesnutt, the son of Charles Chesnutt, took up the new-elite occupation of dentistry; Chesnutt's daughter Ethel married the principal of a Negro high school in Washington, D.C., while John P. Green's daughter, Clara, married a Cleveland pharmacist. This process of amalgamation and transformation of the black elite, of course, was a gradual one, and it would be many years before the old elite was completely eliminated as a distinct social group. But by the eve of the Depression, the transition was virtually complete.[12]

Despite their increasing geographic separation from the black masses, middle- and upper-class blacks took a new interest in the social condition and cultural traditions of the southern migrants after 1915. Part of this concern was reflected in an increased black participation in social welfare organizations, a subject which will be dealt with in the following chapter. The new interest in southern Negro and African folk culture, however, deserves mention in the present context. As August Meier has shown, the origins of these new cultural concerns antedated the Harlem Renaissance by several decades and were ultimately rooted in the changing social and economic organization of black life in the country as a whole, especially in its large cities. The increasing segregation and ghettoization of blacks at the end of the nineteenth and beginning of the twentieth century gradually nurtured a new racial consciousness in blacks, and fostered a philosophy of self-help, race pride, and group solidarity. An incipient interest in folk materials and race history was a natural outgrowth of this new climate of opinion, and a number of black scholars, folklorists, and literary societies began to explore these topics as early as the 1890s.[13]

In Cleveland, however, the ghetto developed later than in Chicago or New York, and the formation of the self-help ideology and group economy was retarded or adulterated in practice. Under these circumstances, it is not surprising that, prior to World War I, educated Negroes in Cleveland were either indifferent or openly hostile to black cultural traditions. At the turn of the century, for example, a delegate to the Cleveland convention of the Ohio branch of the National Association of Colored Women criticized ragtime—a musical form that had originated among black musicians in the South—for its supposed "evil" and "de-

[12] This information was obtained from widely scattered sources and from interviews. Despite their changing occupational interests, most of the children of the old elite remained in recognizably elite positions. Quite exceptional was the case of Herbert D. Myers, George Myers's son, who became a mechanic with the White Automobile and Truck Company.
[13] Meier, *Negro Thought in America*, 256–78.

generating" influence upon black youth. As for African society and culture, it is likely that most blacks would have endorsed the view of novelist Charles W. Chesnutt, who admitted candidly to a friend in 1908 that Africa was nothing more than another "interesting foreign country" as far as he was concerned. These attitudes were not, of course, unique to Cleveland, but middle-class blacks there seemed particularly inclined to such views.[14]

After 1915, the influx from the South, increasing discrimination, and the consolidation of the ghetto helped foster a new racial consciousness among many middle-class blacks in Cleveland. The chief vehicle for this new interest in black folk culture was a unique social institution, Karamu House, originally known as the Playhouse Settlement. Its founders were two white social workers, Russell and Rowena Jelliffe, who had come to Cleveland from Chicago in 1915 at the behest of a local church group. Located for many years near East 38th and Central, Karamu was designed to be a multipurpose social center that would allow young people an opportunity for artistic and dramatic expression and training. Within five years of their arrival, the Jelliffes had established numerous clubs and classes in the cultural arts and helped set up a Central Avenue sports program. During the 1920s they formed a summer camp for ghetto youngsters and were able to purchase an old Central Avenue building which, when remodeled, became Karamu Theater.[15]

Although the Jelliffes had "great respect for what Negroes could bring to their society, culturally and otherwise," the original programs of the Playhouse Settlement were not aimed specifically at blacks. The founders' chief desire was to establish a biracial community center that would "bridge the factor of race, through the media of the theater, dance, and

[14] David A. Gerber, "Ohio and the Color Line: Racial Discrimination and Negro Responses in a Northern State, 1860–1915" (Ph.D. dissertation, Princeton University, 1971), 534–35; Charles W. Chesnutt to Hugh Browne, June 20, 1908, Charles Waddell Chesnutt Papers, Fisk University.

[15] Cleveland Gazette, July 3, 1915; Works Projects Administration of Ohio, "The Peoples of Cleveland" (typewritten manuscript [1942], Cleveland Public Library), 194; Russell Jelliffe to Charles W. Chesnutt [c. 1920], Charles Waddell Chesnutt Papers, Western Reserve Historical Society; Arna Bontemps and Jack Conroy, Anyplace But Here (New York, 1966), 278–86; Katrine M. Baxley, "The House the Jelliffes Built," Oberlin Alumni Magazine (Oberlin, Ohio), 62 (April 1966), 18–22; John Selby, Beyond Civil Rights (Cleveland, 1966), 11–47. Throughout its history, Karamu has had three major functions: it has reflected the cultural interests of the black middle class; served as a social and recreational center for black and, to some extent, white youth; and provided a common meeting ground for blacks and racially liberal whites. In the present context, only the first of these is explored in depth. A thorough history of Karamu, which is beyond the scope of this work, would involve a detailed examination of all three aspects.

the visual arts." In fact, the settlement's programs were integrated from the beginning, and this led to considerable opposition from some whites during the early years. Nevertheless, while the settlement would continue to receive most of its financial backing from liberal whites it soon became evident, as the ghetto enveloped the Central area, that its facilities would be utilized primarily by blacks. A number of elite Negroes lent both their moral and financial support to the enterprise, and the settlement soon became, in effect, a cultural outpost of the Harlem Renaissance. In 1920, six young blacks who had been inspired by the great black actor Charles Gilpin formed the Gilpin Players, an amateur theatrical group which eventually gained national recognition for its excellent productions. Using makeshift facilities, this group of actors began almost immediately to put on plays for the public. Although their earliest performances were "white" dramas, the Players soon began to stage plays that dealt more specifically with the black (especially southern) experience, and as time went on, Negro-content plays became an increasingly important part of the repertoire. "Theater is not a means of forgetting," one of the black actors explained in defending these plays. "It is a means of examining, of re-evaluating. All people have their past in folklore. We need not be ashamed of ours." During the 1920s, the Players staged a number of plays that dealt with aspects of black folk culture, including Ridgely Torrence's *Granny Maumee*, Willis Richardson's *Compromise*, Paul Green's *The No 'Count Boy*, DuBose Heyward's *Porgy*, and Zora Neale Hurston's brief *Sermon in the Valley*. During the following decade they produced a number of Langston Hughes's plays, and for a while the actors benefited from having the black playwright in residence in Cleveland.[16]

The theater program at the settlement also activated an interest in African culture. The very name given in 1927 to the settlement's first permanent auditorium, Karamu Theater, symbolized this new predilection for Africanisms; the term derived from a Swahili word meaning "a place of joyful meeting." Once the new theater had been purchased, the committee set up to supervise its decoration decided on an African motif. Burlap painted with African designs was hung on the walls; the house lights were inserted in carved wooden hemispheres resembling West African chopping bowls; the proscenium was striped diagonally, and a yellow sun with black rays extending from it in all directions was painted on the ceiling. Karamu was also instrumental in establishing the African Art Sponsors, and this group, together with the Gilpin Players,

[16] Interview with Russell and Rowena Jelliffe, September 1, 1971; Selby, *Beyond Civil Rights*, 41–47, 52, 55–60, 82–83, 100–104.

contributed to a fund that helped establish an African art collection at the Cleveland Museum of Art.[17]

The importance of this new interest in the traditional or ancestral culture of the black race, however, should not be overemphasized. Cleveland's middle-class Negroes were not becoming what we would now call "cultural nationalists." In the first place, the black community was far from united in backing these new cultural trends. One group of black ministers objected to the folk characters in some of the plays because they were "not polished enough"; others fulminated for years against Karamu because they believed theater and dance in general had a corrupting effect on youth. Nor was the desire for an African motif shared by all blacks involved in Karamu Theater. A minority stated their distaste for the "primitive designs" that were finally chosen; they would have preferred decorations that were customary and "pretty."[18]

Even among the strongest black supporters of Karamu, in fact, interest in Africa or southern black folk culture was more a symptom of ethnic ambivalence than a revolution in values. The black middle class now found it possible to view or even participate in a play dealing with southern folk culture because they firmly believed that their own way of life was an advance over what was being portrayed on the stage. The president of the Gilpin Players, speaking for the entire group, emphasized this point in 1930. "We are a group of forty people," he said in defense of the Players' enactment of a play with Negro content, "sufficiently removed from the peasant phase of our race to look back upon it, recognize its beauty, and wish to interpret it as beautifully as possible for the general public." The issue is further complicated by the fact that most of the "Negro" plays put on at Karamu during its early years emphasized the humorous, folksy side of black life in the South. Thus the "peasant phase" that was being explored in these theatrical productions usually avoided the bitter side of social reality in the South. As Benjamin Quarles has pointed out, serious black dramatists in the 1920s "faced not only white indifference but also the artistic limitations imposed by Negro audiences" who usually "did not like unpleasant endings, and who insisted that all Negro characters must be fine, upstanding persons, barely a cut below the angels." The new cultural concerns of the black middle class were genuine; but the black middle class, no less than the white theatergoing public, much preferred to be reminded of the smiling

[17] *Ibid.*, 3, 61–65, 67; "Proceedings of the Annual Meeting of the Association [for the Study of Negro Life and History] held in Cleveland, Ohio, October 26–30, 1930," *Journal of Negro History*, 16 (January 1931), 6–7.
[18] Selby, *Beyond Civil Rights*, 56–64.

aspects of black folk culture. What the race's urban bourgeoisie sought, in effect, was a usable past, a tradition of folk culture and ancestral art that they could identify with as a heritage but which also served as an indicator of how far the race had progressed over the decades and centuries. This the early productions of Karamu Theater provided.[19]

This ambiguous but essentially hopeful outlook was not limited to Cleveland. In New York, Chicago, and other cities across the North, the apprehension of the black middle and upper classes about rising discrimination and segregation was more than offset by a belief that the continuing migration of blacks from the South meant not only enhanced profits for their businesses and professions but an improvement for the race as a whole. However guarded or qualified, this optimism about the future of the race was voiced again and again in educated black opinion of the day. Nowhere was this view better reflected than in *The New Negro*, the 1925 volume of prose and poetry, edited by Alain Locke, that was the manifesto of the new black middle class. *The New Negro* contained protest poems by Claude McKay, as well as the grim reminder of W. E. B. Du Bois that "the problem of the 20th century" was still "the Problem of the Color Line." But far more significant was the overriding optimism the writers expressed. James Weldon Johnson spoke of Harlem not as a slum but as "the cultural capital" of the black race; a place where "the Negro's advantages and opportunities are greater . . . than in any other place in the country." Kelly Miller trumpeted Howard University as "the National Negro University." In moving northward, declared Alain Locke, the Afro-American was becoming a "conscious contributor" to the larger life of his society; he had laid aside "the status of a beneficiary and ward for that of a collaborator and participant in American civilization." Wrote Langston Hughes, "We have to-morrow/Bright before us/ Like a flame./ Yesterday, a night-gone thing/ A sun-down name."[20]

The conditions of life of the typical ghetto dweller, of course, differed considerably from that of his or her social betters in the black community. Surveying Cleveland's ghetto in 1930, Charles W. Chesnutt noted that the "upper tenth" frequently owned "handsome, well-furnished homes with many evidences of taste and culture." He went on to

---

[19] *Ibid.*, 81–82, 101; Benjamin Quarles, *The Negro in the Making of America*, rev. ed. (New York, 1964), 201. Although a few of the facts related in this paragraph are taken from Selby's book, the conclusions drawn from them are my own. For an intriguing discussion of the development of black minstrelsy and theater in the late nineteenth and early twentieth centuries and the psychic needs it fulfilled for both white and black Americans, see Nathan Irvin Huggins, *Harlem Renaissance* (New York, 1971), 244–301.

[20] Locke, ed., *The New Negro*, 15, 142, 311, 312, 385.

220 A Ghetto Takes Shape

explain, however, that "the majority live in drab, middle or low class houses, none too well kept up . . . while the poor live in dilapidated, rack-rented shacks, sometimes a whole family in one or two rooms, as a rule paying higher rents than white tenants for the same space." Overcrowded and unsanitary living quarters, the lack of normal recreational facilities, and the closeness of lower-class Negro neighborhoods to gambling halls and red-light districts led to an increase in the incidence of crime and had a deleterious effect on health conditions in the black community.[21]

Crime had always plagued the Central Avenue area, but between World War I and the Depression reports of fist fights, shootings, and robberies in that section of the city became almost a daily occurrence. At the peak of the Great Migration, the city Welfare Department reported a sharp increase in the number of black prisoners committed to the county workhouse. Undoubtedly, the number of serious crimes (the workhouse was designed for lower-level offenders) occurring in the black community also rose in the wake of the migration. No statistics are available for earlier years, but in 1930 the Negro homicide rate in the city was many times that of the white rate. An increase in delinquency was also evident. Although Negroes comprised no more than 6 percent of Cleveland's total population at the time, a study of juvenile court records revealed that 38 percent of the girls committed to the Girls' Industrial School between 1920 and 1926 were Negroes. Almost all of these girls were recent migrants who had accompanied their parents to the city; fully 94 percent had been born in states other than Ohio. Illegitimacy among blacks in the city also probably became more common after the migration. Only 1.6 percent of the white children born in Cleveland in 1923 were illegitimate, while 7.0 percent of all black children that year were born out of wedlock. Three years later the white rate had risen to 1.9 percent and the black rate to 8.0 percent.[22]

[21] Chesnutt, "The Negro in Cleveland," 3. For surveys of social conditions in other northern communities in the wake of the wartime migration, see George Edmund Haynes, *Negro New-Comers in Detroit, Michigan: A Challenge to Christian Statesmanship* (New York, 1918); Abraham Epstein, *The Negro Migrant in Pittsburgh* (Pittsburgh, Pa., 1918); Ira De A. Reid, *Social Conditions of the Negro in the Hill District of Pittsburgh* (Pittsburgh, Pa., 1930); T. J. Woofter et al., *Negro Problems in Cities* (Garden City, N.Y., 1928); Scott Nearing, *Black America* (New York, 1929), 71–126; Abram L. Harris, *The Negro Population in Minneapolis: A Study of Race Relations* (Mineapolis, Minn., [1927]), 12–54; Gilbert Osofsky, *Harlem: The Making of a Ghetto* (New York, 1966), 127–58; Drake and Cayton, *Black Metropolis*, 58–97; Allan H. Spear, *Black Chicago: The Making of a Negro Ghetto, 1890–1920* (Chicago, 1967), 129–80.

[22] "Increase of Negro Prisoners in Cleveland," *Survey*, 38 (September 8, 1917), 509–10; *Proceedings of the Mayor's Advisory War Board, City of Cleveland, from January 1, 1918, to March 31, 1918, with Record of Expenditures of Its Various*

Much of the increase in crime in the ghetto can be attributed to the inferior social conditions which beset the migrants on all sides. But an important attributing factor was the lackadaisical attitude of the Republican administrations and Thomas Fleming toward crime and organized vice in the crowded black sections of the city. Testifying before the City Council in 1917, Harry C. Smith reported despairingly that "Speakeasies, disorderly flats and a gambling den are in full operation. . . . Conditions have degenerated terribly in that vicinity in the last year and a half. . . . Before the big gambling den opened up last year it was bragged up and down Central Avenue that it had protection. Poor Negroes from the South are fleeced in this place. . . . The hands of the police seem tied." A decade later little had changed, and the adoption of a city manager form of government did not lead to a more efficient crackdown on vice in the black community. In 1928 the *Gazette* noted that "dope dealing and peddling, boot-leggers and speakeasies galore, prostitutes and their male 'consorts' " all operated openly in the heart of the ghetto.[23]

An increase in the prevalence of disease among Afro-Americans was common to most northern cities during and after the War. Although whites often claimed that southern migrants could not adapt to the colder northern climate, it seems likely that the most important factor was the overcrowded and unsanitary conditions under which many migrants lived. In 1928, a black physician bluntly stated that there were some dwellings in the Central area, in fact, that "no one can expect to live in and remain in health."[24]

After 1915 there was a marked increase in infant mortality, pneumonia, tuberculosis, and venereal disease among Cleveland Negroes; during one year an epidemic of smallpox also occurred in an area heavily populated by blacks. In 1920, the death rates for the city's black population for pneumonia and tuberculosis were, respectively, 349 and 362 per 100,000 population; comparable rates for whites in the city were much lower: 144 and 83 deaths per 100,000. During the 1920s, the health status of the black community improved only slightly. By 1930 the death rate for pneumonia had dropped to 119 per 100,000. The mortality rate for tuberculosis, however, remained the same for Negroes (while the death

Activities (n.p. [1918]), 22; U.S. Bureau of the Census, *Negroes in the United States, 1920–1932* (Washington, 1935), 377; Howard W. Green, *An Analysis of Girls Committed to the Girls' Industrial School by the Juvenile Court at Cleveland during a Six Year Period, 1920–25* (Cleveland, 1929), 51, 87; Howard W. Green, *An Analysis of Illegitimate Births in the City of Cleveland for 1926* (Cleveland, 1928), 1.
23 Cleveland *Gazette*, September 15, 1917, April 21, 1918.
24 *Ibid.*, April 21, 1918.

rate among whites fell by 40 percent), and on the eve of the Depression syphilis was still six times as prevalent among Negroes as whites. Census-tract data reveal that infant mortality among whites declined steadily from 1919 to 1930 in virtually every part of the city; but in many black neighborhoods the death rate for children under one year of age re-mained the same or, in a few instances, increased slightly during the same period. In 1930 the infant mortality rate for the entire black community was still double that of the white poplulation.[25]

Clearly, the conditions of life which confronted the average black resi-dent in the 1920s gave him less cause for optimism than the middle-class or elite black. To describe the post–World War I ghettos *solely* in terms of the social disorganization that accompanied it, however, is to overlook both the real progress that was made by most of the southern migrants and to neglect important changes in the experiences and perceptions of the average black person living in the North. Historians who have spoken of the "frustrated and disillusioned masses" or the "'horror of slum life" in the ghettos of the 1920s have perhaps been too quick to identify that era with the explosive decade of the 1960s. Social *conditions* of ghetto life indeed may have remained, in many (certainly not all) respects, re-markably unchanged during the last half-century; but the social *per-ceptions* of those who have lived in the ghetto have not. By virtually every measure of socioeconomic progress, the status of black migrants who came north after 1915 constituted an advance over their previous condition.[26]

Most important was the economic opportunity which the migrants en-joyed, at least until the end of the 1920s, when plants began to cut back production and lay off employees. It has already been noted that, in ab-solute terms as well as relative to other groups in the economy, black economic status in Cleveland improved between 1910 and 1920 and did not slip back during the following decade. But this modest achievement does not properly assess the solid gains made by most newcomers to the city, because the conditions they left in the South were much worse than those in the North prior to the migration. The same causes that had led

---

[25] H. L. Rockwood, "Effect of Negro Migration on Community Health in Cleve-land," *National Conference of Social Work Proceedings, 1926* (Boston, 1926), 238–44; U.S. Bureau of the Census, *Mortality Rates, 1910–1920* (Washington, 1922), 258–68; U.S. Bureau of the Census, *Negroes in the United States, 1920–1932*, 388; Howard W. Green, comp., *Natural Increase and Migration* [in Cleveland] (Cleve-land, 1938), 1–14, 66–68. For a general survey, see Eugene Kinckle Jones, "The Negro's Struggle for Health," *Opportunity*, 1 (June 1923), 4–8.

[26] The quotations are from August Meier and Elliott Rudwick, *From Plantation to Ghetto*, rev. ed. (New York, 1970), 226, and Osofsky, *Harlem*, 148.

to the wartime exodus from the South—unproductive land, cotton tenancy, and impossibly low wages—continued in force after 1920. During the 1920s, farm tenancy among South Carolina Negroes remained close to 80 percent, while the pay for picking one hundred pounds of cotton fell from 95 cents in 1924 to 52 cents in 1930. The average black Carolinian was a tenant farmer, sharecropper, or farm laborer, mired in rural poverty and living on an inadequate diet. "Total income for almost all black farmers," writes one historian, "was at or below the subsistence level." Conditions in Alabama, another state which sent large numbers of blacks to Cleveland after 1915, were no better. Rural blacks there were extremely poverty-stricken, and they existed in what amounted to a state of economic serfdom, totally subservient to the white plantation owners who held sway over the lands they worked. By the eve of the Depression, wages for black farm workers in Alabama had dropped to an incredible 50 to 65 cents a day for men and 40 cents for women. But as John Hope Franklin has noted, "Early in the twenties the depression had already begun" for the southern tenants. In moving to the North, the migrants escaped all this—temporarily, at least. Unlike the post-1950 era, when factory employment would become much less important in the overall occupational structure of the country, unskilled labor was still a vital aspect of the economy in the 1920s; and the newcomers to the metropolis during the earlier era were able, despite their lack of skills, to obtain jobs in industry. The assessment of Mary White Ovington in 1911—that for "'the mass of Negroes coming into the city" their new jobs were "an advance over their former work"—was even more true of those who arrived a decade later.[27]

There is also some doubt whether the movement from South to North actually exposed the migrants to a more hostile or dangerous social environment than the one they had been used to in the South. It was E. Franklin Frazier who first emphasized the negative effects of the migration to the city. "In the urban environment," wrote Frazier in 1932, "the migrant is liberated from the control that the church and other forms of association exercised in the rural South. He is released from the gossip of the neighborhood and the fear of being 'churched' if he strays into

[27] I. A. Newby, *Black Carolinians: A History of Blacks in South Carolina from 1895 to 1968* (Columbia, S.C., 1973), 195–204; John Hope Franklin, *From Slavery to Freedom*, 3d ed. (New York, 1967), 495; Arthur F. Raper, *Preface to Peasantry: A Tale of Two Black Belt Counties* (Chapel Hill, N.C., 1936), ch. 11; Charles S. Johnson, *Shadow of the Plantation* (Chicago, 1934), 112; Mary White Ovington, *Half a Man: The Status of the Negro in New York* (New York, 1911), 104. Also useful are Carter Woodson, *The Rural Negro* (New York, 1930), and Pete Daniel, *The Shadow of Slavery: Peonage in the South, 1901–1969* (Urbana, Ill., 1972).

unconventional behavior. Freedom from these controls makes the migrant subject to all the forms of suggestion that the city offers." In the metropolis, the black sociologist concluded, the migrant was too easily "the prey of vagrant impulses and lawless desires." Frazier was particularly disturbed by what he called "the disintegration of Negro family life in the city," which he saw reflected in the statistics recording juvenile delinquency and the number of households headed by women in the black community of Chicago.[28]

For all his insights into the nature of black urban life, Frazier, like many other social theorists of his day, tended to idealize rural life, equating it with stability and normality and contrasting it to the "unnatural" and artificial existence of the city. In reality, the virtues of stability which a number of writers, both white and Negro, found in the rural South during the 1920s may tell us more about these intellectuals than about the nature of southern life. Surveying six hundred rural Alabama black families in 1930, Charles S. Johnson discovered at least as much "social disorganization"[29] there as could be found in northern

[28] Frazier, The Negro Family in Chicago, 75, 76, 147. Frazier continued this theme on a larger scale in The Negro Family in the United States (New York, 1939), 271–390, in a section which he labeled "In the City of Destruction." Since its appearance in updated form in Daniel Moynihan, The Negro Family: The Case for National Action (Washington, D.C., 1965), Frazier's concept of the "matriarchal" black family has either been modified or vigorously rejected by several scholars; see, for example, Lee Rainwater and William L. Yancey, eds., The Moynihan Report and the Politics of Controversy (Cambridge, 1967), and Robert Staples, "The Myth of the Black Matriarchy," in Staples, ed., The Black Family: Essays and Studies (Belmont, Calif., 1971), 149–59. Few of the sociologists critical of Moynihan, however, have bothered to inquire into the historical origins of black family structure.

[29] While using this term as an analytical convenience, I do not accept all the negative connotations that scholars in the past have frequently read into it. If the family structure and life-style of some blacks have developed differently from that of the white middle class, for example, it should not be assumed that they are in all ways "pathological" and hence inferior to white norms. It may be that the gradual development of the matrifocal family among a large segment of the black lower class actually represents a creative adaptation to oppressive economic and social conditions. Unfortunately, in the late nineteenth and early twentieth centuries sociologists and social-work theorists often idealized the values of the white middle class of small-town America, and this tradition has tended to retard a more unbiased inquiry into the nature of black life in the ghetto. See C. Wright Mills, "The Professional Ideology of Social Pathologists," in Irving L. Horowitz, ed., Power, Politics, and People: The Collected Essays of C. Wright Mills (New York, 1963), 525–52; Marvin Gettleman, "Charity and Social Classes in the United States, 1874–1900," American Journal of Economics and Sociology, 22 (July 1963), 418–22; and Kenneth L. Kusmer, "The Functions of Organized Charity in the Progressive Era: Chicago as a Case Study," Journal of American History, 60 (December 1973), 663–69.

ghettos at that time. Disease was widespread; about one-third of the adult population showed some signs of syphilis, and malaria and pellagra were also quite common. Disease and poverty took their toll on family life. Johnson found 13.7 percent of the children of these rural black families were illegitimate, while one quarter of the family units were headed by women. Denied access to all but the most rudimentary educational facilities, 22 percent could neither read nor write. If there was an element of stability in the southern black belt it was an entrenched social perspective born of resignation and despair. "Ain't make nothing, don't speck nothing no more till I die," one black farmer told Johnson. "Eleven bales of cotton and man take it all. We jest work for de other man. He git everything." Said one woman who was forced to raise a large family by herself, "This is a starving land. This is the worst place I ever run on in my life. If you could jest get out of it all you put in it you could live happy. . . . I look at my children sometimes and I'm sorry I ever born a child in the world. . . . How they hold up I can't see." If these conditions bred stoic acceptance among some, they also resulted in a tradition of in-group destructiveness, an aspect of life in the black belt that neither the rural black church nor what Frazier called "the customs of the community" could prevent. "There is a tradition of violence which seems to mark personal relations to a high degree," said Johnson, and he noted an unusually large number of homicides and fatal accidents in the rural black community he studied. "The violence of life," he concluded, "was an inescapable fact in a large number of families in the county." To migrants who had grown up under these circumstances, life in a northern city, despite slum conditions and discrimination, must have seemed preferable to their former home.[30]

It is not at all clear that the movement of blacks to the North resulted in greater family instability or a more "matriarchal" pattern of family life, as Frazier and others have contended.[31] When the condition of black families in Cleveland and other cities, in the wake of the migrations of 1916–30, is studied not in isolation but in comparison to other northern ethnic groups and to southern black families, the results are surprising. (See Table 20.)

[30] Johnson, *Shadow of the Plantation*, 33, 62, 66–68, 126, 129, 186–89, 189–91.
[31] The discussion of the black family in this chapter pertains only to the period of the 1920s. It may be that the wide divergence between blacks and whites and between urban blacks and rural blacks in the proportion of households headed by women is more a product of the post–World War II era than of the Great Migration period. Compare Table 18 with the data in Moynihan, *The Negro Family*, 6–7, which gives census figures for 1960.

TABLE 20. *Percentage of families headed by women, by racial and ethnic group, for urban and rural areas, 1930*

	Native whites of native parentage	Native whites of foreign or mixed parentage	Foreign-born whites	Negroes
Ohio				
Cleveland	14.7	14.0	11.7	17.2
Cincinnati	14.1	23.3	18.4	18.9
All urban areas	12.9	17.1	11.8	17.1
Illinois				
Chicago	13.4	13.8	12.8	19.4
All urban areas	12.4	14.1	12.8	19.3
New York				
New York City	17.7	16.3	12.4	23.9
Buffalo	13.0	16.2	14.2	15.4
Alabama				
Rural farm	5.3	5.5	5.6	13.8
Rural nonfarm	10.3	12.5	9.1	20.9
Urban	12.5	17.5	11.1	29.1
Georgia				
Rural farm	5.8	10.2	7.0	12.0
Rural nonfarm	12.6	11.5	6.9	25.2
Urban	15.5	20.5	11.5	33.7

SOURCE: U.S. *Fifteenth Census, 1930, Population* (Washington, 1933), VI, 95, 303, 362, 921, 1027.

In Cleveland and in most northern urban areas the percentage of black households headed by women was only slightly higher than that of other groups in the population, and the difference between blacks and native whites of foreign or mixed parentage (second-generation immigrants) was frequently negligible. Furthermore, in many rural areas of the South the proportion of black households headed by women was equal or greater than the proportion of such households in the North. One is hard-pressed to prove, on the basis of this data, that the transition of black migrants from the rural South to the urban North caused an unusual amount of family disruption, or that in the 1920s the matrifocal family unit had clearly emerged as a *distinctive* feature of northern black communities. Actually, it was only in southern, not northern, cities that Negroes had a much higher proportion of family units headed by females than did other ethnic and racial groups. In the North, the differential between whites and blacks in this aspect of family life had begun to widen, but the gap was still much smaller than it would be three decades later.[32]

The meaning of the ghetto and its attraction for southern blacks cannot, of course, be measured solely by statistical indexes of socioeconomic progress. "He comes [north] to find work and freedom," said W. E. B. Du Bois of the typical black migrant, "and by freedom he means a chance for expansion, amusement, interest, something to make life larger than it has been on the lonely country plantation, or in the Negro quarter of a southern town." Freedom also meant an opportunity to escape from a situation where "social repression of the Negro [was] a rule of life" to an environment where one was not constantly reminded of the power of white authority. When one black minister in Philadelphia was asked in 1908 why blacks continued to migrate northward, despite the hardships they faced in the city, he gave an answer that was equally applicable to the postwar era. "Well, they're treated more like men up here in the North, that's the secret of it. There's prejudice here, too, but the color line isn't drawn in their faces at every turn as it is in the South. It all gets back to a question of manhood." A black woman who had been a teacher in the South but had moved to New York during the war and taken a job as a textile worker expressed a similar sentiment. Asked if she preferred her new occupation, she replied, "No, I don't. But I just couldn't stand the treatment we got in the south, so I came north to escape humiliation and to live a fuller and freer life."[33]

[32] These conclusions are, of course, tentative. The only sure way of determining the effect of urban life on the family structure of black (or, for that matter, white) migrants would be to trace the lives of a selected group of migrants over a period of years, a task which is beyond the scope of this volume.

One way in which black family life in Cleveland did differ markedly from that of other groups was in the proportion of families having lodgers. Far more black than white families found it necessary to supplement their income in this manner. In 1930, 11.4 percent of the city's native-white households and 10.3 percent of the foreign-born households had at least one lodger. Among Negro families, however, 31.1 percent had at least one lodger and 16.5 percent had two or more lodgers. U.S. *Fifteenth Census, 1930, Population (Families)*, VI, 1025.

[33] W. E. B. Du Bois, "The Black Vote of Philadelphia," *Charities*, 15 (October 7, 1905), 31; Ray Stannard Baker, *Following the Color Line: American Negro Citizenship in the Progressive Era* (New York, 1908), 133; [Joint Committee on Employment of Colored Women in New York and Brooklyn,] *A New Day for the Colored Woman Worker* (n.p., 1919), 12–13. In preparing the report of the Chicago Commission on Race Relations in 1922, interviewers asked a number of migrants the question, "What do you like about the North?" While many mentioned higher wages, far more frequently the newcomers brought up the importance of social freedom and the escape from fear and subordination. See Chicago Commission on Race Relations, *The Negro in Chicago: A Study of Race Relations and a Race Riot* (Chicago, 1922), 100–103.

Even more so than among the black middle class, the consolidation of the ghetto in the postwar era inspired a new racial awareness in the migrants who made up the bulk of the black working class. Coming from a part of the country where the race was both dispersed and repressed, the newcomers suddenly found themselves in the most segregated part of the ghetto. Though fictional, the following description of a migrant's first glimpse of Harlem (taken from a 1925 short story by Rudolph Fisher) must have been a realistic one.

> Gillis set down his tan-cardboard extension-case and wiped his black, shining brow. Then slowly, spreadingly, he grinned at what he saw: Negroes at every turn; up and down Lenox Avenue, up and down One Hundred and Thirty-fifth Street; big, lanky Negroes, short, squat Negroes; black ones, brown ones, yellow ones; men standing idle on the curb, women, bundle-laden, trudging reluctantly homeward, children rattle-trapping about the sidewalks; here and there a white face drifting along, but Negroes predominantly, overwhelmingly everywhere.

It is likely that this kind of experience was repeated many times in the urban North during the decade of the 1920s. On Central Avenue, on South State Street, on a dozen other ghetto thoroughfares, a new racial consciousness was being born.[34]

Like the origins of the ghetto itself, of course, this new awareness of race had been in the making for several decades. After 1915, however, the idea of racial unity, which black businessmen, politicians, and self-help advocates had been trying to inculcate for years, now grew much more rapidly because it was constantly reinforced in everyday life in the black community. The man whose career most clearly reflected the growth of this new racial consciousness was Marcus Garvey. A native of Jamaica, Garvey had in 1914 formed the Universal Negro Improvement Association, an organization that emphasized black pride, the racial unity of all Negroes, and the need to redeem Africa from white colonialist rule. Arriving in New York in 1916, Garvey set about the task of building up his organization. Within six years the UNIA had organized branches in at least thirty cities, and Garvey had established the Black Star Steamship Line, the Negro Factories Corporation (which operated, for a while, several grocery stores, a restaurant, a steam laundry, a printing house, and other small enterprises), and a newspaper, the *Negro World*. The UNIA was strongest in New York City, where 30,000 had joined by 1923.

---

[34] Rudolph Fisher, "The City of Refuge," reprinted in Locke, ed., *The New Negro*, 57–58. See also the description of Harlem in James Weldon Johnson, *Black Manhattan* (New York, 1930), 145, and the autobiographical statement of Horace R. Cayton, *Long Old Road* (New York, 1965), 175.

Chicago had the second-highest membership (9,000); most branches probably had 3,000 or fewer members.[35]

In Cleveland, the UNIA movement was not very strong, and in 1924 the local division was further weakened by a factional split in the membership. Most of Cleveland's Garveyites were probably from the lower class; during the 1920s, however, the leaders of the local branch were LeRoy Bundy, a dentist (and later councilman) and S. V. Robertson, the superintendent of the city's garbage collection unit. The Cleveland UNIA had a Liberty Hall where its meetings were conducted; two branch organizations; and a marching band which performed from time to time in colorful uniforms on Central Avenue. Compared to those of other cities, the local division in Cleveland did not appear very influential, and it is unlikely that the organization's total membership during its first decade ever amounted to more than 1,000.[36]

But Garvey's significance cannot be measured solely in terms of how many individuals actually joined the UNIA. Garveyism was more important as a cultural phenomenon than as a social movement. As one contemporary pointed out, Garvey was popular because he sensed the mood of the black masses and "spoke those things which they would have spoken were they articulate. He at once became the embodiment of their aspirations, the expression of their desires and a collective representative of their aims and yearnings." Garvey visited Cleveland three times before his conviction and imprisonment for fraudulent use of Black Star Line funds removed him from the scene in 1924, and each time he spoke to large and enthusiastic audiences. Through this medium and the *Negro World*, Garvey was able to get his message across to a fairly large proportion of the black lower class in Cleveland and other cities, and it is probable that the number of blacks who sympathized with the Jamaican was much larger than the dues-paying membership of the UNIA.[37]

Most students of the Garvey movement have viewed it chiefly as a psychological escape valve for the frustrations of the black masses.

[35] E. David Cronon, *Black Moses: The Story of Marcus Garvey and the Universal Negro Improvement Association* (Madison, Wis., 1955), 45–47, 60, 173–74, 206, and *passim*.

[36] Cleveland *Gazette*, November 12, 1921, March 4, April 15, 1922; Theodore Vincent, *Black Power and the Garvey Movement* ([Berkeley, Calif.,] n.d.), 204; interview with Dr. William P. Saunders, August 6, 1972.

[37] Cronon, *Black Moses*, 206–07; interview with Dr. William P. Saunders, August 6, 1972; Cellie H. Reid, "Marcus Garvey as a Social Phenomenon" (M.A. thesis, Northwestern University, 1928), 15–16.

The discussion of Garveyism which follows is not related specifically to black Cleveland; but I do not think that the import of Garveyism (as a cultural phenomenon) for the black urban lower class differed much from city to city.

"Garvey's protest," says one historian, "took the form of a complete rejection of the white world through an escapist program of Negro nationalism." More recently two scholars have stated that the Garvey movement "provided a compensatory escape for Negroes to whom the urban promised land had turned out to be a hopeless ghetto." It is likely that some blacks did use the movement as a means of emotional release; the colorful parades and impressive regalia of the UNIA may well have served this purpose. For the most part, however, it is unnecessary to read such psychological meanings into the Garvey phenomenon to explain its popularity. The Garvey movement was essentially the lower-class counterpart of the bourgeois "New Negro" phenomenon. Garvey's rhetoric struck a responsive chord in the black masses of the 1920s because it perfectly reflected the essential ambivilence of their outlook: the peculiar combination of optimism and alienation that resulted from enhanced economic opportunity accompanied by the growth of the ghetto and increased discrimination.[38]

Garvey exalted all things black. He asserted that the Negro race was not inferior to any other and that its African past was a glorious one. He taught that blacks should reject white ideals of beauty, and he banned advertisements for skin whitener and hair straightener from the pages of the *Negro World.* Garvey established an African Orthodox Church and inculcated the novel idea that God and Christ were black. This rhetoric did not provide a "compensatory escape" from the realities of ghetto life, however; on the contrary, it was a logical *effect* of the growth of the ghetto and the new awareness of race that accompanied the migration from rural to urban areas. "He insisted," said Benjamin Mays in analyzing Garvey's religious ideas, "that the Negro was created in the image of God and that in every particular the Negro race is the equal of other races. . . . It is clear that there is nothing compensatory in the way Garvey used the idea of God. He used it definitely to arouse the Negro to a sense of deep appreciation for his race." The emphasis the Jamaican

[38] Cronon, *Black Moses,* xii; Meier and Rudwick, *From Plantation to Ghetto,* 229. For similar interpretations of Garvey, see Franklin, *From Slavery to Freedom,* 490; Quarles, *The Negro in the Making of America,* 195; and the essay by E. Franklin Frazier which has apparently influenced most scholars, "The Garvey Movement," *Opportunity,* 4 (November 1926), 346–48. August Meier, in *Negro Thought in America,* 277–78, was the first to note certain parallels between Garveyism and the New Negro movement (both, for example, were interested in race history and Africa), but Meier goes on to say that "of course the Garvey Movement lacked the dualistic character of the New Negro outlook." I disagree with this latter assessment and believe that an analysis of Garveyism reveals a good deal more ambiguity than has heretofore been acknowledged by historians.

placed on racial ideals and black solidarity may have been extreme, but in most respects they are explainable as a natural culmination of a trend in black thought which—like the ghetto itself—had been developing for several decades.[39]

Yet it would be a mistake to interpret Garvey's emphasis on blackness as "a complete rejection of the white world. . . ." It is far more accurate to say that Garvey *inverted* white standards, substituting black for white but for the most part retaining the dominant values of the larger society. If white America had Red Cross nurses, the UNIA would have Black Cross Nurses; if whites traveled aboard the White Star Line, blacks would journey via the Black Star Line. Garvey portrayed God and Christ as black, but the liturgy and symbolism of his new church closely resembled that of traditional Catholicism. In many ways Garvey's economic and political ideas differed little from the mainstream conservatism of white America in the 1920s. Until the race could build up its own enterprises, Garvey preached, black workers should shun unions and look to their employers as their best friends. The Jamaican had no use for socialists and he urged black workers to accept lower wages as a means of retaining the friendship of white capitalists. Not surprisingly, in the 1924 presidential contest Garvey supported Calvin Coolidge.[40]

Garvey's emphasis on the racial unity of American and African blacks appealed to many urban blacks who were, for the first time, living in a social environment that *resembled* (even if on a rather small scale) an all-black nation. But Garvey's rhetoric about African redemption, like his exaltation of blackness, should be viewed neither as a symbol of despair nor as an escapist fantasy. Once again, the most important aspect of the Jamaican's message was its ambivalence. Garvey's black nationalism served much the same function for the lower class as the study of African and black folk culture did for the middle class: it allowed American Negroes simultaneously to identify with Africa yet still feel they were the most advanced and successful black group in the world. Garvey

[39] Cronon, *Black Moses*, 48, 174–81; Benjamin E. Mays, *The Negro's God as Reflected in His Literature* (Boston, 1938), 184–85.

[40] One is inclined to agree with Harold Cruse (*The Crisis of the Negro Intellectual*, New York, 1967, 330) that "Garvey's nationalism was more bourgeois than it was revolutionary. . . ." For examples of Garvey's generally conservative political and economic values, see Cronon, *Black Moses*, 132–33, 142, 152; on the inversion of white standards in the Garvey movement, see Charles S. Johnson, "After Garvey— What?" *Opportunity*, 1 (August 1923), 232–33. It should be noted, of course, that not all local UNIA chapters were as conservative in their approach to racial questions as their leader was; what is being analyzed here is the central thrust of Garvey's philosophy, not the occasional deviations from it.

did not, as critics and historians have sometimes maintained, advocate mass immigration to Africa as a solution to the racial problems of the United States.[41] He did, however, favor selective and limited migration, not for the purposes of escape but as a means of uniting blacks and rehabilitating and uplifting African society. A proposed UNIA loan of $2,000,000 in 1920 was designed to "start construction work in Liberia, where colleges, universities, industrial plants and railroad tracks will be erected; where men will be sent to make roads, and where artisans and craftsmen will be sent to develop industries." The loan was never raised; but the important thing is the Garveyites' desire to export the American ideal of technological progress to the African homeland. The Jamaican prophet and his supporters never doubted the superiority of American institutions over their African counterparts. In his essay, "The Aims and Objects of the Movement for the Solution of the Negro Problem," Garvey spoke condescendingly of the need to "assist in civilizing the backward tribes of Africa." The American Negro "who is thoughtful and serviceable," the UNIA president concluded, "feels that God intended him to give to his brothers still in darkness, the light of his civilization."[42]

The UNIA program symbolized not despair but hope. It reflected the optimistic belief of the black masses that American blacks had now progressed socially and materially to the point where they could begin to assist the less fortunate of their race who lived beyond the confines of the United States. The attempt to establish commercial linkages between North and South America and the African continent and to colonize Liberia constituted, in effect, an effort at black self-help on a worldwide scale. Segregated more completely than ever before, ghetto dwellers now found it easy to identify to an extent with their African counterparts. Yet they continued to see themselves as Americans as well as Negroes. Perhaps Garvey best summarized the ambivalent identity of his followers when he selected a name for his proposed independent black nation in Africa. "The United States of Africa," he called it.

[41] To be sure, Garvey was at times rather vague on this point. But both contemporary critics and historians (see Cronon, *Black Moses*, 75–76, 200; Meier and Rudwick, *From Plantation to Ghetto*, 228–29) have overstated the emigrationist impulse behind Garveyism. Unlike the followers of "Chief Sam" who journeyed from Oklahoma to Africa in 1914–15, Garvey's supporters did not engage in nor advocate mass emigration to the African homeland. Garvey, in fact, repudiated the "Back to Africa" slogan as "a label tagged on to the U.N.I.A. in ridicule" by his enemies. See Amy Jacques Garvey, *Garvey and Garveyism* (New York, 1970), 135.

[42] Cronon, *Black Moses*, 125, 126–27; Marcus Garvey, "The Aims and Objects of [the] Movement for [the] Solution of [the] Negro Problem," in Amy Jacques-Garvey, ed., *Philosophy and Opinions of Marcus Garvey* (New York, 1923), II, 37–43.

The black ghetto in the 1920s was a paradox of progress and poverty, and the "meaning" of the social changes that the black community was undergoing was to a large extent dependent upon the perspective of the observer. In the fragmented metropolis of the postwar era, most whites simply tried to avoid the ghetto, to escape from it, or to resist its encroachment. For these whites—when they gave the problem any thought—the ghetto was a convenient and altogether suitable place for containing an "inferior" race. But for the black people who were forced to live in it, the ghetto had a much more ambiguous meaning. For the old elite of the black community, the new segregation was an utter disaster, and some of these individuals never were able to reconcile themselves to the fact that blacks in the city were being increasingly set apart from the rest of the population. The new ghetto-based black middle class, though chafing under the burden of social ostracism imposed by whites, tended to view the migration from the South and the growth of the ghetto in a more positive light. The accumulation of wealth among a minority of blacks and the increasing division of the black community along class lines seemed to indicate that, despite handicaps, the race was entering the mainstream of American civilization. The way in which the bulk of the migrants themselves perceived their new urban home is more difficult to discern. Certainly the northern city, with its slums, high rents, and red-light districts must have been disheartening to many of the newcomers. But the area of the country from which they were fleeing was much more scarred by debilitating poverty and deprivation than was the North; and the urban ghetto offered blacks greater social freedom and a more definite sense of racial unity than they had known in the rural South. In contrast to the early 1960s, when (as one sociologist has put it) northern blacks were experiencing "actual gains but psychological losses," the black masses in the northern ghettos in the 1920s could view their status as representing both an absolute and a relative advance over their former condition. The consolidation of the ghetto after World War I produced a growing sense of black unity that would lead to a quest for more political power, but it did not produce the "ghetto revolt" that we have recently witnessed. The twenties can be called the era of the quiet ghetto.[43]

[43] For a brilliant study of the psychological and sociological basis of the black revolt of the 1960s, see Thomas F. Pettigrew, "Actual Gains and Psychological Losses: The Negro American Protest," *Journal of Negro Education*, 32 (Fall 1963), 493–506. Pettigrew notes that in the late fifties and early sixties, northern blacks felt they were falling behind both southern blacks (who were leading the civil rights "revolution") and the newly emergent African nations in making racial progress. In the 1920s, the reverse of this situation held, and northern Negroes

In the long run, of course, many of the positive aspects of black urban life would prove illusory. Industrial employment for Afro-Americans would be severely curtailed in the depression of the thirties, while a new generation of blacks born and raised in the North would find the environment of the ghetto more conducive to frustration than to freedom. A foretaste of things to come were the Harlem riots of 1935 and 1943 and the Detroit riot of 1943, in which blacks rampaged through the ghetto, looting and destroying white businesses in protest against discriminatory practices and slum conditions.[44] One feature of black life that would outlive the decade of the twenties, however, was the sense of common destiny prevalent to some extent in all socioeconomic classes in the black community as a result of the consolidation of the ghetto. In the twenties this new racial consciousness created the Harlem Renaissance and the Garvey movement. Four decades later, in a much more explosive setting, it would produce black revolutionaries and cultural nationalists with fewer ambiguities and a good deal more militancy than Garvey. In both cases, the underlying social foundation of these phenomena was the urban ghetto.

---

could feel with some justification that they were in the forefront of the struggle for racial advancement.

[44] In studying the ghetto rebellion of the 1960s, investigators discovered that the typical riot participant was not a recent migrant from the South but a young black male who "was born in the state and was a life-long resident of the city in which the riot took place." *Report of the National Advisory Commission on Civil Disorders* (New York, 1968), 128. Investigators also discovered that "a significant consequence of growing up in the South was a tendency toward noninvolvement in a riot situation . . ." (*ibid.*, 130). This information helps explain why very few ghetto riots occurred during the earlier decades of the century. Prior to the 1960s, and especially during the 1920–30 and 1945–55 periods, migration from the South was heavy and tended to outpace the rate of natural increase of black population in the North. Thus the typical ghetto resident during these years was not the type of individual most prone to violent rebellion. By the mid-sixties, however, migration from the South had slowed, while an ever-increasing percentage of the black populations of northern cities had been born and raised in the North. This demographic shift may well have laid the groundwork for the rioting which followed.

CHAPTER 11

Toward the New Negro

The influx of black migrants and the hardening of racial lines in Cleveland after 1915 had diverse effects on black leadership, ideologies, and institutions. Among some of the older leaders of the black community, who had pinned their hopes on an integrated society, there was a mounting sense of despair over the rising tide of racism and the consolidation of the ghetto. The newer group of rising black businessmen, politicians, and professionals who relied predominantly on black patronage for their livelihoods greeted these trends with more equanimity. Although somewhat disturbed over discrimination, this newer leadership group—especially the businessmen—viewed the ghetto chiefly in positive terms, seeing in it a clear justification for their philosophy of racial solidarity and self-help.

To some extent they were correct. The consolidation of the ghetto led to increased opportunities for black businessmen. By the mid-twenties, the few remaining Negro entrepreneurs who still catered to a mostly white clientele were an anachronistic remnant from a bygone era; this group continued to decline in both numbers and influence, and the new elite gained power and prestige at their expense. The new-elite philosophy of self-help, however, did not prove applicable to all aspects of life in the black community. Specifically, while the number of secular institutions serving the residents of the ghetto increased in the wake of the migration, the effective control of a number of these organizations remained with the whites who controlled indispensable financial resources. Thus the new elite's reach continued, as it had during the prewar era, to exceed its grasp, and in some respects the tradition of black dependency on white assistance continued into the twenties.

Conservative in both thought and action, the new elite gained the ascendancy during the 1915 to 1925 period. The black community was represented in City Council during this decade by Thomas Fleming, a politician who was extremely cautious and who seldom used his influence to further the collective interests of the black community. By the middle of the twenties, however, the conservative leadership of individuals like Fleming was being challenged by a new group of younger black leaders, the "New Negroes." Under the New Negroes, militancy once again became an important characteristic of black leadership, but this group sought to avoid the strident and divisive approach of the followers of Harry C. Smith. Sensing both the futility of the extreme integrationist stance of some members of the old elite as well as the limitations of the accommodationist, self-help philosophy of their successors, the New Negroes would attempt—with a good deal of success—to transcend the older ideological disputes and develop a more pragmatic approach to the problems that the black community faced. The chief institutional vehicle for implementing this approach was the Cleveland branch of the NAACP.

I

After the Great Migration, the old integrationist leadership that had represented the black community at the turn of the century now spoke for only a dwindling and rather self-conscious minority of the city's Negroes. Some of these individuals (Jere Brown, for example), died before the onset of the migration and were spared the frustrations of the postwar era; others (like Charles S. Sutton) moved away from the city. By the 1920s, Walter Wright and Jacob Reed were in retirement. John P. Green, though in his eighties, continued to practice law but took little part in community organizations or activities. Green increasingly retreated, mentally, into a roseate past. In 1919 he lauded Cleveland as an "asylum from prejudice and proscription" and a "haven of rest to the persecuted and forlorn," even though these descriptions no longed fitted a city that was becoming more and more segregated along racial lines. Although the Republican party was increasingly hostile to blacks in the 1920s, Green preferred to remember the good old days of the Reconstruction era; in 1928 he addressed the Republican National Convention in Chicago and urged blacks to once again give their unqualified support to the GOP.[1]

[1] John P. Green, *Fact Stranger than Fiction: Seventy-Five Years of a Busy Life*

Green's complaisant attitude was not typical of all of the surviving members of the older leadership group, however. The careers of George Myers, Charles W. Chesnutt, and Harry C. Smith demonstrate the different variations that were possible in response to the postwar situation.

Before 1915, George Myers had not worked openly in the struggle against racial discrimination in Cleveland, and the black barber tended to place at least part of the blame for increasing discrimination on blacks themselves—especially lower-class blacks who failed to live up to respectable standards of behavior. Myers had sought to ease the color bar by using his influence with prominent white friends in the city, but he refrained from criticizing Cleveland's white leadership. These attitudes persisted into the postwar era. Myers continued to work behind the scenes in ameliorating racial conditions in the city; in 1927, for example, he persuaded an official in the Department of Public Safety to place black policemen near a swimming pool that was to be integrated for the first time, in order to prevent racial violence. But the barber now became more openly discontented with the policies of the city's white leaders on matters affecting the black community. A new tone of militancy began to creep into Myers's usually circumspect correspondence with leading whites. To some extent, this change can be attributed to Myers's personal experience with racism. In 1923, the management of the Hollenden Hotel informed him that, upon his retirement, all of the black barbers working for him would be replaced by whites. This incident undoubtedly increased Myers's antagonism toward the white power structure of the city; but the barber was well aware, even before then, that Cleveland's traditions of equality and integration were falling by the wayside. In 1926 Myers condemned the local Chamber of Commerce for its lack of concern about the newly arrived migrants. He admonished the white business elite to "Denounce and discourage all forms of segregation, and in all public affairs give the race recognition." He concluded with an emotional plea for racial fairness. ". . . give them decent habitation at a reasonable rental," Myers said of the Central Avenue residents, "coupled with Police protection instead of Police persecution. Establish community centers and play grounds. Teach them how to live, acquaint them with Northern customs and the requisites of good citizenship. Much good will thus be accomplished, as well as a better feeling between the races and we will indeed have a better and greater Cleveland to live in."[2]

---

with Reminiscences of Many Great and Good Men (Cleveland, 1920), dedication page.
[2] George A. Myers to Frank S. Harmon, August 25, 1927; Myers to William R.

At the end of the 1920s, Myers's break with the city's white leadership became complete when he entered vigorously into the struggle to end the discriminatory policies of City Hospital. Myers openly condemned the city welfare director, Dudley S. Blossom, as a racist who thought that most Negroes were criminals. Dismayed at Myers's new-found militancy, the Republican city manager William R. Hopkins accused the barber of having "gone over to Harry Smith bag and baggage." There was more truth to this allegation than Hopkins suspected, for Myers had been working closely with Smith (once his political archenemy) on the hospital issue for almost a year. Throughout the postwar era, Myers remained loyal to the Republican party. But in 1928, just two years before his death, he could proclaim that "I am for my race first . . . and for my party next and reserve the right to tell them [party leaders] when they are wrong." Such had not been the opinion of the George Myers who had helped elect Mark Hanna to the United States Senate thirty years before.[3]

A more important figure than Myers was the noted Cleveland author, Charles Chesnutt. Before World War I, Chesnutt had been a convinced integrationist, and historians have for the most part been correct in labeling him as one of the chief ideological critics of Booker T. Washington. The claim of one scholar, however, that during the first decade of the twentieth century "Chesnutt's sense of identity with the Negro race grew weak . . . [and] as time passed his involvement became that of an interested spectator," must be rejected. If anything, Chesnutt's identification with the race increased and he became more involved in the black community of the city than he had ever been before. During the war, the novelist interceded with Secretary of War Newton D. Baker to have an Army training camp at Western Reserve University integrated, and he also served on the executive board of the Cleveland NAACP for several years. In 1922 Chesnutt was elected president of the Caterers' Association, a Negro social club, and the following year he became one of the directors of a predominantly Negro branch of the YMCA. From 1917 until his death in 1932 Chesnutt served on the board of Cleveland's Urban League affiliate, and for many years he lent his

Hopkins, August 9, 1927; George A. Myers, "Answer to Questionnaire of Cleveland Chamber of Commerce Committee on Immigration and Emigration," in 1926 correspondence, George A. Myers Papers, Ohio Historical Society.
    [3] George A. Myers to William R. Hopkins, December 13, 1927; Myers to Hopkins, December 29, 1927; Myers to Hopkins, February 6, 1928; Smith-Myers correspondence, 1927, Myers Papers; Cleveland *Gazette*, April 19, 1927; George A. Myers to Charles W. Chesnutt, January 16, 1924, Charles Waddell Chesnutt Papers, Western Reserve Historical Society.

support to the Phillis Wheatley Association and Karamu Theater.[4] The significance of Chesnutt's new involvement in the black community should not be overemphasized. Chesnutt must be seen as a complex man who played many roles, a man who, above all else, wanted to avoid the restricted perspective that characterized all too many black leaders of his generation. He was the successful lawyer and court stenographer, who lived an integrated, middle-class existence far from the racial turmoil of his native South; he was the eloquent spokesman for equal rights; he was also the man of letters, writer of short stories and novels which utilized the themes of southern folk culture. Chesnutt continued to fulfill all of these roles during the postwar era. He and his family continued to live in an integrated neighborhood, to attend a "white" church, and to socialize with liberal whites. The author remained on friendly terms with W. E. B. Du Bois and fully supported the NAACP. Chesnutt also took up writing again, after a lapse of almost a decade. He produced two novels but was unable to find a publisher; as a kind of grand old man of black literature, Chesnutt served as a judge of the annual fiction contest conducted by the *Crisis* and found time to encourage younger Negro writers like Benjamin Brawley. In 1928 he received the coveted Spingarn Medal, an award given each year to the Negro who had "reached the highest achievement in his field of activity."[5]

To these aspects of the life and thought of the cultured Cleveland

[4] Julian Krawcheck, "Society Barred Negroes—They Formed Own Groups," Cleveland *Press*, May 30, 1963; Cleveland *Gazette*, November 17, 1917; Charles W. Chesnutt to Sen. Frank B. Willis, May 17, 1922; Charles E. Frye to Chesnutt, February 24, 1923; S. P. Keeble to Chesnutt, March 15, 1924; D. W. Fraekelton to Chesnutt, September 12, 1924, Chesnutt Papers; Minutes of the Phillis Wheatley Association, January 12, 1918, January 8, 1924; Helen M. Chesnutt, *Charles Waddell Chesnutt: Pioneer of the Color Line* (Chapel Hill, N.C., 1952), 262–63. The erroneous statement concerning Chesnutt's lack of involvement or identification with the Negro race is made by S. P. Fullinwider, *The Mind and Mood of Black America: 20th Century Thought* (Homewood, Ill., 1969), 82.

[5] Charles W. Chesnutt to Houghton Mifflin Co., October 8, 1921; Chesnutt to Harcourt, Brace, and Co., November 12, 1921; Charles W. Chesnutt, "Paul Marchand, F.M.C." (manuscript of novel); W. E. B. Du Bois to Chesnutt, September 8, 1924; Du Bois to Chesnutt, December 24, 1924; Du Bois to Chesnutt, September 25, 1926; Chesnutt to Benjamin G. Brawley, March 24, 1922, Chesnutt Papers, WRHS; "The Quarry," manuscript of novel in Chesnutt Papers, Fisk. It is interesting to note that Chesnutt urged Brawley, who had written several books dealing with black life, to diversify his research interests, since "it is well for the colored writer not to segregate himself intellectually." For an outstanding example of psychological and social analysis of a prominent black leader, see Louis R. Harlan, "Booker T. Washington in Biographical Perspective," *American Historical Review*, 75 (October 1970), 1581–99. Harlan's discussion of the complex forces at work in effecting Washington's personality has influenced my understanding of Chesnutt, and his methodology may be applicable to other black leaders as well.

author, however, was now added another ingredient: a new awareness
that America's racial problems—even in the "liberal" North—were deepening rather than improving and that the future was likely to be only a
dismal repetition of the recent past. Chesnutt did not abandon the ideal
of an integrated society; but he now recognized that in the United States
this ideal was not going to be even partially realized for many years to
come. As segregation and discrimination reached new levels of intensity
after 1915, he increasingly came to see the validity of separate black
institutions like the Phillis Wheatley Association. This acceptance by
Chesnutt of the necessity of separate institutions in some areas of black
life was more pragmatic than philosophical. Unlike Jane Edna Hunter,
the founder of Phillis Wheatley, Chesnutt did not favor such institutions
because they were all-Negro but because they were necessary, given the
lack of adequate integrated facilities. Nevertheless, an important shift
in the black novelist's thought had occurred. In 1908 Chesnutt had dismissed as "an idle dream" the idea that Negroes could achieve anything
through racial solidarity; instead he had optimistically believed that
blacks could overcome the strictures of racism through the gradual
process of cultural assimilation. But by 1930, disillusioned with the
growth of the ghetto in his own city, Chesnutt had abandoned such
views in favor of a more pessimistic appraisal. "The white man," he
concluded in an article that thoroughly exposed the deep racial divisions
in Cleveland, "can live down the lowest origin. The Negro's color is
always with him."[6]
    A man with a different point of view was Harry C. Smith. If Chesnutt's
views were complex and multifaceted, Smith's retained their pristine
simplicity. The editor of the *Gazette* continued to seek out and attack
every form of discrimination, no matter how subtle; unlike Chesnutt,
however, he coupled this militancy with a continuing, dogmatic opposition to separate black institutions and persisted for years in denouncing
both Phillis Wheatley and the Negro Welfare Association as retrogres-
sive, Jim Crow organizations. So great was Smith's dislike of separatism
in any form that he seldom used the word "Negro" in his newspaper
without first prefacing it with "so-called." The editor preferred "Afro-
American" to "Negro" because he believed the former indicated black
equality with other ethnic groups and eventual integration into the
larger society, while the latter implied separatism and might be used as

---

[6] Charles W. Chesnutt, "Rights and Duties," unpublished 1908 address, Chesnutt
Papers, Fisk; Charles W. Chesnutt, "The Negro in Cleveland," *The Clevelander*,
5 (November 1930), 27. The entire *Clevelander* article constitutes a thorough (and
often sarcastic) critique of race relations in Cleveland on the eve of the Depression.

a convenient designation, by white racists, for "inferior." Smith continued to equate separatism with accommodation to racism.[7]

There were, however, two noticeable changes in Smith's outlook during the period after 1915: a shift in political allegiance and a new advocacy of black retaliatory violence. Unlike many black leaders, Smith refused to support Woodrow Wilson in 1912, and in 1916 and 1920 he was an avid backer of the Republican candidates for the presidency. During the next four years, however, the black editor became disillusioned with the Harding-Coolidge administration over the issues of American occupation of Haiti and the continued segregation of Afro-Americans in certain departments of the federal government. In 1924 Smith and Walter L. Brown formed an Independent Colored Voters' League to support Robert La Follette's Progressive Party. "No self-respective [sic] Negro," a League pamphlet stated, can vote for Coolidge or Davis. A vote for either is a vote for Negro Degradation." After the demise of the Progressive party, the editor of the *Gazette* found himself in a quandary. Finding "little difference between the two great parties" on the race issue in 1928, Smith endorsed Herbert Hoover only as "the lesser of two evils."[8]

More significant was Smith's opposition to Republican leadership at the local and state level. In 1921 Smith ran as an independent against Eleventh Ward councilman Thomas Fleming. Smith received the endorsement of the Baptist Ministers' Conference, the Cleveland Council of Colored Women, and, surprisingly, given the editor's avowed integrationism, most of the membership of the local UNIA; he ran credibly against Fleming but still went down to defeat. Smith complained afterward of "skullduggery in the election booths" and labeled the election a "farce." Whether these charges were true or not (it is likely they were), they do not entirely explain Smith's defeat. The fact is that Fleming's conservative brand of leadership was simply too strongly entrenched in 1921 for the black councilman to be ousted. Smith also became the focal point of a move for black independence from the regular Republicans at the state level. Smith audaciously ran for the

[7] Cleveland *Gazette*, April 14, June 7, 1919, February 17, 23, 1923, November 13, 1926, May 14, 1927, March 10, 1928. Boston integrationists also opposed the use of the word "Negro," for similar reasons. See John Daniels, *In Freedom's Birthplace: A Study of the Boston Negroes* (Boston, 1914), 163–64; Stephen R. Fox, *The Guardian of Boston: William Monroe Trotter* (New York, 1971), 251.

[8] Cleveland *Gazette*, October 30, 1920, September 27, October 11, 25, 1924, March 17, October 30, 1928; Harry C. Smith to Sen. Frank B. Willis, May 17, 1922; Smith to Willis, May 28, 1922, Chesnutt Papers, WRHS; Independent Colored Voters League, *An Appeal for the Second Emancipation of the Negro* (n.p. [1924]), n.p.

GOP nominations for secretary of state in 1920 and for governor in 1922, 1924, 1926, and 1928. In the first two of these elections, the editor campaigned throughout the state and received the support of a number of black leaders in other cities. Smith complained of the declining amount of patronage blacks received at the statewide level and the failure of GOP leaders, despite increasing numbers of black voters, to support more blacks for political office. The editor hoped his candidacies for secretary of state and governor would "serve notice in a *practical way*" on Republican officeholders in state government that the black vote could no longer be taken for granted. As in the case of the 1921 councilmanic race, however, the editor's quixotic campaign against Ohio's white Republican leadership was premature. It would not be until the 1930s that the Democratic party would offer black voters an attractive alternative to the GOP. Still, Smith must be credited with helping to lay the groundwork for that later rebellion.[9]

Smith's defection from the Republican party was one indication of his lack of faith in the efficacy of white leadership in furthering the rights of Afro-Americans; another was his advocacy of armed resistance against white mobs that threatened the lives and property of blacks. During the racially tense summers of 1917 and 1919, when race riots erupted in a number of cities and towns across the nation, Smith urged black Clevelanders to buy guns and use them if necessary. In an article entitled "We Must Strike Back," the black editor made his position painfully clear:

> Yes, we *have* been too "submissive and spineless" entirely too long, as a result of listening to and accepting the advice of misguided, or designing whites who posed as our friends, and "jim-crow" or weak-kneed "Negroes," who for selfish reasons or fear, preached the "turn the other cheek" course. . . .
>
> We simply must learn the lesson of striking back because the average American has no respect for any individual that fails to do so when conditions warrant it. What our people did during the recent race riots [black retaliation against white mobs] has done more good than all the preaching of the "doctrine of surrender" since the close of the war of rebellion.[10]

---

[9] Cleveland *Gazette*, June 19, August 28, 1920, May 14, October 29, November 12, 1921, March 25, April 8, August 12, 1922, August 9, 1924, June 12, 1926, June 30, 1928; William Giffin, "Black Insurgency in the Republican Party of Ohio, 1920–1932," *Ohio History*, 82 (Winter–Spring 1973), 27–28, 31–33.

[10] Cleveland *Gazette*, November 15, 1919. Smith's advocacy of self-defense brought him under the scrutiny of J. Edgar Hoover (then working for the Justice Department), and in his 1919 report on Negro radicalism Hoover labeled the editorial stand of the *Gazette* "vicious." Arthur I. Waskow, *From Race Riot to Sit-In: 1919 and the 1960's* (New York, 1966), 192.

Smith's militant statements would have found a more congenial reception in Chicago and Washington, D.C., where many blacks were not only giving such advice, but actually putting it into practice in bloody encounters with whites. But in Cleveland, which weathered the tense summer of 1919 without experiencing a race riot, such rhetoric only alienated the editor further from most of the leaders of the black community. Like another trenchant integrationist, William Monroe Trotter, Smith tended to revert to the role of the gadfly in the 1920s. Like Trotter, the Cleveland editor too often personalized the struggle for racial equality; both were quick to criticize and slow to cooperate with other black leaders. Although on many occasions Smith's criticism was warranted, at other times it injured the cause of racial advancement. Smith often criticized the Cleveland NAACP, for example, for not being militant enough in fighting discrimination. While this charge may have been valid in 1918, it certainly was not true ten years later, and the editor's continuing disparagement of the local branch served no useful purpose. "I have known him for twenty-odd years," Robert W. Bagnall, the NAACP's director of branches, wrote of Smith to an NAACP field worker in 1930, "and I have always found him individually interested in the Negro's welfare but unwilling to co-operate with any agency." Smith was a militant fighter for racial justice; paradoxically, the same maverick qualities that made him outspoken in advocating equal rights also limited his ability to advance the principles he believed in.[11]

II

As men like Myers and Smith lost influence in the black community, the business-oriented new elite augmented its power. A similar transition occurred in Chicago's black community (although the process was completed at an earlier date), but in that city there tended to be somewhat greater continuity among the new leadership. In Cleveland the leadership group was, of necessity, much smaller, and the loss of

[11] Cleveland *Gazette*, September 1, 1928 (for a typical attack on the NAACP); Fox, *The Guardian of Boston*, 236–72; Robert W. Bagnall to Daisy Lampkin, March 6, 1930, administrative files (Container C62), Papers of the National Association for the Advancement of Colored People, Manuscript Division, Library of Congress. On black retaliatory violence in Chicago, Washington, and elsewhere, see William Tuttle, Jr., *Race Riot: Chicago in the Red Summer of 1919* (New York, 1970), 226–41; Constance McLaughlin Green, *Washington: Capitol City, 1879–1950* (Princeton, N.J., 1963), 266–67; and August Meier and Elliott Rudwick, "Black Violence in the 20th Century: A Study in Rhetoric and Retaliation," in Hugh Davis Graham and Ted R. Gurr, eds., *Violence in America: Historical and Contemporary Perspectives* (New York, 1969), 402–5.

even a few individuals—by 1920, S. Clayton Green was dead and Nahum
Brascher had left the city—upset the hierarchy of prestige in the black
community and allowed others to move up. During the decade after
1915 the most prominent black leaders in Cleveland were businessmen
Herbert Chauncey and George Hinton, politicians Thomas Fleming and
William R. Green, and social work administrator Jane Edna Hunter.
Although not much is known about the social thought of these individuals, it is clear that all of them played down the need for protest and
agitation. They favored separate black institutions and the creation of a
"group economy" as means to racial advancement.

For some members of the new elite, unfortunately, the philosophy of
self-help and racial solidarity could, upon occasion, degenerate into
little more than a justification for the pursuit of monetary gain. Herbert
Chauncey's enterprises, for example, aided black home-buyers in obtaining loans and provided some additional clerical employment for the
race, but the black entrepreneur severely underpaid his employees in
an effort to squeeze as much profit as possible from his business schemes.
The black real estate dealers and businessmen who founded the Cleveland Realty, Housing, and Investment Company in 1917 billed their
venture as a race enterprise that would "meet the needs" of the migrants.
The firm did provide some employment for black artisans. On the other
hand, the company was not above rent gouging; and when black professionals sought office space in the crowded Central Avenue area, the
managers did not hesitate to eject migrant families on short notice to
make room for more profitable tenants. Furthermore, black real estate
ventures like the CRHI Company, which converted buildings and sometimes whole blocks solely to Negro occupancy, may have to some extent
accelerated the development of the ghetto.[12]

The one person who might have prevented some of these abuses—
black councilman Thomas Fleming—was too personally involved to be
of any help. Fleming was an official of the CRHI Company; little won-
der, then, that he was not among those councilmen who proposed legislation to control rent profiteering during the war. From 1915 to 1927
Fleming was the only black in City Council; as a result he remained the
most powerful black politician in the city. With the exception of a
small amount of political patronage, however, few benefits accrued to
the black community as a result of Fleming's prominence. Under the
black councilman's leadership (if that is the word for it), vice flourished

[12] Cleveland *Advocate*, May 12, 1917; Cleveland *Gazette*, September 7, 1918,
May 14, 1921; interview with Russell and Rowena Jelliffe, September 1, 1971; interview with Dr. William P. Saunders, August 6, 1972.

along Central Avenue, and that area deteriorated into a dingy slum. Fleming could hardly be blamed, of course, for the development of the ghetto, but his attitude often seemed to be one of complete unconcern. Once, when a delegation of concerned citizens questioned him about conditions on Central, the black councilman cavalierly replied that the street was one of the cleanest and best-serviced in the city![13]

Like many black politicians of the 1900–1930 period, Fleming relied on the support of the black electorate while simultaneously maintaining close ties with the white machine. This system, which Martin Kilson has identified as a type of patron-client politics, was the product of the peculiar position of blacks in the northern urban political subsystem at that time; it was not unique to Cleveland. The patron-client relationship gave a measure of legitimacy, as well as enhanced prestige, to the first generation of ghetto-based black political leaders. It also provided some small amount of services and patronage to the black community. In return, the white machine expected utter loyalty in all things political from the elected black officials. Prior to—and in many cases, after—1920, white political support was necessary because the black populations of most cities were as yet too small to elect black candidates by themselves. (This situation was exacerbated by the Progressive "reform" that reduced the number of wards or introduced a system of at-large voting for councilmen. These changes made it more difficult for black voters, even if fairly well concentrated, to swing the election in any given ward.) Fleming's victories in councilmanic races prior to 1921 could not have been achieved without the aid of white Republican boss Maurice Maschke. By the early twenties, Fleming had built up his own political machine—Smith called it the "little black Tammany"—in the Eleventh Ward. But the black councilman remained closely tied to the Maschke organization, and there is no indication that he ever displayed any political independence or disloyalty to his mentor.[14]

Why was black urban politics during the early decades of the twentieth century so boss-ridden? Granted that the newly emerging ghetto-based politicians like Fleming needed white assistance, why did they seek out and emulate the most corrupt of the white politicos? Part of the answer lies in the fact that few white politicians *except* the bosses took

[13] Cleveland *Gazette*, March 25, 1922, April 14, 21, 1928; Cleveland *City Record*, May 15, 1918, July 10, 1918, July 31, 1918.

[14] For a general discussion of the development of patron-client politics in the black ghettos of the North, see Martin Kilson, "Political Change in the Negro Ghetto, 1900–1940's," in Nathan I. Huggins, Martin Kilson, and Daniel M. Fox, eds., *Key Issues in the Afro-American Experience* (New York, 1971), II, 167–85. Kilson does not mention Fleming, but his discussion is applicable to Cleveland.

any interest in the Negro vote during this period. In Cleveland, reform mayors Tom L. Johnson and Newton D. Baker took little interest in the black community (except when whites as well as blacks became alarmed over crime on Central Avenue), and they failed to make even the most perfunctory effort to capture the Negro vote. In the case of Johnson and Baker, part of their lack of interest can be ascribed to the traditionally Republican voting habits of the black electorate. But a deeper reason was the nature of Progressive reform itself. Often elitist, interested in efficiency and the bureaucratization of public services, the typical municipal reformer had an approach to local government that had little appeal to most ghetto dwellers. In New York, blacks found that the Tammany ward heeler was frequently more sympathetic than the would-be reformer, even though the former was a Democrat and the latter usually a Republican. The Tammany official, noted Mary White Ovington in 1911, "is too busy to bother whether the man before him is black or white. The reformer, on the other hand, big with dignity, at times makes him [the Negro] vastly uncomfortable as he lectures upon the Negro problem from the eminence of the superior race." As W. E. B. Du Bois astutely observed, the black voter found himself in a "paradoxical position." He explained:

> Suppose the Municipal League or the Woman's School-board movement, or some other reform is brought before the better class of Negroes to-day; they will nearly all agree that city politics are notoriously corrupt, that honest women should replace ward heelers on school-boards, and the like. But can they vote for such movements? Most of them will say No; for to do so will throw many worthy Negroes out of employment: these very reformers who want votes for specific reforms, will not themselves work beside Negroes, or admit them to positions in their stores or offices, or lend them friendly aid in trouble. Moreover Negroes are proud of their councilmen and policemen. What if some of these positions of honor and respectability have been gained by shady "politics"—shall they be nicer in these matters than the mass of whites?

The mass of black voters, Du Bois concluded, were unwilling to give up these "tangible evidences of the rise of their race" to further reform movements, however intrinsically valuable the changes might be. "And cause after cause may gain their respectful attention and even applause, but when election-day comes, the 'machine' gets their votes."[15]

[15] Mary White Ovington, *Half a Man: The Status of the Negro in New York* (New York, 1911), 203; W. E. B. Du Bois, *The Philadelphia Negro: A Social Study* (Philadelphia, 1899), 383–84.

Another cause of the close association of blacks and machine politics was the political naïveté of many black voters. This was especially true during the decade after World War I, when thousands of unsophisticated southern migrants were added to the voting lists in northern cities. "Dear reader," a black newspaper in Cleveland admonished its patrons in 1918, "your race and family expects you *Not Only to Vote, but to vote a Straight Republican Ticket.* Your X should be under the eagle [the Republican symbol]." Instructions of this sort made it easy for machine politicians to manipulate the votes of black newcomers who (like many of the immigrants from eastern Europe) had never before cast a ballot. This process was assisted by the fact that the machine served an important social function in the ghetto. Councilman Fleming was perpetually providing bail money for prostitutes, petty thieves, and others who had gotten into scrapes with the law. In addition, the headquarters of Fleming's Attucks Republican Club, housed in the same building that contained Starlight Boyd's largest saloon, served as a convenient gathering place for young black males who found the entertainments of the churches too tame to suit their taste. And those who were recipients of the largesse of the black councilman did not forget their benefactor when it came time to vote.[16]

III

Men like Fleming and Chauncy were influential figures during the 1920s, but by the middle of the decade their privileged position was being challenged by a rising group of younger leaders, the "New Negroes." The emergence of this new group reflected the growing complexity of the class structure of the black community. For the most part professionals—doctors and, especially, lawyers predominated—the New Negro leaders had often been educated in white institutions and usually maintained some professional connections with white colleagues. "In Cleveland," a black investigator reported around 1930, "the Negro lawyers are members of the white bar association, attend all its meetings and dinners, and enjoy full and unrestricted membership." In contrast to the prewar era, however, black lawyers and doctors now found themselves increasingly limited to clientele of their own race. Furthermore, they now lived in predominantly Negro neighborhoods. Thus typical

[16] Cleveland *Advocate,* November 2, 1918. On the social functions of the political "club" in aiding the adjustment of black migrants to the city, see W. E. B. Du Bois, "The Black Vote of Philadelphia," *Charities,* 15 (October 7, 1905), 32.

New Negroes had something in common with both the new and the old elite of the black community; it is not surprising, then, that they developed a distinctive ideological stance.[17] The New Negroes tried to transcend the factional disputes that had polarized previous generations of black leaders by emphasizing the positive achievements of the race. Unlike the recalcitrant old upper class, the New Negroes accepted the de facto existence of the ghetto and declined to oppose separate black institutions simply because they were separate; they no longer viewed the struggle for equality solely in terms of integration into white society. On the other hand, the New Negroes usually avoided the accommodationist stance of the new elite; they believed in race pride and racial solidarity, but not at the expense of the equal right to participate in the institutional life of the modern city. Most important, because their relationships with whites were largely professional rather than personal, the New Negro leaders were able to break the paternalistic bonds that had restricted the independence of so many black leaders prior to the Great Migration.[18]

One of the best known of this new group of leaders was Harry E. Davis. A native Clevelander, Davis attended Hiram College and the Law School of Western Reserve University. As a result of his conscientious efforts on behalf of the race, Davis had earned the respect of a wide spectrum of individuals in both the black and the white communities by the end of the Great Migration. Elected to the Ohio House in 1920, Davis was the first Cleveland Negro to serve in that body since 1910. After gaining reelection three times, he stepped down in 1928 to become the first Negro member of the city's Civil Service Commission. Like Fleming, he received the support of the Maschke machine, but Davis managed to remain much more independent than Fleming. In the words of one observer, he was "a machine politician but of the best sort."[19]

---

[17] Carter G. Woodson, *The Negro Professional Man and the Community* (n.p., 1934), 199.

[18] On the New Negro in Chicago (where this group was somewhat more militant than elsewhere), see Allan H. Spear, *Black Chicago: The Making of a Negro Ghetto, 1890–1920* (Chicago, 1967), 193, 197–99, and Tuttle, *Race Riot,* 209–41. For more general comments, see August Meier, *Negro Thought in America, 1880–1915: Racial Ideologies in the Age of Booker T. Washington* (Ann Arbor, 1963), 256–78, and Raymond Wolters's interesting study, *The New Negro on Campus: Black Rebellions of the 1920's* (Princeton, N.J., 1975).

[19] Cleveland *Gazette,* November 6, 1920; Cleveland *Advocate,* August 8, 1921 [?] (clipping in Scrapbook 1, Chester K. Gillespie Papers, Western Reserve Historical Society); Cleveland *Plain Dealer,* January 3, 1928, February 5, 1955 (obituary); Robert W. Bagnall to Daisy Lampkin, July 23, 1930, administrative files

For a while prior to 1915, Davis allied himself with men like Smith and Myers, who opposed the formation of all separate black institutions. In 1911 he had been the youngest of the group of black leaders who took a stand against the creation of a black YMCA. Throughout the postwar era, Davis fought segregation in Cleveland's schools, parks, and other public and semipublic facilities and became a staunch supporter of the NAACP, serving for many years on the National Board of Directors of that organization. He differed from old-line integrationists like Smith, however, in that he ceased, after the 1911 incident, to struggle against the formation or maintenance of all-Negro institutions like the Phillis Wheatley Association. Like many other New Negroes, Davis also deviated from the outlook of the old elite by developing a strong interest in black folk-culture and race history. The black legislator was one of the first to support the activities of Karamu House, and in 1925 he became a member of its Board of Trustees. He also researched the early history of blacks in Cleveland and in 1946 produced *A History of Freemasonry among Negroes*. In contrast to Smith and Myers, Davis coupled the drive for racial equality with an identification with the black race as a group with distinctive cultural and historical traditions.[20]

Another young Negro leader during the postwar era was Chester K. Gillespie. Born in Saylor Park, Ohio, Gillespie attended Ohio State University and the Law School of Baldwin Wallace College. Like Davis, Gillespie sought election to the state legislature during the 1920s; but Cleveland's black population was not yet large enough to support a second black representative, and the young attorney lost every contest. (For a short time, however, he did hold an appointive position as an assistant law director for the city.) Unsuccessful at politics, Gillespie devoted himself to his law practice and quickly became established as Cleveland's leading civil rights attorney. Using the Ohio Civil Rights Law, the young lawyer brought more antidiscrimination suits against Cleveland theater, restaurant, and amusement park owners than any other attorney in the city. In the racist atmosphere of the postwar decade, of course, many of these suits were unsuccessful; but Gillespie's diligence and legal prowess often forced the hand of intransigent white proprietors. "Gillespie got so many court orders against the Hippo-

---

(Container C62), NAACP Papers; Russell H. Davis, *Memorable Negroes in Cleveland's Past* (Cleveland, 1969), 49.

20 Cleveland *Plain Dealer*, February 1, 1911; George A. Myers to Frank S. Harmon, August 23, 1923, Myers Papers; Harry E. Davis to Charles W. Chesnutt, July 10, 1923; Davis to Chesnutt, February 22, 1924, Chesnutt Papers, WRHS; Davis, *Memorable Negroes in Cleveland's Past*, 49; interview with Russell and Rowena Jelliffe, September 1, 1971.

drome," one black resident later recalled with amusement, "that the manger threw up his hands and put a man on the sidewalk to welcome Negroes inside."[21]

Perhaps the best example of the New Negro in Cleveland was Charles H. Garvin, the city's most prominent black physician during the postwar era. Born in Jacksonville, Florida, Garvin attended Atlanta University and the Howard University Medical School. Garvin came to Cleveland in 1916 and within a few years was invited to join the staff of Lakeside Hospital; later he became a professor of urology at Western Reserve University. Garvin defended the right of Afro-Americans to live wherever they pleased, and when he moved into a previously all-white neighborhood in 1926, he courageously endured the bombings and harassment of those who wanted to keep blacks out of their part of the city.[22]

What made Garvin unusual—perhaps unique—was his application of the New Negro concept to the field of medicine. Far more than most educated Negroes, Garvin took the study of African antecedents seriously. He thoroughly researched the history of African medicine and discovered that—notwithstanding the contemporary view of Africa as a primitive, barbaric continent—black Africans had made a considerable contribution to the development of medical techniques. Garvin felt that Negro doctors had a special obligation to study those diseases (such as tuberculosis and pellagra) that most seriously afflicted the race, and he imaginatively related this idea to the literary explorations of the black writers of the Harlem Renaissance. "Heretofore in literature as in medicine," Garvin observed, "the Negro has been written about, exploited and experimented upon, sometimes not to his physical betterment or to the advancement of science, but the advancement of the Nordic investigator." Garvin continued:

> In the past, in only a few instances has the Negro medical man been given an opportunity to make a serious study of his own diseases, that is the diseases peculiar to the black man or at least that attack him differently. The time has come, however when the New Negro doctor realizes that he must be an authority on his own disease peculiari[t]ies as well as the diseases that all mankind are heir to.

[21] Cleveland *Advocate* [n.d.], 1921; Cleveland *Call* [n.d.], 1921 and 1926; Cleveland *Herald*, August 7, 1926; unlabeled clippings, 1924 and 1928, in Scrapbook 1, Gillespie Papers; [Chester K. Gillespie,] "On this Platform I Stand," leaflet, c. 1925, copy in Gillespie Papers; Krawcheck, "Society Barred Negroes—They Formed Own Groups."

[22] Davis, *Memorable Negroes in Cleveland's Past*, 56.

In 1925 Garvin and several other black physicians founded the Cleveland Medical Reading Club, an organization that served as a forum for discussing the problems of black doctors in the community and assisted them in keeping "abreast of advancing medical techniques." Later Garvin served as a board member of a number of community organizations, including the Negro Welfare Association, Karamu House, and the Cleveland NAACP.[23]

Like Charles Chesnutt, Garvin's perspective was complex and sophisticated. For many years, he was the only black doctor in the city serving on the staff of a white hospital; yet he also urged black doctors to devote themselves to the health problems of the race and helped found an all-Negro medical organization. He fought for the right to live in a white, upper-middle-class neighborhood, but still believed in racial solidarity and the study of race history and the African cultural heritage. Seldom did the New Negro's ethnic dualism and pragmatic approach to race problems emerge so clearly in the career of one man.

IV

In the wake of the migration, institutions that served Cleveland's black ghetto increased in both size and number. The black community, however, was ill-prepared to meet the difficulties that accompanied the enormous influx of newcomers after 1915. Under any circumstances the task would have been an arduous one. But for several reasons Cleveland's Negroes were particularly handicapped in dealing with the problems of the migration years. One important factor was the slow growth and moderate size of the black population prior to World War I. Although the Great Migration produced crises in every major black community of the North, Cleveland was less prepared to meet the exigencies of those years than were the black communities of New York and Chicago, both of which had experienced a good-sized influx of newcomers in the decades prior to 1915 and hence had some awareness of the difficulties that the migration would give rise to. A second factor, related to the first, was the underdeveloped condition of black institutions in the Forest City before World War I. Black institutions devel-

[23] *Ibid.*, 57; Charles H. Garvin, "The Influence of African Culture on Modern Civilization," "Medicine in Ancient Egypt," "Ancient African Surgery," and "Malaria and Smallpox and the Early Africans" (manuscripts); Charles H. Garvin, "First Doctors Were Africans," September 26, 1940 (clipping from Cincinnati newspaper); Charles H. Garvin, "The New Negro Doctor" (typewritten booklet), n.p.; Charles H. Garvin, "The Cleveland Medical Reading Club" (manuscript essay), all in Charles Herbert Garvin Papers, Western Reserve Historical Society.

oped late in Cleveland because the Afro-American population was not large enough to support them without white assistance and because they were not needed as urgently as in larger black communities. Thus, like many moderate-sized black communities in the North, Cleveland had almost no functioning structure of secular institutions that could be utilized in a crisis. Finally, most of the leaders who guided the black community during the initial decade of adjustment to the migration were drawn from the accommodationist, business-oriented new elite. Conservative and low keyed, this group tended to favor a course of action which would insure racial peace at any price; in addition, members of the new elite viewed the migration as economically beneficial to themselves and hence were not prone to take seriously any negative effects of the sudden expansion of black population.

The problems of the adjustment of the migrants to life in a large northern city were manifold. Most of the new arrivals were born in Georgia, Alabama, or Mississippi and had been accustomed to a rural way of life. Impoverished and disfranchised, the life-style of many was but a few steps removed from slavery; they lived, as one scholar put it, in the "shadow of the plantation." Recalled Harry E. Davis later of the migrants, "Many . . . came with only the clothing they were wearing, with no preparation for housing, and with little idea of the problems they must inevitably encounter." The newcomers had to be instructed in a number of things that long-time urban residents took for granted: how to make a telephone call, where to board a streetcar, what traffic regulations meant, how to avoid the exploitation of merchants and con men who tried to take advantage of their ignorance of city life.[24]

The rural habits and sycophantic behavior of the migrants often infuriated Negro residents who had been born in the North. Some older black Clevelanders complained of the uncleanliness, slovenly dress, and loud talk which the newcomers exhibited at times. "The [labor] agents," J. Walter Wills complained to the Chamber of Commerce in 1917, "are picking undesirables off the streets and giving them railroad tickets to Cleveland." In a letter to James Ford Rhodes a few years later, George Myers said of the migrants, "Our greatest task is to get them to see themselves from a northern, inste[a]d of a southern standpoint and leave their old condition and customs back in the South. Speaking in the vernacular—to quit being a southern darkey." Old residents feared that the attitudes and habits of the new arrivals could only lead to an in-

[24] Davis, quoted in William Ganson Rose, Cleveland: The Making of a City (Cleveland, 1950), 686; John Selby, Beyond Civil Rights (Cleveland, 1966), 35; Charles S. Johnson, Shadow of the Plantation (Chicago, 1934).

crease in discrimination and segregation which would hurt the entire black community. In 1917 the *Gazette* urged local NAACP officials to go to the steel plants and explain to the newcomers "how to conduct themselves in public places so as to help and not hurt our people of this community." In what seems to have been a universal reaction on the part of an element of the Negro upper and middle class of northern cities, some old residents blamed the migrants for the postwar intensification of racial hostility; they came to glorify the premigration era as a time of racial harmony and good will. Cleveland, of course, had never been completely free of racial prejudice. Discrimination undoubtedly increased after 1915 (to what extent the migrants were responsible for this, of course, is debatable), but older residents were deluding themselves when they claimed that the city had been a Negro Eden before World War I.[25]

Not all black Clevelanders responded to the migration with distrust. Through their churches, especially, many tried to make the newcomers feel at home. "Come, worship and make our church your church," urged the pastor of Lane Memorial CME at the height of the wartime influx, The members of Antioch Baptist greeted the migrants with equal good will. "We stand with outstretched arms welcoming all strangers. . . . Our motto is: 'Strangers but once at Antioch.'" Shiloh Baptist held a fifteen-day revival and the minister noted with satisfaction that "as a result of this great work more than 150 souls were saved." In addition to this religious appeal, individual black churches expanded their services and programs to meet some of the needs of the migrants. The large, well-established Baptist congregations led the way in this regard. During the 1920s, Antioch Baptist increased the number of clubs and organizations devoted to religious, social, and welfare activities, established a Social Service Center, and purchased an old frame building near the church which, when remodeled, became a recreational center.[26]

The response of the black churches to the migration, though laudable,

[25] Wills, quoted in Julian Krawcheck, "Negro Tide from South Swelled City's Problems," Cleveland *Press*, May 31, 1963; John A. Garraty, ed., *The Barber and the Historian: The Correspondence of George A. Myers and James Ford Rhodes, 1910–1923* (Columbus, 1956), 124; Cleveland *Gazette*, January 20, 1917. For the negative reaction among "old settlers" in other cities, see Emmett J. Scott, *Negro Migration during the War* (New York, 1920), 124; Louise Venable Kennedy, *The Negro Peasant Turns Cityward* (New York, 1930), 222–23; St. Clair Drake and Horace R. Cayton, *Black Metropolis: A Study of Negro Life in a Northern City* (New York, 1945), 73–75; Spear, *Black Chicago*, 168; Gilbert Osofsky, *Harlem: The Making of a Ghetto* (New York, 1966), 43–44.

[26] Cleveland *Advocate*, March 31, April 14, 21, 1917; *Antioch Missionary Baptist Church Golden Jubilee, 1893–1943* (n.p. [1943?]), 7.

was hardly sufficient. The secular leadership of Cleveland's black community, however, was slow in responding to the problems engendered
by the wartime migration. In 1916 and 1917 the Cleveland Association
of Colored Men and various ad hoc groups held meetings to discuss the
situation, but little transpired but talk. Noted Henry C. Smith caustically, "It has become a fad . . . to 'discuss the southern influx and the many
problems arising from the same' and stop there." In July, 1917, a statewide organization, the Ohio Federation for Uplift among Colored
People, was formed in Columbus. With committees on "research and statistics, organization and publicity, welfare, labor, and housing," the
organization looked good on paper; in practice, however, it produced
few tangible results and soon became moribund. One of the federation's founders and the delegate from Cleveland, Nahum Brascher, was
far from being the best possible representative of the city's black community. Brascher, a former editor of the conservative Cleveland *Journal*,
was involved in Thomas Fleming's political and real estate dealings and
would shortly leave the city to seek his fortune elsewhere.[27]

The first organization which measurably helped alleviate some of the
problems resulting from the migration was the Negro Welfare Association, an affiliate of the National Urban League, founded in December, 1917, to "advance social and educational conditions" of Cleveland's
black population. Assisted during its first year by a $10,000 grant from
the Mayor's Advisory War Board to help furnish recreation and lodging
for black soldiers returning to civilian life, the NWA carried on a wide
variety of activities during its early years. It investigated and published
reports on conditions in the ghetto, helped migrants find housing, looked
into cases of excessive rentals, and gave some assistance in legal matters
to those who could not afford their own lawyer. The NWA also performed such diverse functions as supervising blacks on parole or pro-
bation and establishing evening classes "for the teaching of English to
adult newcomers who may need such instruction." In 1919 the NWA
leased a large house on Central Avenue to provide temporary board
and lodging for returning black soldiers until they could find employment. The recreational facilities and reading room of the Community
House, as it was called, were open to nonveterans as well, and the center
soon attracted many young people from the ghetto.[28]

[27] Cleveland *Gazette*, March 10, 17, July 21, November 17, 24, 1917, May 25,
1918; Cleveland *Advocate*, August 4, 1917; Nahum D. Brascher to George A.
Myers, October 8, 1917, Myers Papers.
[28] Cleveland *Gazette*, December 22, 1917, March 1, April 5, 1919; National Urban League *Annual Report, 1917–18* (n.p. [1918]), 5, 7; "To the Trustees of the
Negro Welfare Association" [Report of the Executive Secretary of the NWA for

Like its parent organization, the National Urban League, the primary purpose of the Negro Welfare Association was economic improvement. The leader of the NWA stated that their main task was to "point out opportunities in business, industry, and the professions; to conduct an industrial department, through which new opportunities for employment will be sought and efficiency of service promoted." The association was very successful in helping newcomers obtain employment, especially during periods when the demand for laborers was great. During the first two years of operation the NWA found employment for over 80 percent of those who applied for work at its offices, and the organization made a special effort to obtain skilled jobs for Afro-Americans.[29]

Despite these very real achievements, the Negro Welfare Association demonstrated the indecision of much of the city's black leadership during the migration years, as well as the dangers inherent in building "black" organizations with white funds. The NWA came into being too late to help thousands of migrants obtain adequate housing before the winter of 1917–18. Even then, the main drive behind the founding of the organization came not from black leaders but from prominent whites. The idea for the NWA originated in a City Club address by Sherman Kingsley, the white secretary of the Cleveland Welfare Federation; and the Federation provided about 90 percent of the funds for the organization during its early years.[30]

Both Negroes and whites served on the NWA's Board of Trustees, and for many years the organization's executive secretary was William R. Conners, a Negro who had come to the city from the New York office of the Urban League to help organize the local affiliate. During the 1920s, however, the NWA was strongly influenced by white businessmen whose attitudes toward the black migrants were at best paternalistic, at worst exploitative. One of the dominant trustees was the head of a large Cleveland manufacturing concern who had sent labor agents to the South during the war to recruit workers for his firm. Another trustee, a member

---

the period May–August, 1918]; "Accomplishments of the Negro Welfare Association, 1919–1920"; "Negro Welfare Association Annual Report, 1922," Cleveland Urban League Papers, Western Reserve Historical Society.

[29] Cleveland *Gazette*, January 12, 1918, February 1, 1919; Minutes of the Board of Trustees of the Negro Welfare Association, December 14, 1917; "Accomplishments of the Negro Welfare Association from October 1, 1919 to July 31, 1920"; "Accomplishments of the Negro Welfare Association, 1919–1920," Cleveland Urban League Papers; National Urban League *Annual Report, 1920* (n.p. [1920]), 13.

[30] Cleveland *Gazette*, October 20, December 22, 1917; Minutes of the Board of Trustees of the Negro Welfare Association, December 7, 14, 1917, February 5, 1918; "Negro Welfare Association Annual Report, 1922," Cleveland Urban League Papers.

of a wealthy Cleveland family and the city's welfare director during most of the 1920s, refused to force City Hospital to integrate its staff and training programs and instead urged the creation of a separate hospital for blacks. These individuals supported the NWA because of its un-critical stance toward business interests. The Urban League affiliate served as a convenient reservoir of cheap labor for local industrialists; it also sanctioned the use of blacks as strikebreakers, a policy that as-sisted manufacturers in keeping wages down and maintaining control over their labor force. More important, the NWA's close ties with white industrialists and the need for their financial support made it difficult for blacks associated with the organization to protest discrimi-nation in public services or company hiring practices.[31]

As a racial advancement organization, the Negro Welfare Association was also limited in its effectiveness by the theory of social work then in vogue. The NWA (and the Urban League in general) had much in com-mon with white welfare organizations like the Charity Organization Society, in that it fostered the view that poverty and economic dislocation resulted, in many instances, from the failure of the lower class to adopt bourgeois goals and standards. The NWA engaged in a incessant effort to inculcate in migrants the values of thrift, efficiency (a key word of the day), and orderliness. One of the chief purposes of the NWA, William Conners stated in 1917, was to improve the efficiency of black workers. If blacks worked more efficiently than whites, Conners theorized, they might be able to hold their jobs and transcend the "last to be hired, first to be fired" syndrome. During its early years, the NWA established pro-grams designed to help the migrants along the road to middle-class re-spectability. Noting the need for black men to be taught "proper" habits of "expenditure and saving," the association started "thrift clubs" in the ghetto, persuaded black workers to open savings accounts, and in-structed migrant families in the arts of "sanitation and cleanliness in the

[31] Cleveland *Advocate*, March 17, 24, 1917; Cleveland *Gazette*, January 12, 1929; George A. Myers to William R. Hopkins, February 6, 1928, Myers Papers; interview with Russell and Rowena Jelliffe, September 1, 1971. The Detroit Urban League also countenanced strikebreaking. In the words of one historian, the white Employers Association there supported the league because "it was paying for a service." David A. Levine, " 'Expecting the Barbarians': Race Relations and Social Control, Detroit, 1915–25" (Ph.D. dissertation, University of Chicago, 1970), 137. The Chicago Urban League, although also influenced by white industrialists, was less blatantly a tool of management and more active in the social welfare field; it too, however, was hampered by its dependence on white financial assistance. See Arvarh E. Strickland, *History of the Chicago Urban League* (Urbana, 1966), 48–51, 56–67, 72–74; Spear, *Black Chicago*, 169–74; Tuttle, *Race Riot*, 147–48, 149n; and the very interesting general comments in Sterling D. Spero and Abram L. Harris, *The Black Worker* (New York, 1930), 139–44, 465–66.

home." This conceptualization of poverty as a problem in individual cultural adjustment—rather than one of socioeconomic inequality or racism—handicapped the NWA in dealing with the needs of ghetto dwellers because it focused on the failure of the individual rather than the injustices of the social system. The deficiencies of this perspective were less noticeable during the relatively prosperous 1917–27 decade than they would be at the end of the twenties. At that time, the inculcation of efficiency would prove sadly inadequate in preventing discriminatory lay-offs of black workers, and the depression which followed would make a mockery of the notion of "thrift clubs" as a solution to economic insecurity.[32]

Among race institutions established before the war, the Phillis Wheatley Association responded most quickly to the crisis of the Great Migration. Between 1913 (the first year of operation) and 1916, the number of girls utilizing the facilities of Phillis Wheatley steadily increased. When in the latter year Jane Edna Hunter found it necessary to turn away more than fifty "worthy girls," however, she began a campaign for larger quarters. By 1918 she raised $25,000 and was able to purchase and remodel an old Central Avenue mansion. The new structure contained enlarged facilities for job training and temporarily housed close to four hundred girls during its first year of use, twice the capacity of the old home. During the following decade Phillis Wheatley increased its services dramatically. By 1924 the organization's annual budget reached $70,000, and a successful $500,000 fund-raising drive made possible the construction of a nine-story building on Cedar Avenue. Completed in 1928, the new building contained separate schools for instruction in music, cooking, and cosmetology, and could accommodate six times as many girls as the old structure.[33]

Phillis Wheatley served a useful purpose in the expanding ghetto.

[32] Minutes of the Board of Trustees of the Negro Welfare Association, December 14, 1917, March 19, 1918; "Accomplishments of the Negro Welfare Association, 1919–1920," Cleveland Urban League Papers. On the conception of poverty as a cultural problem, see Kenneth L. Kusmer, "The Functions of Organized Charity in the Progressive Era: Chicago as a Case Study," *Journal of American History*, 60 (December 1973), 666–68. A useful study of the development of the Urban League as a national organization is Nancy J. Weiss's *The National Urban League, 1910–1940* (New York, 1974).

[33] Cleveland *Advocate*, May 19, 1917; Cleveland *Gazette*, February 16, 1918, January 3, 1925, April 7, 1928; Minutes of the Phillis Wheatley Association, February 13, June 11, 1917, May 29, September 17, November 12, 1918, January 14, 1919, April 5, September 11, 1923, Phillis Wheatley Association Papers; "Two Women," *Crisis*, 18 (September 1919), 244; "Phillis Wheatley Association," *Southern Workman*, 60 (September 1931), 374; Jane Edna Hunter, *A Nickel and a Prayer* (Cleveland, 1940), chs. 6–9.

Young, unattached black women were an easy prey for both con artists and pimps. Furthermore, employment agencies, unrestrained by any state or federal regulatory legislation, often took outrageous advantage of women who were lured to the North by the hope of economic opportunity. Agents sometimes induced women to accept free transportation to the North in return for signing a contract stipulating that they pay their first two months' wages to the agency. Once in the northern city, the unsuspecting migrant sometimes found herself in debt to the agency; and agents would frequently confiscate the newcomer's baggage (often her only belongings) until she paid the "debt." The Phillis Wheatley Association helped protect girls from this type of ensnarement and assisted them in their adjustment to urban life. Like Karamu, it also provided badly needed recreational facilities for ghetto youth.[34]

The basic program of Phillis Wheatley, nevertheless, was as conservative as that of the Negro Welfare Association, and it involved similar entanglements with white financial backers. The organization could not have been established in 1912 without the financial support of whites who, as a concession, forced Hunter to surrender effective control of the association to a group of wealthy white women. Although Hunter remained the director of Phillis Wheatley throughout the postwar period, white "society women" continued to dominate the Board of Trustees at this time. During the twenties, this elitist leadership was instrumental in raising the funds for the Cedar Avenue building. Blacks paid a price for this beneficence, however. Money flowed into the coffers of Phillis Wheatley at a steady pace because the organization's training program did not, for the most part, threaten the wealthy whites' stereotype of blacks as inferior and suited primarily to menial labor. Most of the girls who graduated from Phillis Wheatley before 1930 became servants of one type or another. "Jane's chief job," a contemporary recalled, "was training domestics." Thus, at a time when one of the most pressing needs of the black community was the upgrading of the occupational status of black women, the program of Phillis Wheatley tended inadvertently to reinforce the belief that Negroes were too ignorant to be anything but servants.[35]

The early history of the Phillis Wheatley Association illustrated the continuing need of black advocates of self-help to compromise their

[34] For a discussion of the problems of migrant women, see Francis A. Kellor, "Assisted Emigration from the South: The Women," *Charities*, 15 (October 7, 1905), 12–13.

[35] Cleveland *Plain Dealer*, May 13, 1917; Cleveland *Gazette*, March 10, 1928; interview, 1971.

philosophy in practice. The black supporters of Phillis Wheatley constantly felt the need to placate and appease the whites who provided the funding for their organization. In a rare committee meeting in 1921 at which no whites were present, a fellow worker touched upon the central dilemma when she praised Hunter as "the only one who can handle the white people and get the money we need in order to run the home." Both Phillis Wheatley and the Negro Welfare Association found it necessary to relinquish a large measure of control to conservative whites. The resulting institutions were odd hybrids indeed: they represented on the one hand the impulse toward black separatism, but were neither controlled completely by nor always in the best interests of the black community.[36]

The first racial advancement organization to break this pattern of dependency was the Cleveland branch of the National Association for the Advancement of Colored People. Most of the local financial support for the NAACP came from blacks, and those whites who did assist the organization were not among the largest contributors. In 1924 (the only year for which complete financial records exist), for example, there were no whites among the six individuals who pledged $100 and only two whites among those who pledged $50. Few whites served on the Cleveland branch's executive committee. Russell Jelliffe, a well-known liberal, was the only white on it prior to 1927. In that year, when the executive committee was expanded from eleven to twenty-seven, only two more whites (David Pierce, of the editorial staff of the Cleveland *News*, and Elizabeth Magee, head of the Consumers' League) were added. So independent was the NAACP's Cleveland branch from white control, in fact, that Robert W. Bagnall felt compelled to instruct the branch president in 1927 that "it is exceedingly advisable that the branch add to its membership as many influential whites as possible and give them some definite work to do toward bettering conditions." While urging increased white involvement, however, Bagnall implied that their role should continue to be peripheral and advisory. Whites should "be induced to use their prestige in arbitrating certain things that may arise and may help procure openings for [national] speakers with white audiences, etc.," but they should not be allowed to dominate the policy-making machinery of the local branch. Thus—at least at the local level—the NAACP was able to eliminate the strictures and restraints that excessive reliance on white financial support entailed.[37]

[36] Minutes of the Phillis Wheatley Association, September 6, 1921, Phillis Wheatley Association Papers.
[37] Cleveland NAACP, 1924 membership list; Robert W. Bagnall to Charles White, February 25, 1927; Bagnall to White, April 1, 1927, branch files (Containers

This independence from white control would prove invaluable in the long run, although it probably hindered the development of the organization during its early years. Until the early 1920s, the Cleveland NAACP was hampered by a small membership and inadequate funding. The branch had been formally established in January, 1914, with 21 members.[38] After a very successful mass meeting (called "the biggest . . . ever held in Cleveland in the interest of Colored people") at which Joel Spingarn was chief speaker, the branch increased its membership to 204. The goal of 500 members by the end of 1914 fell far short, however, and by June, 1915, total membership had increased only slightly, to 254. While it is probable that membership increased during the war, the local branch remained on very shaky financial grounds during this period. Commenting on the unpaid bills left over from the Ohio Conference of the NAACP held in 1919, John R. Shillady, national executive secretary of the NAACP, wrote to Robert Bagnall, "It seems that the Cleveland branch has paid nothing whatever. I should judge that they were not much in sympathy with the movement." At the end of 1920 Cleveland was far behind in meeting its quota as established by the national office; the branch had paid only $1,338 of its apportionment of $1,800.[39]

These circumstances hindered the Cleveland NAACP's effectiveness in the struggle against discrimination during its early years. Prior to 1920, the branch had no definite headquarters where people could report their racial problems. The branch took only a few civil rights cases

G157), NAACP Papers; Cleveland *Call*, April 30, 1927 (clipping in branch files, Container G157, NAACP Papers). Of course, it is not white involvement per se, but paternalistic or exploitative involvement that is restrictive. For a discussion of the difficulties engendered by white domination of the *national* office of the NAACP during the organization's early years, see Nancy J. Weiss, "From Black Separatism to Interracial Cooperation: The Origins of Organized Efforts for Racial Advancement, 1890–1920," in Barton J. Bernstein and Allen J. Matusow, *Twentieth-Century America: Recent Interpretations*, 2d ed. (New York, 1972), 73–76.

[38] A temporary organization preceded the formal founding of the branch in January, 1914. The impetus for the founding of the Cleveland NAACP apparently came less from local incidents than from segregation policies of the federal government under the administration of Woodrow Wilson. See S. P. Keeble to the NAACP, August 28, 1913; Harry E. Davis to Oswald Garrison Villard, September 9, 1913; Villard to G. A. Morgan, September 8, 1913; Nelson L. Ellis to Villard, October 13, 1913; I. A. Lawson to NAACP, September 13, 1913; Frank S. Morgan to Villard, September 14, 1913, administrative files (Container C403), NAACP Papers.

[39] F. E. Young to May Childs Nerney, January 25, 1914 (Container C416); untitled description of formation of Cleveland NAACP by Harry E. Davis, dated April 25, 1914 (Container G157); John R. Shillady to Robert W. Bagnall, June 16, 1919 (Container C74); Walter White to Harry E. Davis, December 7, 1920; F. E. Young to Mary White Ovington, February 26, 1919 (both Container G157), NAACP Papers; *Crisis*, 10 (June 1915), 86.

under consideration, and it failed to organize the black community against the racist films *The Nigger* and *The Birth of a Nation* in 1915 and 1917. During the Great Migration, the branch was headed by Horace C. Bailey, the amicable and moderate pastor of Antioch Baptist Church, and under his leadership the NAACP appeared more interested in holding discussion meetings and organizing social and cultural events than in taking action to oppose discrimination.[40]

Early in the 1920s this situation changed. Through a concerted effort, the branch was able to increase its membership substantially, and at the end of 1922 had sixteen hundred members. The branch collected more money during the first six months of 1922 than it had during the entire preceding year, and within two years it was able to exceed its annual quota by 21 percent. Through quarterly membership drives (often assisted by speakers sent by the national office) and the creation of a women's auxiliary and a college chapter, the Cleveland branch was able to promote greater interest in the organization and place itself on a firmer financial footing.[41]

Although part of this increased vitality can be laid to the population increase of the Great Migration, another important factor was the infusion of new leadership into the local branch in the early twenties. About two-thirds of the members of the branch's executive committee during the postwar decade were professionals, and most of these were young lawyers. Of the remainder, most were white-collar workers of one type or another; one of the most influential of this group was R. K. Moon, a government meat inspector. Only a handful of businessmen took any active part in the Cleveland NAACP; quite exceptional was Edward Jackson, a real estate dealer who served for a number of years as treasurer to the organization. There was a good deal of continuity among this leadership group during the twenties, and the cohesiveness of these individuals was often aided by close professional ties. A number of the attorneys on the executive board, for example, shared law offices.[42]

[40] Cleveland Branch *Bulletin*, 1 (October 1920), 1; Cleveland *Gazette*, January 10, 1914, July 31, 1915, March 31, April 14, 21, May 12, 1917, October 12, December 7, 28, 1918; Larry Cuban, "A Strategy for Racial Peace: Negro Leadership in Cleveland, 1900–1919," *Phylon*, 28 (Fall 1967), 305.

[41] Assistant Director of Branches to Addie Hunton, October 19, 1920; Addie Hunton to James Weldon Johnson, November 20, 1920; "Report of A. W. Hunton, October 6 to November 8, 1922," administrative files (Container C65); Thelma Taylor to Robert W. Bagnall, March 22, 1923; Bagnall to Taylor, April 10, 1923; Charles White to Bagnall, April 13, 1927, branch files (Container G157), NAACP Papers; *Annual Report of the Cleveland Branch . . . for the Year ending December 1st, 1924*, 4.

[42] Information from NAACP Papers.

The persons most responsible for building up the Cleveland NAACP were Harry E. Davis, Clayborne George, and Charles W. White. Davis, whose career has already been discussed, served for many years as legal advisor to the local organization and often acted as liaison with the national office of the association. Davis was from an old Cleveland family, but both George and White were newcomers to the city. Born in 1888 in Surry, Virginia, George attended Howard University as an undergraduate and received law degrees from Howard and Boston universities. He came to Cleveland in the early twenties and soon made a name for himself as an excellent attorney and a vigorous advocate of equal rights. In 1922 George was named to the NAACP's executive committee, and at the end of the following year he was elected president of the branch. Charles White was born in Nashville and attended Fisk University and Harvard Law School. After graduating from the latter in 1924, White came to Cleveland. Described by Robert Bagnall as "capable, efficient, unselfish and earnest," White soon earned a reputation as one of the most independent-minded black leaders in the city. In December, 1926, he was elected president of the Cleveland NAACP, succeeding George, and remained in that capacity for the next three years.[43]

It is clear that, at least during the postwar era, the Cleveland NAACP was guided by New Negroes, and these individuals sought to avoid both the accommodationism of Thomas Fleming and Jane Hunter as well as the overbearing and sometimes counterproductive stridancy of Harry C. Smith. Though militant, the NAACP stressed the need for flexibility and cooperation among different groups and organizations in the struggle against racism. "Every organization," one issue of the *Branch Bulletin* stated, "rightfully aims at the same ultimate end, the advancement of the Negro or the breaking down of race prejudice." This problem, however, has "many sides, all of which are important and must be looked after." The editorial continued:

> This fact is often overlooked by those who insist that our salvation lay in our educating ourselves, or in acquiring wealth, or in battering down the bar of race prejudice with brute force. It is readily admitted that every one of these factors must enter into any program launched for the solution of this perplexing problem, but as important as every one of them is, none is capable of solving the problem alone. We must do, not one of these

[43] *Annual Report of the Cleveland Branch . . . for the Year ending December 1st, 1924,* 2; *Who's Who in Colored America,* 6th ed. (New York, 1942), 202; Selby, *Beyond Civil Rights,* 53, 55; Harry E. Davis to Robert W. Bagnall, December 9, 1926; Bagnall to Davis, December 27, 1926; Bagnall to Daisy Lampkin, July 23, 1930; Charles White to Bagnall, November 26, 1929, branch files (Containers G157 and G158), NAACP Papers.

things, but all of them. We cannot progress far as a race without education, nor can we progress without wealth, nor without courage enough to stand up and fight for our rights. Our progress, to be lasting, must be made along many lines, all developing at the same time, not at the expense of each other, but through a close co-operation of all the forces we can muster along each particular line. The aim of the branch is to bring about just such a co-operation in Cleveland.[44]

To a significant degree, the NAACP was able to realize this goal. The association became the most successful and effective racial advancement organization in Cleveland largely because it avoided the divisiveness that had plagued some previous black efforts at fighting discrimination. At both the national and the local level, the NAACP institutionalized protest. Whereas its predecessors, the Afro-American League and the Niagara movement, were more often than not disparate collections of individuals with an insufficient local base of support, the NAACP was truly an *organization*, functioning from year to year regardless of the personalities involved.

The NAACP struggled against discrimination on many fronts. The activities of the organization in 1924 were typical of the postwar era. In that year the branch brought five suits against discriminatory restaurant proprietors. The racism of some juries at that time was reflected in the fact that the association was able to win only two of these. The threat of legal action, however, was often sufficient to bring proprietors into compliance. The exclusionary policy of the Loew's Ohio Theater was ended when the branch protested to the theater manager. When a case of discrimination at Brookside Park's swimming pool was brought to the attention of the appropriate official, he issued an order to prevent a recurrence of the incident. After an investigation, the branch intervened with the manager of the Higbee Company department store to end that firm's policy of refusing to allow black women to try on articles of clothing. When the association learned that one of the tenants operating a restaurant in a market near East 46th and Euclid was encouraging his help to "doctor" the food served to Negroes, it brought the matter to the attention of the market master, who then informed all the tenants under his jurisdiction that henceforth such discriminatory practices would not be allowed. Finally, upon receipt of a complaint that the Erie Railroad shops on East 55th Street were constructing separate toilet facilities for

<hr />

44 Cleveland Branch *Bulletin*, 1 (October 1920), 3. See also *ibid.*, 1 (November 1920), 1–2; [Charles White,] "'Cleveland Branch of the N.A.A.C.P., Communication to the Executive Committee, February 14, 1927," branch files (Container G157), NAACP Papers.

blacks, both the local and New York offices of the association filed protests with the company's president in New York. After a conference with two of the railroad's representatives in Cleveland, the NAACP persuaded the company to drop the project.[45]

The NAACP did not limit itself to fighting discrimination and segregation in theaters, restaurants, and other facilities, however. It investigated, for example, the occasionally fraudulent claims of real estate and insurance firms doing business in the ghetto, and warned blacks about them. From 1924 to 1926 the local branch actively assisted several black families who, upon moving into all-white neighborhoods, encountered hostility and mob action. In an act of reprisal against Dr. E. A. Bailey, who refused to vacate his home in Shaker Heights, the school board of that community attempted to prohibit the use of its facilities by seventy children—twelve of them black—from nearby Beechwood Village, despite the fact that Beechwood had made an agreement with Shaker that allowed its children to use the Shaker schools. Acting on behalf of the NAACP, Harry E. Davis promptly brought suit against the Shaker officials, and the Court of Common Pleas issued a writ of mandamus requiring the city to carry out the terms of its agreement with Beechwood.[46]

Critics of the NAACP, especially in the 1930s, frequently attacked the association as an elitist organization unconcerned with issues that affected the broad mass of ghetto dwellers. While it is true that, prior to the Depression, the NAACP seldom concerned itself with economic issues, an analysis of activities at the local level shows that the general charge of aloofness from the masses is overstated. After 1920, the Cleveland branch made a special effort to keep working class blacks informed of the activities of the association. From time to time NAACP officials held special meetings with workers in the city's mills and foundries to explain the purposes and objects of the organization, and the branch established an auxiliary composed of a dozen "key men" in Cleveland factories. In addition, the branch intervened in several instances to prevent lower-class blacks from being extradited to the South on trumped-up charges. In one notable case, James Robertson, an iron worker at the Cleveland Hardware Company, through ignorance of his rights signed

<hr>

[45] Annual Report of the Cleveland Branch . . . for the Year ending December 1st, 1924, 1–2; Clayborne George to Robert W. Bagnall, June 10, 1924; George to Walter White, April 21, 1924; "N.A.A.C.P. has Lunch Room Proprietor fined $50 for Discrimination in Cleveland" (press release, June 13, 1924), branch files (Container G157), NAACP Papers.

[46] Cleveland Branch Bulletin, 1 (November 1920), 2; "Cleveland Segregators Try to Oust Colored Children from School" (press release, November 6, 1925), branch files (Container G157), NAACP Papers.

an extradition waiver in 1922 allowing his return to South Carolina. When Harry E. Davis learned that the charges against Robertson were of dubious legality, he immediately wired the governor of Ohio, demanding a hearing on the extradition. NAACP attorneys gained a temporary stay of the extradition order, and after a hearing in a Cleveland court the defendant was discharged. (The local branch was particularly proud of its success in this case, since Robertson was a member of Marcus Garvey's Universal Negro Improvement Association but had received no assistance from his fellow Garveyites. "We took pains," Harry Davis wrote to Walter White, "to emphasize the fact that his connection with the Garvey Movement did not assist him, and that the organization which Garvey was attacking had come to his aid, and in all probability saved him from a long prison or debt sentence in South Carolina.") Apparently at least a portion of the working class viewed the activities of the NAACP as directly related to their own interests. In 1922 almost 40 percent of the local funds for the NAACP came from one-dollar memberships, and it is safe to presume that most of these contributions were from laborers.[47]

V

Before World War I, some Cleveland Negroes had agitated for a separate black YMCA, but they had been unsuccessful. During the Great Migration, however, the need for such an institution became more pressing. Old-line integrationists like Harry C. Smith again opposed the creation of a black YMCA; but when the institution finally came into existence in 1921 it attracted little attention, largely because a facility similar to a "Y" branch—the Negro Welfare Association's Community House—had already been in operation for two years. As early as April, 1920, the NWA proposed to transfer the activities of the Community House to the YMCA, but the NWA board decided to put off the change "until the question of segregation would not loom so large as to prevent success to the movement." Eighteen months later the issue had died down, however, and the changeover was quietly made. In 1923 the "Y"

[47] Cleveland Branch *Bulletin*, 1 (October 1920), 1; Harry E. Davis to James Weldon Johnson, September 15, 1920; George A. Mundy to Mary White Ovington, October 14, 1922; Thelma Taylor to Robert Bagnall, March 22, 1923; "Report of Cleveland, Ohio, Branch of N.A.A.C.P. for the Month of November, 1922"; Harry E. Davis to Walter White, November 15, 1922; "Memorandum for Mr. [James Weldon] Johnson . . . September, 1929"; James Weldon Johnson to Gov. Meyers Y. Cooper, September 5, 1929 (telegram); "Cleve., O., Branch, N.A.A.C.P., Spring Drive for Memberships, 1922," branch files (Containers G157 and G158), NAACP Papers.

branch was moved to a larger, permanent location on Cedar Avenue.[48]

Because of the unusual circumstances which brought it into existence, the creation of a black YMCA caused only a ripple of dissent. The movement to establish a Negro hospital in Cleveland, however, set off a major controversy in the black community that lasted for several years. As early as 1915 Dr. E. A. Dale, a black physician, had proposed the creation of a separate facility, but at that time the black community was far too small to consider financing such an institution; a decade later the idea seemed more feasible. The main proponents of Mercy Hospital (as the institution was to be called) were William R. Green, Herbert S. Chauncey, Thomas Fleming, Jane Hunter, and several black physicians. A number of New Negroes also lent their support, however, and in fact most of the city's black leadership either favored the institution or were noncommittal. In 1927 a campaign was begun to raise $220,000 for the construction of the hospital.[49]

The proponents of the hospital stated that the institution was necessary because of the discrimination in the city's white hospitals; in particular, they cited the fact that no hospital admitted blacks to nurses' training or internship programs. A vocal opposition to the hospital immediately arose, led by Harry C. Smith, George Myers, and a few physicians and ministers. Smith ridiculed the movement for the hospital in terms similar to those used in the debate over the creation of a black YMCA two decades before. Speaking for the die-hard element of the old elite, he perceived the backers of Mercy Hospital as selfish accommodationists, eager for the jobs and titles that the new institution would bring. Noting that one of the doctors supporting the project had recently migrated from Alabama, Smith urged him to "go back South! . . . And . . . *stay there* until you can 'take that red bandanna off your head.' " Some black doctors, the editor fumed, "would harm all of our people in this community almost beyond repair to attain their selfish desires." An elderly black physician agreed: "The men back of this project are *deceivers*. What they want is a job; that is all." Myers, too, condemned those Negroes who would accept segregated facilities if "there is a possible chance for individual profit." He and Smith both felt that the creation

[48] Harry C. Smith to George A. Myers, April 14, 1919, Myers Papers; Minutes of the Board of Trustees of the Negro Welfare Association, April 29, 1920, November 22, 1921, Cleveland Urban League Papers; Cleveland *Gazette*, March 24, 1923.

[49] E. A. Dale and P. H. Green to George A. Myers, June 3, 1915, Myers Papers; Cleveland *Gazette*, November 15, 1919, November 26, 1926, May 21, November 5, 1927; Mercy Hospital Association of Cleveland, *Does Cleveland Need a Negro-Manned Hospital?* (n.p. [1927], pamphlet).

of Mercy Hospital would only lead to further discrimination and "would close the doors of all other Cleveland hospitals to our people. . . ."[50]

Smith and Myers saw the Mercy Hospital issue as a clear-cut case of integration and equal rights versus separatism and self-help. But they were mistaken, for—unlike the 1911 YMCA incident—the black community did not generally divide along these lines. It is probable, of course, that some individuals did favor the proposed institution for the patronage it would bring. It is also true that a few Negroes like Jane Hunter lent their support because they favored separate institutions of any kind. But such accommodationist separatism was not a major force behind the Mercy Hospital movement. The sponsors of the hospital clearly stated that they opposed segregation "that restricts the social, economic, or political life of any group." They conceived of the hospital as a facility which would benefit the entire black community—a place where black patients would be assured admission and where black doctors and nurses could develop the skills that would eventually enable them to be accepted as equals by the white medical profession. Such an attitude more closely resembled that of the "New Negro" than the older, Tuskegee version of racial solidarity.[51]

That this was so was proven by the pragmatic response of the city's black leadership when, in 1929, the black community proved unable to raise the necessary funds for the hospital and the city council vetoed the use of public funds to finance a similar project. Several of those who had originally supported the drive for a black hospital now began a movement—this time fully supported by Smith and Myers—aimed at breaking down the discriminatory policies of tax-supported City Hospital. This new effort elicited a widespread positive response from the city's black population. Charles Garvin, Harry E. Davis, and other prominent blacks entered the fray, and in November, 1929, three Negroes won election to city council by vowing to fight for a change in the city's hospital program. The black population also showed their disaproval of the discriminatory policy of the municipal hospital by voting in large numbers against new hospital bonds. The new city manager, Daniel E. Morgan, soon yielded to the pressure of the black community. In September, 1930, five black women were admitted to the hospital's nurses' training program. The fol-

<hr />

[50] *Ibid.*; Cleveland *Gazette*, April 19, 1927, February 25, 1928, April 13, October 26, 1929; George A. Myers to William R. Hopkins, February 6, 1928; Smith-Myers correspondence, 1927, Myers Papers.

[51] Cleveland *Gazette*, November 26, 1926, quoting Jane Edna Hunter's Phillis Wheatley Association journal, *The Open Door*; Mercy Hospital Association, *Does Cleveland Need a Negro-Manned Hospital?*

lowing year, the first black intern was admitted to the staff. The hospital's policy of segregating Negro patients also came to an end at this time.[52]

The role of the Cleveland NAACP in the dispute over Mercy Hospital was illustrative of that organization's desire to avoid ideological divisiveness without adopting an accommodationist posture. When the hospital movement began getting under way in 1927, the branch found itself "rather hopelessly separated" into two camps. "On the one hand," wrote Charles White of the planned hospital, "it is being bitterly opposed as a self-inflicted bit of jim-crowism. On the other hand, it is being espoused as a very much needed institution for the training of Negro physicians and nurses. . . ." White, seeking a policy that would unite the branch, rejected the "simple assertions" of some opponents that black YMCAs and hospitals should be dismissed simply as "instances of self-segregation." After consulting with the national office of the NAACP, the branch received a ruling from Robert Bagnall that if "the proposed Mercy Hospital is to be a private hospital, serving all groups and appealing to the general public for funds . . . its existence does not run counter to the principles of the National Association." Shortly thereafter, the branch decided to remain neutral on the issue.[53]

The board changed its mind in 1929, however, when black Councilman E. J. Gregg and several other backers of the hospital began to urge the use of *public* funds to create a black medical facility on the East Side. The NAACP came out strongly against this latest plan. In his 1929 *Annual Report*, Charles White made it clear that "our opposition is not to a Negro Hospital privately supported, nor to an East side branch of City Hospital with a mixed staff, designed to . . . serve the whole East

[52] Cleveland Gazette, July 28, 1928, January 12, 1929; George A. Myers to William R. Hopkins, December 13, 1927; Myers to Hopkins, December 27, 1927; Myers to Hopkins, February 6, 1928, Myers Papers; "Local N.A.A.C.P. Head Urges Defeat of Hospital Bonds," Cleveland *Call and Post*, October 27, 1928 (clipping in NAACP Papers); Charles White, "'Cleveland Branch, N.A.A.C.P., Annual Report of President, November 21, 1929," [5–6]; Charles White to Walter White, January 14, 1930, branch files (Containers G157 and G158), NAACP Papers; Charles H. Garvin, "Pioneering in Cleveland," *The Woman's Voice*, 1 (September 1939), 14–16 (copy in Garvin Papers); Thomas F. Campbell, *Daniel E. Morgan, 1877–1949: The Good Citizen in Politics* (Cleveland, 1966), 115–17. The first small breakthrough in the struggle to integrate City Hospital occurred in July, 1928, with the appointment of Dr. John McMorries to the surgical out-patient staff of the hospital. Dr. McMorries, who had practiced in Cleveland since 1916, was the first black doctor ever named to a post at City Hospital. Charles White to James Weldon Johnson, June 23, 1928, branch files (Container G158), NAACP Papers.

[53] [Charles White,] "Cleveland Branch of the N.A.A.C.P., Communication to the Executive Committee, February 14, 1927," 2; Charles White to Robert W. Bagnall, March 28, 1927; Bagnall to White, March 31, 1927, branch files (container G157), NAACP Papers.

side and to which all patients on the east side shall be required to go."
Most people, White stated, failed to understand the distinction on which
their opposition to the plan was based. "We stand against a branch of
the City Hospital which, whether intended or not, will eventuate in a
short while into what to all intents and purposes is a Negro branch of
City Hospital." While the branch sympathized with the plight of blacks
who desired to become nurses or doctors, it "'was not willing to compromise such a fundamental [principle] by acquiescing to the introduction of a pernicious double system of municipality owned and operated
hospitals." Once the City Council had rejected Gregg's proposal, the
NAACP quickly joined with other groups to successfully eliminate discriminatory practices from City Hospital. Throughout the entire controversy the branch had acted responsibly and with a good deal of flexibility to advance the best interests of the black community.[54]

VI

The reaction of the NAACP to the hospital dispute was indicative of the changing political and ideological temperament of black
Cleveland at the end of the 1920s, and the successful conclusion of the
controversy coincided with the rise to power of the New Negroes. Although Thomas Fleming was, throughout the decade, the most influential black politician in the city, it is clear that his conservative brand of
leadership was becoming less and less representative of the views of the
black community. One indication of this was the changing editorial
stance of black newspapers in the city. After the Cleveland *Journal*
folded in 1912, there would never again be an organ in Cleveland that
represented the Booker T. Washington self-help philosophy in its pristine
form. The *Advocate*, which published from 1914 to 1922, was in many
ways the logical successor to the *Journal*. During its early years, especially, the paper preached race pride and "the doctrine of perseverance
and stick-to-it-iveness." The *Advocate's* editor, Ormand Forte, supported
Fleming, gave a nodding approval to the concept of a black YMCA, and
generally refused to criticize Booker T. Washington or his successor,
Robert R. Moton.[55]

The editorial stance of the *Advocate*, however, was never as conserva-

---

[54] Charles White, "Cleveland Branch, N.A.A.C.P., Annual Report of President,
November 21, 1929" [5], branch files (Container G158), NAACP Papers.

[55] Cleveland *Advocate*, September 11, October 30, 1915, March 8, October 21,
1916. For editorials praising either Tuskegee or its headmaster, see *ibid.*, June 12,
July 24, November 6, 1915.

tive as that of the *Journal*. Unlike its predecessor, its tone was not uniformly accommodationist. The paper attacked the racial injustice of the South and called for federal intervention to control what editor Forte called the southern white's "lust for blood." And while refusing to attack Washington, the *Advocate* was also lenient toward Washington's critics. "In spite of everything that might be said against Mr. [William Monroe] Trotter by his bitterest enemies," an editorial proclaimed in 1916, "the fact stands out clearly and unmistakably that he has fought 'in season' and 'out of season' for equal rights for his race." Although it was never a militant paper, the *Advocate* became more favorable to black protest during the Great Migration. Its editorials frequently charged the War Department with racism and in 1917 protested the segregation of black soldiers in separate training camps. By 1918 the *Advocate's* editor revealed the limitations of his support for Washingtonian principles when he vigorously attacked Governor James Cox's proposal to enlarge the facilities at Wilberforce University. Previously Forte had seen nothing wrong with a black YMCA, but he now feared an enlarged Wilberforce would be an "entering wedge for *Separate Education*" in Ohio. "Tuskegee Institute," said Forte, "is all right for Alabama, for it is needed there, but a 'Tuskegee' is not desired in Ohio."[56]

The *Advocate's* flexibility on race issues signaled the beginning of a movement away from the ideological dogmatism that had characterized some elements of the black community on the eve of the wartime migration. During the twenties, the successors to the *Advocate*—the *Call*, the *Herald*, and (after 1928) the *Call and Post* would be much more insistent than the *Advocate* had been in protesting discrimination in restaurants, theaters, and other public accommodations in Cleveland. Unlike the *Gazette*, however, which never ceased its militant agitation for civil rights, these newspapers did not make a fetish of integration. The increasingly attractive approach that they reflected in their editorials was that members of the black community should strive for integration wherever segregation restricted their social freedom or economic opportunity. But neither the *Advocate* nor its successors criticized the Phillis Wheatley Association or other black social-welfare organizations simply because they were institutions designed solely for Negroes.[57]

It was not until the end of the twenties that this view was translated

[56] *Ibid.*, June 24, July 1, August 26, October 21, 1916, September 8, November 24, December 1, 1917, January 12, 1918.

[57] Unfortunately, copies of most black newspapers (with the exception of the *Gazette*) published in Cleveland during the 1920s have not survived. The conclusions in this paragraph are based upon the scattered clippings that have been preserved in a number of manuscript collections.

into political power. Thomas Fleming, the sole black representative on the City Council until 1927, had no desire to use the black vote as a tool to force concessions from the dominant Republican machine. Although Fleming controlled patronage in his Eleventh Ward, he was never able to obtain significant appointments for blacks, and most of the jobs at his disposal were rather minor positions. Within a few years, all this would change, and the political subsystem of the black ghetto would be transformed from a neglected stepchild of the local GOP to a formidable power within the party, able to make its voice heard and to wrest important concessions from the city's white leadership. How did this happen?

As in so many other respects, the underlying cause was the growth of the ghetto. As the black population expanded eastward, it gradually engulfed the Seventeenth and Eighteenth wards, and in 1927 this enabled two new black members, E. J. Gregg and Clayborne George, to join Fleming on City Council. The election of Gregg and George was evidence of an increasing dissatisfaction with the regular Republican organization. Both had run for council as "independent Republicans" in 1925 but had lost, despite credible showings. They then set about building up separate political organizations outside the regular party caucuses. George established the East End Political Club in the area just beyond East 79th Street in which middle-class Negroes were settling in increasing numbers. He founded his organization "on those principles which the N.A.A.C.P. has advocated for some years, namely, that the Negro should use his ballot effectively for men and measures without respect to party label." In 1927 both George and Gregg ran as independents again, and Gregg was elected with Democratic support. "The whole of Cleveland," Charles White proclaimed in the wake of election, "is now awake to the fact that the Negro's vote can no longer be classed as solidly for the Republican party or for any party. These gratifying results were achieved by a unity that was outstanding and by an independence that has given rise to a new respect for the Negro vote."[58]

During the next year Gregg and George caucused with the Democratic minority in the council, and Democratic leaders made an effort to sway them to their side of the aisle permanently. W. Burr Gongwer, the local Democratic boss, appointed forty-two blacks as precinct committeemen

[58] Cleveland *Gazette*, November 19, 1927; Charles White to Robert W. Bagnall, November 15, 1927, branch files (Container G158), NAACP Papers. After 1924, Cleveland councilmen were elected from four large districts on the basis of proportional representation. Party organizations at the ward level remained intact, however, and in many respects the old ward boundaries continued to function as the basic political units.

in wards 11, 12, and 18, an arrangement more generous than that offered by the Republican machine. Whether Gregg and George actually considered joining the Democratic fold permanently, however, is doubtful; it is likely that they were using their relationship with the Democrats as a threat to force concessions from the GOP. In January, 1928, Republican council votes elected Harry E. Davis to the Civil Service Commission, and a year later the Republicans backed a known independent, Dr. Russell S. Brown, minister of Mt. Zion Congregational Church, for the council seat vacated by recently indicted Thomas Fleming. Shortly thereafter the rebellious black councilmen rejoined the Republican caucus.[59]

This episode marked the beginning rather than the end of black political independence in Cleveland, however. Fleming was soon convicted and imprisoned on bribery charges, which eliminated him once and for all from the political scene. The path for new black political leadership was now completely unencumbered. In the councilmanic elections of November, 1928, George was reelected, lawyer Lawrence O. Payne succeeded to the seat held briefly by Dr. Brown, and LeRoy Bundy, a black dentist and sometime-entrepreneur, replaced E. J. Gregg. In this same election Mary B. Martin became the first Negro to gain a seat on the Cleveland Board of Education; the previous year, lawyer Perry B. Jackson had won election to the state legislature.[60]

Under the leadership of Bundy, a militant advocate of equal rights who had played a controversial role in the black community of East St. Louis over a decade before, the three black councilmen now moved quickly to transform their votes into an effective political instrument.[61]

[59] Cleveland *Plain Dealer*, January 3, 1928; Cleveland *Gazette*, February 16, 23, March 9, October 19, 1929; Giffin, "Black Insurgency in the Republican Party of Ohio," 36–37.

[60] Thomas W. Fleming, "My Rise and Persecution" (manuscript autobiography [1932], Western Reserve Historical Society), 89–100; R. O. Huus and D. I. Cline, "Election Fraud and Councilmanic Scandals Stir Cleveland," *National Civic Review*, 18 (May 1929), 289–94; Cleveland *Gazette*, November 9, 1928, February 23, November 9, 16, 1929; Davis, *Memorable Negroes in Cleveland's Past*, 47.

[61] Of the New Negro leaders who rose to power at the end of the 1920s, Bundy was clearly the most dynamic. He grew up in Cleveland (his father, Rev. Charles Bundy, was a prominent minister) and received a degree in dentistry from Western Reserve University. Before World War I, Bundy moved to East St. Louis, Illinois, where he set up his dental practice, became engaged in a number of entrepreneurial schemes, and rose to prominence in the local black community. Bundy soon became involved in politics and allied himself with the local Republican boss, Mayor Fred Mollman. Described as an "aggressive political agitator," Bundy managed to win favorable patronage concessions for the black community while simultaneously incurring the hatred of many East St. Louis whites. In the aftermath of the bloody race riot of July, 1917, many whites attempted to make Bundy the scapegoat.

They were greatly aided in this task by their strategic position in the new council: only fourteen of the twenty-five seats were held by Republicans, and this gave the black councilmen a balance of power in that body. The integration of City Hospital was only the first of a series of victories that flowed from the enhanced political power of the black vote. In 1930, the black "triumvirate" (as Payne, George, and Bundy were labeled by the press), effectively marshaling the black vote, brought about a stunning primary-election defeat of an organization candidate for county prosecutor who had threatened to crack down on the East Side policy rackets, a "business" that had become an especially important source of black employment with the onset of the Depression. At the same time, all three councilmen won election as ward leaders, thereby significantly increasing the amount of patronage available in the black community. Winning reelection in 1931, the black councilmen once again put their balance of power to good use, refusing to support the Republican machine's candidate for council president until all three black representatives were given committee chairmanships. In 1932, at a time when the GOP suffered massive defeats at the local and state level as well as in the national elections, the black political leadership of Cleveland still managed to engineer the election of Chester Gillespie to the state legislature. And during the next three years the blacks who served on City Council continued to use their voting leverage to wring concessions from city hall and to enhance their own power within the party.[62]

Charged with murder and conspiracy, the black dentist eventually won acquittal and returned to Cleveland, where he became involved in the Garvey movement. It appears, however, that Bundy's interest in Garveyism was temporary and perhaps opportunistic. His militant agitation for equal rights and enhanced black political power in East St. Louis (and his support of labor unions there) was hardly typical of most of Garvey's followers, and in 1929 he was elected to the Cleveland City Council on a platform pledging to fight for the integration of City Hospital. Tremendously ambitious, Bundy was nevertheless a master political strategist; he was probably one of the most successful black politicians of his day. Cleveland *Journal*, May 20, 1905; Elliott M. Rudwick, *Race Riot at East St. Louis, July 2, 1917* (Carbondale, Ill., 1964), 119–32, 147, 185–90, 216n; interview with Dr. William P. Saunders, August 6, 1972.

[62] Cleveland *Gazette*, April 19, June 19, July 26, 1930, November 14, 1931, January 23, November 12, 1932, November 11, 18, 25, 1933, January 6, 1934; Maurice Maschke, "The Memoirs of Maurice Maschke," Cleveland *Plain Dealer*, September 5, 1934; Russell H. Davis, "The Negro in Cleveland Politics," Cleveland *Call and Post*, October 29, 1966. For a detailed discussion of black politics in Cleveland during the 1929–45 period, see Christopher G. Wye, "Midwest Ghetto: Patterns of Negro Life and Thought in Cleveland, Ohio, 1929–45" (Ph.D. dissertation, Kent State University, 1973), ch. 8. The strategic political position of blacks in Cleveland during the 1929–35 period was in many ways similar to that of Chicago during the

VII

The triumph of the New Negroes did not, of course, culminate in the destruction of racial inequality in Cleveland, nor did it lead to an appreciable diminution of the slum conditions which continued to mar the quality of black life in the city and which would lead to increasing discontent in the years ahead. These aspects of what Gunnar Myrdal called "an American dilemma" were far beyond the capability of a few black councilmen—however strategically powerful—to solve. In fact it was becoming more and more apparent that these problems were beyond the ability of local government in general to solve, and the next generation of concerned citizens would look increasingly to the federal government and national protest organizations as a means of altering the racial status quo.

Nevertheless, a watershed had been reached; the first years of the Depression marked the conclusion of an important phase in the history of black Cleveland. The consolidation of the ghetto as a physical entity was complete. A process at least fifty years in the making had finally run its course, and in innumerable ways the average black citizen was more isolated from the general life of the urban community than he had ever been since the founding of the city. Yet it was this very isolation, and the sense of unique goals and needs that it fostered, that helped unify the black community and provided the practical basis for the future struggle against racism in all its manifestations. During the next half-century, the black ghetto would undergo many changes—but this paradox would endure.

---

regimes of Mayor William Hale Thompson. In both cases blacks held the balance of power in city government and were able to use this leverage to their advantage. See Drake and Cayton, *Black Metropolis*, 346–51; Harold Gosnell, *Negro Politicians: The Rise of Negro Politics in Chicago* (Chicago, 1935), *passim*; Kilson, "Political Change in the Negro Ghetto," 185–89.

A Note on the Analysis
of Occupational Data

With few exceptions, historians have generally failed to follow the early lead of sociologists such as W. E. B. Du Bois and St. Clair Drake, who urged the systematic study of black occupational structure. The position of blacks in the economy has usually been studied in isolation, without relating or comparing Afro-Americans with other groups. Scholars have also too readily accepted the Census Bureau's classification of jobs. One traditional Census Bureau category, "manufacturing," is too broad for all but the most general purposes, while two other, "trade" and "transportation," are utterly useless because they include everything from the most menial laborers to the highest paid managers of large industrial firms. Finally, although some historians have noted the changes in black occupational structure produced by such dramatic events as the "Great Migration" of 1916–19, there has been little attempt to systematically trace changes over a more prolonged period of time.[1]

[1] W. E. B. Du Bois, *The Philadelphia Negro* (Philadelphia, 1899), 97–146, and St. Clair Drake and Horace R. Cayton, *Black Metropolis: A Study of Negro Life in a Northern City* (New York, 1945), 214–62, both survey black occupations in great detail. Since these studies of black urban life were chiefly sociological rather than historical in nature, however, neither concerned itself much with the changes that occurred in black occupations over the long run. The same can also be said for other early ghetto studies, such as Mary White Ovington's *Half a Man: The Status of the Negro in New York* (New York, 1911), John Daniels's *In Freedom's Birthplace: A Study of the Boston Negroes* (Boston, 1914), and William A. Crossland's *Industrial Conditions among Negroes in St. Louis* (St. Louis, Mo., 1914). In *Harlem: The Making of a Ghetto* (New York, 1966), Gilbert Osofsky mentions the depressed state of black occupations in New York City in 1890, but he fails to follow this up by discussing any changes in this pattern that may have occurred during the following forty years. Allan Spear's *Black Chicago: The Making of a Negro Ghetto, 1890–*

In this book I have attempted to rectify these deficiencies by systematically surveying male and female occupations in Cleveland's black community over a sixty-year period; by comparing blacks with immigrants and native whites (and, in some instances, comparing conditions in Cleveland with other cities); and by utilizing a more functional occupational classification system than that used by the Census Bureau.

The classification system used throughout this book is based upon that developed by Alba M. Edwards.[2] In 1937 Edwards compiled an *Alphabetical Index of Occupations by Industries and Social-Economic Groups* that exhaustively categorized every occupation tabulated by the Census under nine subheads ranked from 0 (the highest category) to 8 (the lowest):

0. Professional persons
1. Farmers (owners and tenants)
2. Proprietors, managers, and officials (except farmers)
3. Clerks and kindred workers
4. Skilled workers and foremen
5. Semiskilled workers
6. Farm laborers
7. Other laborers
8. Servant classes

In adapting it to the present purposes, I have made several modifications in Edwards's classification system. While retaining his general rank order of occupations, I have combined several of the categories. Since after 1870 there were fewer and fewer farm owners, tenants, or farm laborers in Cleveland, categories 1 and 6 were eliminated as separate groupings. Categories 1 and 2 were combined, as were 6 and 7. The result is the following ranking of

---

1920 (Chicago, 1967), represents a considerable methodological advance over Osofsky's treatment of the job structure. Spear systematically (rather than impressionistically) analyzes both male and female occupations during the first two decades of the twentieth century. Unfortunately, however, his discussion is rendered less valuable by his use of the Census Bureau's unwieldy classification system; and, unlike Drake and Cayton, Spear does not compare the job status of blacks with that of the foreign-born or native white populations of Chicago.

Although it is not primarily a study in black history, a recent outstanding exception to the lack of historically oriented studies of black occupations is Stephan Thernstrom, *The Other Bostonians: Poverty and Progress in the American Metropolis, 1880–1970* (Cambridge, 1973), 176–219. Thernstrom surveys black occupations in greater detail and over a longer period of time (ninety years) than any other scholar. I would question, however, his conclusion that there "was virtually no improvement in the occupational position of black men in Boston between the late nineteenth century and the beginning of World War II." By skipping from 1900 to 1940 in his analysis of occupational data, Thernstrom may have inadvertently overlooked a significant—if temporary—upward trend in black occupations during the 1916–30 period.

[2] Alba M. Edwards, *An Alphabetical Index of Occupations by Industries and Social-Economic Groups* (Washington, 1937), 5–7 and *passim*.

occupations, as used in this book (with some changes in the titles of categories):

Occupational category	Rank	Edwards's rank
Professionals	1	0
Proprietors, managers, and officials	2	1, 2
Clerical workers	3	3
Skilled workers	4	4
Semiskilled workers	5	5
Unskilled workers	6	6, 7
Personal and domestic servants	7	8

In a handful of cases I have placed a given ocupation in a category different from that adopted by Edwards. It seemed more appropriate, for example, to categorize newsboys as unskilled laborers than (as Edwards does) as clerical workers. I do not think that the mere fact that newsboys handle newsprint in the course of their work justifies their being grouped under the clerical category! Likewise, apprentices to skilled trades are listed as skilled workers rather than semiskilled workers. Apprentices do not, of course, earn the same pay as journeyman artisans; but they should still be ranked, I believe, with the occupational grouping that they will enter upon the completion of their training. Other deviations from Edwards's ranking system include boarding and lodging house keepers (listed as proprietors rather than semiskilled workers), bakers (skilled workers rather than semiskilled workers), whitewashers (semiskilled rather than unskilled), chauffeurs (personal service rather than semiskilled), deliverymen (unskilled instead of semiskilled workers), messenger, office, and bundle boys (personal service instead of clerical workers), and barbers, hairdressers, and manicurists (skilled instead of semiskilled). This last category may seem somewhat arbitrary, but it is defensible, I think, when one considers that prior to about 1910 the barbering trade offered one of the more visible routes of upward mobility in the black community. A number of black barbers owned their own shops, many gained prestige from their association with wealthy whites, and a few became—by the standards of the black community—well-to-do. In 1903 one Negro barber in Cleveland was even elected to the state legislature. After 1910 the prestige of barbering began to fall off rapidly as black barbers turned more and more to the less lucrative Negro trade of the ghetto. Still, quite a few of these individuals actually ran their own shops and might more properly be considered proprietors than either semiskilled or skilled workers. But since it is necessary, in this analysis, to lump all barbers together in one category, I have chosen the middle course and listed them as skilled tradesmen.

The following list of occupations by socioeconomic category is selective and includes only the most common job designations; for the categorization of all other jobs, the reader should consult Edwards's *Alphabetical Index of Occupations*.

Professionals

clergymen
dentists
lawyers
musicians and teachers of music

nurses (trained)
physicians and surgeons
teachers

Proprietors, managers, and officials

building contractors
garage keepers and managers
merchants and peddlers
retail dealers
undertakers

boarding- and lodging-house keepers
hotel keepers and managers
restaurant, cafe, and lunchroom
    keepers
saloon keepers

Clerical workers

clerks (including clerks in stores)
commercial travelers
insurance agents and officials
real estate agents and officials

salesmen
agents
bookkeepers, cashiers, and accountants
stenographers and typists

Skilled workers

apprentices to trades (before
    1910, all apprentices)
bakers
butchers
blacksmiths
brick and stone masons
carpenters
stationary engineers
foremen and overseers
machinists
milliners
molders

painters, glaziers, and varnishers
    (except those in factories)[a]
plasterers
plumbers
shoemakers and cobblers
tailors
tinsmiths
wheelwrights
locomotive engineers and firemen
barbers, hairdressers, and manicurists
policemen

Semiskilled workers

semiskilled operatives (all)
bartenders
laundry operatives
brakemen
undifferentiated iron and
    steel workers (as listed in 1870
    and 1890 censuses)

housekeepers
whitewashers
dressmakers and seamstresses
nurses and midwives (as listed
    in 1870 and 1890 censuses)
saw mill employees

[a] In the 1870 and 1890 censuses, the undifferentiated category "painters, glaziers, and varnishers" is counted as skilled work.

Unskilled workers
laborers (all, except those listed under domestic and personal service)
longshoremen and stevedores
porters in stores

newsboys
messengers, packers, and porters (as listed in 1890 census)
draymen and hackmen

Personal and domestic servants
chauffeurs
livery-stable keepers and hostlers (as listed in 1870 and 1890 censuses)
charwomen
elevator tenders
janitors and sextons
laborers (domestic and personal service only)

launderers and laundresses (except those in laundries)
porters (except those in stores)
servants
messenger, office, and bundle boys
waiters

In a few instances, in compiling occupational data from the 1870 and 1890 censuses, it was necessary to omit certain job categories altogether. The following occupations were either too vague or too general to be of use:

1870 census
officials and employees of government
billiard- and bowling-saloon keepers and employees
hotel or restaurant keepers and employees
officials and employees of express companies
officials and employees of railroad companies
officials and employees of street-railroad companies
officials and employees of telegraph companies
1890 census
steam railroad employees
street railroad employees

The occupational index. By means of a proportionate weighting of the percentages of a given segment of the work force (blacks, native whites, etc.) employed in different occupational categories, it is possible to calculate a single number, the occupational index, which measures the average occupational standing of a group in a particular year. In this study the occupational index is used to compare the relative position of blacks in the economy at any given point and to trace changes in black occupational structure and status over a period of decades. It must be emphasized that the occupational index measures the mean occupational status of the *entire group* (blacks, for example) in a given year and that changes in the index over a period of time indicate alterations in this mean. The occupational index, traced over time, is not a measure of *individual* mobility. It does not tell us what *proportion* of blacks in the community at any given point were advancing or declining occupationally or whether intergenerational mobility was high or low. On the other hand, it should be pointed out that the use of the occupational index is superior to that of the study of individual mobility in one respect. The index measures the mean occupational standing of *all* members of a group living in a city at a given time. Individual mobility studies record changes in occupational rank only for that minority that remain in a city for ten years or more. Thus while the index is limited in some ways, it is still a useful research tool, when supplemented by a detailed study of changes in specific occupations.

The procedure for calculating the occupational index is simple and straightforward. The first step is to compute the percentages of the total occupations of a given group that fall into the different occupational categories, ranked from 1 (professional workers) to 7 (domestic and personal servants). Next, multiply each percentage by the rank that it is categorized under, and add these products together. The index is then obtained by dividing this sum by the sum of the percentages of the seven categories and multiplying the entire result by 100. Or, to state this in mathematical terms:

$$\text{The occupational index} = 100 \times \frac{1a + 2b + 3c + 4d + 5e + 6f + 7g,}{a + b + c + d + e + f + g}$$

where $a =$ the percentage of the group in the professions,

$b =$ the percentage ranked as proprietors, managers, and officials,

$c =$ the percentage in clerical work, etc.

Theoretically, the occupational index used in this book can range from 100 (a hypothetical case in which all members of a group are professional workers) to 700 (a case where all workers are personal or domestic servants). In actuality, the occupational index almost always falls between 300 and 600.

Supplementary Tables

TABLE 21. *Area of birth of Ohio Negroes, 1900 and 1910*

Area of birth	1900		1910	
	Number	Percentage	Number	Percentage
Ohio	56,232	58.4	59,194	53.6
Middle West outside Ohio	2,218	2.3	2,714	2.8
Northeast	1,996	2.1	2,834	2.5
Upper South and Border	32,190	33.6	40,227	36.4
Lower South	3,026	3.1	4,565	4.1
West	50	0.1	114	0.1
Not specified or born abroad	764	0.8	1,149	1.0
Total	96,476	100.0	110,797	100.0

SOURCE: U.S. Bureau of the Census, *Negro Population in the United States, 1790–1915* (Washington, 1918), 75–79; U.S. *Twelfth Census, 1900* (Washington, 1902), I, pt. I, 702–5.

NOTE: *Middle West:* Michigan, Ohio, Indiana, Illinois, Iowa, Kansas, Wisconsin, Minnesota, Nebraska, North and South Dakota; *Northeast:* New England states, Pennsylvania, New York, New Jersey; *Upper South and Border:* Virginia, Kentucky, Tennessee, North Carolina, Maryland, West Virginia, District of Columbia, Missouri, Oklahoma, Delaware; *Lower South:* Georgia, South Carolina, Alabama, Mississippi, Louisiana, Texas, Florida, Arkansas; *West:* all other states.

TABLE 22. Area of birth of Cleveland Negroes, 1910 and 1920

Area of birth	1910		1920		Increase		
	Number	Percentage	Number	Percentage	Number	Percentage of Total	Percentage increase 1910–20
Born in Ohio	3,125	35.7	5,740	16.9	2,615	10.0	84.2
Born in other states	4,890	57.8	27,950	80.3	23,060	88.1	472.0
Foreign born	295	3.5	414	1.2	119	0.4	40.6
Others[a]	254	3.0	655	1.9	401	1.5	158.0
Total	8,564	100.0	34,759	100.0	26,195	100.0	307.0

SOURCE: U.S. Bureau of the Census, *Negro Population in the United States, 1790–1915* (Washington, 1918), 32.
[a] Includes those of undetermined nativity and those born in U.S. territories and possessions.

TABLE 23. *Increase in white and Negro populations in selected northern cities,* 1910–20

City	Negro population 1910	Negro population 1920	Negro increase, 1910–20 Number	Negro increase, 1910–20 Percentage	percentage increase in white population 1910–20
Detroit	5,741	40,838	35,097	611.3	107.0
CLEVELAND	8,448	34,451	26,003	307.8	38.1
Chicago	44,103	109,458	65,355	148.2	21.0
New York	91,709	152,467	60,758	66.3	16.9
Philadelphia	84,459	134,229	49,770	58.9	15.4
St. Louis	43,960	69,854	25,894	58.9	9.4
Cincinnati	19,639	30,079	10,440	53.2	7.9
Pittsburgh	25,623	37,725	12,102	47.2	8.3

SOURCE: U.S. Bureau of the Census, *Negroes in the United States, 1920–1932* (Washington, 1935), 55 (Table 10).

TABLE 24. *Area of birth of Ohio Negroes, 1910–20*

Area of birth	1920 Number	1920 Percentage	Increase, 1910–20 Number	Increase, 1910–20 Percentage of total
Ohio	66,836	36.3	7,642	10.6
Middle West outside Ohio	5,489	3.0	1,775	2.5
Northeast	4,843	2.7	2,009	2.8
Upper South and Border	62,674	34.0	22,447	31.2
Lower South	42,621	23.1	37,609	52.3
West	362	0.2	248	0.3
Not specified or born abroad	1,347	0.7	198	0.3
Total	184,172	100.0	71,928	100.0

SOURCE: U.S. *Fourteenth Census, 1920* (Washington, 1922), I, 637–41; U.S. Bureau of the Census, *Negro Population in the United States, 1790–1915,* 75–79.

NOTE: *Middle West:* Michigan, Ohio, Indiana, Illinois, Iowa, Kansas, Wisconsin, Minnesota, Nebraska, North and South Dakota; *Northeast:* New England states, Pennsylvania, New York, New Jersey; *Upper South and Border:* Virginia, Kentucky, Tennessee, North Carolina, Maryland, West Virginia, District of Columbia, Missouri, Oklahoma, Delaware; *Lower South:* Georgia, South Carolina, Alabama, Mississippi, Louisiana, Texas, Florida, Arkansas; *West:* all other states.

TABLE 25. *Census tracts with highest Negro percentages, Cleveland, 1910–30*

Census tract	Percentage Negro		
	1910	1920	1930
I-3	24.4	62.6	67.4
I-2	19.7	32.7	36.6
H-7	19.6	45.7	54.9
H-9	14.7	50.8	88.8
G-9	13.8[a]	18.5	17.4
G-1[b]	8.5	16.3	4.4
I-1[b]	8.4	5.4	0.7
J-1	6.2	25.4	63.3
I-6	5.9	42.0	53.0
L-6	5.6	6.8	8.9
G-7	5.1	3.8	0.7
I-5	3.1	26.0	25.5
H-8	3.1	28.5	52.4
J-2	2.8	32.5	48.7
M-6	2.8	20.8	81.1
M-2	2.8	2.3[a]	13.7
M-7	2.2	8.7	90.6
M-9	1.8	4.2	32.7
M-3	1.8	7.9	81.0
I-4	1.6	20.7	28.7
L-9	1.5	9.5	70.9
M-5	1.3	10.1	70.0
R-5	1.1[a]	5.0	4.0
M-4	0.9	6.4	76.1
I-8	0.8	20.9	75.7
M-8	0.4	7.1	78.3
I-7	0.4	38.5	75.5
J-3	0.4	11.7	49.1
N-7	0.4	3.3	30.6
N-1	0.4	3.5	25.4
G-4	0.3	6.4	16.4
S-2	—[c]	17.2	19.6
S-8	—[d]	12.4	13.8
U-1	—[c]	3.4	1.5

SOURCE: Howard W. Green, *Population Characteristics by Census Tracts* (Cleveland, 1931), 216–18, 231–32.
   [a] Estimated; tract combined with one other tract for the year indicated.
   [b] Denotes tract whose population declined drastically during the twenties due to industrialization.
   [c] Accurate estimate impossible; tract combined with two or more other tracts for year indicated.
   [d] The tract was not used by the Census Bureau for the year indicated.

TABLE 26. *Index of relative concentration of Negro males in selected occupations, Cleveland, 1870–1930*

Occupation	1870	1890[b]	1910	1920	1930
Professionals					
Physicians and surgeons	0	82	50	56	53
Lawyers	0	33	74	19	38
Teachers	60	—	—	22	15
Clergymen	50	—	—	235	210
Musicians and music teachers	—	—	286	74	155
Proprietors, managers, and officials					
Building contractors	—	—	108	52	37
Manufacturers and officials	—	24	8	—	—
Retail dealers	19	9	18	20	29
Restaurant, lunchroom, and café keepers	—	32	—	95	81
Clerical workers					
Clerks in stores	—	—	20	49	28
Clerks (not in stores)	—	28	54	31	30
Salesmen	—	11	10	5	13
Insurance agents	0	—	6	15	52
Skilled workers					
Bakers	36	0	12	45	18
Blacksmiths	71	21	26	41	25
Brick and stone masons	78	153	133	84	58
Carpenters	81	48	45	42	41
Foremen and overseers	—	—	29	26	12
Compositors, linotypers, and typesetters	—	—	5	27	10
Machinists	—	19	18	23	15
Painters, glaziers, etc. (not in factory)	129[a]	45[a]	44	38	59
Plumbers	0	11	16	15	24
Shoemakers	74	9	16	18	55
Tailors	11	8	27	36	48
Pattern and mold makers	—	—	15	3	1
Barbers, hairdressers, and manicurists	1,620	1,010	463	180	139
Policemen	—	51	51	31	10
Semiskilled workers					
Semiskilled operatives in foundries and rolling mills	—	4[b]	33	105	65
Painters, glaziers, etc. (in factories)	—	—	7	43	46

Occupation	1870	1890	1910	1920	1930
Unskilled workers					
Longshoremen and stevedores	—	25	15	—	—
Porters in stores	—	514[c]	770[d]	480	392
Draymen, hackmen, and teamsters (all)	94	156	373	194	169
Domestic and personal service					
Chauffeurs	—	—	886	320	186[e]
Porters (except in stores)	—	—	2,900	1,380	1,000
Servants	260	2,120	1,320	432	317
Messenger, bundle, and office boys	—	—	120	79	93
Waiters	—	—	1,930	420	416

SOURCE: Thomas Goliber, "Cuyahoga Blacks: A Social and Demographic Study, 1850–1880" (M.A. thesis, Kent State University, 1972), 67–90 (data for black occupations in 1870); U.S. Census Bureau reports, 1870–1930.

NOTE: An index of 100 indicates that the proportion of blacks in an occupation was the same as the proportion of all males in the city in that occupation. Indexes below 100 indicate black underrepresentation in an occupation; indexes over 100 signify overrepresentation.

[a] Includes all painters and glaziers, whether in factories or not.
[b] Undifferentiated iron and steel workers.
[c] Messengers, packers, and porters.
[d] Laborers, porters, and helpers in stores.
[e] Includes truck and tractor drivers.

TABLE 27. *Index of relative concentration of Negro females in selected occupations, Cleveland, 1870–1930*

Occupation	1870	1890	1910	1920	1930
Professionals					
Teachers (all categories)	25	38	38	27	18
Nurses (trained)	—	—	23	14	8
Proprietors					
Boarding- and lodging-house keepers	244	305	152	173	129
Clerical workers					
Clerks in stores (including saleswomen)	—	13	9	20	11
Clerks (not in stores)	—	8	12	11	8
Stenographers and typists	—	0	3	2	5
Skilled workers					
Milliners	—	—	17	9	—
Semiskilled workers					
Housekeepers	—	85	112	105	132
Textile operatives (all)	—	0	—	31	13
Laundry operatives	—	0	13	510	416
Dressmakers and seamstresses (not in factory)	97	64	135	150	197
Unskilled workers					
All unskilled laborers	—	71	—	194	100
Domestic and personal service					
Charwomen	—	—	342	144	99
Laundresses (not in laundries)	781	605	503	643	514
Servants	65	141	300	432	421

SOURCE: Goliber, "Cuyahoga Blacks," 67–69; U.S. Census Bureau reports, 1870–1930.

TABLE 28. *Home ownership by racial and ethnic group, Cleveland, 1890*

	Total number of families	Percentage of families owning homes
Negroes (total)	690	14.8
Mulattoes only	329	17.9
Native whites (total)	17,938	30.3
English and Welsh immigrants	4,293	36.2
German immigrants	15,126	50.6
Irish immigrants	5,014	41.6
Italian immigrants	152	8.5
Norwegian, Swedish, and Danish immigrants	224	24.5
All Others	9,181	39.4
Total	52,947	39.1

SOURCE: U.S. Bureau of the Census, *Report on Farms and Homes: Proprietorship and Indebtedness* (Washington, 1896), 582, 598, 605.

NOTE: The category "Negroes (total)" includes mulattoes. The category "Native whites (total)" includes native whites of native parentage and native whites of foreign or mixed parentage.

Bibliographical Essay

Most of the chapters in this volume contain footnotes that are bibliographical in nature, and some of these footnotes include commentary on the references cited. It would be superfluous, then, to once again list every source in a formal bibliography. The sources which follow are those which bear directly upon the history of black Cleveland. For more complete citations and references to black communities in cities other than Cleveland, the reader should consult the extensive documentation in the text itself.

Unpublished-manuscript collections

Cleveland is virtually unique in having a large number of collections of manuscripts by blacks. Most of these are part of the black history collection at the Western Reserve Historical Society in Cleveland. Unpublished manuscripts used in this study include: the Walter L. Brown Papers, the Charles Waddell Chesnutt Papers, the Lethia C. Fleming Papers, the Charles Herbert Garvin Papers, the John Patterson Green Papers, the Phillis Wheatley Association Papers, the Cleveland Urban League Papers, the Walter B. Wright Scrapbooks, the Chester K. Gillespie Papers, and Thomas Fleming's 1932 autobiography, "My Rise and Persecution" (all at the Western Reserve Historical Society); the Charles Waddell Chesnutt Papers at Fisk University; the George A. Myers Papers at the Ohio Historical Society (Columbus, Ohio); and the Papers of the National Association for the Advancement of Colored People, Manuscript Division, Library of Congress. A small portion of "The Peoples of Cleveland," an unpublished Works Projects Administration study written in 1942 (copy in the Cleveland Public Library) also deals with black Cleveland.

Of these manuscript collections, the most valuable are the Green Papers, the Myers Papers, and the Papers of the National Association for the Advancement of Colored People. The Myers collection, in particular, is very large and contains correspondence not only with black leaders in Cleveland and other cities in Ohio but with influential Negroes in many other parts of the country as well. Most of the material in the NAACP Papers relating to Cleveland is in

the branch files (Containers G157 and G158), but there is some correspondence of value in Containers C65, C74, and C403. The Chesnutt Papers at
Fisk are also very useful, although many of the most important letters in this
collection are reprinted in Helen M. Chesnutt, *Charles Waddell Chesnutt:
Pioneer of the Color Line* (Chapel Hill, 1952). There is some interesting material relating to blacks in the medical profession in the Garvin Papers.

Cleveland before 1870

Sources on the early history of black Cleveland are not as plentiful as for
later periods. The *Annals of Cleveland* (Cleveland, 1937–38), a digest of the
city's early newspapers, contains occasional references to blacks and much
information on the slavery controversy. The Cleveland *Leader*, the city's
leading newspaper during the second half of the nineteenth century, is the
best general source of information on black activities and white racial attitudes. For a discussion of the Black Laws in Ohio, see Helen M. Thurston,
"The 1802 Constitutional Convention and [the] status of the Negro," *Ohio
History*, 81 (Winter–Spring 1972); Frank U. Quillin, *The Color Line in Ohio*
(Ann Arbor, 1913); and Charles T. Hickok, *The Negro in Ohio, 1802–1870*
(Cleveland, 1896). Franklin Johnson, *The Development of State Legislation
Concerning the Free Negro* (New York, 1918) contains a useful chronologi-
cal listing of legislation passed by Ohio and other states. The growth of aboli-
tionism and sympathy for the Negro in the Western Reserve is traced in A. G.
Riddle, "Rise of the Anti-Slavery Sentiment on the Western Reserve," *Maga-
zine of Western History*, 6 (1887); Karl Geiser, "The Western Reserve in the
Anti-Slavery Movement, 1840–1860," Mississippi Valley Historical Society
Proceedings, 5 (1911–12); and William C. Cochran, *The Western Reserve
and the Fugitive Slave Law* (Cleveland, 1920).

*North Into Freedom: The Autobiography of John Malvin, Free Negro,
1795–1880* (Cleveland, 1966), a reprint of the 1879 edition, edited by Allan
Peskin, is the only important first-person narrative written by a Cleveland
Negro in the nineteenth century. Though somewhat sketchy at points, it pro-
vides valuable information on the early years of the black community, and
Peskin's introduction and notes are useful in explicating the text and placing
Malvin's life in the proper context. There is additional information on
nineteenth-century black leaders in Harry E. Davis, "Early Colored Residents
of Cleveland," *Phylon*, 4 (July 1943), and in Russell H. Davis, *Memorable
Negroes in Cleveland's Past* (Cleveland, 1969), a volume of brief sketches of
prominent Cleveland Negroes. The early years of black politics in Cleveland
are discussed in Russell H. Davis, "The Negro in Cleveland Politics: Negro
Political Life Begins," Cleveland *Call and Post*, September 11, 1966. A valuable source on the residential patterns, occupations, and family structure of
Cleveland's early black community is Thomas J. Goliber's "'Cuyahoga Blacks:
A Social and Demographic Study, 1850–1880" (M.A. thesis, Kent State Uni-

versity, 1972), a study based chiefly on an analysis of manuscript census data. Unfortunately, there is no adequate general history of Cleveland that would help put black Cleveland in historical context. James H. Kennedy's *History of the City of Cleveland* (Cleveland, 1896) is a fair survey of the city's early years, but it contains only a few brief references to the Afro-American population. Slightly more useful, but still quite inadequate, is William Ganson Rose's *Cleveland: The Making of a City* (Cleveland, 1950), a volume that is more a collection of facts than a history.

The black community in transition, 1870–1915

In the late nineteenth and early twentieth centuries, Cleveland's white newspapers, the *Leader* and the *Plain Dealer*, began to take less interest in the city's black community and hence are of decreasing value as sources of information on blacks. Invaluable for an understanding of black Cleveland during these years are the city's black newspapers, the *Gazette*, the *Journal* (1903–12), and the *Advocate* (1914–22). The *Gazette*, which began publication in 1883 and did not cease until the death of its editor, Harry C. Smith, in 1941, is an excellent source, not only on black Cleveland but on the black communities of other Ohio cities as well. Because of Smith's militancy, the *Gazette* is usually the best source of information on civil rights activities and discrimination. The *Journal* and the *Advocate* were more more conservative in their approach to race problems and less prone to print news about black protest. All three newspapers contain a wealth of data on the social and cultural life of the city's Afro-American population.

Quillin, in *The Color Line in Ohio*, underestimated the degree of racial prejudice in Cleveland in 1913, although he was correct in stating that race relations were more harmonious in the Forest City than in most Ohio metropolises. An excellent corrective to Quillin is David Gerber's "Ohio and the Color Line: Racial Discrimination and Negro Responses in a Northern State, 1860–1915" (Ph.D. dissertation, Princeton University, 1971), which surveys discrimination, school segregation, racial violence, and several other variables of racial prejudice in a spectrum of Ohio cities.

There is probably more primary source material for the study of black leadership in Cleveland during the late nineteenth and early twentieth century than for any other city. The most valuable printed works include John P. Green, *Fact Stranger than Fiction: Seventy-Five Years of a Busy Life with Reminiscences of Many Great and Good Men* (Cleveland, 1920); Chesnutt, *Charles Waddell Chesnutt*; John Garraty, ed., *The Barber and the Historian: The Correspondence of George A. Myers and James Ford Rhodes, 1910–1923* (Columbus, 1956); and Jane Edna Hunter, *A Nickel and a Prayer* (Cleveland, 1940), which tells the story of the early years of the Phillis Wheatley Association from the point of view of the organization's founder. Useful on the relationship of George A. Myers with Mark Hanna is Henry E.

Siebert's "George A. Myers: Ohio Negro Leader and Political Ally of Marcus
A. Hanna" (Senior Thesis, Princeton University, 1963). Cleveland's first
black councilman, Thomas W. Fleming, tells the story of his political career in
"My Rise and Persecution" (manuscript [1932], Western Reserve Historical
Society). For brief sketches of lesser known black leaders, such publica-
tions as William J. Simmons, *Men of Mark* (Cleveland, 1887); Clement Richardson et al., eds., *The National Cyclopedia of the Colored Race* (Montgomery, Ala., 1919); and the various editions of *Who's Who in Colored
America* (first published in 1927) proved useful, as did Davis's *Memorable
Negroes in Cleveland's Past.* A scholarly article dealing with Cleveland's black
leaders is Larry Cuban, "A Strategy for Racial Peace: Negro Leadership in
Cleveland, 1900–1919," *Phylon*, 28 (Fall 1963). In overstressing the conservatism of Cleveland's black leaders during this period, Cuban carries a
good point too far. Most of Cleveland's influential blacks were not militant,
but they were not as uniformly accommodationist as Cuban implies.

The Great Migration and after, 1915–30

Cleveland's black weeklies, the *Gazette* and (prior to 1922) the *Advocate*,
contain extensive information on all aspects of the black response to the Great
Migration; and there are some clippings from the *Call*, the *Herald*, and the
Call and Post in the Chester Gillespie Papers and the George Myers Papers.
Langston Hughes's *The Big Sea* (New York, 1940) contains a discussion of
increasing white hostility during World War I, and the Cleveland Chamber
of Commerce's *Investigation of Housing Conditions of War Workers in Cleveland* (Cleveland, 1918) gives information on the housing and wages of black
workers. John B. Abell, "The Negro in Industry," *Trade Winds*, March,
1924, surveys black workers in a dozen Cleveland firms.

For surveys of some of the more deleterious effects of the migration, see
H. L. Rockwood, "Effect of Negro Migration on Community Health in Cleveland," National Council of Social Work, *Proceedings, 1926* (Boston, 1926),
and two studies by Howard W. Green: *An Analysis of Girls Committed to
the Girls' Industrial School by the Juvenile Court at Cleveland during a Six
Year Period, 1920–25* Cleveland, 1929), and *An Analysis of Illegitimate
Births in the City of Cleveland for 1926* (Cleveland, 1928). Also useful is
Gordon Simpson, comp., *Economic Survey of Housing in Districts of the City
of Cleveland Occupied Largely by Colored People* (Cleveland [1931]).
Green, who served as director of the census in Cleveland for a number of
years, also compiled several volumes of population data that are indispensable
for the study of the growth and distribution of the black population of Cleveland during the 1910–30 period. They include *A Study of the Movement of
the Negro Population of Cleveland* (Cleveland, 1924); *Natural Increase and
Migration* (Cleveland, 1938); *Nine Years of Relief in Cleveland, 1928–1937*
(Cleveland, 1937); *Population Characteristics by Census Tracts, Cleveland,*

Ohio, 1930 (Cleveland, 1931), which contains data from 1910 and 1920 as well; and *Population by Census Tracts, Cleveland and Vicinity, with Street Index* (Cleveland, 1931).

On the growth of the black church in Cleveland after 1915, data from the Cleveland *Gazette* should be supplemented by the scattered references in the Cleveland Foundation's *Cleveland Year Book, 1921* (Cleveland, 1921); George F. Bragg, *History of the Afro-American Group of the Episcopal Church* (Baltimore, 1922); John T. Gillard, *The Catholic Church and the American Negro* (Baltimore, 1929); and the *Antioch Missionary Baptist Church Golden Jubilee, 1893–1943* (n.p.[1943?]), which describes the growth of Cleveland's largest black congregation. A critical history of the development of Karamu House is badly needed. John Selby's *Beyond Civil Rights* (Cleveland, 1966) focuses too much on the lives of the founders of Karamu, Russell and Rowena Jelliffe, and not enough on the institution itself. There is some information on Karamu in Arna Bontemps and Jack Conroy, *Anyplace But Here* (New York, 1966). The histories of the Cleveland Urban League and the Phillis Wheatley Association are best approached through the unpublished minutes of the board of directors of those organizations, held at the Western Reserve Historical Society. There are ample materials on the early years of the Cleveland branch of the National Association for the Advancement of Colored People (including rare copies of the *Annual Reports* and the *Branch Bulletin*) in the NAACP Archives at the Library of Congress.

The best general sources on segregation and discrimination in Cleveland during the postwar period are the Cleveland *Gazette* and the branch files of the NAACP Papers. On hospital segregation and the attempt to build a separate black medical facility, see the Mercy Hospital Association of Cleveland pamphlet, *Does Cleveland Need a Negro-Manned Hospital?* (Cleveland [1927]), and Charles Garvin, "Pioneering in Cleveland," *The Woman's Voice*, 1 (September 1939). The successful conclusion of the drive to integrate City Hospital is discussed in Thomas F. Campbell, *Daniel E. Morgan, 1877–1949* (Cleveland, 1966). On the decline of equality in the Cleveland public schools, see Alonzo G. Grace, "The Effect of Negro Migration on the Cleveland Public School System" (Ph.D. dissertation, Western Reserve University, 1932), and Willard C. Richan, *Racial Isolation in the Cleveland Public Schools* (Cleveland, 1967). For an excellent, overall survey of racism in Cleveland on the eve of the Depression, see Charles W. Chesnutt, "The Negro in Cleveland," *The Clevelander*, 5 (November 1930).

William Giffin's valuable article, "Black Insurgency in the Republican Party of Ohio, 1920–1932," *Ohio History*, 82 (Winter–Spring, 1973) contains information on Cleveland as well as several other cities. While not dealing specifically with the period surveyed in this volume, Christopher G. Wye's "The New Deal and the Negro Community: Toward a Broader Conceptualization," *Journal of American History*, 59 (December 1972) and Wye's dissertation, "Midwest Ghetto: Patterns of Negro Life and Thought in Cleveland, Ohio, 1929–1945" (Kent State University, 1973), proved most useful in understanding the historical development of Cleveland's black community. A recent publication which deals extensively with the institutions and personalities, both prominent and obscure, of black Cleveland is Russell H. Davis, *Black Americans in Cleveland* (Washington, D.C., 1972). The first half of this volume contains much useful information on the period prior to 1930.

Index